The Black Power Movement

The
Black Power
Movement

Rethinking the Civil Rights–Black Power Era

Edited by

Peniel E. Joseph

Routledge
Taylor & Francis Group
New York   London

Routledge is an imprint of the
Taylor & Francis Group, an informa business

Portions of the "Introduction" were published in different form in "An Emerging Mosaic: Rewriting Postwar African American History," in *A Companion to African American Studies*, edited by Lewis R. Gordon and Jane Anna Gordon (Malden: Basil Blackwell, 2006).

Chapter 8, "Rainbow Radicalism: The Rise of Radical Ethnic Nationalism" originally appeared in *Black Power: Radical Politics and African American Identity* by Jeffrey O. G. Ogbar (Baltimore: Johns Hopkins University Press, 2004).

Chapter 10, "Black Studies, Student Activism, and the Black Power Movement," originally appeared in *The Journal of African American History* 88, No. 2 (Spring 2003): 182-203.

Published in 2006 by
Routledge
Taylor & Francis Group
270 Madison Avenue
New York, NY 10016

Published in Great Britain by
Routledge
Taylor & Francis Group
2 Park Square
Milton Park, Abingdon
Oxon OX14 4RN

© 2006 by Taylor & Francis Group, LLC
Routledge is an imprint of Taylor & Francis Group

Printed in the United States of America on acid-free paper
10 9 8 7 6 5 4 3 2 1

International Standard Book Number-10: 0-415-94595-X (Hardcover) 0-415-94596-8 (Softcover)
International Standard Book Number-13: 978-0-415-94595-0 (Hardcover) 978-0-415-94596-7 (Softcover)

Library of Congress Cataloging-in-Publication Data

Catalog record is available from the Library of Congress

Taylor & Francis Group
is the Academic Division of Informa plc.

Visit the Taylor & Francis Web site at
http://www.taylorandfrancis.com

and the Routledge Web site at
http://www.routledge-ny.com

CONTENTS

ACKNOWLEDGMENTS

Many people and institutions helped make this anthology possible. First, I would like to thank all of my contributors. The University of Rhode Island, my former employer, provided valuable support through two Council of Research Grants in the summers of 2001 and 2004. Thanks as well to all my former colleagues at URI's History department and Afro-American Studies program.

Fellowships from the Woodrow Wilson International Center and the Ford Foundation provided time and resources to work on this anthology.

Thanks as well to the following individuals whose work continues to inspire me: Sonia Sanchez, Lewis R. Gordon, Robert Self, Robin Kelley, Gerald Horne, Yohuru Williams, Ernest Allen Jr., John Bracey, James Smethurst, Sundiata Cha-Jua, David Roediger, Tim Tyson, Robert Chrisman, Askia Muhammad Toure, Les Owens, and Femi Vaughan. Rhonda Y. Williams deserves special thanks for her advice, suggestions, and support.

Kimberly Guinta, my editor at Routledge, has shepherded this project with enthusiasm and professionalism. Takisha Jackson provided invaluable editorial assistance as this book went to press. Thanks as well to Karen Wolny for believing in this book from the start and to Daniel Webb for editorial assistance.

Without friends and family, of course, this work would have been impossible. Thanks to Kerith, Dawn, and Caitlin Joseph. Shout-outs to Daryl Toler and family, Chris, Ina, Savio, and Djuna Pisani and Michael, Natalie, Storm, and Miles Williams.

Props to the following friends for their steadfast support: Salvador and Jess Mena; and Mark and Orion Barnes.

Much love and appreciation goes to Catarina da Silva who has lived with this project.

Finally, this book is a small dedication of my love and affection for my mom.

LIST OF ILLUSTRATIONS

PREFACE

A few days after the fortieth anniversary of the landmark 1965 Voting Rights Act marked the commemoration of a more tragic, but no less significant, event: the Watts rebellion. At first blush Watts was shocking, less so for its unrepentant violence many believed, than its timing, which came on the heels of President Lyndon Johnson's August 6 signing of legislation to ensure black enfranchisement. Less than a week later, Watts shattered the racial peace that seemingly existed outside the South. Popular memory, burnished by subsequent histories, surrounds Los Angeles's week-long orgy of violence as the end of a more innocent age that gave birth to the violent, angry, and punitive rhetoric of the Black Power Movement.

This popular narrative denies the harsh realities of America's postwar racial politics. Indeed, racial violence—sometimes physical, other times "hidden" in unequal educational, residential, judicial, and economic outcomes between blacks and whites, thrived in postwar America, forming beachheads in virtually every part of the country. The first half of the 1960s bore witness to these unsavory aspects of America's racial landscape with violence in Oxford, Mississippi, Birmingham, Alabama, and Harlem, New York, preceding the Watts uprising. Taking place during the Civil Rights Movement's high tide, these riots were dismissed as aberrations.

They weren't. The racial uprisings, self-defense movements, and cultural pride celebrations subsequently associated with Black Power era radicalism were far from a decisive break from a more hopeful era. Rather, they were the direct results of a troubled and contested, but no less heroic, past that has been left largely unchronicled. "The riot was a rebellion," writes Walter Mosley, "a naturally formed revolution, an unconscious expression of a people who had lived entire lives, many generations, in a state of enforced unconsciousness."[1]

But many were conscious. Not only in Watts, but in urban cities such as Baltimore and Newark and embattled hamlets in the South. Black Power's roots go deeper than the now almost-forgotten spectacles of violence that flared with remarkable consistency during the 1960s and encompass the collective activism, anger, and hope of black Americans who agitated for full citizenship by any means necessary. It is to their story that we now turn.

INTRODUCTION: TOWARD A HISTORIOGRAPHY OF THE BLACK POWER MOVEMENT

PENIEL E. JOSEPH

America first heard the words "Black Power" in 1966 as they echoed from the Mississippi Delta. During the second week in June, Martin Luther King Jr. and Stokely Carmichael led hundreds of demonstrators through the state of Mississippi in defiance of white terror and violence and to continue James Meredith's solo "March Against Fear" begun on June 5. Four years earlier, Meredith had become a household name as days of rioting and violence intended to keep him from enrolling at the University of Mississippi pushed the Kennedy administration to the brink of civil war with the citadel of the Old Confederacy. In 1966 a determined Meredith vowed to walk across Mississippi alone to combat "the pervasive fear" that plagued the state's black residents. Meredith was ambushed on the second day of his trek and civil rights leaders gathered at his hospital bed in Memphis, where they vowed to take up his banner and continue his March Against Fear. Clashes over armed self-defense, interracial cooperation, and political tactics began immediately and marked the long walk through Mississippi, setting off ongoing debates between King and Carmichael. Over a decade into his public activism on behalf of black Americans, King was an internationally recognized civil rights leader. Carmichael possessed no such international reputation, having spent the past several years—in between successfully completing a philosophy degree at Howard University—engaged in the thankless

1

task of door-to-door organizing in the rural South. Reporters enthusiastically played up the generational differences between the men, with the 24-year-old Carmichael cast as the 37-year-old King's latest foil. Tension increased when King and Carmichael were interviewed walking at the head of the march. When asked whether the Meredith incident would shake the movement's resolve, King professed unwavering commitment to nonviolence while Carmichael casually proclaimed his tactical rather than philosophical support.

In the sweltering Mississippi heat, Student Nonviolent Coordinating Committee (SNCC) activist Willie Ricks regaled his friends with tales of the growing militancy of southern blacks. Ricks's assignment had been to sprinkle the march route with SNCC's new slogan—"Black Power"—while downplaying the King-led Southern Christian Leadership Conference's more mainstream "Freedom Now." On June 16, reacting to police harassment against demonstrators, Carmichael introduced the slogan "Black Power" to the black freedom struggle. "This is the twenty-seventh time that I've been arrested. I ain't going to jail no more. The only way we gonna stop them white men from whuppin' us is to take over. What we gonna start saying now is Black Power!" This slogan would propel Stokely Carmichael into history.

As the crowd chanted "Black Power" in unison, the rhythmic call and response between speaker and audience electrified some, frightened others, and marked a turning point for the African American freedom movement.[1] The national media seized on Carmichael's words as the signpost of a new militancy. Martin Luther King Jr. distanced himself from the slogan and a triumphant Carmichael emerged as the spokesman for an entire generation of black radicals. For many journalists and political analysts the Meredith March represented a stark line between civil rights and the coming Black Power Movement (BPM).[2]

Black Power and the Heroic Period of the Civil Rights Movement

The preceding narrative has been generally accepted as the starting point for the Black Power Movement. At its core, this movement attempted to radically redefine the relationship between blacks and

American society. Black Power activists trumpeted a militant new race consciousness that placed black identity as the soul of a new radicalism.[3] For example, Black Power activists fought for community control of schools, Black Studies programs at colleges and universities, welfare rights, prison reform, and jobs and racial justice for the poor. Simultaneously, many activists focused on increasing black political power through conferences, community organizing, independent schools, and the strategic use of electoral politics. Local and national issues converged with the movement's international ambitions as well. In the 1950s African independence movements helped fuel a renewed black American anticolonialism. By the early 1970s a broad coalition of Black Power activists had succeeded in placing the quest for African independence at the forefront of black consciousness. Moreover, black feminists organized in small, but robust groups that made important inroads among black activists and intellectuals. Although all of these activities reflect the era's richness and diversity, in the popular imagination Black Power is often reduced to symbols associated with its advocacy of self-defense (i.e., the Black Panthers).[4]

The Civil Rights Movement (CRM) is generally accepted as comprising the years 1954–1965. These years contour the beginning of the demise of legal segregation and the acquisition of black voting rights. The sit-ins, protests, marches, beatings, and boycotts that highlight this period represent the *heroic period* of the Civil Rights Movement in both public memory and historical scholarship.[5] However, such a characterization removes from the spotlight important civil rights-era political organizations and figures (some of whom simultaneously participated in more conventional civil rights struggles) that went beyond the call for civil rights to advocate radical systemic social and political change. Furthermore, such a description creates a situation in which the BPM can be conveniently blamed for the demise of the Civil Rights Movement, rather than being viewed as an alternative to the ineffectiveness of civil rights demands in critical areas of American life.

From this perspective, Black Power simultaneously triggered the demise of civil rights and the New Left's apocalyptical descent into destructive "revolutionary" violence. 1968, the year of Tet, May Day revolts, the assassinations of King and Bobby Kennedy, and the election of Richard Nixon have all become signposts (interpreted after the fact) for the end of a more hopeful era. Such narratives of declension diminish continuities between postwar black freedom struggles and late 1960s- and 1970s-era black radicalism. A complementary flaw conflates the entire New Left with the much written about Students for a Democratic Society (SDS), marking that group's demise in 1968 as the end of the era while bypassing what historian Van Gosse has described as the 1970s' "movement of movements." Cumulatively, this scholarship posits a good 1960s, filled with hope and optimism reflected in SNCC's early interracialism and SDS's youthful idealism, and personified by Martin Luther King Jr., with a bad 1960s, characterized by the omnipresent Black Panthers, urban rioting, and black separatism.[6] New scholarship alters this narrative by substantively examining the multilayered roots of Black Power-era radicalism, arguing that civil rights and Black Power, while occupying distinct branches, share roots in the same historical family tree.[7]

The Long Black Power Movement

Historical case studies by Komozi Woodard and Timothy Tyson have helped reperiodize the Black Power Movement. Woodard's *A Nation Within a Nation: Amiri Baraka (LeRoi Jones) and Black Power Politics* provides an in-depth examination of Black Power's impact on the local, national, and international levels.[8] Woodard's case study of the rise of black political power in Newark, New Jersey, during the 1960s and 1970s illustrates the rich insights and potential that is emerging from the recently developing historiography of the Black Power Movement. Indeed, after reading Woodard's study it becomes evident that Newark stood at the nexus of black nationalism, consciousness-raising, and municipal elections that comprised major strains of Black Power activism. Woodard simultaneously documents the impact of grassroots activists on local elections, the pivotal role of black nationalism and the Black Arts in building and sustaining local and national political momentum, and efforts to turn this newfound power toward the international arena through support for anti-colonial efforts in southern and western Africa.

A Nation Within a Nation also enriches Black Power historiography by highlighting the importance of international anticolonial efforts (in addition to the assassination of Malcolm X) in the radicalization of large segments of African Americans during the 1960s and 1970s. More importantly, it provides clear and substantive detail regarding the successes and failures of Black Power activists in a major city. Organizing the Committee for a Unified Newark (CFUN) on the heels of his influential, although short-lived, Black Arts Repertory Theater and School, Amiri Baraka utilized black cultural nationalism as a tool for community building and cultural awareness. Black nationalism in Newark produced tangible benefits, with the city's Black Power Movement, birthed in the aftermath of the 1967 rebellion, successfully electing African American Mayor Kenneth Gibson in 1970. Perhaps the study's most important contribution is in its detailed depiction of 1972's National Black Political Convention. This important gathering has been neglected in most accounts of the era.[9] Attended by a cross-section of the African American community, the convention highlighted the brief unity between black radicals, politicians, and cultural workers during this period and its final declaration included support for African liberation struggles, guaranteed income for the poor, and the restructuring of black urban communities.[10] For even serious scholars of the era, this story serves as an instructive departure from the usual Black Power narrative that inevitably reduces the era to a series of montages featuring angry militants brandishing rifles.[11] Despite these undeniable strengths, Woodard's study gives less attention to Black Power's demise. While providing new details about setbacks in the Black Power experiment in Newark, New Jersey, little is said about the clashes between black nationalists, pan-Africanists, and Marxists that roiled the series of national and international coalitions (Congress of African People, National Black Political Assembly, African Liberation Support Committee, Black Women's United Front), that Woodard describes as the "Modern Black Convention Movement."

If Woodard's study of Black Power in Newark sheds new light on the practical effects of cultural nationalist organizing in a major northeastern city, Timothy Tyson's history of racial militancy in the South during the 1950s moved Black Power historiography forward by turning back to the past. *Radio Free Dixie: Robert F. Williams and the Roots of Black Power,* Tyson's case study of black protest led by Robert F. Williams in Monroe, North Carolina, revises narratives of civil rights and Black Power by focusing on the two phases' distinct relationship and interaction. Williams's defiant resistance against white terror in the South crossed borders and boundaries not typically associated with civil rights struggles of the 1950s. For example, Williams toured Cuba in 1960, bringing along a contingent of black intellectuals, activists, and cultural workers. Williams's advocacy of armed self-defense made him a hero to scores of blacks living in and outside of the South during the 1950s and 1960s.

Yet this portrait of racial assertiveness was only one layer of Williams's multifaceted approach to the black freedom struggle. Arguing that Williams's militancy influenced Black Power activists including Black Panther cofounder Huey P. Newton, *Radio Free Dixie* stretches the periodization of conventional civil rights history by locating a central influence of Black Power radicalism in the hotbed of black southern racial militancy. Tyson's work also forces historians to reexamine the intersection between the Cold War, black radicalism, and the Civil Rights Movement.[12] By illuminating the strong connections that existed between civil rights activists, black radicals, and the Third World, *Radio Free Dixie* highlights the fluidity and historical breadth and depth of the postwar black freedom movement. Indeed, as suggested by the book's subtitle, the immediate roots of the Black Power Movement reside in the postwar era and civil rights and Black Power "grew out of the same soil, confronted the same predicaments, and reflected the same quest for African American freedom."[13]

Radio Free Dixie, however, suffers from some constraints inherently tied to its biographical form. At times, Williams's importance feels overstated, to the extent that Malcolm X and Harlem represented an arguably greater matrix for Black Power politics than Williams's North Carolina base. Indeed, readers may be left with the impression that Williams was a forerunner of Malcolm X, when in fact the two men's activism paralleled and intersected and Malcolm's influence far exceeded that of Williams. Malcolm X, perhaps more than any single individual figure, reflects the "roots" of Black Power—including its intersection with Cold War politics, its eclectic black nationalism, ties to the Old Left, and internationalism.[14]

Nevertheless, both Woodard and Tyson's works marked a significant turning point in Black Power scholarship, each study in its own way, suggesting that the roots of Black Power required investigating the impact of Cold War politics on black activism. On this score both works echo the search for a deeper understanding of postwar black freedom struggles. Over the past two decades studies ranging from groundbreaking histories of W.E.B. Du Bois and the black response to the Cold War to detailed narratives of sharecroppers in Birmingham, Alabama, and black tobacco workers in Winston Salem, North Carolina, have reinterpreted the black freedom movement's regionalism, worldliness, class composition, gender tensions, and goals and strategies. Ultimately, they chronicle a "long civil rights movement" (from the Great Depression through to the 1980s) that fundamentally alters historical and contemporary understanding of the civil rights revolution. [15]

New works depicting a "long Black Power Movement" complement and expand the scope and depth of these inquiries by extending the chronology of Black Power beyond the 1960s and delving back into postwar black political radicalism and civil rights militancy whose antecedents included Depression-era radicals who interpreted events in Birmingham and Harlem, Haiti and Ethiopia, as interrelated.[16] If this new chronology goes forward by looking back, it gains equal momentum by looking ahead, stretching its gaze toward the 1970s' panoramic political activism, to reveal a "second wave" of Black Power activism where a mosaic of students, feminists, trade unionists, welfare rights activists, black nationalists, Marxists, panAfricanists, and politicians participated in a Black Public Sphere that stretched from Newark, New Jersey, to Dar Es Salaam, Tanzania, and beyond.[17]

Black Power Studies

The publication of recent works on the Black Power Movement has opened up new fields of inquiry in the historical study of the Civil Rights Movement and African American history that may be best described as "Black Power Studies."[18] Although numerous studies have been written about civil rights during the last two decades, Black Power has received far less scholarly attention.[19] "Black Power Studies" highlights connections between two historical periods, characterizing the civil rights and Black Power era as a complex mosaic rather than mutually exclusive and antagonistic movements. While the individual subject matter, organizations, and approach of these recent works vary, they converge in at least four important ways.

First, this new scholarship reperiodizes the Civil Rights–Black Power era by pushing the chronology of black radicalism back to the 1950s and forward into the 1970s.[20] Arguing that the "origins" of Black Power rhetoric, ideology, and militancy are to be found by taking a fresh look at domestic and international events during the *heroic period* of civil rights, "Black Power Studies" transforms civil rights scholarship by placing militant organizers side-by-side with nonviolent moderates.[21] In locating threads of Black Power radicalism in the political activities of students and activists of the postwar era, these works revise contemporary historical understanding of black freedom struggles. The new BPM historiography extends the historical gaze beyond civil rights activities of the 1950s and 1960s by highlighting the importance of little known black activists, organizations, and events that stretched into the 1970s and in the process rewrites the history of the Civil Rights–Black Power era.[22] Recent case studies illustrate that there is much historical information and insight to be gained from the substantive examination of black organizations that stretch the borders of standard periodization. Indeed, emerging scholarship suggests that black organizing, protests, conferences, and activism at the local, national, and international level *increased* during the first half of the 1970s, a phenomenon that refutes the standard chronology of Black Power, New Left, and other radical social and political movements associated with 1960s-era political activism.[23]

Second, they place early Black Power activists at the center of Cold War intrigues. Tyson's biography of Robert Williams highlights this approach, by placing Williams in the midst of Cold War global antagonisms between the United States and Cuba (and later China and Africa). James Smethurst's groundbreaking history of the Black Arts Movement expands this approach to cultural and political organizations of the early Cold War era, locating proto-Black Power activism within a Cold War cultural milieu in which black radicals were confronted by the "black list," "red squads," and worse.[24]

Third, this new scholarship documents both the iconic and unglamorous. Social history's focus on "ordinary people" infuses works that highlight local activists in regions and locales not typically associated with Black Power. Yet, since even the movement's icons and well-known organizations and events have received relatively little attention (an ambiguous exception is the Black Panther Party), scholars have produced new histories critically assessing and evaluating figures often briefly mentioned in other works but rarely thoroughly investigated.[25]

Finally, new works on the Black Power era contribute to, and expand the scope of, a larger contemporary discussion about the legacy of civil rights; a debate that, more often than not, ignores or demonizes the Black Power era. This is to say that "Black Power Studies" is, in part, a response to the ecology of contemporary race relations; an environment that historians Sundiata Cha-Jua and Clarence Lang have described as the "new nadir."[26] Cha-Jua and Lang point to increased rates of black incarceration, unemployment, residential segregation, and illiteracy as indicators of the most miserable climate for a segment of black America since the late nineteenth century. In this sense, much of the new scholarship investigating the Black Power era exists in a historical environment in search of new strategies, tactics, and resources for black political mobilization. New voices, many born during the Black Power era (at least between its conventional dates of 1965–1975), have sought to place this era's radicalism within a long black activist tradition. Historical works and popular memory ignore the radical humanism behind the movement, and in doing so, discredit the memory and contemporary legacy of an era that encompassed radical trade unionists, welfare mothers, black feminists and nationalists, however tenuously. Thus, Black Power in contemporary scholarship and historical memory plays a significant, if undermentioned, role in the fierce debates, discussions, and dialogue known as the "culture wars." Characterized as a fever dream filled with violent rhetoric, revolutionary posturing, and the worse kind of misogyny, Black Power serves as a metaphor for not only the excesses of the 1960s, but provides a kind of fictive explanatory power for contemporary urban crises: ranging from alarming rates of inner-city unemployment and incarceration to debates over links between race, crime, and the urban "underclass."[27] Consequently, in both conservative and liberal analyses of the 1960s, Black Power contains virtually no redeeming qualities, except perhaps for its promotion of black pride.[28] In the process, the movement's rich political history is forgotten, its intellectual insights buried, contemporary relevance abandoned, and grassroots activists dishonored.

The best of the new wave of scholarship explores how the era's culture and politics informed one another. For a generation of scholars who have come of age in an American social and political landscape marked by the rise of Hip Hop culture, the decline of the Civil Rights Movement, and conservative appropriation of that movement's icons and ideals, Black Power offers radical activists whose lives and works resonate with intellectuals seeking to come to grips with a mean season of racial setbacks in American life. The Black Panthers, of course, personify the era's radicalism for many, but more obscure groups have drawn passionate interest. And that fascination with Black Power symbols extends toward the Black Arts as well; just witness the spate of new works on the era and the way in which poets such as Sonia Sanchez and Amiri Baraka informed the black radical cultural *zeitgeist* of the 1990s.[29]

The Black Power Movement: Rethinking the Civil Rights–Black Power Era seeks to critically engage an ongoing conversation about the uses and abuses of the black freedom movement (sometimes boiled down to "civil rights") that has, up until recently, largely excluded Black Power. Among the questions asked by this book are: What did the term "Black Power" mean to grassroots activists and organizations? What was the relationship between civil rights and Black Power and what influences, origins, and histories do these movements share? How did international events, specifically decolonization movements in Asia, Africa, and Latin America, impact domestic civil rights struggles? What events, organizations, and activists provide the immediate historical context for Black Power? How did issues of violence and self-defense influence Black Power ideology and organizations? What was the Black Power Movement's intellectual legacy? How did black women respond to, influence, and transform the movement? What was the relationship between culture and politics during the era? How did efforts to build Black Studies provide an educational, political, and social base for far-reaching transformations at the local, national, and international levels? How did contact with Third World activists and intellectuals affect the Black Power Movement? What led to the decline of the Black Power Movement? What is the significance of Black Power radicalism to contemporary black politics? The efforts to fully answer these and many more questions will constitute Black Power Studies' intellectual challenge, historical contribution, and scholarly mission.

Substantively, this scholarship chronicles the rise of the Black Power Movement through an examination of the political, social, and cultural development of several converging groups. These include: Malcolm X and the cadre of radicals, locally, nationally, and internationally, whom he consorted with and influenced; civil rights era radicals such as Robert F. Williams; cultural workers such as Amiri Baraka (LeRoi Jones) who would combine their struggles around African American identity and art with politics in what became known as the Black Arts Movement; student radicals who would influence the Student Nonviolent Coordinating Committee (SNCC) and would go on to play major roles in Black Power activism; scholar-activists of the Institute of the Black World (IBW); black feminists involved in guerrilla theater, grassroots protests, and intellectual activism; students and faculty committed to the establishment of Black Studies programs across the nation; and, finally, organizations such as the Student Organization of Black Unity (SOBU) and African Liberation Support Committee (ALSC), which were increasingly attracted to international and pan-African perspectives. Drawing from social, political, cultural, and intellectual history, these works examine the wide-ranging implications of postwar black activism by shedding light on the deep connections between black activists and grassroots communities, black radicals and the Third World, the Black Arts and the international arena, and black urban politics and black nationalism. Ultimately, the Black Power Movement left a legacy that altered black political discourses, culture, and consciousness. More specifically, the BPM was institutionalized through the creation of Black Studies departments and programs at American universities and through the rise of black elected officials.

Early Black Power Activism

Scholar James Edward Smethurst's *The Black Art Movement: Literary Nationalism in the 1960s and 1970s* breaks new ground by placing postwar black radicalism within the context of the development of overlapping political, intellectual, and cultural currents that led to the rise of the Black Arts. More convincingly than any other study to date, Smethurst argues that understanding the Black Arts and Black Power Movements requires a deep, substantive appreciation of the history of black radicalism. This includes following the at times surprising trajectory of some of the most radical elements of the postwar black freedom movement, where veterans of civil rights unionism and Popular Front strategies mentored young black nationalists, tutored independent intellectuals and artists, and introduced future Black Arts icons to Left-wing history, organizations, and institutions. At times, the relationship between seasoned black leftists and militants took on eclectic new dimensions, perhaps most remarkably in the editorial control black radicals exerted over *Muhammad Speaks,* turning the Nation of Islam's ostensibly sectarian newspaper into one of the era's most cosmopolitan periodicals.[30] Yet, as Smethurst suggests, the coming together of seemingly irreconcilable trends was not as unusual as it seemed; in political centers such as New York City, Marxists and black nationalists fraternized (while maintaining sharp political differences and organizations) and produced activism that "had a certain practical synergy even if they were opposed on an ideological level."[31]

Periodicals that provided radical coverage of Cuba and the larger Third World, such as *Muhammad Speaks, The Baltimore Afro-American, Soulbook, Freedomways,* and *Liberator,* became vital conduits for early Black Power activists. Simultaneously inspiring and regaling readers with bold declarations of African independence and denunciations of Afro-American ignorance, this literature deepened black knowledge of the outside world. Additionally, international publications such as *Revolution* and *Presence Africaine* served a similar purpose.[32] *Freedomways Reader: Prophets in Their Own Country* is the rare collection of some of the pivotal journal writing from the period.[33] Featuring writings by some of the leading black radical activists and intellectuals of the era, this anthology represents a valuable resource for the study of the intellectual history and cultural and political criticism of the era.

Indeed, Cuba became a repository of black American support for the Third World during the age of civil rights.[34] Shortly before the American embargo that would end diplomatic relations between the United States and Cuba, blacks were among the groups of American radicals who founded the Fair Play for Cuba Committee (FPCC). FPCC's black members included the novelist James Baldwin, the writer John Henrik Clarke, and the journalists William Worthy and Richard Gibson. In the summer of 1960, Fair Play sponsored a group of black writers and activists for a tour of the island. This trip would have lasting consequences for those who attended, most notably Harold Cruse, Julian Mayfield, Tom Feelings, Robert Williams, LeRoi Jones, and John Henrik Clarke. At least five of these visitors would write lengthy essays about their trip once they returned to the United States.[35] Cuba inspired this group of black intellectuals and activists with an example of revolutionary politics that contrasted with the spectacle of antiblack violence associated with domestic civil rights struggles during the late 1950s and early 1960s. At times, the island provided safe harbor, perhaps most famously when Robert Williams fled there after being unjustly pursued by local and federal authorities. In short, black Americans' tour of Cuba in 1960 set the stage for the increasing identification of African Americans with colonized peoples all over the world. Impressed by the political, cultural, and economic restructuring taking place on the island, black radicals became some of Cuba's biggest American advocates.[36]

Narratives of the Civil Rights Movement have rightfully underscored the founding of the sit-in movement and the subsequent organization of SNCC as a watershed event.[37] For example, Clayborne Carson's case study of SNCC demonstrates how local activism, far removed from the national spotlight reserved for mobilizers such as Martin Luther King Jr., fostered a movement culture that drew on indigenous black southern organizing traditions. However, this "black awakening" did not take place in a vacuum. In 1960, the same year that sit-ins ignited the direct action phase of the civil rights era, Fidel Castro captivated thousands of African Americans in Harlem, meeting with Malcolm X and defying the Cold War's racial and ideological boundaries.[38] That year also witnessed increasing numbers of African nations enjoying the bittersweet realities of independence;

none more poignantly than the Congo, led for two months by the radical Prime Minister Patrice Lumumba. The Congo Crisis of 1960–1961 resulted in the murder of Lumumba and increased awareness and outrage on the part of black Americans, hundreds of who protested in and outside the United Nations in February 1961.[39] Thus, many of the same activists and students influenced by SNCC's courageous organizing in the South were equally impacted by events taking place around the world.[40]

New scholarship on the Deacons for Defense and Justice highlights a local civil rights landscape that defies conventional portraits of black southern activism. Historian Lance Hill's recent case study of the Deacons examines the unheralded black working-class men who formed self-defense units for civil rights activists in large swaths of the South. From humble beginnings in Jonesboro, Louisiana, the Deacons became a scourge of the Klan and white supremacists in Louisiana and Mississippi. Ironically, white pacifists, along with black militants in the Congress of Racial Equality (CORE) aided the organization's growth. At the local level, CORE activists confronted levels of white terror and violence that mandated creative, improvised solutions be grafted onto organizational orthodoxy. "The experience of the Deacons," writes Hill, "lays bare the myth of nonviolence, testifying to the crucial role of defensive violence in securing the law of the land."[41] What Hill provocatively characterizes as the "myth of nonviolence" dovetails into a larger reconsideration of longstanding civil rights tropes that depict a world filled with polarities between pacifism and violence, nationalism and integration, and personified by divergent historical conceptions of Malcolm X and Martin Luther King Jr.[42]

Local Militants in a Global Black Revolt

Black radicalism at the local level impacted the international political arena. The story of black expatriates in Kwame Nkrumah's Ghana reflects the cross-currents between early Black Power militants, the Cold War, and civil rights. Educated in the United States and advised by a coterie of radical Caribbean, African American, and African intellectuals, Nkrumah offered a welcome relief for black radicals engaged in antiracist struggles. Perhaps the most famous black American to reside in Ghana during the 1960s was W.E.B. Du Bois, but he was not alone.

According to Kevin Gaines, Ghana represented "an inspirational symbol of black power" for African Americans, especially those increasingly identifying with Third World Independence Movements.[43] Key black activists lived in Ghana, including the labor unionist Vicki Garvin, the scholar St. Claire Drake, the poet Maya Angelou, and the writer Julian Mayfield.[44] Far from being isolated by their relocation to Africa, black radicals found themselves in the middle of major controversies that included Malcolm X's 1964 tours of Africa. In short, the impact of black Americans' active participation in Ghana between 1957 and 1966 "reflected an important trend in black politics, however foreclosed or forgotten."[45]

The African Liberation Support Committee (ALSC) represents perhaps the most powerful merging of local Black Power activism with international imperatives.[46] Radical advocates of anti-imperialism and the liberation of Africa, ALSC successfully organized the first African Liberation Day (ALD) in 1972 to promote awareness of the Third World, raise money for liberation efforts in Portuguese controlled southern Africa, and sent groups overseas to observe global struggles for racial justice. Understudied relative to the organization's influence, the ALSC was a pivotal part of the increasing internationalism and class-consciousness exhibited by significant portions of African American activists, workers, intellectuals, and students during this era.[47]

Forging a New Vision

Sisters in the Struggle: African American Women in the Civil Rights-Black Power Movement, edited by the historians Bettye Collier-Thomas and V. P. Franklin, represents a significant contribution to studies of postwar African American history. This collection explores the distinct, yet overlapping, phases of the black freedom struggle from the 1950s through the 1980s. An outstanding example in this regard is Sharon Harley's essay on Gloria Richardson. Harley argues that Richardson's leadership in the Cambridge, Maryland, desegregation battles of the early 1960s has been ignored by historians because it defies conventional periodization of the Civil Rights–Black Power era. According to Harley, the Cambridge movement's willingness to utilize self-defense prefigured the demise of the southern movement's dominance in the public sphere.[48] Harley's discussion of Richardson is notable for utilizing one of the few prominent women leaders of the movement as a vehicle for both historical analysis and conceptual reperiodization. In truth, Richardson's struggles in Cambridge provides one important example of numerous instances that have received inadequate attention, or been relegated to history's dustbin, for defying standard chronology and understanding of the civil rights era.

Recent works focusing on local people and unknown political organizations have provided nuance to the era, including the racial and ethnic diversity of individuals associated with Black Power activism. Grace Lee Boggs's *Living For Change* documents the political activism of the Chinese-American activist who, as a Marxist theoretician and colleague of C.L.R. James and, later, as the wife and political partner of Detroit activist James Boggs, placed an indelible stamp on Black Power politics in theory and practice.[49] And Diane C. Fujino's *Heartbeat of Struggle* is the first comprehensive biography of Yuri Kochiyama, the Japanese-American radical who traced her revolutionary politics to meeting Malcolm X during the 1960s.[50] Whereas the black freedom struggle's makeup has historically been multicultural, by the late 1960s this rich ethnic mosaic took on new depth and breadth, "giving rise to a visible movement of radical ethnic nationalism and new constructions of ethnic identity."[51]

The Us Organization influenced much of these newly developing "rainbow" nationalisms by staunchly upholding a return to indigenous cultural roots as the key to contemporary progress. Scot Brown's *Fighting For US: Maulana Karenga, the US Organization, and Black Cultural Nationalism* breaks new ground in the study of Black Power activism.[52] Erroneously referred to as "United Slaves" in many historical accounts of the era, the group's name was actually a literal reference to "us" blacks in contrast with whites. Brown argues that Us, known primarily for its notorious and ultimately deadly conflicts with the Black Panthers, has had its historical image shaped in large part by detractors who were unaffiliated with the organization. Arguing that Us was a driving force behind early, and ultimately short-lived, Black

Power coalition efforts such as the Los Angeles Black Congress, Brown's study offers a major revision of conventional narratives of cultural nationalism, black radicalism, and the Us–Panther conflict.

Into the Fire: Black Power Activism in the 1970s

New works on the BPM examine the impact of the movement on local struggles that continued into the 1970s. For example, in an examination of Boston's school desegregation crisis during the early 1970s, Jeanne Theoharis argues that "struggles for education in Boston eschews the prevalent dichotomy made between integrationist and Black Power strategies."[53] While campaigning to "integrate" the city's public schools, Theoharis asserts that black activists were influenced by Black Power militancy in waging their struggle.

The historian Robert Self's *American Babylon: Race and the Struggle for Postwar Oakland* expands discussion of the era by placing the Black Panther Party (BPP) and the development of Black Power within the sweep of Oakland's postwar black freedom movement.[54] Self's study is particularly noteworthy for its creative illustration of the ways in which the politics of space within a deindustrializing predominately black urban terrain impacted Black Power organizing efforts and strategies. Both Self and Theoharis successfully connect the Black Power era to local struggles waged by African Americans over community control, school desegregation, and political representation.

In *Black Politics/White Power: Civil Rights, Black Power, and the Black Panthers in New Haven*, historian Yohuru Williams examines one of the BPP's most successful local chapters through a case study of New Haven's civil rights activism.[55] The New Haven Panthers represented both the best and worst aspects of the BPP's combative legacy. Buoyed by the success of its community programs that included breakfast for children, New Haven seemed poised to serve as a model for the Panthers' ambitious program of transforming some of America's toughest black urban communities. External repression and internal vulnerabilities turned New Haven into the sight of race controversy and radical coalitions in the aftermath of the murder of Alex Rackley, a Panther wrongly suspected of being a police informer.[56] The subsequent trial made international celebrities of the "New Haven Nine" and Yale University attracted both pro-Panther partisans and a variety of radical efforts, including antiwar demonstrations. Thus, we witness the type of activism in New Haven during the 1970s more typically associated with the preceding decade. By examining the way in which the BPP's local influence in New Haven refracted through a national political climate passionately divided over Black Power, Vietnam, and the very meaning of American democracy, Williams critically analyzes the Panthers' impact on grassroots black activists during the late 1960s and early 1970s.[57]

Two recent anthologies on the Panthers have deepened historical understanding of both the Black Panthers and the Black Power Movement.[58] *The Black Panther Party [Reconsidered]* provides the most comprehensive look at the group to date. *The Black Panther Party [Reconsidered]* contains essays by political scientists, historians, and ex-Panthers that explore the group's enduring significance. Most significantly, the anthology begins "the process of systematic scholarly investigation" of the group's successes, failures, and contemporary legacy.[59] Collectively, these essays offer up new evidence regarding the group's internal structure and dynamics, its eclectic fusion of black nationalism and Marxism, gender dynamics, relationship with the New Left, and internationalism. *Liberation, Imagination and the Black Panther Party,* highlights the organization's legacy on the New Left, black radicalism and the global impact of the group during the 1960s as well as the contemporary era. Ultimately both works situate the Panthers within a larger historical tableau where the Black Power Movement represented an "oppositional discourse that exposed the hegemony of Americanism as incomplete, challenged its universality, and imagined carving up its spaces differently."[60] Despite the strengths of these works, without a definitive organizational history and with few published studies of local chapters, much about the Panthers and their legacy remains to be considered and analyzed in the future.[61]

New scholarship on Black Power's contentious relationship with black women has added complexity to an era widely assailed as reflexively misogynistic.[62] Tracye Matthews provides the most detailed study to date of the role of black women in the Black Panthers.[63] Matthews argues that during the organization's first five years black women's roles were transformed in many ways. Notwithstanding the organization's sexism, according to Matthews, black women carved a space of genuine agency and political power, albeit one that was constantly under threat.[64] Recent scholarship has expanded the focus on black women during the era beyond the Panthers to include black feminist organizations.

Kimberly Springer has written the first case study of Black Power-era black feminist organizations. Springer revises standard historical understanding of the black freedom movement and Black Power by documenting the legacy of radical black feminist organizations, most notably the Third World Women's Alliance (TWWA).[65] An outgrowth of SNCC's Black Women's Alliance, TWWA defies conventions associated with black women during this era. Comprised of black and Latino activists who were militant nationalists, feminists, and socialists, TWWA's grassroots activism and consciousness-raising provides an example of the breadth of the politics of the Black Power era. The group's publication, *Triple Jeopardy,* was a forerunner to "race, class, and gender" studies that have transformed a variety of contemporary academic disciplines, including history. On this score, Benita Roth has argued that black feminism "is at the center of the story of second-wave feminism" rather than a marginal development. Roth focuses on black study groups and the watershed publication of Toni Cade Bambara's edited anthology, *The Black Woman,* in 1970. For Roth, activists such as Bambara, Frances Beal, and Barbara Smith comprised the core of a group of black feminists whose writings and political activism transformed the feminist movement.[66] Finally, Duchess Harris's examination of the late 1970s group of radical black lesbian feminists known as the Combahee River Collective (CRC) is one of the first to examine the group's legacy within the context of Black Power-era activism.[67]

While all of these approaches are vital, innovative work exploring Black Power's impact on unfamiliar and untraditional black female spaces, such as welfare and tenants rights activists in urban cities, promises to open up new fields of critical inquiry and historical narratives.[68] All of these studies point to the importance of reassessing the legacy of Black Power-era politics and black women's roles in the transformations, struggles, successes, and failures that subsequently took shape. Most important, they shed light on understudied elements of black political activism that thrived during the 1970s.

During the 1970s, many black activists became disillusioned with their involvement with party building and electoral participation. Beginning with the Freedom Now Party in 1963, the Mississippi Freedom Democratic Party in 1964, and the Lowndes County Freedom Organization (nicknamed the Black Panther Party) in 1966, black radicals sought political power as a tool for racial justice and economic empowerment. The mayoral victories of Carl Stokes and Richard Hatcher in 1967 and Kenneth Gibson in 1970 promised new levels of black political power in urban areas. 1972's Gary Convention, a highpoint of Black Power-era politics, attempted to coalesce a wide-range of ideological and organizational participants into a cohesive national political force.[69] Black activists could not maintain the political leverage that made them vital constituents in new emerging black urban political machines in Newark, Atlanta, and Los Angeles.[70] Yet in many instances black mayors continued to enjoy the fruit of nationalist rhetoric concerning political power long after it became obvious that "black faces in higher places" would not qualitatively transform urban ghettos. Despite these setbacks, Black Power remained a formidable presence during the mid-1970s.[71] Black Power activists were instrumental in the organization of the Sixth Pan-African Congress (6-PAC) held in Dar Es Salaam, Tanzania, in 1974. In many ways, this conference and its resolutions represented the highpoint of Black Power's resonance during the 1970s while simultaneously showcasing the political fractures that would lead to the movement's decline.[72]

This "second wave" of Black Power activism, one that featured alliances between grassroots activists and politicians, burgeoning independent black political and cultural institutions, and the flowering of a contemporary black feminism, profoundly influenced the decade's "movement of movements." Smeared as "identity politics" by the Right and Left, movements for racial, economic, gender, and environmental justice reflected a political landscape where radical voices were no longer muted. Loud, contentious, and angry debates ensued around Affirmative Action, the Equal Rights Amendment, and welfare rights, to name a few, that fundamentally challenged white supremacy in institutions, politics, and social movements.[73]

Significant gaps in the historical literature of the Black Power era deserve special mention. Despite the spurt of new works on Black Power, the movement's origins have not been documented in a satisfying manner. Perhaps surprisingly, even the era's iconic activists have, with notable exceptions, yet to be accorded substantive historical analysis. A historical archaeology of Black Power will need to focus on the lives and activism of key figures (Malcolm X, Kathleen Cleaver, Stokely Carmichael, Angela Davis, and Sonia Sanchez, for example) whose political activism and intellectual thought have, more often than not, received insufficient scholarly attention.[74] Of course, this will still tell us only part of the story. Local studies of Black Power activists who fit outside of conventional historical interpretations—faceless and unglamorous, women and men, multiracial and multiethnic, middle-aged and senior citizens, southern and international—will go a long way toward providing a more accurate picture of the movement's scope and depth. The historian Clarence Lang has rightfully cautioned against allowing continuities between civil rights and Black Power to collapse two distinct periods into one, largely indistinguishable, era.[75] Although civil rights and Black Power activists certainly claimed unique worldviews, intellectual philosophies, and political tactics, the distinctiveness of each era becomes less stark depending on where one looks. For example, northern black freedom struggles in the postwar era reflect a militant edge usually associated with Black Power radicalism of the 1960s. Similarly, Black Power activism in the South during the late 1960s and early 1970s suggests that civil rights-era organizing traditions, ostensibly abandoned by the push toward black militancy and racial separatism, were in fact updated with a new face and political edge.[76] Such distinctions seem miniscule but reflect the hegemony of three decades of scholarship (and public memory and political discourse) that have framed civil rights and Black Power as a progressive regression from hope to anger to chaos. The power of this narrative declension, particularly its relative inattention to 1970s-era Black Power radicalism, is widespread enough to impact aspects of otherwise revisionist histories of the movement.[77]

Looking Forward by Turning Back

Reimagining the historical periodization, organizational diversity, intellectual parameters, and political depth of the Black Power Movement requires rewriting postwar African American history. Postwar black freedom struggles, although varying by region and locale, spanned the entire breadth of American society and beyond. Local struggles shaped the national character of specific protests, boycotts, demonstrations, and labor organizing in ways that complicate historical understanding of the Cold War, civil rights, and Black Power eras. Black radicalism contoured these activities, providing key intellectual, political, and cultural institutions that nurtured both self-described civil rights and Black Power activists.[78]

The Black Power Movement rewrites postwar black freedom struggles by locating the Black Power Movement in its appropriately dynamic local, national, and international historical context. Jeanne Theoharis reframes conventional understanding of the Watts riots by examining radical black community activism before the uprising. According to Theoharis, Los Angeles' postwar black radicalism centered on school desegregation (as well as jobs and fair housing) as a vehicle for educational opportunity and economic advancement. By illustrating a preriot era of militant community organizing, Theoharis challenges assumptions that allow Watts to neatly demarcate the end of civil rights activism and the onset of Black Power. Komozi Woodard deepens understanding of Black Power's historical trajectory. Examining the transformations in radical black activism between the 1961 United Nations "riot" and 1972's watershed Gary Convention, Woodard documents LeRoi Jones's evolution to Amiri Baraka to trace the contours of Black Power radicalism. Rhonda Y. Williams expands and enriches the examination of Black Power and gender with an essay that uncovers new aspects of the movement's effects at the local level. Specifically, Williams examines how Black Power radicalism impacted and paralleled local black women's struggles in Baltimore, Maryland. Fighting for community-based issues including bread and butter economics in a postwar urban landscape that regarded them as nonpersons, grassroots black women, many of them low-income, creatively adapted aspects of Black Power political organizing to further their own local causes that ranged from jobs and community education to public housing and welfare rights. Inspired by Black Power radicalism, black women in Baltimore—ranging from nuns to Black Panthers to social workers—added militant discourse in service of a rhetorical arsenal promoting human rights.

Kimberly Springer analyzes the contentious relationship between Black Power activists and black feminists. Despite their relatively small numbers, Springer argues that black feminists altered the landscape of the black freedom struggle through groundbreaking intellectual contributions that elevated gender matters to the same pantheon that Black Power activists placed race and class. Stephen Ward's discussion of Frances Beal considers black feminism through the groundbreaking Third World Women's Alliance. For Ward, Beal and TWWA provide clues into a complex and contested history of black women equally committed to feminism and Black Power.

Simon Wendt's examination of the Deacon for Defense and Justice and other, less well-known, civil rights-era self-defense organizations, sheds new light on conceptions of nonviolence. According to Wendt, the Deacons complemented civil rights organizing by providing protection for white and black rights workers. Yet, Wendt challenges the notion that the Deacons' militancy represents a direct bridge to Black Power radicalism and groups such as the Black Panthers, arguing instead that self-defense units during the civil rights era pivoted on a pragmatic view of nonviolence that their very presence helped facilitate.

Yohuru Williams explores the NAACP's hostility toward Black Power through Roy Wilkins's evolving relationship with the Black Panthers. An eloquent critic of Black Power and the era's leading militants, by the early 1970s Wilkins was among a prominent group of liberals defending the Panthers against state-sanctioned murder. A Cold War anticommunist liberal, Wilkins broke ranks with the American political establishment in the face of mounting evidence that the Panthers were being systematically destroyed by unconstitutional and illegal methods.

Jeffrey O. G. Ogbar looks at how the Black Power Movement inspired indigenous groups, including Native Americans, Chicanos, and Puerto Ricans. This "Rainbow Radicalism" produced eclectic political and cultural groups drawn to Black Power styled radicalism.

Although not credited as a forerunner to contemporary discussions and organic manifestations of multiculturalism, Black Power-era political and cultural advocacy helped set the stage for present day discussions of racial diversity. Keith Mayes's evocative history of Kwanzaa looks at the way in which black community activists around the country kept this Black Power-era holiday alive even after the decline of the movement that created it. More than a simple extension of Maulana Ron Karenga's creative adoption of cultural nationalism, Mayes situates Kwanzaa's enduring success and contemporary relevance in the local efforts of unnamed urban activists who educated a skeptical black public about a holiday that eventually became mainstream enough to enjoy corporate sponsorship.

My own chapter traces the modern roots of contemporary Black Studies by examining how early Black Power activists pushed for a new kind of radical intellectual movement in periodicals, study groups, and political organizations. Beginning with an important beachhead at San Francisco State College in 1967, Black Studies grew into a political movement that amplified and reflected Black Power's themes of self-determination and race consciousness and became one of the movement's most enduring legacies.

* * *

Recent studies have stressed the importance of local history to understanding the complexity of the black freedom struggle. John Dittmer and Charles Payne's exemplary case studies of civil rights struggles in Mississippi have expanded the depth of historical research on the movement and the breadth of conceptual frameworks. In essence, these works have redefined the very way that scholars approach postwar black freedom struggles. Following earlier works by Clayborne Carson on SNCC and William Chafe on local activism in Greensboro, North Carolina, historians of civil rights have shifted their gaze away from national, mostly male leaders, to a landscape populated by ordinary people: rural and urban, educated and unlettered, women and men, whose slow, patient, and resilient activism, folk culture, freedom songs, home cooking, and quiet courage transformed the United States. Both Dittmer and Payne's portrait of Mississippi resist triumphant, one-dimensional narratives of the movement. Instead, they offer indelible portraits of multilayered activism forged in a black organizing tradition that valued hard work, political principles, and self-help in the cause of human dignity.

Two recent anthologies, *Freedom North* and *Groundwork,* have amplified these scholarly efforts to recast postwar black freedom struggles. Substantively, both works go beyond the intellectual parochialism that has too often placed the Civil Rights Movement in a kind of time warp: one where civil rights and Black Power are viewed as two fundamentally dichotomous eras. By concentrating on grassroots activists and organizations that shaped a movement without geographic borders, this scholarship casts postwar African American history as an almost half-century long black freedom movement that—although highlighted by distinct strains, political differences, and conflicts—featured connections and continuities previously missed.

This anthology embraces and builds on this complexity, by outlining a panoramic view of the black freedom struggle, highlighting previously undocumented traces, origins, and evolutions of Black Power radicalism. In doing so, the following chapters tell of women and men from rural hamlets to urban cities who—as tenants rights organizers, college students, feminists, nationalists, and independent political activists—gave the Black Power era meaning. If some of the destinations in the ensuing stories seem unfamiliar, it is because, collectively, they map out unexplored intellectual terrain and new historical routes.

"ALABAMA ON AVALON"

Rethinking the Watts Uprising and the Character of Black Protest in Los Angeles[1]

JEANNE THEOHARIS

> Los Angeles hurt me racially as much as any city I have ever known—much more than any city I remember from the South. It was the lying hypocrisy that hurt me. Black people were treated much the same as they were in any industrial city of the South.... The difference was the white people of Los Angeles seemed to be saying, "Nigger, ain't we good to you?"
>
> —Chester Himes, African American novelist who moved to Los Angeles in 1941[2]

> California is a state where there is no racial discrimination.
>
> —Governor Edmund Brown, 1965[3]

On February 20, 1941, posting signs that read "This is no coon's day," a mob of white students held a mock lynching on the front lawn of Fremont High School. [4] Five hundred teenagers gathered around a bonfire to burn six black students in effigy, having circulated a poster that explained, "We want no niggers in this school. This is a white man's school. Go to your own school and leave us to ours." Located in South Los Angeles, Fremont High School had been built in the 1920s as a haven for white students when black migration to the city was integrating these neighborhoods. Well into the 1930s, white students performed minstrel shows as part of the high school's enter-tainment. Thus, the presence of six African American students desegregating Fremont High School in 1941 was unprecedented and, for many white families, unwanted.

Hearing rumors that such a riot had occurred, Charlotta Bass, the editor of the black newspaper the *California Eagle*, went down to investigate the scene. Fremont's principal J. P. Inglis called the riot "unfortunate." Although informing the participating students "they shouldn't have done it," Inglis pursued no disciplinary action against them. Referring to the Fremont incident as "Alabama on Avalon," Bass decried the principal's reaction, "They shouldn't have done it—what amounted to a juvenile translation of the Gestapo in Germany, the Ku Klux Klan in Alabama.... What amounted to the heart-breaking failure of democracy."[5]

Unwilling to accept this sort of fear-mongering, an interracial group of mothers called a meeting and formed Mothers of Fremont High School District (later renamed Mothers and Citizens Committee for Democracy in Education) to "fight race hatred at Fremont high school."[6] A few weeks later, 15-year-old African American student Robert Summerrise spoke to a mass meeting about his experiences at Fremont:

> They used to throw orange peels and apple cores at me, and the only way I could eat lunch was to go way out on the bleachers. Pretty soon some kids told me that I had better leave school or there would be trouble. So I went to the Principal. I told him what had been going on. He said that this term was the first time so many colored kids had been going to the school (six). He said I might like it better if I went to Jeff or Jordan. I asked if he could call an assembly or something like that to tell the kids not to pick on us colored fellows, but he said it would be nice if I left the school and that I would be happier someplace else.[7]

The Mothers and Citizens Committee came up with four modest recommendations for the Board of Education to begin to address the situation: a general student body meeting at Fremont and across the city to acquaint students with black history and the rights of all citizens; an invitation by the administration of Fremont High School to any black student who might have left the school because of intimidation to return; a statement by the Board denouncing the Fremont incident; and an investigation committee by the Board that included student and community representatives.[8]

Despite this organizing, there was little response by the school district. Indeed, this mock lynching seems to have had a chilling effect on African American attendance at Fremont High School as the school returned to being a nearly all-white school through 1946.[9] On March 16, 1947, history repeated itself.[10] Six hundred white students went on strike to protest the presence of six new black students at the school. Posting signs that read "Niggers if you value your life, stay out" and "Jiggs not wanted," they hoisted two black effigies onto a lamp post. This hate strike followed weeks of harassment of black students. The previous Thursday, a group of black girls was pelted with rotten apples and threatened with death if they returned to school on Monday.[11] When Charlotta Bass attempted to drive up to the school to investigate, "our car was rammed by a jeering group of half-growns who yelled 'no niggers are wanted here.'"[12] The principal, Herbert Wood, took measured action against the striking white students, making each student sign a statement that "recognized the rights of Negro students to attend school" in order to return to Fremont.[13] But the president of the school board called the event a "trumped-up case of racial discrimination"[14] and many school authorities and white citizens thought the attention to the events at Fremont was part of a communist conspiracy.[15]

These incidents at Fremont High School—in their blatant and violent racism and in the grassroots organizing they produced—provide a different perspective for understanding the racial politics of Los Angeles. L.A. was a destination for more than a half million African American migrants in the postwar period in part because of the opportunities the city offered. Yet, legalized segregation, overt racism, along with an active and varied black freedom movement were equally part of the Southern California experience.[16] In many postwar history texts and in the public imagination, the 1965 Watts uprising serves as the dividing line between the heroic civil rights movement and the movement's militant and northward turn—a literary device to signal the shift from civil rights to Black Power.[17] Often Watts is cast as the first black political action outside of the South, and the uprising seems to derive from an alienated, apolitical community, which offers little ground for political organizing to develop. Indeed, the placing of Watts in the North is not specifically about region but about an imagined dichotomy between a righteous nonviolent movement that flowered in the South and the various forms of black anger and Black Power politics that took place in the rest of the country.[18]

In many accounts, then, the Northern black struggle appears only after the Watts riot, when Martin Luther King Jr. is chastised by the young rioters and allegedly realizes that the Voting Rights Act had not solved black people's problems in the North. This version paints local and national civil rights leaders, and Rev. King in particular, as naïve and out-of-touch with the gritty realities of ghetto blacks.[19] Simultaneously, the Watts uprising is used to introduce Black Power—and through it, Black Power comes to be seen as an angry, emotional and disorganized response of underclass black communities post-1965. Cast through the misconception that sustained political action was largely absent in the urban poor North, Black Power is shown born out of fire and looting as opposed to indigenous political organizing, organic theorizing, and varied tactical strategies.[20] In short, Black Power is framed as the absence of political organizing.[21] The Watts riot often becomes a way for historians to introduce the racial struggle in the North through a declension narrative in which the movement loses its righteous drive and disintegrates amidst spontaneous violence, internecine struggles between militant groups like Us and the Black Panthers, intense government repression, and white backlash. Anti-civil rights backlash in the North is described largely as a reaction to the riots and the black militancy that develops in their wake.

By portraying Watts as "a dense, squalid ghetto" where "residents went about the cathartic business of destroying their neighborhood" sharp contrasts are drawn between accomodationist middle-class leaders who are portrayed as "out of touch" with the black majority viewed as hard-edged ghetto dwellers who then become the foot soldiers of Black Power.[22] The term "Watts" serves as a social demarcation of black South L.A—not simply the neighborhood called Watts where only 9 percent of the city's African Americans lived in 1960, but a culturally foreign black bantustan encompassing the entirety of poor black L.A.[23] Gerald Horne asserts in his seminal study of the uprising, that one of the causes of the Watts rebellion was that "few took pride in or care of their community, and that became a root of many of its social problems."[24]

This portrayal of Black Power and political organizing in the urban North squares with a turn in the social sciences toward a theory of urban crisis. Numerous social scientists and historians have linked structural changes in the economy, black Northern migration and urban segregation with a decline of community institutions and the development of a pathological set of behaviors among an isolated and poor black community.[25] The urban black poor are often portrayed as a socially disintegrated, postindustrial underclass too busy surviving and too alienated from mainstream culture to theorize and mobilize against their oppression.[26] Rioting makes sense within this paradigm because it is the spontaneous and angry political action expected from an estranged class of people. Some scholars have suggested that blacks in L.A. were physically and psychically distanced from the civil rights movement and that, as a result, the riots "filled an ideological void in black L.A."[27] The logic is tautological: these black communities were too alienated for any long-lasting political organization and had to resort to rioting to express their frustration; thus, the riot proves that there was no sustained black activism in L.A. because, if there had been, there would be no reason for a riot. Moreover, this line of reasoning inadvertently echoes the very discourse of black "negative attitudes" that was used by city officials to justify school inequities in postwar L.A.

Seeking to complicate and expand our knowledge of black Los Angeles, a growing body of L.A. history has enlarged the story of the uprising and the racial landscape of Los Angeles more generally: pulling the timeline backward, documenting the rabid racialization of pre- and postwar L.A, charting the economic and political forces at play in the city, and painting a portrait of black L.A. before, during, and after World War II.[28] Yet in these works, the uprising still appears to arise out of a generational and ideological gap between middle-class leaders and underclass youth, the latter of whom turned to crime, gangs, violence, and for a brief moment (a militant but ineffective) Black Power to voice their disaffection with U.S. society. Pre-Watts activism is treated largely as middle-class activism that is then rebuked by the poor who rise up in 1965. While drawing attention to the weight of structural problems unaddressed by the city, these works largely maintain a notion of "black community transformation" which produced an alienated class of people estranged from political action. This scholarship perpetuates a linear trajectory and stark break between civil rights and Black Power. It misses the robust complexities of ground-level activism, the connections in movement goals and in the ideological critique of racial liberalism that spanned both periods, and the opportunity to reperiodize and reformulate notions of the black freedom struggle and postwar American politics more generally.

If we begin the story of the black freedom struggle in Los Angeles with the 1941 "Alabama on Avalon" riot, the trajectory of the movement and the meanings of the Watts uprising take on a much different look. This chapter focuses on African American organizing around school inequity in the two decades before 1965 and, in so doing, challenges the use of the Watts uprising as a dividing line between the righteous civil rights movement and the underclass Black Power one. Black Angelenos understood themselves as part of the black liberation struggle and had been waging a movement in the city for decades. The black community was a diverse one, of longtime residents and new Southern migrants, of a well-established black elite and also vast numbers of poor people, but those differences were not always divisions. At times, they prompted alliances in spite of class and ideological distinctions. Thus the presumed binary between middle-class organizing and underclass anger that often predominates in portraits of L.A. is hard to sustain when looking at grassroots activism that led up to the riot. Many African Americans from across class and generational lines took action in the postwar period, attempting to widen the space of opportunity and freedom for themselves and their families. Local chapters of the National Association for the Advancement of Colored People (NAACP), the Congress of Racial Equality (CORE), and the Nation of Islam (NOI), among others, played prominent roles in that struggle—and people moved between organizations and worked in coalitions well before 1965.[29]

Cultural and political nationalism and self-determination were a strand of the movement throughout these decades, developing in

tandem with and as a result of local people's experiences in the movement and in the face of white resistance in L.A. Indeed, this period in
L.A. provides an important window into the ingredients that shaped
Black Power: the potent mix of intense and growing racism in the
city, a concomitant public hypocrisy that L.A. was a racial promised
land, and a public justification of racial inequity through explanations
of cultural pathologies within the black community. These formed
the racial landscape of Los Angeles in which Black Power would
grow. If one aspect of Black Power would be a sharp critique of racial
liberalism, examining these two decades of L.A. activism provides us
a window onto the early roots of this critique.

This story of black activism in L.A. is focused particularly, though
not exclusively, around activism for educational equity.[30] It does not
have the space to do justice to the myriad ways Angelenos organized
around discrimination and exclusion within jobs and public space in
L.A. and pressed for political representation. People took numerous
actions during these decades to break open unions, integrate work-
sites, and protest racially exclusive housing and redevelopment
schemes—ways they moved to secure a stable economic future as the
city's industrial base shifted and shrunk. Although focusing on school
activism gives only a limited view of black organizing during this
period, it provides an important window onto the ways that community members saw schools as a primary vehicle for their children's
upward mobility. It also demonstrates how struggles for racial equity
and desegregation in L.A. were thwarted by blaming black students
and parents for their poor values while denying segregation (just
"natural boundaries").

Moreover, it returns desegregation to the Black Power narrative by
showing the continuities and cross-fertilizations of what are traditionally seen as the ideologically and temporally distinct civil rights and
Black Power movements. Desegregation meant disrupting a system
that could cordon off black children in a set of separate crowded
schools through the use of white and black taxpayer money and then
blame black children for their own educational inadequacies. This history reveals the political context that nourished black nationalism and
why celebrations of black culture, history, and community were a
necessary repudiation to these widespread beliefs of cultural inferiority.

Looking at school activism in L.A., where racial segregation was often justified through "culture of poverty" arguments, provides a way to dismantle the enduring belief about the lack of thoughtful political action among poor and working-class urban blacks.[31] Complicating the dichotomy between civil rights and Black Power, between the black poor and the middle class, this history shows how people of varying ideological positions both came together and went in different directions to address the profound racial inequities in the city's schools. This, then, is not a story of ghetto nihilism and alienation but of two decades of vibrant and frustrated struggle in the city that laid the groundwork for the 1965 uprising and for emergent militant organizations like the Black Panther Party and the Us Organization.[32] It was this panoply of action and the accompanying disillusionment with the lack of progress—with the virulence and slipperiness of white resistance in Southern California and the stark lack of concern shown by the nation at large—which formed the basis for the riot. Moreover, the consistent resistance activists encountered—made even more public with the 1964 passage of Proposition 14, which repealed the state's Fair Housing Act—disrupts the still-prevalent assumption that white backlash developed as a response to the race riots of the mid-1960s and the onset of Black Power.[33]

* * *

Los Angeles offers no easy contrast with the legalized and brutal segregation believed to be particular to the South.[34] Segregation, and in particular school segregation, had been upheld by the California courts. The California Supreme Court's 1924 *Piper v. Big Pine School District* again affirmed the constitutionality of segregating children: "it is not in violation of the organic law of the state or nation ... to require Indian children or others in whom racial differences exist to attend separate schools." In the 1920s the rejuvenated Ku Klux Klan had solidified a supple base of supporters in L.A., holding open air meetings in suburbs like South Gate, Maywood, Lynwood, and Long Beach.[35] Interracial marriages remained illegal in California until 1948, and well into the 1950s most public swimming pools were segregated—at one YMCA in South L.A., blacks could only swim on Tuesdays.[36] Many hotels and other business establishments barred black patrons, and restrictive covenants formed a legal wall around

South Los Angeles that black Angelenos could not scale. Thus, California had affirmed segregation in daily interaction and the law, not unlike the state of Alabama.

Born February 4, 1908, in St. Louis and active in the NAACP since she was a teenager in Kansas City, Marnesba Tackett moved to L.A. in 1952.[37] She had wanted to leave the South where she and her husband had been living; her husband chose Los Angeles. On arriving, she looked for the local branch of the NAACP and paid her dues. "When I came to L.A. I found the same kind of discrimination that I had found in Kansas City, in Detroit, and very little better than what I found in the South."[38] Despite its reputation for racial *bonhomie*, Los Angeles became increasingly segregated in the postwar period for African Americans.[39] While blacks had comprised only 3 percent of the city's population until World War II, the black population grew from 63,744 in 1940 to almost 763,000 in 1970. Yet, black Congressman Gus Hawkins explained, "things went backwards rather than forward."[40] Most white Angelenos, aided with federal housing loans after the war, were resolute in their commitment to living in all-white communities, and black neighborhoods grew more and more overcrowded after the war.

Marnesba Tackett was soon elected chair of the NAACP education committee and embarked on a project to examine textbooks for stereotypes and lack of exposure to African American history and culture. Racist images were plentiful in L.A. school books and, foreshadowing later nationalist calls for more black books in the curriculum, the NAACP committee focused its efforts on changing the curriculum, providing positive images of blacks and introducing black writers into the curriculum. In the early 1950s, the L.A. NAACP pressed the issue of segregation within the city's schools.[41] The Board of Education vehemently denied the charge, claiming that they were color-blind and kept no records of racial distribution of students or teachers. The NAACP would have to produce its own studies to demonstrate that segregation existed in L.A. The need to *prove* segregation would be a persistent one, and thus civil rights groups demanded on countless occasions that the Board of Education administer a racial census to determine the obvious segregated nature of L.A. schools.[42] The Board resisted calls for such a census, asserting they did not want race inscribed on individual student records and claiming that black parents would object to this.

Strategic research also formed part of an organizing strategy to mobilize black L.A. The NAACP had received numerous complaints from black teachers who could not find work.[43] In 1957–1958, the Urban League conducted a study of teachers and found that 85 percent of black teachers were teaching black students and, as a result, concentrated in a few schools. Slightly under 5 percent of teachers in L.A. were black people, which meant that most teachers in black schools were white, as were the principals. Malcolm X described such a system in his critique of school segregation: "a school is segregated when it is controlled by people who have no interest in it whatsoever."[44] Black teachers requesting school transfers were often denied, and many black teachers who lived on the Westside had to travel to the Eastside to gain a teaching job. Teacher hiring within L.A. public schools included an oral examination and a principal's interview that allowed for a significant measure of discrimination in hiring. Very few blacks held positions in school administration; in 1962, there were only two black high school principals in the entire system, and most black schools had no black people in any administrative posts.

School segregation worsened in L.A. after the Supreme Court's landmark *Brown v. Board of Education* decision.[45] As the *California Eagle* subsequently reported, "More Negro children attend all-Negro schools in Los Angeles than attend such schools in Little Rock."[46] Indeed, the 1960 census revealed that Los Angeles was more segregated than any city in the South.[47] School segregation did not simply reflect racialized housing patterns but was a systematic method of solidifying those residential patterns and distributing educational resources. Black schools were tremendously overcrowded, many forced to have double session days to accommodate all of their students. Yet, as Tackett noted, there were a "great number of empty classrooms in other sections" of the city.[48] Even though black teachers were channeled into black schools, the majority of educators in those schools were still white, and a number of white teachers still used corporal punishment against black students into the 1960s. Teachers and administrators often called black students "monkeys or even thugs and tramps."[49] Textbooks were old and often contained "happy slave tales" and demeaning portrayals of black people, history and culture.[50] College preparation classes were rare in black schools; the NAACP Education Committee reported that given the "feeling that the Negro student in particular is best equipped and qualified in the manual fields rather than the academic," black students were often directed toward manual and nonacademic programs.[51]

Given this systematic inequality, other groups also began to mobilize against disparities in the city's schools. In 1961, the Southern California American Civil Liberties Union (ACLU) began pressuring the Board around issues of school segregation.[52] Tackett, who also joined the ACLU, credits ACLU activists John and LaRee Caughey for this push, particularly around the issue of school overcrowding. In 1961, Martin Luther King Jr. made the first of many trips to speak to an L.A. Freedom Rally. Organizers expected 12,000 people to rally but more than 28,000 showed up. According to the LAPD, it was "the largest assembly of Negroes in Los Angeles within memory."[53] Although many of King's trips to L.A. were intended to generate support for Southern civil rights struggles, King highlighted issues facing African Americans in Los Angeles, and King himself made the connections early in the 1960s between Southern struggles and the L.A. movement.

In June 1962, the ACLU, NAACP, and CORE all called on the Board of Education to address widespread segregation and discrimination in the district against students and teachers. While some members dismissed the charges altogether, Board member Georgiana Hardy called for the convening of a special Ad Hoc Committee. Subsequent access to school records, according to ACLU activist John Caughey, showed that the Board had been "reliably informed about where Blacks were" in the district and thus had misrepresented its own knowledge of school segregation in LAUSD [Los Angels Unified School District]."[54] District lines had not been drawn arbitrarily. As Tackett explained, "In the Wilshire Olympic corridor where if the line had been drawn east and west instead of north and south, they would have integrated the schools in that area automatically. In the Southern area, there were places down toward Carson where if they had drawn the lines a little differently, we would have integrated the schools."[55]

Local actions continued apace. In September 1962, for instance, a group of black and Japanese families living near the all-white Baldwin Hills Elementary School tried to enroll their children and were refused. The NAACP began picketing. NAACP leader Theodore Wright explained, "These families live much closer to the Baldwin Hills school than the Marvin Ave. School, which is nearly 96% Negro. Some live only about two blocks from Baldwin and as long as seven blocks from Marvin."[56] Several days later, a group of black students tried to enroll at the white Huntington Park High School and also were rejected. After a week of picketing, fifty black students were given transfers to Baldwin Hills Elementary School, and the NAACP stopped the pickets.

The L.A. chapter of CORE became increasingly militant in this period, pioneering new campaigns of confrontational direct action. Revitalized in 1955 by the white pacifist Herbert Kelman and the black social worker Henry Hodge and counting thirty active members by 1960, L.A. CORE drew hundreds more as its direct action campaigns against housing and school segregation mounted. By 1964, several hundred people made up the chapter's membership. Seeing the interconnections between housing and school segregation, L.A. CORE targeted both public authorities and private business interests. For instance, in April 1962, CORE led a 34-day sit-in against a developer, which resulted in a black family getting to buy a home in Monterey Highlands, Monterey Park. CORE also targeted all-white housing tracts in Torrance, holding demonstrations, in the face of violence, for nearly a year. In July 1963, 1,000 people, mostly African Americans, marched for integration in Torrance.[57]

Issues of police brutality also inspired organizing that crossed ideological lines. The NAACP brought a tabulation of police brutality to the attention of the Police Commission in 1961 but "didn't get results."[58] On April 27, 1962, the 29-year-old unarmed secretary of the local Nation of Islam, Ronald Stokes, was killed and six other Muslims were wounded by police officers in a melee in front of Muslim Temple 27. Yet despite an autopsy that established that Stokes was shot at close range and had been stomped, kicked, and bludgeoned while dead or dying, the public inquest into Stokes's death found that the police shooting was "justified" in "self defense."

Making an emergency trip to L.A. to hold city authorities account-able for Stokes's death, Nation of Islam minister Malcolm X worked with the NAACP branch, local ministers such as Rev. J. Raymond Henderson and Rev. Maurice Dawkins, Cyril Briggs and emerging political leaders such as Mervyn Dymally to publicize the issue. They held a joint mass meeting that drew over 3,000 people at Second Avenue Baptist Church. Loren Miller who owned the *California Eagle* and had previously helped successfully litigate *Shelley v. Kramer* for the NAACP, and Earl Broady provided legal assistance for the fourteen young NOI members charged with resisting arrest and assaulting the police. And Celes King of the NAACP and a bail bondsman by trade provided $160,000 bail for the Nation of Islam members who had been arrested. Working with local activists, Malcolm X helped to gather 10,000 signatures on a petition to the United Nations over police brutality.

Mayor Sam Yorty lashed out at the local branch of the NAACP for its "agitation," claiming that "they are bringing about the very condition they are complaining about."[59] The local NAACP struck back, claiming the Muslims were "scapegoated"; and in a public forum with the mayor, NAACP head Roy Wilkins called attention to the city's "long reputation" under Chief Parker for police brutality.[60] After working on a case-by-case basis, the NAACP and CORE again brought grievances around a pattern of police abuse to public attention in 1963. Drawing significant attention to the issue of police brutality in L.A. in 1962 and 1963, this coalition of activists, across ideological lines, pushed the city to create a blue ribbon committee but little change in police practice. NAACP President Christopher Taylor blasted the committee's report, "We're right back where we started from. ... They have ignored all complaints of the community, and now they can keep on doing the same thing."[61]

Shortly after getting out of jail in Birmingham, in May 1963, Martin Luther King Jr. returned to L.A. and spoke to an overflow crowd of more than 35,000 people at Wrigley Field. Calling for full freedom "in Birmingham and Los Angeles," he declared, "You asked me what Los Angeles can do to help us in Birmingham [Alabama]. The most important thing that you can do is to set Los Angeles free because you have segregation and discrimination here, and police brutality."[62]

The turnout at these events and the tenor of the coverage in L.A.'s black newspapers suggests that black residents in L.A. saw themselves as part of larger black freedom struggle that linked Birmingham to Los Angeles. Moreover, the coalition of activists and groups that joined together to organize around the Stokes murder and fact that King stressed the need for the movement in L.A. two years before the Watts riot challenges the misconception that the civil rights movement and King himself turned their attention to the issues of police brutality and Northern injustice only after the Watts uprising.

Seeing the necessity for a more coordinated civil rights effort, a coalition of 76 community and political groups formed the United Civil Rights Council (UCRC), in response to King's visit to L.A.[63] Marnesba Tackett was unanimously selected as the education chair for the UCRC. According to Mary Tinglof Smith (the only pro-integration Board member), "Tackett directed the full force of her large grassroots committee against school segregation. Angered by the board's do-nothing tactics, she demanded immediate action."[64] In early June 1963, the UCRC drew up a list of demands that included redrawing district lines for purposes of desegregation; transferring students attending overenrolled schools on half-day sessions to underenrolled schools; diversifying the curriculum; and revising the transfer and promotion process to provide better distribution of black teachers throughout the entire district and more possibilities for career advancement for black teachers. These demands represented issues the community had been pressing for more than a decade. Attacking the Board's claim of colorblindness, Tackett compared Los Angeles schools to "those of Alabama and Mississippi" in order to break down the false distinction between Jim Crowism in the South and "colorblindness" in a city like L.A.[65]

Tackett's activism and leadership in these school struggles complicate prevalent ideas of L.A.'s middle-class leadership. The Tacketts were middle class—Marnesba had a successful real estate business and was 55 years old when she came to head the UCRC education committee. Yet the UCRC increasingly moved beyond the bounds of respectable protest, and Tackett's leadership was characterized by a vociferous critique of liberalism in the city and by pulling a range of people, including many young people, into these direct action protests. Given her public stature beginning in 1963, the FBI contacted Tackett every six weeks for the next four years. This pattern continued until 1967 when they asked her to be an informant for some "communistic organizations" like the Us Organization and the Black Panther Party. Tackett told the Bureau instead, "I know those organizations. They have been so supportive and I just praise them to high heaven." Having banked on exploiting what they perceived as differences within the movement, the FBI ceased contacting her after this. Tackett saw the differences being tactical, more than ideological, asserting "we all want the same thing." Still, although she was friends with the emerging Black Power leaders Ron Karenga and Tommy Jacquette, she thought their embrace of armed self-defense suicidal. "Because the whole idea of attempting to get equality by fighting for it is only going to end up in defeat. Because we do not own the ammunition. We do not build the rockets. We do not manufacture the guns."[66]

The UCRC asked for a response to its school proposals within ten days. Most of the Board actively opposed desegregation while maintaining that the problem did not exist. Board member Charles Smoot declared, "I say no de facto segregation exists.... I resent pressure put on the board.... We represent majorities."[67] And J. C. Chambers asserted that if there was not much black history being taught in LAUSD, it was because there was "not much of it to teach." These attitudes effectively absolved the Board from having to do anything while maintaining the idea that any differences in education were the result of cultural inferiority.[68] A year after its convening, the Board's Ad Hoc Committee still had not issued any report or recommendations.

Black leaders were making many direct comparisons between L.A. and Birmingham—to the venal racial climate that existed in both cities and the confrontational direction the movements were taking. Such rhetorical strategies sought to demonstrate the gravity of the situation in Los Angeles and to highlight the righteousness of the struggle that black Angelenos were waging. Rev. Maurice Dawkins, former president of the NAACP chapter, wrote an *L.A. Times* piece threatening Birmingham-style demonstrations if decisive action around schools was not taken. Yet, the liberal Board of Supervisors member Kenneth Hahn (not unlike clergy in Birmingham) decried confrontation. Hahn distinguished the liberal racial politics of L.A. from those of Birmingham and believed that confrontational politics were unnecessary and alienating. In early June, a conference of city and county officials, businessmen, and black leaders was held in Hahn's office "to avert any violent demonstrations similar to those that have torn cities apart in the South."[69] A group of black leaders including Tackett and NAACP President Christopher Taylor then issued a statement "To Men of Good Will" purposefully echoing King's "Letter from a Birmingham Jail": "All deliberate speed has meant no speed at all. The spirit of Birmingham means integration now in every way."[70]

On June 24, 1963, despite criticisms from many white politicians and some black residents, more than 1,000 people joined the UCRC in a Freedom March from the First African Episcopal Church through downtown and ending at the Board of Education, which still had not responded to the UCRC. This was the first in a series of marches that continued all summer to pressure the Board around school inequity. Birmingham-styled, confrontational nonviolent tactics were on full display in L.A. As Marnesba Tackett recalled, "There was so much resistance [here in L.A.] that I really did not have time to work actively [on behalf of events in the South]."[71] The UCRC grew increasingly frustrated with this lack of action and with the Board's continuing suggestion that there needed to be more discussion of the issue. "We've talked enough. We're breaking off negotiations!" asserted Tackett after the Board defeated a voluntary student transfer plan 6–1, committed an extra $737,000 for remedial classes for black children, while still having no report from the Ad Hoc Committee regarding their demands.[72]

In response to this obstinacy, the UCRC called for more demonstrations and political action against recalcitrant Board members, opposed support for future school bond issues, and supported legal proceedings against the Board.[73] In August, the UCRC held a silent protest in the boardroom to dramatize their decision that further talks with the school board were fruitless. National civil rights leaders joined the UCRC's fight. James Farmer of CORE and James Forman of SNCC (Student Nonviolent Coordinating Committee) came to L.A. to lead a march of more than 600 to the Board of Education building.

There Tackett declared, "We have been the victims of subterfuge and delay."[74] Tackett and other community activists highlighted the polite hypocrisy that preserved L.A.'s segregated school system. Malcolm X waged a similar critique in his speech "The Ballot or the Bullet": "In the North, they do it a different way.... [W]hen Negroes become too heavily concentrated in a certain area, and begin to gain too much political power, the white man comes along and changes the district lines. ... And usually, it's the white man who grins at you the most, and pats you on the back, and is supposed to be your friend. He may be friendly, but he's not your friend."[75] The UCRC continued to speak out against the profound racial inequities imbedded in the school system and the hypocrisy that protected it.

A coalition of civil rights groups, the NAACP, ACLU, CORE and UCRC, highlighted the examples of Jordan High School (98 percent black) and South Gate High School (less than 1 percent black), which were less than two miles apart, to demonstrate the intentionality of school inequality in Los Angeles.[76] Five black students had desegregated South Gate High School in June 1963 and faced eggs, bricks, Confederate flags, and racial epithets.[77] Despite the Board's claims that Jordan and South Gate were simply "neighborhood schools," many black students lived closer to South Gate than Jordan, and many whites to Jordan rather than South Gate. Black community leaders pressed the Board to rezone using only commuting distance as the determinant. Tackett explained, "The education at South Gate was so much better, there was no comparison. Alameda Street, the boundary which separated them, was called 'the line.' ... We noticed that the school board kept expanding Jordan's boundary as more black children moved into it instead of sending them to South Gate." Alameda was a "natural boundary" separating segregated high schools at 103rd, Manchester, and Slauson streets, but not at Vernon, where black elementary schoolers were expected to cross it to get to school.[78] Jordan High School was also located on its own eastern boundary line, next to a group of junkyards, and community leaders initially pushed to close Jordan completely because of its poor location. The Board's persistent claim of "natural boundaries," then, echoed the hypocrisy decried by Chester Himes.

Activism intensified in September 1963, particularly among young people. Jordan High School students protested "Jim Crowism" on the first day of school. Days later, eight CORE members conducted a weeklong hunger strike in front of the Board of Education. A week later, hundreds of students marched on the Board of Education.[79] On September 12, 1963, the report of the Ad Hoc Committee on Equal Education Opportunity was finally issued. After 15 months of hearings, the report rejected most of the NAACP and UCRC's proposals and placed responsibility for whatever problems did exist outside their purview. In the preface, they wrote,

> [T]here are no easy answers and no speedy solutions to these problems which include de facto segregation in our schools; the present segregated housing patterns of the community; the high incidence of low economic status among minority people … and the lack of hope and motivation among some of these families which leads them into negative attitudes toward education and the demands the school makes on their children.[80]

The language of *negative attitudes toward education* provided L.A. a way to shirk responsibility for any racial patterns within its schools. Relying on the Board's staff as an objective source of information on discrimination within the system, they concluded, "We are not disposed to urge that free citizens of any race be forced into educational environments not of their own choice." By blaming black and Latino families for their values and motivation and suggesting that this was the real reason for minority student underachievement, the Board provided a palatable justification for the existence of racially different educations—a group of culturally deficient students, not a segregated system. The district would raise the budget of compensatory and remedial programs for black and Mexican American children but not address segregation.[81] In the face of this assault on black culture and values, activists moved toward avenues that would celebrate, promote, and preserve black history and culture.

In response, while decrying the Board's "failure to obey the law of the land," CORE and the UCRC held numerous interracial sit-ins, sleep-ins, and study-ins throughout the fall. Hundreds of student protesters marched, lined the halls of the Board of Education building, and disrupted meetings throughout the fall.[82] Young people took the lead in these confrontations, filling the streets, halls, and meetings. Hundreds of students conducted study-ins along the corridors of the Board of Education in November, and held a sing-in to disrupt a Board meeting. Board member Tinglof Smith recalled the numerous small actions young people took to confront school authorities. "As the hearings dragged on, the student integrationists became more and more impatient.... I remember the 'study-in' with students, nose in book littering the sides of the long corridors in the board building.... On another front there was talk of seven students volunteering to chain themselves to the chauffeured automobiles allotted each board member."[83] The notion that activism pre-Watts was strictly older generation and conciliatory is a troubling act of historical amnesia.

Such confrontational tactics were not popular in a city proud of its liberalism like Los Angeles. In November, national director of CORE James Farmer was barred from speaking at the University of Southern California (located on the edge of South L.A), because the dean deemed him "too controversial."[84] That same month, CORE launched "Operation Jericho," going door-to-door in Watts to counter petition campaigns by South Gate residents to prevent school desegregation.[85] At the end of the month, the Board acquiesced to South Gate parents and refused to redraw the school boundary between South Gate and Watts and ruled that no South Gate children would be bused out of the area. They made available 34 high school transfers for black students to attend school in South Gate and Huntington High Schools—a move Tackett characterized as "virtually no change from the past."[86] The *Eagle* called the decisions a "fraud of the worst kind, designed to maintain the present segregation on the one hand and to allay criticism on the other."[87]

Given the Board's public posture around "open enrollment," the UCRC then called for the busing of black and Mexican American children attending overcrowded, double-session elementary schools to vacant slots in full-day white schools. (Many schools serving black and Latino children had grown so crowded that they were forced to operate two different sessions per school day—some students attending in the morning, others in the afternoon.) When the Board allocated only $80,000, covering less than 800 of the more than 5000 students on double-session days, a group of parents decided to take matters into their own hands and create their own busing program that would begin operating with private funds in the fall of 1965.[88] Other activists were taking different directions, prioritizing cultural and historical reclamation in an attempt to ward off damaging school curriculum and public attitudes about black cultural deficiencies. Ron Karenga, who would later form the black nationalist group the Us Organization, began teaching an adult Swahili class at Fremont High School in 1964.

An examination of the black newspapers the *L.A. Sentinel* and the *California Eagle* during this period makes clear the variety of actions in the years leading up to the Watts uprising and the interconnections between various strands of the movement often viewed as divergent, for example, the NAACP and the Nation of Islam. Nearly every week they detailed numerous grassroots actions happening within the city. This was front-page news, not overshadowed by events happening in the South but often connected by the paper's journalists to movements in Birmingham, Selma, Greensboro, and Jackson. The *Eagle* gave Tackett a "Woman of the Year" award in 1964, referring to her as "small of stature but a self-starting dynamo in the fight against segregation in the city's schools." Accepting the honor, Tackett told the audience to "get out their walking shoes because there are a lot more demonstrations against the do-nothing policy of the School Board coming up."[89] Such coverage meant that many black people who were not directly involved in these movements were nonetheless well informed of the struggle—similar to a place like Birmingham, where many African Americans were affected by the movement even though they did not participate. As Celes King, who had been active in the L.A. NAACP since 1951 and became vice president from 1964 to 1966, explained, "So with all the expectancies out there, and the models in the other part of the country where they appeared to be making progress, here in L.A. we were supposed to be the satisfied blacks. Well, they really weren't satisfied."[90]

This burgeoning mass movement had to turn its organizing energies to defeating an ominous proposition on the ballot in 1964. Proposition 14 sought to repeal the state's 1963 Rumford Fair Housing Act banning racial discrimination in the sale of property. Civil rights activists had worked hard to see the Fair Housing Act passed, and now this new proposition threatened to return the right of Californians to discriminate in the sale of their property.[91] According to ACLU activist John Caughey, those "that had supported UCRC efforts for reforming the schools now saw a need to concentrate on defeat of the realtor's proposition."[92] Initially these groups (including the Caugheys and Tackett) actively sought to prevent Proposition 14 from getting on the ballot; then to press for it to be on the November rather than June ballot (when realtor groups sought to rush it into the June election); and finally to oppose its passage. The NAACP, UCRC and CORE, along with student groups from a number of L.A. colleges, conducted voter registration workshops, called for a boycott of Southwest Realty Board for backing the initiative, and worked to pressure Governor Edmund Brown to come out against the proposition.[93] Martin Luther King Jr. came to L.A. in February 1964 to join the fight against Proposition 14, saying its passage would "be one of the most shameful developments in our nation's history."[94] Supporters of Proposition 14 picketed King's speech, likening it to communism. Angry white Angelenos also picketed the opening of the Western Christian Leadership Conference office, carrying signs reading "King Has Hate, Does Travel" and "Thank God for Chief Parker." King returned to L.A. in late May to join with 15,000 people in a giant interfaith rally against Proposition 14 in California and for passage of the Civil Rights Act in Washington, DC.[95]

Supporters of Proposition 14 drew on many "culture of poverty" images that had been deployed previously to justify patterns of racial inequity. L.A. County Young Republican President Robert Gaston asserted, "Negroes are not accepted [in white neighborhoods] because they haven't made themselves acceptable."[96] Indeed, in a language palatable to white moderates, the campaign to pass Proposition 14 took up the discourses of culture, family, and pathology that had historically thwarted the black freedom movement in L.A. Calling the 1963 Fair Housing Act "the Forced Housing Act," supporters of Proposition 14 raised contrasting images of black and white families—happy, suburban Anglo families and dysfunctional and deviant families of color. Such ideas were not new but would prove resilient in the November election. A scant four months after Lyndon Johnson had signed the Civil Rights Act, California voters passed Proposition

14, repealing the state's Fair Housing Act. Three of four white voters supported it, and the measure passed two to one.

Proposition 14's passage sent a collective chill through black California. Despite the passage of the Civil Rights Act and a president who had gone to bat for civil rights, these national commitments did not seem to extend to California. While it would later be overturned in court, the message behind Proposition 14's overwhelming approval was clear: black people were not welcome in many neighborhoods in California and liberal politicians like Lyndon Johnson and Edmund Brown were not willing to do much about it. But its venom was insidious in nature: unlike Selma or Birmingham where many opponents of racial equality were forthright in their defense of segregation, Proposition 14's ugliness lurked just beneath the surface. And thus it could be willfully ignored by those who would claim surprise when nine months later, the arrest of Marquette Frye sparked seven days of rioting in the largely black neighborhoods of South L.A.

The story of the Watts uprising cannot be fully understood without foregrounding this activism and the effect of Proposition 14. It sapped the organizing energies of a broad array of community activists. Forcing them to defend one of the gains they had labored to secure, it literally took valuable organizing energy away from movements around housing and education. In an interview three days after the Watts rebellion, the renowned African American psychiatrist Alvin Poussaint identified Proposition 14's passage as one of the root causes behind the rebellion.[97] Simultaneously, it demonstrated the success of political discourses of family values, crime, delinquency, and community pathology in forging a post-civil rights political movement and in preventing social change in a city like Los Angeles. Submerging race in a lexicon of family and crime, culture, and behavior had dominated the city's response to black demands for school and housing desegregation and would prompt a conservative rebirth bringing Ronald Reagan to the governorship in 1966 and Richard Nixon to the U.S. presidency in 1968.[98]

* * *

I doubt that a single Negro in Los Angeles would agree that conditions are improving. We don't walk down the same street. You may think the courts are the same, arrests are the same, getting insurance is the same. But it isn't. The real Negro leaders have been trying to speak to you for years ... You won't listen.

—James Baldwin at a press conference in L.A., May 1963[99]

On August 11, 1965, the California Highway Patrol pulled over 21-year-old Marquette Frye for drunk driving. Frye had grown up in Wyoming before moving to California in 1957. He drew a sharp contrast: "The school curriculum was better. The kids' vocabularies were better.... In Wyoming ... there were only about eight Negroes in school ... and we were accepted by the whites. When we came to California, we got into an all-Negro school ... I made 'A's and 'B's back in Wyoming. But here I kept getting suspended for fighting."[100] Frye ended up dropping out of Fremont High School.

When another officer arriving on the scene began hitting Frye and his mother, the crowd that had gathered began throwing stones and bottles. This escalated to looting and burning buildings. In response, the police cracked down on the rioters and on the community at large. As Cynthia Hamilton, who was a 15-year-old attending Fremont High School, later explained, "the city used the incident to quarantine the entire community."[101] The city curfew only covered black L.A.—an area that the media then began calling "Watts," although it covered the neighborhoods of Watts, Central, Avalon, Florence, Green Meadow, Exposition, and Willowbrook. That this swatch of 250,000 residents could be effectively cordoned off from the rest of the city is a testament to the degree of segregation in L.A.

The uprising lasted seven days—tens of thousands of African Americans as well as thousands of other Angelenos participated.[102] Thirty-four people died, and hundreds were injured, many at the hands of the police; 14,000 National Guardsmen had been called out and 4000 black people had been arrested. Forty-five million dollars' worth of property had been damaged. Nonetheless, John Caughey described the period after the riot as one of activism and organization: "The riot also spread awareness that discriminations were rife. Concern to get at the underlying causes and to prevent a recurrence produced activity reminiscent of the early months of UCRC, but on a larger scale."[103]

The public reaction to the riot quickly turned to surprise. Despite an active black freedom movement in the city for decades, local and state officials were *astonished* by the anger evident in the riots. Governor Brown, on vacation when the riot happened, flew home immediately. Telling reporters that "nobody told me there was an explosive situation in Los Angeles," he maintained that California was "a state where there is no racial discrimination."[104] Police Chief William Parker and Mayor Sam Yorty professed similar ignorance.[105] The surprise expressed by many politicians, city officials, businesspeople, and other California residents after the Watts uprising needs to be understood in part as the surprise of intransigence—a willful shock. This had not been an invisible movement with small grievances and unpublicized demands but one that had challenged the fabric of L.A. society: schools, housing, jobs, policing. Surprise, then, became a way to deny the longstanding nature and significance of those grievances—to erase a pattern of racial struggle within the city.

The riot was more targeted than public officials suggested. For instance, the Urban League's Watts project was unscathed, the only building not burned on the block.[106] Some—but not all—white businesses in South L.A. were burned (such as the 4300 block of Central Avenue that restricted African Americans from renting business fronts and 37 of the 40 savings and loans associations that charged higher interest rates in South L.A.); some—but not all—black establishments were spared. Aimed largely at commercial interests, most housing was untouched. Stan Myles, a black student at Cal-State Long Beach, explained that people were "not lawless"; community members volunteered to man street corners where traffic lights had gone out and drivers followed their lead. But it became easier to describe rioters as indiscriminate and criminal (although most arrested had no previous record) than to grapple with the substance of the uprising. Chief Parker, for instance, likened rioting blacks to "monkeys in a zoo."[107]

According to NAACP vice president Celes King, the profound hope and accompanying disappointments over the lack of racial progress in the city laid the groundwork for the riot. "[I]n order to talk about the Watts riot, it's impossible not to, say, go back and look at some of the conditions that tended to create the atmosphere.

Some of those things dealt with a level of expectance that was moving along in our community ... A lot of things were creating a thing called hope, and hope is the kind of thing that, when the bubble explodes, problems occur too."[108] The anger and frustration that burst forth during the riot did not reveal nihilism but demonstrated the expectation that had grown within African Americans in the city. Celes King posted bond for hundreds of people; to do this, he risked his business because he eliminated the standards usually used to agree to post bail for someone. That the vice president of the NAACP was willing to bail people out of jail, to affiliate himself and his economic future with the rioters, is telling. Celes King elaborated, "The community was, I would say, generally supportive of the blacks that were the so-called rioters."[109] The Los Angeles Riot study conducted by UCLA on black attitudes about the riot found that 58 percent of the black people surveyed felt that favorable results would follow the riot, 62 percent considered the riot a Negro protest, and 64 percent thought the attack was deserved. This is not to say that every black Angeleno saw the riot as a form of protest (a significant minority of the black community clearly did not) nor even that those who did linked it directly to the activism in the city of the previous decades. But to understand how nearly two-thirds of black Angelenos surveyed saw the riot as "deserved" necessitates seeing both the inequities in the city and the history of struggle to address these by other means.

Martin Luther King Jr. traveled to Watts to assess the situation, and many commentators quote an encounter between King and the young rioters to illustrate the untenable gap between the civil rights movement and the emerging Black Power one. "We won," they told King, "because we made them pay attention to us." Although this quote is usually used to highlight the disjuncture between Rev. King and these ghetto youth, it reads much differently in the context of a two-decade struggle against school and housing segregation in the city. Despite a multifaceted movement, the city's schools were more segregated and unequal in 1965 than in 1950—and black students continued to be blamed for their poor values and low motivation. Getting the city even to pay attention, let alone address these inequities, remained a crucial problem. King's reaction to the uprising and the way he framed his "shock" also must be understood as partly calculated for he, too, had been raising fundamental questions about the lack of economic and social justice in Los Angeles and across the nation to little avail. As Alfred Ligon, owner of the black bookstore Aquarian Bookstore and Center, explained, "It was only because of the [Watts] uprising that they became interested in the blacks."[110] The massive public attention to the Watts riot allowed King, as well as local leaders, a new platform to expound on these issues.

The uprising produced an avalanche of study, of scholars and journalists who journeyed to Watts to unearth the real ghetto story. The African American writer Maya Angelou, living in L.A. at the time, described the misconceptions of nihilism and destitution perpetuated by the media about the character of the rioters and by extension, of Black Power. Angelou described an encounter with a French journalist:

> If he had visited the area one day before it exploded, if he had gone to the right bar or pool hall or community center, he could have met someone who heard his accent and, realizing he was a stranger, might have invited him home. He could have been sitting in a well-furnished house dining on great chicken and greens, receiving all the kindnesses. Then he really would have been befuddled if, on the following day, he heard of the conflagration and had seen his host of the day before struggling with the heavily armed police.... [This journalist] wrote an account of the Watts riot allowing his readers to hold on to the stereotypes that made them comfortable while congratulating themselves on being in possession of some news.[111]

Angelou's observation was supported by one study that showed two-thirds of the men arrested and convicted for their participation in the riot were employed, with a third making over $300 per month.[112]

Governor Brown established a commission to study the causes of the riot. In December 1965, the McCone Commission issued its report on the causes of the uprising, largely attributing it to black pathology that had developed from the history of slavery and a "dull devastating spiral of failure that awaits the average disadvantaged child." Advocating more remedial programs, the Commission blamed black students who they described as "unprepared and unready" for their own segregated schools: "the very low level of scholastic achievement we observe in the predominantly Negro schools contributes to de facto segregation in the schools.... We reason, therefore, that raising the scholastic achievement might reverse the entire trend of de facto segregation."[113] Although the report recommended massive public and private spending, it did so in the context of describing an alien and dysfunctional black community who exhibited un-American values and antisocial behaviors. While the Watts uprising brought temporary funding (and the War on Poverty) to South L.A., these "culture of poverty" assumptions limited how systemic the change would be and lent further urgency to local activists to reclaim black culture and pride.

The vast majority of studies ignored the long-standing demands and social movements within the city; even those that foregrounded social inequality did so outside of the frame of a black community organized and organizing for social change. Indeed, they portrayed the "community" as estranged from those who did engage in politics and disregarded the presence of a long-standing black struggle in the city. By framing activism in the city outside of a righteous black freedom movement, black Los Angeles was pictured as implicitly less deserving of racial justice and educational equity. This historical erasure helped further the marginalization of South L.A. as a culturally foreign place, and it cast groups that developed in the wake of the riot such as the Black Panther Party and the Us Organization as a product not of progressive activism amid a hostile racial climate but of an alien and alienated black community. By doing so, the growing militancy, the emphasis on cultural pride and reclamation, the continued importance of eliminating school segregation and diversifying the curriculum, and the embrace of self-defense that characterized Us, the Panthers, and the school walk-outs of the late 1960s, were delegitimized as surprising and extremist. Indeed, Black Power in Los Angeles evolved out of a genealogy that includes, rather than reacts to, what is often deemed "civil rights protest"—out of a mounting critique of racial liberalism by community activists in the city over three decades and an activist politics of confrontation that long preceded the uprising.

2

AMIRI BARAKA, THE CONGRESS OF AFRICAN PEOPLE, AND BLACK POWER POLITICS FROM THE 1961 UNITED NATIONS PROTEST TO THE 1972 GARY CONVENTION

KOMOZI WOODARD

For hundreds of years we have been the footstool of other races and nations of the earth simply because we have failed … to recognize and know ourselves as other men have known themselves and felt that there is nothing in the world that is above them except the influence of God.

—Marcus Garvey, *Philosophy and Opinions*

Afro-Americans were caught up in an assertive drive for a viable, collective identity adapted to the peculiar conditions of their development in the United States and their African background. Further, it was a drive to recover a cultural heritage shaped by over 300 years of chattel slavery and a century of thwarted freedom.

—Harry Haywood, *Black Bolshevik: Autobiography of an Afro-American Communist*

During the Black Power Movement, Amiri Baraka (LeRoi Jones) and the Congress of African People (CAP) provided an important window into the international dimensions of the black freedom struggle of the 1960s. Black Power organizations such as the Black Panther Party, National Welfare Rights Organization, Student Nonviolent Coordinating Committee (SNCC), the League of Revolutionary Black Workers, the African Liberation Support Committee, the National Black Political Assembly (NBPA), and the Congress of African People served as vital links between the local struggle for Black Power and the global fight for African Liberation. This chapter explores Amiri Baraka's politics during his leadership in the Congress of African People, especially his political trajectory between his arrest at the so-called United Nations Riot in 1961 and his rise to national leadership at the Gary Convention in March 1972.

The Black Power movement developed during a distinct period in international relations. For Third World radicals, the Cold War offered danger and opportunity. These radical activists interpreted global events in unique ways. Racial oppression and black resistance have a long history. In New Jersey, Colonel Tye led the Ethiopian Regiments in guerrilla warfare against divided white slaveholders in the midst of the American Revolution. During the Cold War, with the United States and the Soviet Union locked in a global struggle for power and influence, Third World radicals such as Ahmed Babu and Malcolm X felt that liberation struggles might make use of the dispute between superpowers to forge ahead for freedom. Of course, it would take daring to employ such a strategy. If the federal government could terrorize and hound W.E.B. Du Bois, Claudia Jones, and Paul Robeson, then it might frighten, intimidate and silence black leadership in general. For the younger generation, the difference between the civil rights establishment and the black nationalist militants seemed clear. During the Congo Crisis in the 1960s, Malcolm X openly voiced the sentiments of the blacks who were developing political opposition to America's role in the death of Patrice Lumumba and the Congolese people. Malcolm X declared that the days of white supremacy and Western imperialism were numbered. However, although Malcolm X's forces openly denounced U.S. policies in the Congo, the buzzwords for Martin Luther King Jr. and the

American Negro Leadership Conference on Africa were civility and caution. In fact, the White House was attempting to *intimidate* and *condition* black leadership to accept its exclusive hegemony over foreign affairs, including colonialism and independence in Africa. There were many avenues for the expression of such threats, including the national media. Thus, the *Washington Post* lectured the civil rights establishment: "Insofar as the civil rights leaders allow their movements to become hostage to the uncertain and confused events in Africa, they can provide heedless comfort to their enemies.... There ought to be the utmost caution in statements that can enable bigots to assert that race is a stronger bond than citizenship."[1] In other words, the establishment would "protect" African Americans from extremist "bigots" only if black leadership accepted a subordinate role in matters of public policy and foreign affairs. The right of full citizenship did not extend to African American leaders when it came to these political affairs; and clearly white terror would be employed in order to enforce those rules of the game. Malcolm X would pay a high price for his political and intellectual independence; and the new wave of leadership would have to decide how it would respond to the limits on black thinking imposed by white power during the Cold War.

Piero Gleijeses reports that "After the U.S.-Belgian raid on Stanleyville, the leaders of the American Negro Leadership Conference on Africa asked for a meeting with President Lyndon Johnson, who handed them over to Secretary Rusk. 'What the President hopes is that you might find a way of making the point that we do not think it is a good thing at all to encourage a separate Negro view of foreign policy,' National Security Adviser Bundy told Rusk. 'I get loud and clear that the President wants to discourage emergence of any special Negro pressure group (a la the Zionists) which might limit his freedom of maneuver,' noted an NSC official."[2] Thus, the civil rights leadership was being *conditioned* to proceed with extreme caution in international politics, particularly when voicing opinions regarding Africa. However, a new breed of leadership emerged that openly denounced the U.S. role in the Congo, along the lines of Malcolm X's condemnations of White House policy.

The 1961 pro-Lumumba protest at the United Nations, the so-called UN Riot, marked the birth of the New Afro-American

Nationalism, one of the formative influences in the development of Black Power. A generation of black activists identified with the charismatic leader of the independence movement in the Congo, Patrice Lumumba. For political and cultural workers watching the rise of African independence, Patrice Lumumba held a singular fascination. Lumumba rose from simple origins in a remote Congolese village; and like Malcolm X he held no university degrees to heighten his claims to leadership. However, with courage and determination, by 1960 Lumumba had become a man of the people and a burning symbol of African nationalism. Many of the students empathized with Lumumba, a young man with high aspirations despite the humiliations of white colonialism. At one point, the young Lumumba had wandered into a segregated white area in his homeland, and a white woman called him a "dirty monkey." Such experiences resonated with young black people from South Africa to the United States. Moreover, Lumumba sent clear signals that the days of African timidity were over. Lumumba's leadership would not be intimidated by Belgium colonialism or Western imperialism and he insisted that the Congolese not replace Belgian colonialism with a new imperialism.[3]

However, the United States made no secret of backing secessionist forces aiming to dismember the Congo in order to keep its tremendous mineral wealth in the hands of Western capitalism. Soon after Lumumba's election to prime minister of the Republic of the Congo, violence erupted in the new nation. During an international tour, Patrice Lumumba spoke in several cities in the United States. Howard University students warmly received Lumumba in July 1960 when he addressed students about the crisis in the Congo and when he spoke in New York City on July 24, stressing the strategic value of his nation's resources, blacks were drawn to Lumumba and the fate of the mineral rich Congo. In effect, for a generation of students whose attention was riveted on the struggle to control Africa, the Congo Crisis was a crash course in world political economy.

As the situation worsened, Belgian interests usurped power in the Congo and outrageous reports from Africa brought news of the death of Lumumba's daughter, and soon thereafter, about the brutal intimidation and bullying of the imprisoned Premier Lumumba. For African Americans, Patrice Lumumba was the Nelson Mandela of his era.

John Henrik Clarke explained the overwhelming attraction for Lumumba for Black America: "Patrice Lumumba became a hero and a martyr to Afro-American nationalists because he was the symbol of the black man's humanity struggling for recognition.... When the Congo emerged clearly in the light of modern history he was its bright star. Lumumba was a true son of Africa and was accepted as belonging to all of Africa, not just the Congo. No other personality has leaped so suddenly from death to martyrdom."[4]

Indeed, the protests were international, with demonstrations erupting from the West to the East. Demonstrations, some of them bloody, developed in the major Western capitals: Dublin, Bonn, Belgrade, Rome, and Paris. In the East students roared in Colombo, Sri Lanka; Bombay and New Delhi, India; Karachi, Pakistan; and, Malaya, Malaysia, with the largest demonstration reported in China where Premier Zhou En Lai led one rally, attended by 100,000 in Beijing. In Africa, students demonstrated their anger in Casablanca, Morocco; Khartoum, Sudan; and Accra, Ghana. "Lumumba believed in his mission," wrote the Algerian revolutionary Frantz Fanon, he "continued to express Congolese patriotism and African nationalism in their most rigorous and noblest sense."[5] Ghanaian President Kwame Nkrumah charged that the United Nations schemed to murder Lumumba, and particularly attacked Britain, France, and the United States. In a wire to President Eisenhower, President Sekou Toure of Guinea condemned the role of the United States in the Congo. In line with the African condemnations, Cuba's representative criticized the United Nations.[6]

In the United States, there were demonstrations in Washington, D.C., where a number of students from Howard University were arrested and in Chicago, blacks carried signs insisting, "Shame on the West!"[7] The most dramatic upheaval took place in New York City. On Wednesday evening, February 15, 1961, at the United Nations headquarters, a group of African Americans, the women wearing black veils and men black armbands, shocked the nation by expressing their outrage right on the floor of the Security Council. While the U.S. Representative Adlai Stevenson spoke, "About sixty men and women burst into the Security Council Chamber, interrupting the session, and fought with guards in a protest against the United

Nations policies in the Congo and the slaying of Patrice Lumumba, former Congo Premier." After the violent clash between the demonstrators and the UN police force, twenty people were treated for injuries by United Nations medical personnel.[8]

Outside of the UN headquarters there was another contingent of the demonstration on the north side of 42nd Street, chanting: "Congo, yes! Yankee, no!" Amiri Baraka, Calvin Hicks, and Mae Mallory were beaten and arrested in front of the United Nations. According to Baraka, the police came at them with clubs flying and "Mae [Mallory] put up a terrific battle and the police were sorry they ever put their hands on her. It took several of them to subdue her." Mounted police, seeking to prevent protestors from taking the demonstration to Times Square attacked at the corner of 6th Avenue and 43rd Street. A mass rally was held in Harlem to protest police repression and one of the protest groups was led by the jazz singer Abbey Lincoln. [9]

The controversial demonstrations split African Americans into two camps. Whereas civil rights establishment leaders Roy Wilkins of the NAACP and Ralph Bunche of the UN condemned the protest, the demonstrations announced the emergence of a New Nationalism. This new trend formulated in international solidarity with the emerging nations of Africa, and its heroes were shared by a number of student groups around the world. Second, this new breed was not confined to Harlem; as indicated by the Lumumba protests, there were circles emerging in other American cities not only on the East Coast but also in the Midwest and on the West Coast. Third, these new militants placed African liberation at the center of their concerns and claimed African politics as part of their political interests. And, finally, there was an intense revival of the search for a meaningful black identity that was somehow closely connected with the independence struggles in Africa.

A number of young people drawn together by the demonstrations soon discovered common political and cultural interests. Speaking of poets such as Askia Muhammad Toure, Baraka recalls that, "When I first came in contact with them, it was as a political activist, [later] we all found out we were poets." Many of those young artists would find community fighting for a "Cultural Revolution" in the Black Arts Movement.[10]

Of course, the black artists' interest in Third World politics did not begin with the Congo Crisis. Just a year earlier, Baraka had joined veteran black writers including Julian Mayfield, John Clarke, and Harold Cruse in Havana to meet Fidel Castro and to celebrate the first anniversary of the Cuban Revolution. It was in Cuba that Baraka met his hero, the militant freedom fighter Robert F. Williams of the controversial Monroe, North Carolina, NAACP. Under repeated violent attack, the Monroe NAACP met white terror with armed self-defense. Beginning with the "Kissing case" Williams employed the tactic of exposing white terror and repression in the international arena to force the hands of U.S. justice. Washington refused to facilitate the prison release of two little boys who kissed a white girl in a children's game in North Carolina until Williams took the case to French public opinion. In Cuba, Williams would find a wider field of international pressure points to expose American racism. Later, Williams would meet Mao Zedong in China and draft a number of Mao's historic statements in solidarity with the African American struggle against white terror, including one in response to the assassination of Martin Luther King Jr.[11] Meeting Robert F. Williams and Fidel Castro was a formative experience for the 25-year-old Amiri Baraka. As Harold Cruse observes, "The great transformation in LeRoi Jones was brought on by the Cuban Revolution." And Baraka concurs in his autobiography: "The Cuban trip was a turning point in my life." At the same time, "In Havana it was noted that Jones made a very favorable impression on the revolutionary intelligentsia of the Castro regime," reports Cruse.[12]

The generational difference was marked. Although Cruse was perhaps the most skeptical of any of the writers, for Baraka the encounters not only in Cuba with Fidel Castro but also on his long political journey with such leaders and writers, Mohammad Babu of Zanzibar, Ngugi wa Thiong'o of Kenya, Walter Rodney of Guyana, as well as Robert F. Williams and Malcolm X, challenged his identity both as a writer and as a man. As far as Baraka was concerned he was on the path to finding himself, and it all revolved around the sense of kinship that he felt with that generation of radicals in Cuba, Africa, and Asia. In scholarly terms, Baraka's generation was forming "an imagined community" not only of an African American nation but also of a "fictive kinship" of Third World revolutionaries. In political terms, the African revolutionary Amilcar Cabral termed that odyssey of identity and struggle, a "Return to the Source."

Within a few years, elements of the United Nations protests, scattered across the country, would give birth to a forceful Black Power Movement. That movement would bear the birth marks of support for the Cuban Revolution, African liberation, and armed self-defense against white terror and intimidation. It was also characterized by a mounting quest for African American identity and black self-determination.

* * *

By the 1970s Baraka had graduated from those fledgling groups at the UN demonstration; he was at the helm of one of the most formidable Black Power organizations in the United States, the Congress of African People, a group that crystallized and institutionalized the thrust of the annual National Black Power Conferences between 1966 and 1968. The Congress of African People was founded at a summit meeting of 3000 black people in Atlanta, Georgia, on the Labor Day weekend of 1970. CAP featured a broad united front of Black Power and civil rights leadership, symbolized by the public embrace of the Nation of Islam representative Louis Farrakhan and the National Urban League leader Whitney Young as well as Jesse Jackson and Betty Shabazz. Leading up to the African Congress, the Southern Christian Leadership Conference (SCLC) leader Ralph Abernathy and many other civil rights leaders supported Baraka's campaign for black political power in Newark. This unity would pave the road to the largest black political convention in U.S. history, the March 1972 Gary Convention.

As one of the organizers of CAP, Baraka was immediately launched into the national and international political arena. In the aftermath of the CAP conference, Baraka's itinerary on September 22, 1970, included a day of diplomatic meetings in New York City with representatives of Sudan, Guinea, and Tanzania: Ambassador Fekreddine Mohamed at the Sudanese Mission at 11:30; Al Hajj Abdoulaye Toure at the Guinean Mission at 12:30; the First Secretary at the Ugandan Mission at 1:30; and that afternoon he met with Ambassador Salim Salim at the Tanzanian Mission.[13]

The origins of Baraka's agenda in international politics during this period are both general and specific. In general, Baraka was carrying a traditional responsibility of African American leadership. The most underestimated component of the black freedom movement was that it was a revolutionary school, with an apprentice system. In other words, those formal and informal sessions between activists and artists such as a young LeRoi Jones with masters and veterans such as Langston Hughes, John Coltrane, Margaret Walker, Ossie Davis, Max Roach, James Baldwin, Martin Luther King Jr., President Sekou Toure, President "Mwalimu" Nyerere, Amilcar Cabral, Fidel Castro, Robert F. Williams, and Malcolm X were essential to his political transformation. Young black leaders received an unconventional education; they were nurtured in the rich and complex legacy of black politics, including its controversial international traditions dating at least as far back as Maria Stewart and David Walker. That baton had been carried by generations, from Ida B. Wells, W.E.B. Du Bois, and Marcus Garvey to Claudia Jones, Vicki Garvin and Paul Robeson to Fannie Lou Hamer, Martin Luther King Jr., Queen Mother Moore, and Malcolm X.

Even in a generally conservative business town such as Newark, New Jersey, there was a long international tradition ranging from the Irish revolutionary politics and street fighting of James Connolly to the Moorish Science Temple Movement of Noble Drew Ali. Connolly immigrated to Newark, worked as a machinist at Singer Sewing Machine, and led socialist and labor organizations until he returned to Ireland and fought in the 1916 Easter Rebellion in Dublin. Ali worked on the railroad in Newark and migrated to Detroit where his movement spread from city to city: laying the foundation for one wing of Marcus Garvey's broad united front and the Nation of Islam.[14] (The influence of the Moorish movement culture on Baraka's Newark Congress of African People could be seen in their nonmeat vegetarian diet in the 1970s.)

By the 1950s Paul Robeson and the National Negro Labor Council (NNLC) had a profound impact on the politics of black Newark. Robeson was a pioneer in the support for African liberation, and his work in that area was not limited to his partnership with W.E.B. Du Bois in the well-known Council on African Affairs. Robeson and the

NNLC were outspoken champions of liberation struggles all over Africa, and they linked American support for colonialism in Africa to its support for Jim Crow racism in the United States. Among NNLC strongholds was the New Jersey Negro Labor Council (NLC) headed by Ernest Thompson of Orange, New Jersey. The New Jersey NLC had a dramatic impact on the politics of Black Newark and established a tradition of connecting the struggle for African American representation in the city and the state with the global fight for African liberation and human rights. That tradition built a powerful bridge between local movements for black rights and the international politics of African liberation. In historic terms, this was the foundation for New Jersey as a stronghold for the 1970s African Liberation Support Committee (ALSC) and for the link between Black Newark's 1972 congressional district and, later, the election of U.S. Representative Donald Payne who would specialize in African affairs in Congress.

In terms of the specific origins, the best place to start is with Baraka's links to Paul Robeson, Langston Hughes, and Malcolm X. Baraka was ousted from the Air Force in the early 1950s for reading and subscribing to "subversive" publications, including one publication not often mentioned: Robeson's important newspaper, *Freedom*. Of course, Robeson is well known as a champion for liberation movements and his linkage of radical politics and culture. What does not receive enough attention is that Robeson represents a profound turning point for cultural nationalism. Prior to Robeson the political theories of cultural nationalism were basically elitist along the lines outlined by the historian Wilson J. Moses.[15] However, Robeson's emphasis on the revolutionary nature of African American folk culture was a dramatic break with the old cultural nationalism that focused on the Anglophile aspirations of "civilization" and cultural refinements of elites. Robeson's cultural theories, expanding on those of Du Bois, laid the basis for Baraka's cultural politics in his important 1963 publication, *Blues People*. In New York, Baraka was profoundly influenced by Hughes and a brief look at the Hughes papers at Yale University illustrates how much attention the veteran of the Harlem Renaissance paid to the emerging poet. When Baraka arrived in New York, he recalls that the first poetry reading he attended featured Langston Hughes accompanied by a jazz band. The influence of the Harlem Renaissance is easily charted around the world from Haiti's *Indigenism,* to Cuba's *Negrism*, to French West Africa's *Negritude;* that cultural development was anthologized by Hughes and outlined in a book studied by Larry Neal and others in the Black Arts Movement, Janheinz Jahn's *Neo-African Culture.*[16]

In addition to the specific influence of Robeson and mentoring of Hughes, there was the direct guidance of Malcolm X. By Baraka's January 1965 meeting with Malcolm X, the poet had published his groundbreaking *Blues People* (1963) and his Obie Award-winning play, *Dutchman* (1964). As an emerging voice in American culture, Baraka sought political guidance from veteran leaders at the cutting edge of the black struggle. Following the 1964 uprisings in Harlem and Brooklyn, Baraka refused to renounce violence, and he made some controversial statements insisting on black self-determination of Harlem. In January 1965 Malcolm and Baraka met with the leader of the 1964 Zanzibar Revolution, Ahmed Mohammad Babu. They conferred from 8 p.m. until 8 a.m. discussing the nature of a global political strategy against Western imperialism: How could they build an international united front against their oppression? According to Babu, a key issue in the unresolved all night debate was whether the main enemy was racism or capitalism: race or class? How could they make the best use of the conflicts between the major world powers in order to buy enough time to fashion some autonomous space for African liberation? Like Robeson before him, Malcolm had publicly called for a Bandung strategy, a united front against colonialism.[17] Within a month of their meeting, Malcolm X was assassinated. In the aftermath of Malcolm X's murder, there was profound demoralization, enormous political confusion, and violent repression; in that context Baraka plotted how to carry the baton of international struggle. Of course, Baraka was not alone in that mission. A new generation of leaders would launch a Black Power movement, the daughters and sons of "the shining black prince," each one trying to represent the legacy of Malcolm X: Angela Davis, H. Rap Brown, Nikki Giovanni, Stokely Carmichael, June Jordan, Huey P. Newton, Kathleen Cleaver, and Amiri Baraka. Baraka, Sonia Sanchez, Askia Muhammad Toure, June Jordan, Don L. Lee (Haki Madhabuti), and Nikki Giovanni took some leadership in the Black Arts Movement that quickly became a national force. Thus, Baraka's first major role in national leadership after the death of Malcolm X was in cultural politics.

When Huey Newton was wounded and arrested in a shooting incident with the police in Oakland, the immediate response of the Black Arts Movement was "Black Arts for Black Panthers." Alongside Sonia Sanchez, Baraka was in San Francisco to help launch the first Black Studies program at what was then San Francisco State College. Over time, Baraka would become a major force in the Black Studies movement, arguing that either black identity was international or it was a sell-out to U.S. imperialism: "To be an American, one must be a murderer. A white murderer of colored people."[18] In that logic, for Negroes to qualify as Americans, they had to first "murder" themselves. As far as Baraka was concerned, Black Studies by definition was global, meaning it had to include not only African American history and "the Black Atlantic" but also "African History, Realistic World History, Eastern Philosophies-Religion, Islam-Arabic-African Religion and Languages, Black Art—past and contemporary, ... Black Psychology, Revolutionary Consciousness, ... War, ... Eastern Science, Black Science, Community Workshops (How To) in Black Power, Business and Economics: Keys to a new black world . . ."[19]

While in the Bay Area, Baraka toured both Oakland to see the Black Panther Party for Self-Defense and Los Angeles to visit the Us Organization. From the late 1950s to the early 1960s, Newton and the Bay Area militants had been involved in discussions of Cuban politics, and against the wishes of Berkeley campus officials they had fought for the right to hear Robert F. Williams and Malcolm X. Such debates and discussions crystallized into new and innovative Black Power organizations in the aftermath of the August 1965 Watts uprising. After Watts, a new group formed to carry out the legacy of both Malcolm X and the Watts Rebellion; it was the Us Organization—as Malcolm X had insisted "us as opposed to them." On the first anniversary of the Watts upheaval, when the Us Organization held a rally at its Los Angeles headquarters, Newton served as one of the guest speakers. Us's leader, Maulana Ron Karenga was once a fellow student in militant Bay Area discussion circles with Newton and Bobby Seale among others. Baraka was impressed with the political and cultural developments on the West Coast. It looked as if the Black Panther Party might spread nationally and that numerous local Black Power groups might sign on as local branches of a united front Black Panther movement. Because many of the young activists were under attack, unity was a major theme of that day. With the increasing endorsement of SNCC leaders Stokely Carmichael and H. Rap Brown, it seemed possible that many of the Black Power organizations might be able to unite under a Black Panther banner. In that context, Baraka wondered how he could use those models for a Black Power organization in Newark.

Soon after Baraka returned to his hometown of Newark, New Jersey, he endured a savage beating from police during the July 1967 uprising. In his own autobiographical account, Baraka recalls:

> The blood felt hot in my face. I couldn't see, I could only feel the wet hot blood covering my entire head and face and hands and clothes. They were beating me to death.... I was being murdered and I knew it. . . . But then I could hear people shouting at them. Voices calling, "You bastards, stop it. Stop it. You're killing him." From the windows black people were shouting at the police.... They started throwing things.[20]

The reporter Ron Porambo conducted his own investigation of the incident and turned up an eyewitness, a black police officer, who said he was:

> ... standing about thirty feet away when they snatched [Baraka] out of that little truck, knocked him to the ground and began to beat him so viciously that I don't know how that little man is still living today. I started to get over and butt in, but I just knew they were going to kill him from the way they were beating him and I figured they'd just kill me, too. *Man, I was crying.* That was all I could do without committing suicide.[21]

The anonymous black officer never found his voice in the courtroom. Thus, he told Porambo that "he didn't testify at the trial because 'it would have been just another *nigger* telling lies on the whole Newark police force.'"[22] White terror was so powerful at that moment in Black America that Baraka did not believe he would survive his imprisonment.

However, not only did he survive prison; a movement rose out of the ashes of the Newark Rebellion. Baraka's leadership and organization came to symbolize the politics of black urban militancy: "Black Power, the power to control our lives ourselves. All of our lives, Our laws. Our culture. Our children. Their lives. Our total consciousness, black oriented." Baraka made a plea for a different kind of black revolution, linking political power to the reordering of the world: "We want power to control our lives, as separate from what [others] want to do with their lives. That simple."[23] Speaking of the new revolutionary black man, he wrote: "He will reorder the world, as he finds his own rightful place in it. The world will be reordered by the black man's finding such a place. Such a place is, itself, the reordering. Black Power. Power of the majority is what is meant. The actual majority in the world of colored people."[24] As Baraka spread his ideas of black self-determination, circles of black people gathered to defend him from the police and from the legal system. Poets and writers from Allen Ginsberg to James Baldwin rallied to support Baraka's legal defense. Even more importantly, local activists involved in his legal defense, began thinking about building a new Black Power organization, the United Brothers.

As the smoke cleared from the Newark uprisings in July 1967, the United Brothers, the United Sisters, the Black Community Defense and Development (BCD) and the Spirit House formed a circle of Black Power groups that merged by 1968 into the Committee for a Unified Newark (CFUN). Those groups were the forerunners of CAP.[25] They fashioned a Black Power politics distinguished by the Modern Black Convention Movement, with its demands for Black self-determination, Pan-Africanism, African liberation, and later, women's emancipation and socialism. The Modern Black Convention Movement (MBCM) took shape in a series of interconnected black summits, conventions, assemblies, conferences, congresses, and united fronts in the decade between 1966 and 1976 that developed a process of *agenda building* from below.[26] At the local and national level hundreds of community organizations, worker's leagues, block clubs, student associations, women's groups, and circles of artists and intellectuals convened at mass assemblies in black communities to fashion their principles and demands into an independent black political agenda. The Black Agenda may be distinguished from many of the other conference resolutions because the grassroots ultimatum of that movement was not simply rhetorical; the agenda was a plan of action. Black Power politics used that agenda to produce a long-term strategy for liberation that included running candidates for public office to galvanize the black community in the short term.

From Los Angeles and Oakland to Detroit and Newark despite their differences, many Black Power groups shared certain fundamentals and their political trajectories established a common pattern. Each organization claimed to be the true heir of Malcolm X; each group supported African liberation movements; each concluded that Black America suffered as an internal colony of the United States; and each demanded black self-determination. Furthermore, many organizations embraced black nationalism, incorporating significant elements of Marxism.

In 1967, on the heels of the Detroit and Newark uprisings, a National Black Power Conference unfolded in Newark attended by H. Rap Brown, Jesse Jackson, Maulana Karenga, and Baraka. Brown was the newly elected chair of the Student Nonviolent Coordinating Committee and Jackson, the Chicago-based civil rights activist. Baraka arrived with his head bandaged, calling for black self-determination and insisting on the right of self-defense and joined with a SNCC and Black Panther maneuver to get the United Nations to look at the violent repression of African Americans as a human rights violation, insisting that the oppression of Black America was a colonial question.

Together with other Newark leaders, Baraka created a Black Arts cultural group, the Spirit House Movers and Players, and a Black Power political group, the United Brothers. In the face of daily physical intimidation and terror from the Newark police department, Newark's Black Power Movement fostered African American resistance, claiming black Newark block by block. Within a few months, the United Brothers called for a black political convention. Local people sensed that this new politics was an expression of the street fighting that had begun in July 1967. At the Spirit House, Baraka's theater group performed plays by writers such as Ben Caldwell, author of "The First Militant Preacher." Those actors and poets also chanted a new kind of haunting spiritual at their performances, inquiring: "Who Will Survive America?"

In late March 1968, Dr. Martin Luther King Jr. visited Newark on a tour to launch the Poor People's March on Washington. Although his advance man, James Bevel, told Baraka that King would visit, Amiri and Amina Baraka were surprised when King showed up at the front door of the Spirit House in the heart of the ghetto trailed by a media crowd and flashing light bulbs.

Similar to Malcolm X, King suggested to Baraka the absolute necessity for a united front of black leadership. Baraka listened respectfully to King, and then explained what he was doing in Newark politics. Afterward, when King spoke at South Side High School (now Malcolm X Shabazz H.S.), he insisted that black was beautiful and called for black political power in cities like Newark. A few days later, King reiterated his internationalist stand against wars of aggression and colonialism in a speech in Washington, D.C., where he described racial oppression in the United States as *internal colonialism*. King had become outspoken on international politics, especially after his condemnation of the Vietnam war. And even much earlier, King had advocated Third World solidarity with independence struggles, trumpeting Gandhi's resistance to British colonialism and insisting that African Americans and Algerians were "brothers." By 1967, King was sounding closer to Malcolm X in his denunciations of the urban crisis, poverty, and international politics. Tragically, in that context, King was assassinated in Memphis on April 4, 1968. Just as the murders of Lumumba and Malcolm X were meant to terrorize Black America and to kill its will to fight racial oppression, the brutal assassination of King was meant to silence the African American freedom song.

In response to King's murder, urban uprisings exploded in more than 100 cities, including Washington, D.C., and Newark. The phenomenal spread of Black Power represented another major response to King's death. In New Jersey, a press conference that Baraka called in Newark, started a long march to black political power in that state. Why was black political power such a formidable task in New Jersey? African Americans had made little progress in the former slave state of New Jersey; in fact, the Garden State had held slaves into the 1850s.

Jim Crow racism was deeply rooted in New Jersey from Paul Robeson's hometown in Princeton, where planters' sons had brought their
slaves with them to college, to its largest urban center, Newark, where
graduates from Lincoln University aspired to jobs as waiters. While
there had been a considerable number of black slaves in New Jersey's
agricultural economy, as late as 1950 the whole state of New Jersey
had no black elected official. When outspoken Newark community
leader Irvine Turner arose to city council representative in 1953, he
became the first African American in New Jersey history. Turner was
supported by the controversial Negro Labor Council, and he resisted
a great deal of red-baiting, insisting that the right of black political
representation included self-determination in the choice of ideological creed and political allies. Significantly, Turner was nominated at
an independent community political convention that was the forerunner of the Lowndes County Black Panther movement and the Modern Black Convention Movement of the 1960s and 1970s. As late as
1959 when Honey Ward, a member of the meatpackers union and a
golden gloves champion, was elected Central Ward chair of the
Democratic Party in Newark and Preston Grimsley was elected First
Ward chair of the Democratic Party in Orange, they became the first
black ward chairs of any political party in the history of that state.
Both Grimsley and Ward were remnants of the Negro Labor Council. By 1956 the Negro Labor Council had been destroyed by federal
persecution. However, government repression failed to chill the fire
of liberation politics in Newark; and by 1967 Honey Ward was a
mentor to Baraka and a leader of the United Brothers.[27]

After two elections and two long years of street fighting in
Newark's tough political arena, the United Brothers rallied 1000
African Americans to its Newark Black Political Convention in June
1968 and hundreds of African American and Puerto Rican delegates
to the November 1969 Black and Puerto Rican Convention. During
the course of these struggles, the Puerto Rican Young Lords Party
and the United Brothers signed a mutual defense pact against armed
white terrorists, insisting that an attack on one group was an attack on
both groups. Throughout this time, support for Puerto Rican independence and African liberation were linked, and by June 1970 a
number of the Black and Puerto Rican Convention's candidates were

elected to positions on the city council and the chief executive position of mayor. Newark's first black mayor, Kenneth Gibson, attended the initial meeting to establish the United Brothers and the first summit to establish the Congress of African People.

With Gibson in City Hall, Baraka tried to persuade the mayor to use his offices to establish close relationships with Africa; to suggest the importance of those ties, Baraka and CAP arranged for the Tanzanian ambassador to pay a special visit to Newark. At the founding of the Congress of African People its program called for complete support for African liberation struggles, including the donation of boots to rebel fighters on the continent. In fact, Baraka was so successful in his call for black unity and support for African liberation at the Atlanta summit that the FBI immediately began developing "imaginative" and "innovative" attacks on him and his organizations because they viewed him as a possible "black messiah," in the same vein as Malcolm X or King.

By 1971 Baraka was invited to Tanzania by President "Mwalimu" Julius Nyerere and his political party to celebrate the nation's tenth anniversary of independence. With Baraka in the leadership of CAP, and with Ahmed Babu in President Nyerere's cabinet, the time was ripe for building a united front against racism and colonialism, perhaps along the lines that Babu, Baraka, and Malcolm X had considered in January 1965. Step by step, CAP developed close relationships with liberation groups from Africa to the Caribbean. One important asset that CAP had in developing this platform was that one of its founding leaders, Balozi Zayd Muhmmad of the BCD, had cultivated United Nations connections since the 1950s. Many of the African liberation groups toured black communities from coast to coast, explaining the history of their particular countries and expressing solidarity with indigenous struggles in the United States. As CAP developed into a stronger national organization, it established national tours for visiting representatives of the African liberation groups from Zimbabwe to Angola.

During the 1970s CAP became a Non-Governmental Organization (NGO) at the United Nations. In line with Malcolm X's strategy, CAP established cordial relations, as Malcolm X had, with not only President Nyerere of Tanzania in East Africa but also President

Sekou Toure of Guinea in West Africa. Moreover, CAP established connections with numerous liberation groups in the Caribbean, Africa, and the Middle East. By the early 1970s, CAP forged ties with Maurice Bishop and the New Jewel Movement in Grenada; Amilcar Cabral of the PAIGC liberation group (Partido Africano da Independencia da Guine e Cabo Verde) in West Africa; and a number of the leaders of the liberation movements in Zimbabwe, South Africa, Namibia, Angola, Mozambique, and Palestine. Indeed, CAP was instrumental in establishing the African Liberation Support Committee to help end colonialism in Angola, Mozambique, Guinea-Bissau, Namibia, and Zimbabwe; if the assessments of Walter Rodney and St. Claire Drake are correct, then the ALSC was the most important American group in this regard since Du Bois and Robeson's Council on African Affairs.

Consequently, streams of international and national figures visited Baraka and either performed or lectured in Newark about African and African American art, music, dance literature, politics, and liberation. As a result, Newark showcased grassroots Black Studies and African culture and politics. More important, the sense of political and cultural kinship, created by Black Power, the Black Arts, and the African liberation movements sent hundreds of leaders and artists to help build and sustain the Modern Black Convention Movement in Newark.

Conditions were ripe for forging links between the Black Power Movement and African radicalism. On this score, important meetings were held in Washington, D.C., between Tanzanian diplomats and CAP representatives to launch the Tanzanian Exchange Program that encouraged progressives from the United States to immigrate to Tanzania to help build socialism. When some black nationalists objected to progressive white applicants for the program, the Tanzanian government explained that as far as they were concerned socialism was a nonracist philosophy and they encouraged both progressive black and nonblack technicians in their efforts.[28]

Around this time, CAP's publishing arm, Jihad, secured the permissions to print essays by the PAIGC leader Amilcar Cabral, Tanzanian President Nyerere, and a few works by Guinean President Toure. Later, Jihad published the internationally known Guyanese historian

Walter Rodney's important critique of Tanzanian socialism and of the pitfalls of some forms of Pan-Africanism.

Between 1972 and 1974 the strength of these Pan-African politics was expressed in each new national organization. Significantly, at the 1972 founding of the National Black Political Convention in Gary, Indiana, the summit meeting expressed close connections to African liberation rooted in their memories of the Atlantic slave trade. Breaking out of the earlier limits of civil rights leadership, the Gary Agenda on foreign policy insisted, "Because the history and culture of Black people is fundamentally related to our African Birthright, we are concerned about the movement of colonized African countries from subjugation to independence and from neo-colonized states to fully independent ones." Although the Gary Agenda attacked Western imperialism, headed by the United States, for its policies on the African continent, it also criticized the West "in Vietnam, the Middle East, the Caribbean and other places in the Third and Pan-African World."[29]

Linking the fight for independence in the Third World with the black awakening in capitalist America, the Gary Agenda argued that, "the economic impoverishment of the black community in America is clearly traceable to the historic enslavement of our people and to the racist discrimination to which we have been subjected since 'emancipation.' Indeed, much of the unprecedented economic wealth and power of American capitalism has obviously been built upon this exploitation of Black people." The Gary Agenda called for reparations, for pressure on white churches, corporations and institutions to make meaningful investments in black communities, and for the "exploration of alternative forms of economic organization and development of a system that promotes self-reliance, cooperative economics, and people's ownership and control of [the] means of production and distribution of goods." Above all, the Gary Agenda concluded that there would be no full economic development for African Americans "without radical transformation of the economic system which has so clearly exploited us these many years." As far as the National Black Assembly was concerned, "We have been—and are now—a colony, living in the midst of a society committed to values other than the development of the human spirit."[30]

After Gary, in cities such as Newark, Detroit, Cleveland, Baltimore, Philadelphia, and Pittsburgh, the NBA, CAP, and ALSC acted as bridges between local community struggles and the fight for African liberation. Community groups decided to cook dinner for African leaders when they arrived at the United Nations and that developed into an annual dinner for African diplomats in New York City. Neighborhood clubs held African fashion shows to raise funds for African liberation movements and high school groups sponsored educational programs to end colonialism in Africa. Those communities also elected a new wave of black political representatives to speak for constituents with Africa on their minds. Thus, the Black Power movement had established a strong bridge between its local and national fight against racial oppression and the global battle for African liberation and independence.

In short, in the decade between the 1961 Congo Crisis protest at the United Nations and 1972's Gary Convention, Amiri Baraka and a community of activists developed from fledgling protest groups scattered across Black America and condemned by the civil rights establishment, into the formidable Black Power movement, backed by many civil rights leaders. By the Gary Convention, Black Power played a leading role in rallying many of the chief civil rights organizations and black elected officials, with Coretta Scott King, Jesse Jackson, Julian Bond, and Michigan Congressman Charles Diggs. The Congress of African People, the African Liberation Support Committee, and the National Black Assembly advocated an agenda for African liberation, national independence and NGO status in the United Nations. Within a broad thrust for African liberation support in Black America, Baraka and CAP reflected an important moment in radical Pan-African politics.[31]

Unfortunately, within a few years, events in Africa and in Black America produced major setbacks. Although these reverses changed the cast of characters bridging Black America and Africa, the new developments could not stop the momentum for African liberation support in the United States. In West Africa, Amilcar Cabral of Guinea-Bissau was assassinated in early 1973 soon after his influential visit to speak at the United Nations and talk to Black Power leaders in the United States. In Tanzania, there was an additional stumbling block when Ahmed M. Babu was arrested along with many African American radicals in the aftermath of the assassination of Tanzania's Vice President Sheikh A. Karume. This was a major loss because Karume had been the first African president of Zanzibar following the Zanzibar Revolution; and he became one of two vice presidents after the unification of Zanzibar and Tanganyika into the United Republic of Tanzania in 1964.

By 1974, ALSC entered a crisis period, punctuated by bitter, sectarian struggles between proponents of black nationalism and those of Marxism that began in 1973. That conflict set off a chain reaction within CAP along similar lines. In some ways, 1974 marked the beginning of the end of Black Power as a national movement. The movement galvanized around the legacy of Malcolm X had reached a turning point at which perhaps half its leadership questioned the very foundations of the Black Power experiment. With that declension the acrimonious debates not only led many of the Black Power groups to unravel but also weakened the movement's major publications, institutions, and a number of the Black Studies programs in colleges and universities. The June 1974 Sixth Pan-African Congress in Dar Es Salaam, Tanzania, only sealed the split in the Black Power movement when the American delegation debated those issues in Africa.

While ALSC was effectively liquidated in 1975 by an ultra-Left-wing bloc that closed the national headquarters, global developments from 1974 through 1976 raised the African liberation struggle to unprecedented heights. The wars of national liberation in Portugal's Africa colonies paved the way for revolution in Portugal and the independence of Guinea-Bissau, Cape Verde, Mozambique, and Angola. Tragically, a prolonged and horrific civil war erupted in Angola, with one group supported by America's CIA and the South African military.

Nonetheless, in June 1976 the Soweto uprising baptized a new generation in the long march to South African freedom. And Zimbabwe forged its independence from white minority rule after a long war of liberation. By that time, Black America's Africa consciousness was both mature and widespread enough to propel the anti-Apartheid movement; a movement that, in the United States especially, became a major front in a global struggle to isolate the

South African regime economically and politically. Few people observing the 1961 United Nations protest during the Congo Crisis would have predicted that African liberation would win its major battles within the next two decades. Ultimately, Black Power sparked a new political consciousness among African Americans and it transformed the stance of black political leadership in foreign affairs. These achievements can be traced back partially to the political development of Amiri Baraka and the Congress of African People. Baraka's political evolution touches upon the contours of two generations of black radicals who were political activists, cultural figures, and international leaders. Baraka's multiple relationships—which ranged from unglamorous grassroots activists to African dignitaries and black American icons—provides a pivotal illustration of Black Power's substantive victories, contentious debates, and historical legacy.

3

BLACK WOMEN, URBAN POLITICS, AND ENGENDERING BLACK POWER

RHONDA Y. WILLIAMS

American society can learn much from Black women. Black women have borne the burdens of so many other living things.

—Sister Mary Roger Thibodeaux, from *A Black Nun Looks at Black Power* (1972)[1]

Power concedes nothing without demands.... The limits of tyrants are prescribed by the endurance of those whom they oppress.

—Stokely Carmichael quoting Frederick Douglass, Morgan State College (1967)[2]

In the 1960s, grassroots organizer Goldie Baker raised her children in Lafayette Courts, an inner-city public housing complex in downtown east Baltimore. Her neighborhood, and the city, not only buzzed with the activity of civil rights organizations and Great Society programs but also Black Power groups. A tenant, welfare, and education rights activist, Baker believed in black self-determination, political power, economic security, respect, and human dignity. However, unlike some black women, Baker did not join nationally recognized Black Power organizations. Instead, Baker and numerous other black women, many of them low-income, engaged in battles around home-, family-, and neighborhood-based issues either as individuals or as members of local community organizations. Their lives and grass-roots struggles, then, not only provide plentiful evidence of social welfare protests in extraordinarily rich activist decades, but also possess the narrative power to enrich and complicate the history of the Black Power era by elucidating how black women outside of traditional organizations interacted with and engendered Black Power politics in the 1960s.[3]

For Baker, an awareness of black empowerment and struggle came early. Her mother, Margaret Dockins, and her maternal grandmother, Emma Dupree, served as her teachers. Dockins and Dupree migrated from Dillon, South Carolina, to Baltimore—the northernmost southern border city and an East Coast industrial and commercial port. In Baltimore, they became domestic laborers, the primary jobs open to workers of their gender and race. "My mother and my grandmother and them, they always fought for their rights anyway down in the South. When they came to Baltimore, I guess they thought they was going to, you know, have more rights (chuckles) … but they weren't." Baltimore may have boasted the largest free black population on the eve of the Civil War and might have been north of South Carolina, but race still shaped employment, politics, neighborhoods, social relations, and opportunity throughout the late nineteenth and twentieth centuries. As residents in their new city, Baker's mother and grandmother joined the Progressive Party, protested slum conditions, and fought for "Negro representation" and people's rights. Because of their affiliations and activism, her mother and grandmother were "harassed" and "branded Communists" in an era that boasted world war, increasing conformism, and anticommunist scourges targeting critics of American domestic policies.[4]

Goldie Baker grew up witnessing her mother and grandmother's strident activism as black working-class women and their daily struggles as mothers to provide for their families. Her family's inability to afford a babysitter meant Goldie Baker often attended these interracial meetings and protest campaigns. Postwar economic prosperity did not extend to all equally—or, for that matter, alter many black people's economic status. In Baker's case, familial financial challenges not only

exposed her to economic inequality, but also provided her with concrete examples of black women's and poor people's struggles for
empowerment. "By me being involved with going to all those meetings, then I learned that you had to fight, poor people and colored
people (at that time, you weren't called black people) had to stand and
fight for every little right that they could, you know, that they would
get." Her mother and grandmother went door to door in the black
community trying to mobilize people to act. "And our people were so
scared, colored people were so scared. They'd stand in the door" mute
while her mother and grandmother tried to convince them "to come
out and fight for their rights. They didn't understand that. They was
afraid of white people. They had thought we were terrible people
because we talked back to white people."[5] When Baker became active
herself decades later in the 1960s, she noticed a familiar fear. But she
also witnessed—and interacted with—organizations and individuals
who aggressively spoke truth to white power, contested marginalized
people's oppression, and organized around bread and butter issues.

In the 1960s, numerous black women including public housing
tenants, welfare mothers, and nuns mobilized outside of, but in the
context of, Black Power radicals. These women protested racism, a
discriminatory state, and an economic system that kept people
impoverished. They called for black pride and demanded power,
social rights, and the dignity denied to their communities, their families, and themselves as black women, mothers, and often their families' primary financial providers. In fact, their activist ethos in many
ways echoed—and in some cases, preceded—the myriad ideologies
and initiatives of the Black Power era. Yet because these grassroots
black women, many of them low-income, neither jibed with the popular and simplistic media-cultivated image of armed black men, nor
joined nationally known freedom organizations or black militant
groups, their economic and political activism has remained relatively
invisible within narratives of Black Power.[6]

In the age of rights, antipoverty, and power campaigns, black
women in community-based and often women-centered organizations, like their female counterparts in nationally known organizations, harnessed and engendered Black Power through their speech
and iconography and as participants of tenant councils, welfare rights

groups, and a black female religious order. An examination of their articulated motivations and practices not only provides a picture of 1960s' struggles that often defy clear-cut categorizations but also expands historical understanding of Black Power politics by exposing its precursors, influences, overlaps, and coexistence with other activist traditions. Examining Black Power in this way simultaneously highlights how male predominance has been sustained in historical scholarship and nationally known organizations, and challenges accepted renderings of organizational politics. For, quite often, black women's activism, although central to the sustenance of many grassroots efforts and organizations, has failed to be recognized—not just by scholars but by the very people in the neighborhoods and cities where they struggled. But they were right there, in cities, seeking rights and power in order to alter the material conditions of people.

The Arrival of "Black Power"

Gloria Richardson emerged as a black radical in 1963 in Cambridge, Maryland—a city on the Eastern Shore about 63 miles south of Baltimore. According to the historian Sharon Harley, Richardson's militancy represented a pivotal moment. Her "refusal in 1963 and 1964 to accept nonviolence as the primary strategy in civil rights protests, foretold the death of the nonviolent Civil Rights Movement most closely associated with Martin Luther King, Jr."[7] Richardson became involved in black rights struggles through the encouragement of her teenage daughter, Donna Hayes Richardson, and other young activists' direct and confrontational style of protest.[8] At age 39, Gloria Richardson joined sit-in and picketing campaigns sponsored by the Cambridge Nonviolent Action Committee, a Student Nonviolent Coordinating Committee (SNCC) affiliate, to contest exclusion from and discrimination in theaters, restaurants, bowling alleys, and other businesses. She also helped mobilize black women poultry workers on the Eastern Shore in Maryland.[9] But the Cambridge Movement—unlike some SNCC chapters in the Deep South—had an expanded agenda: one that saw racial equality as probable only with economic justice, access to good jobs, improved education, better housing conditions, and improved health services.

Richardson also participated in the Northern Negro Grass Roots Leadership Conference organized by Reverend Albert B. Cleage Jr. in Detroit in November 1963—three years before the rallying cry of Black Power nationally.[10] Disenchanted with an intransigent status quo, racial liberalism, and nonviolence activism that did not transform black people's daily conditions, Richardson expressed a belief in rights, self-defense, and aggressive action. In an *Ebony* magazine profile titled "Gloria Richardson: Lady General of Civil Rights," the writer described the five-foot-seven, 138-pound Richardson as "sharp-tongued," a "tigress," who drew criticism from white and black middle-class business people and homeowners because "of her militant, uncompromising leadership."[11]

Richardson's experiences, like those of Baltimore's Goldie Baker, reveal not only black people's concerns beyond integration and equality before the law, but also Black Power as the "latest in a series of efforts to contest the injustices that existed in almost every dimension of life between black and white Americans."[12] As is clear, the clarion call of Black Power in 1966 did not necessarily propel women like Baker and Richardson into activism. The urgency of harsh daily realities provoked them to act; and the rights and power organizations of the day helped to electrify the political terrain. In other words, the unfamiliar narratives of black women expose unresolved community problems—especially the ones that women frequently had to navigate—and, in so doing, convey an often overlooked genealogy and the engendering of Black Power goals.[13]

Shortly after SNCC chairman Stokely Carmichael championed the phrase to a national audience in Greenwood, Mississippi, in 1966, Black Power "formally" arrived in Baltimore. The Congress of Racial Equality (CORE), founded in Chicago in the 1940s, embraced Black Power as a rallying cry and a concept that challenged racial liberalism by moving their agenda beyond integration as a goal, equating "moderation with stagnation," and demanding "far more militancy."[14] Preparing to hold its annual convention and kick off its first "Target City" in Baltimore, the national CORE organized under the banner, "To Organize for Economic and Political Power."[15] The conference was not all cooperation. Arguments emerged over whether Black Power rhetoric should be adopted, and the "Big Three"—the

NAACP, Urban League, and Southern Christian Leadership Conference (SCLC)—boycotted some convention sessions in protest.

Black Power was a multifaceted, at times elusive, concept that eventually spurred new alliances as well as divisions and inflected the political context in which people lived and organized.[16] For instance, national CORE leader Floyd McKissick argued that "Black Power is not Black Supremacy; it is a united Black Voice reflecting racial pride in the tradition of our heterogeneous nation. Black Power does not mean the exclusion of White Americans from the Negro Revolution; it means the inclusion of all men in a common moral and political struggle."[17] The CORE-Target City's *Soul Book,* the conference program published in 1966, defined Black Power as "a working convention for community power." On the back cover of the *Soul Book* appeared the following: "Black Power means the organization of the Negro community into a tight and disciplined group" to secure leadership, improve self-image, and achieve political, economic, and consumer power.[18] Many of these definitions and aims vocalized by avowed Black Power groups also surfaced among black women engaged in their own community-based efforts.

Despite the multiple meanings of and intraracial disagreements over whether to embrace Black Power—for some black and white people, Black Power forebode black chauvinism, violence, and separatism—CORE stood by its expressed commitment to foster power in the fight against urban discrimination. The Target City project vowed to contest "glaring discrimination in housing, education, employment, and police malpractice" and to demonstrate "how the power of the black poor could be mobilized for their own advancement."[19] CORE's Target City, and the general demand for poor people's power, brought to light entrenched economic inequality and the government's failure to address it in increasingly black cities.[20] As Walter Percival Carter, a former CORE chair and then executive board member, recognized, civil rights legislation had not empowered black urban citizens in their daily lives. "We had broken the public accommodations aspect of civil rights down and we knew the real civil rights battles would be fought right there [in neighborhoods] where these people are whipped by everything—housing, unemployment, lack of opportunities, improper schooling."[21] These issues, while emerging anew on the "cutting edge" of black politics in the 1960s, echoed the deep-rooted struggles of grassroots black women—women similar to Baker's mother and grandmother in 1940s' Baltimore, Richardson in early 1960s' Cambridge, and eventually Baker herself.

Baltimore's CORE, which found itself in the spotlight in 1966, had a history before the annual convention and the implementation of the national CORE's Target City program. CORE's Baltimore chapter was founded in 1953. At that time, four of its six executive committee members were women and the majority of its base was white—at least until 1963, when blacks and whites were equally divided. In 1964 blacks became the majority. During the 1950s, Baltimore CORE had waged several direct action campaigns in downtown dime stores, at Northwood Shopping Center near the black Morgan State College, and at the Gwynn Oak Amusement Park, which excluded African Americans. The latter campaign lasted over eight years. In the 1950s, the chapter experienced internal discord and declined. Not until 1961—the year the Route 40 Freedom Riders came through Baltimore—was Baltimore CORE revitalized.[22]

As the 1960s progressed, the rhetoric and proponents of civil rights, antipoverty, and power politics in Baltimore shared the urban stage where inequality continued to thrive.[23] For instance, just like CORE members, the Black Panther Party (BPP), and antipoverty activists, Dr. Martin Luther King Jr. also began to discuss war, poverty, and a war on poverty. By 1967, King had advocated "power for poor people"—arguing in his newly released book, *Where Do We Go From Here: Chaos or Community?*, that "the impact of automation and other forces have made the economic question fundamental for blacks and whites alike."[24] In the post-1940s era and even following the passage of civil rights and voting rights legislation, working-class black people continued to confront urban renewal and fewer housing opportunities, schools in need of greater resources, rising crime and drugs, a dwindling tax base, deindustrialization and a lack of living-wage jobs, and increased economic and residential segregation. Neither access to stores and amusement parks, the freedom to ride a bus without being Jim Crowed, nor the vote immediately addressed these concerns. So when CORE and other groups issued calls for economic and political power, many people paid attention, including white politicians.

The Republican mayor, Theodore R. McKeldin, welcomed CORE's Target City program to Baltimore, saying the campaign could make a potentially long, hot, and disruptive summer safe. A white politician who supported racial progress during his first stints as mayor and governor in the 1940s and 1950s, McKeldin had won his elections with black votes. And in the 1960s, he continued to back change, but in an orderly, lawful, and cooperative fashion. "In an oblique reference to black power," McKeldin implicitly made his views about aggressive action and confrontation known. Addressing CORE's convention delegates, McKeldin argued, "The world is not going to be saved by intercontinental missiles, atomic bombs, or any kind of power but the power of God." Probably to McKeldin's chagrin, his statement produced "chants of 'black power'" from the audience.[25] Despite his aversion to Black Power radicalism, the mayor nevertheless believed that practical accomplishments could be gained with the help of Black Power activists organizing for improvements in inner-city neighborhoods, schools, and housing.

Groups foregrounding Black Power sentiments increased in Baltimore—some more militant and aggressive than others. For instance, CORE's Target City spurred organizational offshoots as a result of internal instability and conflicts between local and national officials over Baltimore-based campaigns.[26] According to James Griffin, a former Baltimore CORE chair appointed to the school board in 1968: "All kinds of confusion and in-fighting developed after a while."[27] People like Walter Carter and Sampson Green left CORE and formed Activists for Fair Housing, and Benjamin "Olugbala" McMillan, a CORE member, opened the Soul School in west Baltimore. As cultural nationalists, Soul School members focused on the artistic and literary contributions of black people, black consciousness, pride, the "collective psyche," and their relationship to black freedom.[28]

Other black organizations incorporated a revolutionary nationalist stance that critiqued black oppression on race and class grounds and sought to transfer power to black people, who were deemed colonial subjects in U.S. inner cities. Union for Jobs or Income Now (U-JOIN), "a civil rights organization," opened an office in east Baltimore under the guidance of Walter Lively and worked toward empowering low-income black people in inner cities. In 1966, U-JOIN sponsored the founding of the Mother Rescuers from Poverty, the city's first welfare rights organization, which sought rights and power for poor women. A year after the national Black Panther Party formed in Oakland in 1966, a BPP branch opened in Baltimore. Proving a prescient statement, at least for a time, the white reverend of Baltimore's St. Francis Xavier Church, Henry J. Offer, recognized in early 1968 that Black Power had a broad appeal: "Black power is here to stay, whether you like it or not."[29]

Engendering Black Power

An examination of the activities and speech deployed by some grassroots black women activists in public housing communities reveals the reach of Black Power rhetoric, if not, at times, these activists' direct interactions with Black Power advocates. The Soul School, which sat on a street bordering Murphy Homes public housing complex, provided educational programming and served as a political meeting place. A former resident of Murphy Homes and tenant council leader, Gladys Spell, recalled that the Soul School would teach young people about themselves. Ultimately, the Soul School "got so they would teach the children to be so militant, you know, until some of the parents had to stop sending them over there. But Soul School was over there, and them brothers they had a tough look."[30]

The Soul School, however, was not just home to "tough" brothers. Women also participated in the cultural center's activities. Male and female junior and senior high school students gathered there on Saturdays to organize a citywide Black Student Union.[31] In the late 1960s, Oblate Sister Judith (Brenda Williams), a member of a black nun order founded in nineteenth-century Baltimore, taught courses there.[32] And in June 1969, Gladys Spell and the youth committee invited Soul School members to display their African art at the tenant council's Black Seminar series. Held in a crowded recreation room, the event became heated when McMillan "insulted everybody with a white face," according to Spell.[33] White people had no space in the Soul School's vision of Black Power. Seen as "oppressors" and "blue-eyed devils," white managers and staff were simply not welcome.[34]

A black mother of four and public housing tenant, Marian Johnson actually adopted the popularized veneer of Black Power militancy through speech and the persona she assumed—comparable to that of the publicly feared, armed Black Power brothers who protected the black community.[35] Johnson was a Community Action Agency (CAA) worker and a part-time student at Coppin State College. The CAA was a War on Poverty program established by the Office of Economic Opportunity. In 1967, Johnson and her children moved into Brooklyn Homes, one of the few remaining white-only public housing complexes in the city. Seeking to intimidate black residents who broke the color barrier, white supremacist organizations staged protests at Brooklyn Homes, burned crosses, and handed out hate literature. On one such evening, Johnson called her mother who arrived with Johnson's brother-in-law and father's friend. Both men were armed. Despite her mother's pleas to leave for the evening, Johnson refused. "I just will not be scared or intimidated by a bunch of bigots in white sheets," Johnson stated. Vowing to protect her children and her new government-subsidized home, which represented improved housing conditions, the 25-year-old Johnson decided to keep a weapon in the house for protection. Johnson's picture in the *Baltimore Afro-American* prominently evoked the stylized gun-toting stance of Malcolm X, the Black Panther Party, and popular notions of self-defense: with a shotgun on her lap, she sat guard at the front window of her public housing apartment. She dictated her story to the *Afro-American,* like Malcolm X did to Alex Haley. The opening lines of the *Afro-American* article—with the byline, "By Marian Johnson as told to Michael Davis"—read: "The Ku Klux Klan had better think twice before attempting to march on the home of Mrs. Marian Johnson in the Brooklyn Homes housing project."[36]

Another public housing activist Shirley Wise, who described herself as the Malcolm X of public housing, lived in the same complex as Goldie Baker—Lafayette Courts in east Baltimore. Wise and her family were among the first residents to move into the complex in 1955. In the early 1970s, Wise became the chair of public housing's resident-initiated, citywide Resident Advisory Board (RAB). As RAB chair and a dedicated professional "agitator," Wise found herself arguing for more tenant control, criticizing public housing officials for obfuscating issues, and challenging the housing author-ity's operating procedures and proposed policies. Wise's forthright style made more moderate black tenant leaders uncomfortable. But for Wise, the right of tenant participation meant that residents should be empowered to shape public housing policy. Not afraid to challenge white or black powerbrokers, Wise spoke her mind and rocked the boat with fervor.[37]

Such strategic deployment of self-defense and the powerful iconic figure of Malcolm X to deal with the pressing daily issues of housing, safety, and potential white violence exhibited the allure of Black Power at the grassroots—in these two specific cases among black women public housing tenants. But although Johnson and Wise deployed the visual and verbal rhetoric of familiar Black Power icons, there were other black women who actually joined the organizations, such as the BPP, that helped to generate those iconic images.

By mid-1969, the Baltimore BPP, which had previously garnered little public attention, adopted an aggressive militaristic strategy—just as the national BPP began stressing community-based programming over masculinist flourish.[38] During this troublesome and deadly year for Black Panthers across the nation—one marked by Federal Bureau of Investigation (FBI) and police infiltration—the Panther Central Committee unleashed an internal purge designed to eliminate an "internal criminal element."[39] Baltimore's BPP became a target for reorganization. Midyear, the Central Committee sent in full-time comrades from Oakland and New York to address organizational and administrative inefficiencies.[40] Baltimore's branch captain, Warren Hart, was demoted for not organizing sufficient political education classes, an "over-emphasis of para-military procedures," and failing to place "stress on security and avoidance of police infiltration."[41] Fearing that police would assassinate local BPP leaders like the recently mur-dered Chicago Panthers Fred Hampton and Mark Clark, local activ-ists formed the Baltimore Committee for Political Freedom.[42]

By April 1970, police arrests and infiltration had destabilized the Baltimore chapter. Like in New Haven, Connecticut, where police arrested Black Panthers, charged them with murdering a suspected police informant, and held them over in the "trial of the century," Baltimore Panthers confronted a similar situation. Police arrested numerous Panthers and charged them with murder in two different incidents—one for the shooting death of a police officer and the other for the murder of a suspected agent provocateur. Steve McCutcheon, who police sought in the informant's death, fled to Philadelphia. According to McCutcheon, authorities had "targeted damn near the entire branch on charges of murder and conspiracy."[43]

Before its eventual decline, the Baltimore BPP managed to attract a core group of activists; however, most seemed to be men—as Steve McCutcheon, also known as "L'il Masai," noted the scarcity of women comrades in a 1969 diary entry. Perhaps the new masculine emphasis on paramilitary stylizing and action by the Baltimore Panthers in 1969 turned some women off.[44] But for black men and former war veterans like Irving "Ochiki" Young, the Panther men's valiant public stance proved attractive. A college student who grew up in the Douglass Homes "project," Young decided to ally "myself with helping oppressed people." The Panthers appealed to him "as, you know, men because they had the guts to stand out in front of everybody and say we tried everything their way and got no place.... They were out there to prove to this system that black people were about business and we want some changes now."[45]

In Baltimore, as across the nation, Black Power was publicly deployed through black male images. McKissick of CORE maintained: "1966 shall be remembered as the year we left our imposed status of Negroes and became *Black Men* ... when black men realized their full worth in society—their dignity and their beauty—and their power."[46] Men like Malcolm X, Huey Newton, Bobby Seale, L'il Bobby Hutton, Stokely Carmichael, and H. Rap Brown, who exuded manhood and "potent masculine street bravado," took center stage.[47] By the late 1960s, the now familiar depiction of Black Power—incarnated in images of men wielding guns, berets, leather jackets, and no-holds-barred rhetoric—had taken on a life of its own. But black men activists did not have to wield guns for politicians and police to react; an aggressive stance and fiery rhetoric were enough. Carmichael and Brown, dubbed the "twin priests of violence" by Maryland's Governor Spiro Agnew, and well-known Baltimore-based black men leaders such as Walter Lively and Walter Carter became local white officials' favorite black demagogues.[48]

While it remains unclear how many women were members of Baltimore's BPP, some women undoubtedly did join. These women participated in community free breakfast, liberation school, and clothing programs and performed various organizational tasks, exposing the fluidity of roles and the multiplicity of duties and giving some credence to the former national BPP communications secretary Kathleen Cleaver's claim that "the women who filled the ranks of our organization did not have specifically designated sex roles."[49] Although not universally true, Cleaver's statement does reflect the reality of some BPP women.[50] Reeva D. White served as the Baltimore branch's first communications secretary, a position later filled by another woman named Connie who later married L'il Masai McCutcheon. And Sherry Brown, who moved to Baltimore from Ohio, became the branch's lieutenant of finance in August 1969.[51] In September 1969 after a rally in a park in east Baltimore, police arrested Sister Sandy and Sherry Brown whom they beat with a baton. Women suffered beatings alongside Panther men, accruing "no comfort or benefits from stereotypes of women as fragile and weak and needing to be protected."[52] At the very moment that Panther women in Baltimore confronted the brutality of police power, Panther women in an interview in *Movement* magazine argued: "The sisters have to pick up the guns just like the brothers. There are a lot of things the sisters can do to change society."[53] In the highly publicized 1970 roundups in Baltimore, police arrested women and men in the informant murder case. And black female youth responded by helping to organize protest campaigns among students.[54] In numerous ways then, local black women Panthers' experiences and organizational roles, at times, not only reflected those of well-known (and not so well-known) Panther women but also other grassroots women activists throughout the nation in the 1960s and 1970s.

Black Nuns and Community Power

At the grassroots level in mid-1960s Baltimore, some black nuns also incorporated a community control and self-determination stance—one that presaged 1960s' Black Power struggles, unveiled interaction with Black Power ideology, and, as with the activism of women such as Baker, Johnson, and Wise, exposes yet another space of Black Power activism outside of familiar and popular organizations such as the BPP. One such nun was Oblate Sister Judith who taught at the Soul School. The Oblates of Providence was founded in 1829 by four freeborn black women from Santo Domingo (Haiti).[55] Sister Judith, however, maintained that eventually she had to leave the Oblate Sisters because of her Black Power activism.[56]

In contrast, another black nun, Sister Mary Paraclete Young, an Oblate Sister who became principal of the 140-year-old St. Frances Academy in 1967, laid claim to Black Power by marshaling the history of the black sister order. Sister Young maintained that the Oblate Sisters founded the order "for our people." Historically, the Oblate Sisters were "instrumental in educating the children of the black community"—primarily black girls whom black nuns taught to face "the problems of racial discrimination that exist even in the church."[57] Their order, schools, and orphanages served black people, partially the result of the black nuns' commitment to the black community and the discriminatory practices of white Catholics who harbored an aversion to "black women in habits."[58] While facing exclusion in the religious and secular worlds, the Oblate Sisters operated its order in a nondiscriminatory fashion; its founding rules stated that no prospective nun could be turned away because of race. And in 1967—the same year that Black Power began to heat up urban communities—a white woman interested in civil rights joined the order.

Black nuns such as Sister Young and Sister Mary Roger Thibodeaux, who resided in Philadelphia, did not see Black Power as contradictory to their spiritual vision. Neither did other black theologians. For instance, in *Black Theology and Black Power* in 1969, James H. Cone interpreted Black Power as "the freeing power of the gospel to black people under white oppression."[59] A nun for over 20 years, Sister Young argued in 1969 that "Black power includes self-respect, self-identity, and self-determination. We've just found a name for what we've been doing all these years."[60] Sister Thibodeaux, who traveled the country presenting lectures on Black Power, reaffirmed Young's stance, going so far as to say Yahweh approved of the cultural, political, and, in this instance, religious stance of black people seeking progress and equality. In 1972's *A Black Nun Looks at Black*

Power, Sister Thibodeaux wrote: "Black Power is not foreign to Yahweh and Yahweh is not foreign to Black Power. There is a covenant of friendship there. The cause of Justice is and always will be in strict accordance with the Will of God." And she challenged Catholicism, the clergy, and more broadly the church to become fearless and acquire the "courage displayed during the beginning stages of the Black Power Movement."[61]

Like Cleage, Cone, and other ministers in the Civil Rights and Black Power movements who sought to make religion relevant to black freedom struggles, outspoken black nuns similarly linked their efforts and their religious order's history to black empowerment, psychological reconditioning, and improvement of black communities.[62] Moreover, Thibodeaux—like her sisters in public housing in the 1960s—conveyed a familiarity with and sympathy for the names, poetry, and pictures of more well-known Black Power political icons. She wrote in her book, for instance:

> Black people are proud of Mayor [Richard] Hatcher. We are proud of Bishop Harold Perry and quote the late Dr. Martin Luther King with appropriate respect. We are concerned about Angela Davis and would like to see Eldridge Cleaver [who fled the United States to avoid arrest] back on the American scene. All this is Black pride speaking out to America![63]

In the mid-1960s, Perry became the first black priest in the twentieth century elevated to bishop in the Catholic Church, and Hatcher became the first black mayor of Gary, Indiana—representing the entrée of black leaders into the predominantly white realms of city hall and the Catholic Church.

In her section on "Nuns and Black Power," Thibodeaux also criticized the narrow-mindedness and misinformation emanating from some churches regarding the Black Power Movement. Expressing critiques similar to Cleage's (whose book, *The Black Messiah,* was advertised on the back cover of her book), Thibodeaux wrote: "Religious congregations have been great disappointments to the Black Power Movement. Although professing to be the chief allies of the cause they have produced some of the least knowledgeable people in the area of Black Power."[64] A few stanzas later, she pleaded: "Let

Black nuns speak to us. Their messages are sincere and honest. They are striving to HELP the cause—not hinder it."[65]

Sister Young saw her activism as the fulfillment of a religious mission and racial legacy, and stressed the historical educational mission of the Oblates to help the cause of black liberation. In Baltimore, the order decided to turn St. Frances Academy, the city's oldest black educational institution, into a community school and unsuccessfully applied for Model Cities funding in 1969. Sister Young maintained the order was denied government support for, she felt, "political reasons ... [But] we are still working because if I don't get it one way, I'll get it another." And she asserted: "I am a militant because I don't see any other way."[66] Two years later, Young still worked to realize the order's vision of the school as a community institution. The order prepared a proposal entitled, "An Oasis in the Ghetto," formed an organization "to build a school that educates a community," and proposed daycare for preschool children, a tutorial program, and an adult education program.[67] In 1971, however, Young argued that white people who opposed the community school concept still did not want "to grant full self-determination for blacks."[68] St. Frances Academy closed between 1972 and 1974 "for repairs and reorganization," and by 1979 was in the midst of the third phase of a $2.4 million restoration and expansion project supported primarily by private donations. Upon reopening, the academy extended its community outreach, and accepted boys into the school.[69]

Bread, Butter, and Respect

The demands that many black women made at the grassroots level reflected the desire for self-determination, which could only be achieved if they had the basic material necessities for living, such as shelter, safety, health, food, and income. While some women became involved in public housing activism and community education campaigns, other black women united in organizations like the Mother Rescuers from Poverty—"because that's who we were, rescuing other women from poverty," stated Margaret "Peggy" McCarty, the organization's chair and, then, a separated mother of seven children.[70]

As low-income citizens, Mother Rescuers from Poverty, a group of primarily black women, discussed their citizenry rights alongside empowerment, self-determination, respect, and dignity, and attacked the government's neglect of poor people. McCarty argued that the government should help provide them with "the tools to work with," otherwise "how can we better ourselves with nothing, you know?" She insisted:

> We got to be educated. You know, we got to have proper finances. We got to have proper clothing. We got to have the tools to work with, so that our kids can see that there is a better way to live, a better life.... Our goal was to get off of welfare. That was our goal. Yeah, we had goals too. We didn't want to live in shacks. We didn't want to live around all them rats, and filth, and dirt. We wanted the world to see that black people didn't want this. People didn't want this. We wanted a better life for ourselves and our children.[71]

Also a member of the National Welfare Rights Organization's (NWRO) National Coordinating Committee, McCarty saw herself and other welfare rights activists as warriors on an urban battlefield.[72] In 1967 at a NWRO rally in Washington, D.C., McCarty critiqued a regressive welfare bill, advocated political power for black people, and contested government power. After arguing that "lousy, dirty, conniving brutes" designed the bill, she continued: "I'm black and I'm beautiful and they ain't going to take me back" to slavery. Finally, McCarty stated that if officials would not listen to welfare recipients' voices, maybe they would respond to "force." Beulah Sanders, vice chair of NWRO, also threatened the government, saying protestors should tear down the Capitol if government officials "don't listen."[73] Both McCarty and Sanders's statements and actions evoked civil rights protest campaigns, the urban uprisings of the mid-1960s, and Malcolm X's by-any-means-necessary sentiment. Moreover, their agenda against racial oppression, economic inequality, and poverty resonated not only with the demands of Richardson, Baker, and her foremothers, black women public housing activists, and King, but also several items on the Black Panther Party's Ten-Point Platform, including the right to "fit shelter for human beings" and the demand for "land, bread, housing, education, clothing, justice, and peace."

Not surprisingly, McCarty maintained that both the modern Civil
Rights Movement, which she learned about after joining up with U-
JOIN, and the Black Power Movement influenced her politics. "I
mean you begin to feel like you were a part of something big now,"
McCarty said of civil rights. "That it was not just you isolated in Baltimore. You belonged to something that was powerful. Who doesn't
want power?" And though she categorized organizations like the Black
Panther Party as "too militant" for her (even though she befriended at
least one Baltimore Panther member who was arrested and acquitted
in the 1970 police informant shooting case), McCarty maintained
Black Power offered "a sense of identity, a sense of our culture, a sense
of self-worth ... a sense of belonging, a sense of respect and dignity for
ourselves." But she also argued that the conditions of her life not only
made her more receptive to rights and power claims, but also motivated
her and many other low-income women to act.[74]

Although primarily a black women's organization that challenged
race, class, and gender hierarchies, the Rescuers (like NWRO) did
attract black men, some of whom served as a protective force at demonstrations and a few who mobilized alongside black women against
the injustices of the welfare system. Clarence "Tiger" Davis was
one of them; his life experiences had led him into the arms of CORE,
U-JOIN, and eventually the Rescuers. Davis had returned home from
a military stint in Europe in 1964, and at 21 years old he found himself searching for answers to black people's troubles. Although he
respected the NAACP, he did not want to join them. By 1965 he was
a married father of three. Struggling financially and without health
insurance, Davis became embarrassed when his wife, Barbara, applied
for public medical assistance when their fourth child was born. "I was
pissed that she got that card." Davis believed he was not living up to
his obligations as a man, husband, father, and provider. His views on
racism, men's familial responsibility, and public assistance shaped his
political organizing. In the mid- to late 1960s, he worked with
CORE, U-JOIN, and the Rescuers, because he too believed that poor
people had a right of access to welfare programs that should help
them become "self-sufficient."[75]

Low-income black women also demanded representation and
voice in policy-making arenas, including the welfare agency, public

housing administration, and Model Cities program. In 1967, as city officials met to develop a proposal to present to the Department of Housing and Urban Development, U-JOIN and its supporters, including McCarty, signed a protest letter demanding a role in the local Model Cities demonstration project. At a press conference, McCarty argued poor people did not want the program if their ideas—such as a comprehensive plan that included housing, welfare, and jobs—were not taken seriously. And she warned, "We'll get 'their' program, if we don't take a stand."[76]

An Explicit Critique of Male Authority

Just as the examination of black women's community-based initiatives exposes the complexity of Black Power-era politics on the ground, so, too, do some of these women's voices unveil the existence of explicit gender critiques and feminist sensibilities. For black women's use of Black Power iconography and their actual interaction with male activists operated alongside critiques of patriarchal authority with regard to the family, community, and government. The story of Salima Marriott not only provides another example of the overlaps among housing, welfare, Black Power, and women's struggles, but also the opportunity to examine increasingly widespread gender critiques by black women during the Black Power era. For instance, in 1972, National Welfare Rights Organization executive director Johnnie Tillmon compared welfare to "a super-sexist marriage," maintaining that single-mother Aid to Families with Dependent Children recipients ended up trading "in *a* man for *the* man. But you can't divorce him if he treats you bad."[77]

A Baltimore native who grew up in the Cherry Hill Homes public housing complex and a graduate of the all-black Morgan College in Baltimore, Marriott became a pan-Africanist in New York where she moved with her husband shortly after they married. While there, Marriott, a mother of two who worked as a caseworker for the welfare department, became involved in education and antiwar activism. After her marriage soured, she returned to Baltimore with her two children. "It was two years later, a little more than two, and really the New York experience really shaped my life. ... You know, it was so different. I was such a different person. It wouldn't have been so obvious, but it was in the middle of the Black Power movement and I come back to Baltimore with this nappy hair and African clothes and all that stuff." She had even named her son, born in 1967, Patrice Kenyatta for Patrice Lumumba (Congo) and Jomo Kenyatta (Kenya). Marriott argued: "Integration was never anything that was a goal for me. So the [Civil Rights] Movement never excited me. I became excited with Black Power. That's what I wanted. I was excited about identification with Africa and the Third World."[78]

On her return to Baltimore, Marriott rekindled a relationship with an old boyfriend—a college graduate, chemist, and ex-offender who, after serving his jail time for selling marijuana, found a support system among Islamic nationalists. Marriott had also met Soul School members and Black Panthers through her activism around educational issues and support of student protests. "Here's how we linked ... with them," she recounted of her Panther connection. "There was a student uprising at Eastern High School [an all-girl high school] in Baltimore. ... And they, ultimately, some of them ended up in the Panther Party." She also knew Panther member, Paul Coates, "because he owned the bookstore in the neighborhoods where I ultimately lived."[79]

Her familiarity with black nationalist organizations in the late 1960s and early 1970s spurred her growing black feminist consciousness. Like Tillmon's famous quote about "The Man" and other explicit gender analyses in the 1970s expressed by black women artists, intellectuals, and groups, Marriott disapproved of women's mistreatment and male dominance.[80] In particular, Marriott said her experience "with the nationalist community," especially with Islamic groups in Baltimore and D.C., helped her recognize male chauvinism. Around the early 1970s, when Marriott decided to go back to school for an advanced degree, she began severing her ties with those nationalist organizations. She did stay in touch with the Soul School and even began exploring electoral politics, but the future state delegate said of the other groups: "I just didn't want to affiliate with those sexist type organizations." Marriott grew to believe "that this Black Power movement ... really just wanted to relegate us to be the secretaries."[81]

Concerned about women's welfare, wanting to help low-income black women access resources and gain power, and raising her children alone, Marriott had also taken a job at the Baltimore welfare department when she returned from New York. As a caseworker, Marriott helped her clients organize a welfare rights chapter. When she returned to school, she pursued a master's degree in social work. For one of her field placement requirements, Marriott chose to work with the Baltimore Welfare Rights Organization (BWRO), which followed in the footsteps of Mother Rescuers from Poverty. But she left after finishing her year-long placement.[82] In later years, she would characterize as "inappropriate" male leadership of groups that focused on predominantly women's issues such as the NWRO under George Wiley and the BWRO under Bob Cheeks, who became the group's first male director in the mid-1970s.[83]

In Marriott's second field placement after the BWRO, she and about ten black women social workers formed a group called Black Women Concerned about Urban Problems, because they "felt that the [black] Association of Social Work was not relevant and it was chauvinist" and "that those men in there were really trying to get their own jobs and stuff." That was around 1972, and as far as Marriott knew, "not a lot of black women organized trying to do something" like that.[84] But while Marriott and her colleagues may have well been unique in the formation of a new group to support black professional women in Baltimore, they were part of a national trend. For, by 1972, a number of diverse black women's organizations and agendas existed, and some of them had explicitly feminist pedigrees already years in the making.[85]

Black Women's Expansive Power Agendas

Black women's activism complicates our knowledge of the Black Power era in another way as well. Just as many of them operated outside of familiar organizations, incorporated various Black Power ideologies, or contested gender politics in the Black Power era, so, too, did others break ranks by refusing to envision or enact their politics in what they viewed as either rigid or exclusionary ways. As their varied statements and efforts plainly and suggestively show, some of these black women activists at the grassroots viewed their daily struggles for material well-being, representation, autonomy, and respect as part of a quest for not only citizenship rights and self-determination but also as a matter of human rights. In this sense, they battled not only "crimes against black humanity," but also laid claim to women's and poor people's humanity in a society that seemed to revel in their dehumanization.[86] For these women, empowerment meant rejecting knowledge and practices "that perpetuate[d] objectification and dehumanization" and replacing them with "an alternative vision of power based on a humanist vision of self-actualization, self-definition, and self-determination."[87]

For Sister Young, the acceptance of Black Power in its cultural nationalist and community empowerment forms did not preclude a conception of Black Power as a broad-based human rights struggle. Young told a newspaper reporter that when St. Frances Academy offered a black history course, students had to be convinced of its relevance. For Young, it only underlined how much work had to be done to bring about self-pride in black communities. Sister Young maintained: "All their lives they see black houses that are inferior, black jobs that are inferior, black schools that are inferior. But you have to be able to accept oneself in order to accept others."[88] The academy sat in a community full of vacant and deteriorated housing; the conditions represented a human tragedy. For such reasons, Sister Young defined the Black Power Movement as a "human movement": "It's the only place Christ is today ... You can't let a white say you're inferior because that's not the truth. That's not Christian, and I've got to say it and even die if necessary to convince the man of the truth."[89]

Goldie Baker worked with Black Power proponents and advocated empowerment and self-determination, but she maintained that such beliefs supported both black people's rights specifically and social justice broadly. As a result, she insisted upon describing herself as a human being interested in liberation: "If you fighting for my rights and all the poor people's rights, I'll join you.... That doesn't mean I'm a black nationalist. It means I'm a human being."[90] Baker recalled how her mother and grandmother, who battled Jim Crow and black inequality, taught her to fight for the rights of the disfranchised, discriminated against, and poor—what they called "human rights." So

Baker said "to each its own. They all got their own concept." But she argued that:

> If you got any kind of hatred against a group of people … I can't deal with it. I don't say anything about the Muslims or the Black Power movement or anybody else. They talk about white people being white devils and they the slave master and all that kind of stuff. That's fine.… In their mind or in their movement or in their struggle that's what [white people] are. All I'm saying is if the white people are willing to fight for an issue that's going to affect any class of people … I'll fight with them. I don't have to have no hatred. I ain't got no control over what you hate or how you feel. I know how I feel.[91]

Peggy McCarty also vocalized and accepted some tenets of Black Power, but expressed discomfort with the black separatism of some cultural nationalists. She praised Malcolm as a "great orator, very intelligent" and approved of the Nation of Islam's emphasis on "mending the family, because it was something I always wanted"—of course, without being lorded over or seen as subservient to any man. And she lauded the group's antiracist efforts and calls for black pride, but she did not approve of mandatory racial exclusivity. Commented McCarty: "The racial thing—that bothered me, because I have always seen people as people. And I've always loved people. It didn't matter what color they were."[92] Even though Baker and McCarty did not support attempts to silence black voices that protested white supremacy or offered black people alternative worldviews, they disapproved of what they deemed hatred and separatism—whether espoused by whites or blacks.[93]

Conclusion

Black women's grassroots struggles—alongside other freedom and equality campaigns—help reveal the politics at work in communities and expose what power meant to local actors. The often unknown or unacknowledged political articulations and activism of these disparate groups of black women—public housing residents, tenant leaders, welfare rights activists, nuns, and Panther women—expose the varied, complex, and hidden histories of the Black Power era. Moreover, their myriad struggles contribute to our knowledge of how race, gender, and economic status combined to influence black women's and black men's activism in urban areas as well as circumscribe public images and historical renderings of Black Power. In popular and scholarly narratives, men and male images usually predominate. But black women wanted power too—both before and after 1966—and they waged battles to secure it. The local struggles of women to secure stable futures for themselves, their families, and communities by seeking racial equality, improved living and economic conditions, better education, political representation, and organizational control reflected not only their historic and contemporary daily concerns—and the methods for addressing those concerns—but also a general belief that they had a right to secure power to make critical decisions affecting their lives.

In the decades rich with social movements, these black women activists clearly saw a purpose and a need for black freedom organizations and Black Power advocates in the struggles against racism and exclusion. They interacted with rights and power proponents, listened to speakers, and adopted the iconography and various freedom languages of the day. Their needs often provided the foundation for, and dovetailed with, Black Power organizations' goals. And their activism often paralleled numerous urban-based Black Power era initiatives.

Just as important, the activism of these black women also exposes the diverse viewpoints and campaigns among women at the grassroots, including the expansive character of political struggle in the name of marginalized people as human beings. Such an expansive focus, which recognized the large constituency of "have-nots," did not translate into a naïve dismissal of race. On the contrary, in Baltimore, the black women who did express such a focus fully recognized the power of race as a factor in black people's lives alongside gender, economics, and even residency. But they also argued that people—as human beings—deserved the basic necessities of survival to secure better, more fulfilling lives. Clearly such black women at the grassroots level were not the only ones to view their pursuit for rights and power as a quest for human dignity.[94] But in cities languishing under the historic weight of inequalities, and eventually pregnant with activism in the 1960s, numerous black women at the grassroots level stepped out, and with the power they could muster, struggled to improve themselves, their families, their communities, and ultimately, the human condition.

BLACK FEMINISTS RESPOND TO BLACK POWER MASCULINISM

KIMBERLY SPRINGER

The Negro Problem. The Woman Question. Two phrases used to encompass the dilemmas progressive social movements historically grappled with as they attempted to deal with difference, or how to situate women and blacks within rubrics for social and economic revolution. For the old guard Left, Marx did not adequately deal with the race problem. How was the progressive Left to deal with African Americans, while completely ignoring the presence of African American radicals? Women were also left untheorized, although Engels broached the subject of the home as a reproductive sphere and women's unpaid domestic labor. Still, women were a question, a conundrum, often set aside with a dismissive, "Women? What about them?"

There are striking similarities between the denial of blacks' and women's basic human rights that were challenged in the Abolition, Suffrage, and Civil Rights Movements. A similar case can be made for the rise of the Women's Liberation Movement, which took many cues from Black Power's radicalism. But what of black women? What of those who were both a "Negro" problem and a "Woman" question? Are we to believe that black women, occupying both social positions, were, therefore, a problematic question? In short, as Deborah King observes, "We learn very little about black women from this analogy.

The experience of black women is apparently assumed, though never explicitly stated, to be synonymous with that of either black males or white females; and since the experiences of both are equivalent, a discussion of black women in particular is superfluous."[1]

Polls taken during the 1970s to measure black women's attitudes toward feminism found that black women, in fact, were more likely to agree with feminist values than white women.[2] What made this possible, particularly during the Black Power era? Surely, more black women participated in Black Power organizations than in women's movement organizations? No one, to date, has completed a comparative analysis of these two movements' organizational numbers, particularly as they pertain to black women. However, lacking concrete demographics, defining black feminism as antithetical to black nationalism denies the possibility that black women are equally, if not more, in tune with feminist principles than white women. Moreover, media depictions of women's movement rallies, in particular as relayed by television and photographs of the era, show predominately white women marching, protesting, and struggling for equality. Finally, there was—and remains—the issue of some black women's aversion to the label "feminist." Though not universal among black women, nor confined by race, feminism as a label or identity often undermined black women's "true blackness" if they dared claim it.

Yet, black women did form feminist organizations, join predominately white feminists' movement groups, and espouse feminist ideals within black nationalist organizations. Therefore, this essay concerns black feminists' influence on the Black Power Movement through the literary arts and social movements.

Komozi Woodard outlines five phases in the process of black nationality formation in the United States: slavery; pre–Civil War; the Jim Crow era; the Great Migration from the rural South to the industrialized North; and the black migration between 1940 and 1970.[3] Black women had an often-unrecognized voice in each phase. Sojourner Truth and Francis Ellen Watkins Harper spoke to slavery's immorality, as well as black women's contradictory gender roles in the institution. Nineteenth-century literary figures and abolitionists, such as Harriet Jacobs, passionately advocated for the black community's freedom. Anna Julia Cooper addressed the need for black education and full citizenship after Reconstruction's failure. Woodard notes the prevalence of colonial uprisings after World War I and the rise of Garveyism globally, so it would be remiss not to acknowledge the contributions of women, such as Amy Jacques Garvey and Claudia Jones, in articulating black identity's revolutionary potential, whether domestically or abroad.[4] In each period, black women mobilized, giving voice to race *and* gender concerns, even if they prioritized one over the other depending on the pertinent issue.[5] If we take the years between 1965 and 1975 as working dates for the Black Power Movement, black women's assertions of feminist consciousness, through their writings and organizations, fit squarely within the period.[6]

It would be presumptuous to assume that black women's physical attendance in a movement or organization is proof of black feminist political presence. Instead, I define a black feminist presence as *a vocal, explicit avocation of both race- and gender-related issues.* These issues can be seen on personal, organizational, and societal levels, ranging from black women's untapped leadership skills to sexism as it impacts individual black women and the entire black community.

Some adamant proponents of the Black Power Movement might maintain that it is ahistorical to impose a gender framework on black men and black organizations active during the 1960s and 1970s.[7] After all, people do evolve and there are black men from the Black Power era who might contest, offer revisionist narratives, or repudiate sexist abuses in the movement.[8] However, it is useful for contemporary scholars to question the reach of the concept "The Black Man," as articulated during the Black Power Movement.[9]

Given the racist abuses black men experienced at the hands of white supremacy, it is not surprising that black liberation struggles have been, and continue to be defined, with a discourse that equates black freedom with a reassertion of black patriarchy. Still, a conversation about gender and sexism in the black liberation movement is crucial to understanding black nationalism's past and planning for its future. It is also imperative that we complicate the category *gender* in examining the Black Power era. This complication is not about "male-bashing" or how black men have done black women wrong. Instead, examining gender includes black masculinity's construction at the time and expectations of black women—both of which were informed by black feminist ideology. Such an approach is complementary and offers a more holistic picture of black struggle.

Black women were major participants within social movements of the late 1960s and early 1970s. However, some black women also opted to develop black feminism as a dynamic theory and practice that promoted black liberation. For black feminists, Black Power's chief flaw was sexism. Similarly, they questioned the efficacy of racism in a women's movement purporting to speak for *all* women. Black women asserted a gender/race analysis, whether they adopted the feminist label or not, in mixed-sex black nationalist organizations and in single-sex black feminist organizations. To paraphrase the Combahee River Collective, a prominent black feminist organization of the era, black women struggled with black men around issues of sexism and with white women around issues of racism. In neither case did black women surrender.

Black feminists' response, then and now, is more than a litany of sexist incidents. Black women had a range of responses to gender discrimination during the Black Power era and black feminism is but one of them. This unique political viewpoint is demonstrated in formal black feminist organizations, but also in black feminist literary and theoretical voices of the time. For the rest of this chapter, I want to, first, define what feminism meant for black women in the 1970s. I then take a look at the works of Toni Cade Bambara, Ntozake Shange, and Michele Wallace as example of defining, if controversial, moments in coming to a public discussion of gender discrimination within black communities. I conclude with a brief discussion of black feminist organizations' development parallel to Black Power and women's movement organizations in the late 1960s and 1970s. Overall, a black woman-centered perspective in social movement organizations and the arts challenged a strictly masculine picture of black revolutionary struggle.

What's in a Name? [10]

What is feminism? Mainstream feminists consistently engage in such debates and black feminists are no different, only their question makes race a priority. On one level, there is the issue of whether black women should call themselves feminists at all. Many in the civil rights and black nationalist movements feared that feminism, derided as a "white woman's thing," was divisive to the struggle for black liberation. Joined with that fear was the concern that if black women engaged in the women's movement or with feminist ideology, their energies would be diverted from the "real" struggle. The idea that black women could only focus on one issue or struggle at a time is considered a "monist" approach to politics.

King describes monist politics as the tendency to focus narrowly on one issue to the detriment of a plurality of issues that could broaden a political agenda. More specifically, monism prioritizes one form of discrimination over others.[11] Thus, Fidel Castro and his compatriots could claim that with the elimination of capitalism Cuba ended all forms of discrimination, including classism, racism, and sexism. Although capitalism fell in 1959, doubt remains as to whether contemporary Afro-Cuban women (as both Afro-Cubans and women) experienced significant improvements in their social and economic lives. While much freer in many respects than African American women, Afro-Cuban women's postrevolutionary experiences offer a compelling demonstration of monism's limits.

The definition of black feminism is varied, but there seem to be a few common tenets applicable to defining what black women during the Black Power era meant by black feminism. Beverly Guy-Sheftall offers the following premises:

- Black women experience a special kind of oppression and suffering in this country which is racist, sexist, and classist because of their dual racial and gender identity and their limited access to economic resources.
- This "triple jeopardy" has meant that the problems, concerns, and needs of black women are different in many ways from those of both white women and black men.
- Black women must struggle for black liberation and gender equality simultaneously.

- There is no inherent contradiction in the struggle to eradicate sexism and racism as well as the other "isms," which plague the human community, such as classism and heterosexism.
- Black women's commitment to the liberation of blacks and women is profoundly rooted in their lived experience.[12]

This assessment, although formulated in the 1990s, encapsulates contemporary black feminism as influenced by the Black Power/Women's Movement era.

Black feminists used a range of definitions to speak to a wide array of experiences. The Third World Women's Alliance (TWWA), for example, echoed many of the contours Guy-Sheftall delineates. The TWWA evolved from first the Student Nonviolent Coordinating Committee's (SNCC) Black Women's Caucus and, later the Black Women's Liberation Committee.[13] Both earlier formations sought to explore issues distinct to black women and how the frameworks of the civil rights, Black Power, and women's movements applied to their situation. How, for instance, might black women reframe the women's movement's demands for "Safe & Legal Abortion" to take into account black women's experiences with the denial of reproductive rights and coerced sterilization?[14] How did a black feminist analysis respond to some black nationalist rhetoric equating abortion with genocide? How could the civil rights movement's freedom framework apply to black women's experiences as behind-the-scenes leadership, which found them relegated to the background because they were neither male nor clergy?

The TWWA suggested coalescing seemingly disparate movement agendas through Third World, socialist, and feminist struggle. The organization's goals included: creating sisterhood through Third World solidarity; promoting Third World unity around economic, social, educational, and political issues; collecting, interpreting, and disseminating information about the Third World; establishing solid relationships with Third World men based on "human love and respect"; and training Third World women for leadership in the revolutionary struggle.[15] The TWWA's black feminism, as reflected in their newspaper *Triple Jeopardy*, was a radical humanism that embraced issues that stressed race, class, and gender matters. Also crucial was the willingness to include struggle with black men as integral to the TWWA's goals and ideology.

The Black Power Movement, although varied by organization, attempted to redefine black women's role as childbearers for the revolution. Certain groups issued calls for black women to, figuratively and literally, walk behind black men. Contrary to popular myth, while black feminists certainly did not comply with these demands, neither did they cede the terms of the liberation movement to black masculinism.[16] Black feminists, such as those in the TWWA and Combahee, pushed male Black Power activists to recognize the strength of black and Third World women. Contrary to sociologists (e.g., E. Franklin Frazier, Daniel Patrick Moynihan), who attempted to create a competition between black men and black women by reinforcing a separate spheres ideology, organizations such as the Chicago-based National Alliance of Black Feminists (NABF) clearly defined black feminism as, "… the belief that women have the *right* to full social, political, and economic equality."[17]

During the Black Power era, black women encountered stumbling blocks in defining black feminism. In addition to black women's relationships to black men, black women also longed for a feminism that would address their relationships to one another. When white feminists used the word "sisterhood," it set off warning bells for black feminists whose collective historical memory included the plantation mistress/slave relationship, the racism of some nineteenth-century suffragists, and contemporary workplace manipulations that mirrored anything but sisterhood. These relationships, based on economic exploitation, forestalled a sisterly allegiance between white and black women, although there were women who worked together effectively to struggle for abolition, enfranchisement, workers' rights, and civil rights.

Given the contentiousness black women faced in attempting to work with white women, many black women, particularly within the feminist movement, assumed sisterhood among women of the same race would be inevitable. Yet, contemporary black feminists only had to look back to the struggles over leadership in the club women's movement for a reminder that black women, too, needed to deal with difference.[18] Class was a persistent marker of difference with the potential to disrupt black feminist notions of sisterhood. With the rise of the contemporary lesbian and gay movement, black women also had to figure out how sexual orientation fit into their concepts of a black feminist sisterhood. Struggles over class manifested in debates over, for example, the best way to spread black feminism's message. Would women lacking the time to commit to activism and having varied education levels, be more likely to pick up a free newspaper, such as *Triple Jeopardy,* or an edited anthology, such as Barbara Smith's *Home Girls: A Black Feminist Anthology?*[19] Were the assertiveness training workshops, held by the National Alliance of Black Feminists, merely mimicking bourgeois, white middle-class ideas about women's inability to communicate effectively with men? Did the agendas of the NABF and the San Francisco/Bay Area-based Black Women Organized for Action (BWOA) only speak to women's aspirations to climb the corporate ladder, resulting in the neglect of poor and working-class women's issues around welfare and accessible health care? From within black feminists came contests over leadership and direction of organizations rooted in concerns about how black feminism would address class as an issue in black communities.

Homophobia was also detrimental to black feminists' usage of sisterhood as an organizing principle. Still considered a psychological disorder by the American Psychological Association until 1973, black lesbians faced not only the medicalization of their desire through the label "homosexual," but they also faced social sanctions from their own communities. If they "kept it to themselves," black lesbians might be able to safely travel within and maintain their good standing among blacks. However, those who spoke out and asserted that acceptance of different sexual orientations was integral to black struggle encountered derision through name-calling and life on the political margins.

Black feminists were not immune to homophobic socialization and, thus, many organizations manifested behavior that ran counter to notions of sisterhood. For example, although at their first national conference the National Black Feminist Organization had a president, Margaret Sloan, who was a self-identified lesbian and led a workshop discussing lesbian issues, some attendees still felt free to voice their homophobia in open forums. Black feminists were surely right that being feminists, they would face lesbian-baiting from outside the organization, but giving in to that fear by attempting to exclude lesbian concerns and experiences could only retard progress black women could make regarding female sexual agency.

In short, it would be more accurate to speak of multiple *definitions* of black feminism. At its most basic, black feminism encompassed the liberation of black women from white supremacy and patriarchy—a radical humanism that could provide liberation. At its most complex, black feminism needed to, in addition to challenging racism and sexism, tackle poverty and patriarchy as it impacted *all* black women. A slight to one was a slight to all, but for black feminists to recognize this they would have to go through the growing pains that accompany the evolution of any revolutionary ideology.[20]

Black Feminists' Literary Responses to Masculinism

Writers are at the forefront of social movements in articulating grievances and, ideally, suggesting fruitful paths for the future. Through poetry, plays, music, and prose, writers expounded upon the ideals of Black Power through the Black Arts Movement, which "celebrated the folk culture of blues people and preached black revolution."[21] Interestingly, although they are mentioned as active during the time period, black feminist writers are often separated from the Black Arts Movement. This may be because, while they celebrated blackness, they also offered a critique of sexism within the movement and the community. Toni Cade Bambara, Ntozake Shange, and Michele Wallace, considered briefly here, each offer poignant examples of the personal and political difficulties in challenging gender discrimination and voicing a coherent black feminist position.

The black feminist premises discussed earlier capture many items on the 1970s black feminist agenda as proposed by women such as Toni Cade Bambara, editor of the groundbreaking anthology, *The Black Woman*. In her introduction, Bambara drew attention to Third World struggles, reclaiming black women's history, discussing sexuality, and "set[ting] the record straight on the matriarch and the evil Black bitch" and its relationship to black women's struggle.[22]

A number of the writers in the volume were active in both black and feminist organizations, demonstrating the intersections of theory and practice so crucial to black feminism's development. Bambara, Grace Lee Boggs, Audre Lorde, Ann Cook, Pat Robinson, Abbey Lincoln, and a host of other writers provided black feminism's first contemporary manifesto. *The Black Woman* offers compelling examples of the issues black feminists included on their agenda for a black liberation that would address race and gender, including interpersonal relationships, poverty, employment, and birth control.

Ntozake Shange's choreopoem *for colored girls who've considered suicide/ when the rainbow is enuf* (1975) inspired similar debate because of her portrayal of black men. Shange celebrated black women's survival in the face of physical and emotional abuse at the hands of black men. Represented by a range of colors, the women in Shange's choreopoem laughed, danced, cried, and sang their way through their experiences of racism and sexism. One woman described her experience of the stage presentation of Shange's choreopoem:

> I managed to make it back to the city on Sunday to see *Colored Girls....* Needless to say, it was *magnificent.* I felt as if I could've (and have been) any one of those women. I hope you can get them to come up to Boston. I also hope I can get a chance to see it again as well as a few of my friends whom I recommended it to. Some interesting things went on during the course of the play in terms of audience response. There was laughter (nervous and otherwise) during a segment on rape and throughout the play I noticed males laughing at the derisive (and quite accurate) statements the author made about men. I wonder if the laughter was nervous (unlikely, since most men don't find anything wrong with their attitudes toward women), detached (the "I don't treat my women that way" rationalization) or condescending (the self-righteous, macho response—which gets my vote). I would be interested to compare the responses of different types of audiences . . .[23]

For this woman, audience reaction demonstrated the long road the black community had yet to travel before taking sexism seriously. However, the aspects she found uplifting—the very celebration of survival and labeling of sexism—put black men on guard, particularly given the negative reflections of black men in the play.

Michele Wallace's *Black Macho and the Myth of the Superwoman*, in the wake of the mildly controversial but critical success of Shange's play, caused a massive uproar in the black community. Wallace's central argument was that the black community was in serious jeopardy if black men continued to enact patriarchy in the form of black "macho" and black women maintained the self-sacrificing role of "superwoman." Reviewed widely in popular and academic periodicals, as well as featured on network television's *Phil Donahue Show*, Wallace ventured into treacherous territory in terms of the vitriol she experienced as a result of her publication.

In Marlon Riggs's documentary *Black Is, Black Ain't*, Wallace and others note the theoretical flaws with her work and the naiveté with which she, as a 28-year-old woman, decontextualized a particularly virulent expression of sexism through an autobiographical approach.[24] However, the problematic aspects of her book do not detract from the political trashing that turned personal. The backlash had a profound impact on Wallace and, as noted in black women's letters to the National Alliance of Black Feminists, served as an important catalyst for black women who saw sexism and the image of black women as superhuman as detrimental to the black body politic.[25] For women who were not intimidated, the dialogue around Wallace's book opened up channels for frank discussions of gender in black communities that were, before this point, considered private "family" matters.

There are other examples of black women writers who bravely tackled the black community's dirty laundry, making public patriarchal abuses. Toni Morrison's *The Bluest Eye* (1970) and Alice Walker's *The Color Purple* (1982) are two notable examples that dealt with incest and physical violence that tore at the seams of black family life. Particularly notable about these works is the way in which black men were re-centered at the expense of trying to deal with very real issues of sexism and abuse within the black community. Not unlike today, when black women challenged sexism and abuses of patriarchal power during the Black Power era, they were met with a backlash chorus labeling them "man-haters."[26]

The writers discussed earlier in this chapter never claimed that black men were evil. These writers did, however, demand accountability for sexism as it occurred in black families, communities, and organizations that advocated liberation. A sophisticated vision of liberation would not only be focused on how to dismantle external systems of oppression, but also be concerned with ending injustice within black communities. Whether contributing to a black feminist framework or prying open the Pandora's box of gender, these writers stepped forward to insert a female voice into the Black Power discussion of the time.

Black Feminists' Organizational Response

Finding predominately white women's liberation groups unresponsive to issues of racism, and some black liberation organizations unresponsive to issues of sexism, black women formed their own organizations. Unlike historically single-sex organizations, black feminist organizations were not the female auxiliary or branch of male organizations. In doing so, they followed in the footsteps of several black women's groups active since the end of the Civil War in advocating for a simultaneous race and gender analysis toward black liberation.

For a moment, however, it is important to recognize that there were black women who articulated a black feminist perspective, or at least a gendered perspective, who chose to fight sexism within Black Power organizations. For example, black women waged battles against sexism within groups such as the Committee for a Unified Newark (CFUN). In 1971, women within the organization launched a Women's Division that took up the task of demanding organizational equality for women, particularly as related to attempts to impose, " ... traditional African concepts of polygamy for the manipulative and vulgar purposes of American adultery and sexual exploitation."[27] These struggles against permissive interpretations of African-centered principles spiraled into a broader attack against male chauvinism at the local and national levels. The evolution of Black Women's United Front (BWUF), in addition to struggling for organizational equality, also tackled issues such as rape against female inmates and forming defense committees for women who fought back and often murdered their prison guard rapists.[28] Moreover, black women, such as those working within the Black Panther Party, offered critical analysis around black women's culpability in perpetuating their own oppression, making consistent self-critique a necessary aspect of revolutionary consciousness.

If many black women found their early political bearings in civil rights and Black Power organizations, they looked outside these groups to address sexism. Margaret Sloan, president of the National Black Feminist Organization, recalled the sexual division of labor she encountered as a young woman seeking to become active in the Chicago branch of the Congress of Racial Equality (CORE).[29] Combahee River Collective activist Barbara Smith doubted whether she could continue as an activist when Black Power advocates challenged her early antiwar involvement. Patriarchal attitudes were not new, but the virulence and prevalence in black nationalist rhetoric gave her pause.[30]

Francis Beal started a black women's consciousness-raising group within SNCC toward the end of that organization's existence that flowered into the TWWA. Highlighting the racial implications of gender issues such as coerced sterilization and self-image, the small group eventually reached out to, first, black working women and later Third World women, who were often also involved with nationalist struggles. Discussing the political strategy of the era, the historian Komozi Woodard notes:

> The black nationalists of the 1960s viewed the members of liberation movements in the Third World not only as allies but as brothers and sisters in the struggle. Identifying with the battle for self-determination in Africa, Asia and Latin America, the politics of cultural nationalism proposed a strategy of black liberation involving struggles for regional autonomy in urban centers' in alliance with oppressed people of color in the United States, particularly Puerto Ricans and Mexican Americans.[31]

Fittingly, the TWWA on the East Coast incorporated the concerns of Puerto Rican and Palestinian nationalist women, while a later TWWA West Coast organization united with Asian and Chicana nationalist women. On both coasts, Black, Puerto Rican, Palestinian, Asian, Native American, and Chicana women found common ground in their assertions of multifaceted political radicalism.

Conclusion

Neither archived organizational records nor interviews with black feminist activists yield any evidence of significant encounters or joint actions between black feminist and black nationalist organizations, though there were plenty of black feminists, such as attorney Flo Kennedy, active with Black Power groups. Although anecdotal, this lack of interaction at the organizational level speaks perhaps to both black nationalists groups' reticence to deal effectively with sexism and women who spoke about it, as well as black feminists' reluctance to directly confront black masculinism. Most often, black feminists recall tensions with black nationalist women who questioned their motives and dedication to black liberation struggles.

Despite limited direct organizational contact, black feminists added ideals of gender equality and antisexism to the social activist milieu of the Black Power era. They did so through literary contributions that are lasting documents of black feminist *and* nationalist revolutionary goals. Bambara's *The Black Woman*, Wallace's *Black Macho*, and Shange's *for colored girls* contested the rising masculinism of the Black Power era that sought to relegate women to the periphery of struggle and into a private sphere that black women, always workers, were never fully embedded in. The controversy generated by discussions of gender during the Black Power era, and the retrospectives emerging now, demonstrate the vital importance of black feminism's role in offering solutions to the Negro problem and answers to the Woman question.

5

THE THIRD WORLD WOMEN'S ALLIANCE

Black Feminist Radicalism and Black Power Politics

STEPHEN WARD

One of the unifying and most important features of the emerging scholarship on Black Power is the recognition that the movement was multidimensional and involved a wide range of activities, organizations, and programs. Refuting popular interpretations of the Black Power era as a destructive, and often violent, deterioration of black political activity, this scholarship is beginning to document the vibrant political, cultural, and intellectual worlds that flourished under the banner of Black Power.[1] This work is also painting a richer and more redeeming picture of Black Power than is presented in some histories of the Civil Rights Movement, which have tended to cast Black Power as an unfortunate and misguided departure from civil rights struggles. By uncovering diverse expressions of Black Power politics, scholars are demonstrating how the period's "cultural and political formations," in the words of Komozi Woodard, "galvanized millions of black people in the broadest movement in African American history."[2] Although the historical study of Black Power is still in its early stages, and therefore has yet to fully stake out the broad interpretive and historiographical contours of the field,[3] this body of recent work (to which the present volume is an important contribution) is breaking new ground in the study of black politics and culture in postwar America.

This chapter highlights the place of radical black feminism among the intellectual and political currents of the Black Power Movement.[4] It traces the evolution of a New York-based black feminist collective during the late 1960s and early 1970s from its origins as a women's caucus in the Student Nonviolent Coordinating Committee (SNCC) to the Third World Women's Alliance (TWWA). Locating the group within a nexus of Black Power groups, ideas, and political projects, this history highlights the activism and intellectual work of Frances Beal, the TWWA's central figure, arguing that her political trajectory offers a window into the ways that black women activists developed a feminist consciousness and political program within, and as a part of, Black Power's ideological development.

By placing Frances Beal and the Third World Women's Alliance within a narrative of the Black Power Movement,[5] this chapter makes two related claims. First, it contends that black feminism is a component of the Black Power Movement's ideological legacy. I aim to challenge the notion that black feminism and Black Power were ideologically incompatible or locked in an inherently antagonistic relationship. To the contrary, the TWWA's feminism was not simply a critique of Black Power politics but, rather, a *form* of it. The members of TWWA were simultaneously feminist activists and Black Power activists, and they crafted a multipositioned political space through which they fashioned feminist politics that also theorized and enacted central ideological commitments of the Black Power Movement as part of their feminist politics. That is, they built on and extended elements of Black Power politics.

My second claim is about the character and contours of Black Power-era feminism. Using the example of the TWWA, I want to suggest that a central objective of Black Power-era feminism was to create an autonomous political identity for black women activists, and a hallmark of this identity was its expansive and generative character. In their struggle to define themselves as thinkers and activists within the spaces of Black Power politics, Beal and her comrades sought to build an organization that included black women (and ultimately all women of color) as active agents of political struggle and social

change. In the process they developed political analyses that identified and theorized the intersections of race, gender, and economic
exploitation in American society. Accordingly, the group's evolution
from a caucus of black women in SNCC to the TWWA—an organization of black, Latina, and Asian American women—was not a
reversal or abatement of their political vision or of their political identities as black women activists, but, rather, a strengthening and
expansion of them.

In making these claims I do not wish to minimize, deny, or evade
the masculinist posturing that pervaded Black Power, nor do I intend
to downplay the significance of black women's critiques of sexism and
gender relations in the movement. Indeed, the discussion here illustrates some of the ways that black feminists challenged the reaction-
ary gender politics, sexist rhetoric, and misogynistic tendencies that
marred much of the movement. However, such interventions were
not the whole of black feminist politics. As the historical example of
the TWWA suggests, the sexism of the Black Power Movement was
a significant impetus for black feminist organizing, but this alone
does not account for the emergence of Black Power-era feminism.
Nor does it fully represent the ideological depth of black feminist
thinking. In other words, black feminist organizing of the 1960s arose
largely as a response to an increasingly misogynistic and male-domi-
nated political culture, but its growth and evolution into the 1970s
reflected a wider commitment to progressive political action and a
sustained engagement with the struggles of African American communities. Thus, we might more appropriately see black women's confrontation with sexism within the Black Power Movement (and
racism or marginalization within the women's movement) in the
1960s and 1970s as a starting point and a platform for the creation of
a broader black feminist political space.

Frances Beal, "Double Jeopardy," and Black Power Politics

Though less well known than many of her contemporaries, Frances
Beal was a central figure in the resurgence of black feminist thinking
and activism of the Black Power era. She is perhaps best known as the
author of "Double Jeopardy: To Be Black and Female," a pioneering

essay that helped to lay the foundation of black feminist thought in the 1960s and 1970s. Published in 1970, it helped to clarify key issues and ideas that were then emerging as critical components of an autonomous black feminist consciousness and political agenda.[6] In fact, Beal helped to theorize the connection between racial and gender oppression. She argued that racism and sexism worked in concert to create a particular set of experiences, concerns, and problems in the lives of black women that not only deserved consideration as distinct political questions, but also were central to the broader struggle for black liberation. Thus, Beal's essay helped to expand the boundaries of Black Power thought. Furthermore, by articulating a notion of multiple or simultaneous forms of oppressions—of race, gender, and capitalist economic exploitation as intersecting and mutually reinforcing systems—"Double Jeopardy" anticipated conceptual frameworks of contemporary black feminist thought such as intersectionality.[7] The essay has been widely anthologized and stands as one of the most recognized writings of the era. But to grasp fully the essay's historical import requires an explication of Beal's intellectual and political trajectory.

The daughter of politically progressive parents, Beal was raised in communities in western New York and later New York City during the 1940s and 1950s that nurtured her intellectual curiosity and laid the foundation for her politics. Her political commitments were crystallized by the Civil Rights Movement and sharpened by her experiences as a student activist and member of SNCC. Beal was a student at the University of Wisconsin between 1958 and 1960, where she served as vice president of the student chapter of the NAACP and participated in solidarity demonstrations at local five and dime stores in support of the sit-in movement in the South.[8]

In August 1960, Beal and her husband moved to Paris. She earned a degree from the Sorbonne and participated in the African American expatriate community, meeting figures such as Richard Wright (and befriending his daughter Julia Wright Herve), and helping to organize the efforts to bring Malcolm X to speak. Beal credits her years in Paris for the development of her international and anticolonial consciousness, as she met students from newly independent African and Caribbean nations and frequently engaged in lively discussions about colonialism and African independence. Furthermore, living in Paris during the early 1960s Beal witnessed first hand the bitter debates over colonialism and the national liberation struggle in Algeria and she also encountered the works of Franz Fanon (reading his *The Wretched of the Earth* in its original French edition, years before the English translation captured the political imagination of black American militants).[9]

Beal returned to the United States in 1966, taking a position as a research assistant with the National Council of Negro Women (NCNW) in New York and shortly thereafter joining the New York chapter of SNCC. Over the previous five years, she had worked with SNCC during visits home in the summers. By 1967 she was a member of SNCC's New York chapter and had assumed a leadership role in the newly formed International Affairs Commission spearheaded by SNCC veteran James Forman. The commission reflected SNCC's growing global awareness and identification with the Third World, and Beal's international experience made her particularly suited for this post.[10]

Specifically, the formation of SNCC's International Affairs Commission was one expression of the organization's transformation during the mid-1960s from civil rights to Black Power. During this period SNCC (like the Congress of Racial Equality and other civil rights groups) moved away from and eventually rejected the tactics and goals of the mainline Civil Rights Movement, namely, nonviolence, interracial organizing, and liberal integrationism. By 1967 SNCC had embraced Black Power and its broad political commitments, which included the internationalization of black protest, a rejection of nonviolence, and the embracing of self-defense; call for racial unity and the reclaiming of an autonomous black cultural heritage; and independent black politics. During the second half of the 1960s members of SNCC and other activists across the country attempted to act on these and other ideas as they built a movement for Black Power.

Contested Gender Ideology: Nationalism, "Black Manhood," and the Role of the Black Woman

Fueled largely by a resurgence of black nationalism during the second half of the 1960s, the Black Power Movement produced an

increasingly masculinist sensibility and political language. Much of
the rhetoric and ideas coming from various streams of nationalism
both marginalized black women activists and adversely shaped gender
dynamics within the movement and organizations such as SNCC.[11]
During the mid-1960s, these issues frequently surfaced in black political discourses and intellectual debates, as activists and analysts of
black politics debated black gender relations and the relative roles of
black men and women in the family, community, and political struggle.[12] For example, between July 1965 and August 1966 several articles, commentaries, and letters in the *Liberator* magazine, an
important venue of black thought, revealed a running dialogue on
black women's position and participation in black social, political,
and cultural life.[13] Addressing topics such as the "Role of the Afro-
American Woman" and "Black Men vs. Black Women," this dialogue
highlighted the tensions embedded in the frequently posed question:
"What is the role of black women in the black liberation struggle?"
For many, the answer was clear: black women should play a supportive but subordinate role. Indeed, the very question was founded
on—and ultimately served to reinforce—the assumption that men
were the natural and appropriate protagonists of the struggle. Many
black women activists, of course, challenged the very foundations of
the question, recognizing this to be an inherently paternalistic query
based on the assumption that men and women were predisposed to
play distinct (and invariably unequal) roles. Kathleen Cleaver, who
was a member of SNCC and then served as communications secretary
of the Black Panther Party (a post she created), simultaneously
exposed and rejected this thinking with her succinct response: "No
one ever asks what a man's place in the Revolution is."[14]

During the mid- and late 1960s, overt calls for black women to
recede into the background in deference to male leadership were tied
to the ostensibly revolutionary objective of reclaiming "black manhood." As a symbolic call to arms, a declaration of militant political
commitment, or a metaphor for collective dignity, the struggle to
reclaim "black manhood" galvanized black women as well as men
within the emerging political communities of the early Black Power
Movement. But this metaphor and the male-centered political framework that it represented could be, and too often was, used to silence

and discipline the activism of black women. For example, women who were considered overly assertive or who assumed leadership roles were accused of undermining black manhood and labeled "castrators." Such thinking called for a guarded and truncated "female" political space, of which the family and reproduction were central sites. Indeed, these nationalist discourses underwrote a patriarchal vision of nation-building in which the highest calling for women was to "have babies for the revolution" and birth control was considered genocide.[15] The Nation of Islam, for example, decried "the sins of birth control" and "the deadly pill" in a series of front-page articles in *Muhammad Speaks* during the summer of 1965.[16] By the fall of that year, the *Moynihan Report* further intensified public discussion of black gender dynamics by popularizing the idea of a "black matriarchy" and the notion that patterns of female dominance had undermined black men and harmed black communities.[17]

Beal recalls that in 1967 and 1968 she and other black women noticed some of these ideas being expressed in SNCC. In response, they began raising questions about gender dynamics in the organization and pushing for discussions about sexism.[18] SNCC was by then mired in an organizational crisis that would ultimately lead to its demise, but the group still provided the space for political discussion and ideological debate. This proved essential for the intellectual and political development of black women activists, who were emboldened to act on their own specific ideas, analyses, and experiences.[19] As Beal recalled: "It was almost as if becoming a feminist and being able to articulate those thoughts and ideas liberated the rest of me to be able to have confidence to say I have some real political thoughts of my own."[20] For example, at the end of 1968 Beal presented a position paper on sterilization abuse and reproductive rights at a SNCC staff meeting in New York. This proved to be a catalyzing moment in two important ways: it was the genesis of her essay "Double Jeopardy"; and it sparked the formation of a black women's caucus in SNCC, which was the beginning of the Third World Women's Alliance.

Beal's paper grew out of the collective development of feminist consciousness among black women in New York SNCC and signaled Beal's emergence as a radical black thinker. Her choice of subject matter, sterilization abuse, was significant for at least four reasons.

First, it was timely and particularly prescient. At the end of the 1960s, the practice of coerced and involuntary sterilization of poor black women was widespread, though largely hidden from public view.[21] However, during the early and mid-1970s, a series of high profile cases exposed extensive sterilization abuse of poor black women across the South and in urban areas such as New York, Boston, and Los Angeles, implicating the federal government as well as local and state agencies.[22] Second, Beal's decision to address sterilization abuse is significant because it reflected a willingness to speak publicly about the social and political dimensions of an intimately private experience.[23] This proved to be a vital step both in the expansion of black women's gender consciousness and in their struggle to broaden the scope and terrain of black political struggles. Third, Beal recognized that other women of color, domestically and internationally, were also being subjected to sterilization abuses, and she framed black women's experiences with these oppressive practices within a broader, Third World context. In particular, Beal exposed the alarming rates at which Puerto Rican women were sterilized, both in the United States (particularly New York) and on the island,[24] implicating America as a colonial and domestic exploiter of black and Puerto Rican women. This forecasts the ideas of Third World unity and anti-imperialist internationalism that animated the Third World Women's Alliance. Finally, by broaching the topic of women's reproduction, Beal addressed the most important issue of the women's liberation movement: reproductive rights. Beal's paper was written against the backdrop of the emerging women's liberation movement (which played a part in creating the cultural and political context from which black feminism emerged). However, her attention on the practice of forced sterilization of black (and Puerto Rican) women, as opposed to the fight for access to safe abortions and birth control, demonstrates how the feminism of black women often deviated from the feminism of white women.[25]

The discussions occasioned by Beal's paper led to the formation of a women's caucus within SNCC named the Black Women's Liberation Committee (BWLC). Although SNCC was falling apart as a national organization, the BWLC reflected a lively strain of political energies. Ideologically, the group represented the crystallization of an autonomous feminist political perspective among black women in SNCC's New York office. Politically and practically, the BWLC served as a vehicle that continued the evolution and expansion of a radical black women's political identity. The group began meeting and solidifying its structure in January 1969, with former Tuskegee activist and antiwar organizer Gwen Patton serving as chair along with Mae Jackson, SNCC organizer and poet, as secretary.[26]

In its first weeks, the BWLC quickly set out to build an agenda for black women activists that reflected the group's engagement with Black Power politics. The group put forward an ambitious national program that included setting up "Liberation Schools" for children and organizing "a network of women to give draft counseling services to our young men."[27] The idea of liberation schools, which would be popularized months later by the Black Panther Party during the summer of 1969, emerged among Black Power formations as an attempt to build parallel institutions that would respond to the needs of black communities. Similarly, the idea of establishing draft counseling centers to encourage and assist black men to avoid the draft reflects a broader antiwar and anti-imperialist position that grew in SNCC during the mid-1960s and was widespread among Black Power activists. Patton herself was a founding member of the Student Mobilization Committee Against the War in Vietnam (SMC) and the National Black Anti-War, Anti-Draft Union (NBAWADU).[28]

While these two large projects highlighted elements of the group's broad political vision,[29] the BWLC's first organizing effort reflected the group's primary objective of creating a space for discussion among black women activists and the development of black feminist consciousness. Shortly after its founding, the BWLC issued a call for an organizing and planning meeting in Atlanta for black women in SNCC during March 1969. The purpose of the meeting was to bring together "the most active women who have been involved in the Movement for ... the past eight years." In a letter announcing the meeting, Patton projected thirty attendees from across the country, and she identified by name three SNCC veterans: "Mrs. Fannie Lou Hamer, Mrs. Diane Bevel, and Miss Faye Bellamy."[30] Patton attached a series of provocative and wide-ranging questions to serve as the basis for discussions during the meeting. Covering various theoretical, political, and ideological issues, the questions spoke to core concerns of black women's political activity, including notions of gender and social identity; black male-female relationships; and women's roles in the black liberation movement.[31] Patton invited participants to add further questions to the ones that she posed, all toward the objective of serious reflection: "we are calling a group of women to sit down for the *sole* and *soul* purpose of knocking our heads together to find answers."[32]

From the Black Women's Liberation Committee (BWLC) to the Black Women's Alliance (BWA): Consciousness-Raising and Organization Building

The Atlanta gathering apparently did not materialize as planned, but instead a smaller group of BWLC members met on the East Coast during April to engage some of Patton's questions.[33] The resulting conversation was an example of the group's most significant activity in these initial months, namely the creation of a dialogic, collective process through which the members of BWLC developed their ideas. For example, some of the language, ideas, and formulations discussed at this meeting found their way into Beal's "Double Jeopardy" and in an essay by Patton titled "Black People and the Victorian Ethos," both of which were published in Toni Cade Bambara's 1970 anthology, *The Black Woman*.[34] More broadly, the gathering facilitated the BWLC's continued efforts to work out its ideological positions and organizational identity with respect to intellectual currents (and ideological tensions) in the Black Power Movement.

The discussion began with the question, "Just what is the Black Women's Liberation Committee?" The conversation around this question highlighted the need for an autonomous vehicle for black women's political activism. In particular, it revealed what would become a driving concern for the group as it evolved into the Third World Women's Alliance, namely the organization's attempt to articulate a theoretical and political understanding of black women (and eventually all women of color) as agents of revolutionary change. Anticipating the TWWA's internationalism (especially as it would be represented through coverage in the organization's newspaper

Triple Jeopardy), they talked about the need to "look closely at other revolutionary struggles" to develop a "historical analysis of other women who have actually fought in liberation struggles and find out what their role in that struggle was." Furthermore, studying the history of revolutionary struggles also yielded another lesson: "unless the woman in any oppressed nation is completely liberated, then a revolution cannot really be called a revolution."[35] This forecasts one of the central components of the TWWA's political analysis and practice: using revolutions in the Third World as models, they would argue for the inclusion of women's liberation as a central plank in the broader black political program.

A significant part of the discussion turned to the rise of cultural nationalism and its espousal of unequal gender relations. "Nothing [is] wrong with cultural nationalism" or with "brothers exerting themselves," Patton said. "I think that's beautiful. The most beautiful thing that Black Power did was to get black brothers up there on the stages. It was good to see Stokely Carmichael, Rap Brown, etc." However, she rejected the notion that black men's ascendancy required women's subordination. "It doesn't make sense that in order for a man to be strong, I have to be weak." Patton was also critical of "all these people running around here in these dashikis and that kind of carrying on talking about African history," referring to the selective readings by some cultural nationalists to justify placing women in subordinate positions relative to men in black family and political life. "I don't understand what kind of African History they been reading … All these big time kings that they're talking about are the same kings that sold us into slavery."[36]

Other points of discussion dealt with more personal dimensions of black women's lives such as black family structure (including debates over the *Moynihan Report*) and reproductive rights. Drawing from her personal experiences, Beal identified the lack of adequate day-care centers as a particular means of oppression ("an oppression that society at large perpetrates") for many women. The availability of safe, clean child-care facilities, she said, "would liberate a woman to go out and become a full, participating productive member of society." Another participant in the discussion raised "the whole idea of birth control" and its impact on the black struggle. She challenged the notions, advanced by some Black Power activists, that women should "have babies for the revolution" and that birth control was genocide. "I think that what is going to happen," she said, is that birth control "will free black women to participate in the revolution. Black people are always going to have children, we don't have to get into hang-ups that if we use birth control we won't be able to build our nation." Beal added her opinion that the lack of information about birth control could keep a woman "attached to her home, keeping from exerting herself in society." She underscored this idea by stating: "I think that a woman will not be free until she becomes a productive member of society." Interestingly, Beal made sure to separate housework from the category of productive labor. With her personal history informing her analysis, she described housework as a "very degrading, dehumanizing kind of work for anyone to do," revealing that "I did it for a number or years while the children were small. It's not satisfying in the least. There's nothing that you notice about housework except what's not done." To underscore her call for women's independence, Beal added: "You just can't live your life as some satellite of some man."[37]

Beal's comments reveal some dimensions of the complex relationship that she and other black women activists had to the broader women's liberation movement. Some feminists, for example, would be uncomfortable with Beal's sharp distinction between housework and productive activity. At the same time, her call for women's independence and her rejection of the traditional family roles of male breadwinner and female homemaker echoed key ideas emanating from the women's liberation movement. Similarly, the BWLC meeting bore some resemblance to the consciousness-raising groups of the women's liberation movement, even while it represented an important ideological departure from that movement. Serving both as a method of developing theory and as a movement-building strategy, consciousness-raising involved women sharing their personal experiences in small group discussions. It was a process of radicalization that helped women discern the social origins of their personal problems, generate a consciousness of collective oppression, and identify a basis of collective political action. As such, consciousness-raising was directly related to the principle of "the personal is political," a central theoretical insight of the women's movement that asserted an organic relationship between personal and social experience.[38] The comments cited earlier from the BWLC meeting reveal how Beal and the other members drew political insights from their individual experiences—both in their personal and family relationships and as activists—and began a collective effort to theorize their experiential and emotional responses to oppression.

One outcome of the BWLC's consciousness-raising efforts was the decision to expand the scope and membership of the organization. The gender dynamics of Black Power (and SNCC in particular) had been BWLC's primary point of departure when the group formed as a women's caucus in SNCC at the end of 1968. However, through their conversations and activities over the course of the ensuing year, the members of the organization increasingly came to see the need to form a black women's organization beyond SNCC. By 1970, they decided to expand the group from a SNCC caucus to an autonomous black women's organization that would include "women from other organizations, welfare mothers, community workers, and campus radicals."[39] Now independent from SNCC, the BWLC changed its name to the Black Women's Alliance (BWA).[40]

The Black Woman and the Articulation of a Collective Political Identity

When it emerged in 1970, the BWA did not yet have a fully developed, cohesive ideology, but it was developing a decidedly anticapitalist and anti-imperialist framework. Thus, the BWA occupied a dual position among the larger ideological crosscurrents of the Black Power Movement: it was part of the network of black Left thinkers and activists; and at the same time the BWA represented one thread of intellectual and political activity within a wider fabric of black feminist politics. In popular as well as scholarly accounts of this period, black feminism is too often obscured within the broader space of Black Power radicalism. Nonetheless, the force and impact of this black feminist politics was most dramatically announced with the publication in 1970 of Toni Cade Bambara's *The Black Woman*. Indeed, the evolution of the BWLC from its early activities in January 1969 to its transformation into the BWA in 1970 can be understood as one of the many expressions of black feminist consciousness and organizing that the book documents.[41]

In the summer of 1969, when she was completing *The Black Woman*, Bambara did not know Frances Beal. But she was familiar with the BWLC and through their mutual network of activists learned that Beal was interested in the forthcoming anthology. So Bambara wrote to Beal inviting her to contribute to the volume, requesting a piece on the BWLC or some other "hard-headed, cold-blooded" essay that would address itself "to the Struggle, to the Black Woman and the Movement, to the Revolution." Beal had already prepared such an essay, having accepted an invitation to contribute to *Sisterhood is Powerful*, edited by Robin Morgan. (Beal would receive several more invitations in the coming months.) Beal contributed "Double Jeopardy: To Be Black and Female" to both collections. The prospect of publishing in Bambara's project likely appealed to Beal because it was, in Bambara's words, "an anthology of the Black Woman—a long overdue book."[42]

Published in August 1970, *The Black Woman: An Anthology*, represented a pathbreaking showcase of black women's intellectual production. Alongside works by recognized black women writers and thinkers, such as Nikki Giovanni, Audre Lorde, and Paule Marshall, readers found selections from college students, community activists, and political organizers. The collection brought together seasoned writers and first-time authors, musicians, and political theorists. Through poetry, short works of fiction, and essays—some autobiographical and others analytical—*The Black Woman* addressed a variety of topics and presented a wide range of thought, experience, and creative expression. Several of the contributors, including Beal and Patton, addressed many of the issues that the BWLC/BWA had grappled with, such as: the myth of a "black matriarchy" and notions of family and motherhood; the debates regarding the role of black women in the contemporary black struggle; the possibility of redefining gender roles beyond dominant white patriarchal models; birth control and the debates over women's reproductive rights; and discussion of the nature of black female/male relationships.

Published in the midst of the Black Power Movement, the book presented a compelling collage of contemporary black women's writings, concerns, interests, and politics. *The Black Woman* therefore stands as an important intellectual artifact of the period.[43] Its appearance coincided with a range of other works inspired by Black Power. For example, Floyd Barbour's anthology *The Black Seventies* (a follow-up to his 1968 anthology *The Black Power Revolt*); George Jackson's autobiographical political treatise *Soledad Brother;* and the inaugural issue of the journal *Review of Black Political Economy* also appeared in 1970. Looking forward to the 1970s, each of these works emanated from the Black Power Movement and in some way attempted to chart a particular ideological lens (for instance, revolutionary nationalism or Pan-Africanism) or arena of struggle (such as economic development or prisons). Bambara's anthology served a similar function. As several scholars have noted, *The Black Woman* helped to create the space for a wide community of black women thinkers to articulate ideas and develop a body of thought.[44] The book therefore played a critical role in the broader construction of a political language and identity for black women activists, which was a central goal of Black Power-era feminism. Thus, *The Black Woman* represents an important stage of the broader project to which the members of the BWA also belonged. As the BWLC and then BWA sought to construct its political identity—first through ideological development, then through building an autonomous organization dedicated to black women's liberation—the organization developed an expansive vision of black women's political agency. As this vision grew, so did the composition of the organization.

The Third World Women's Alliance

In the summer of 1970, two women who were members of the Puerto Rican Socialist Party and active in the Puerto Rican independence movement asked the BWA about joining the organization. This forced the members of the BWA to think more concretely about their call for Third World solidarity and its implications for the organization's membership and political orientation. This led to a debate within the organization in which some members argued against permitting nonblack women into the group. They reasoned that the historically unique situation of African American women demanded that they remain an all-black organization. The BWA could form coalitions with other groups, they said, but should not allow nonblack women to become members. Others held that women of color faced many of the same social and political circumstances and that these commonalities outweighed their cultural and historical distinctions. Ultimately, a majority of the group agreed with this position, and in the summer of 1970 the organization was expanded to include "all third world sisters" and became the Third World Women's Alliance.[45]

The change in membership did not represent a qualitative change in focus. In fact, the change reinforced rather than altered the group's politics. Specifically, the organization's "Third World" orientation remained grounded in, and responsive to, black political struggles. This is apparent from a pamphlet that the group circulated, "Third World Women's Alliance: Our History, Our Ideology, Our Goals." The writing and distributing of this pamphlet was one of the TWWA's first tasks. It contained a history of the organization (tracing its evolution as the BWLC and BWA); an outline of the group's goals; a discussion of its ideological platform; and three statements, each presented in the form of a question, addressing the organization's relationship to the struggles for black, women's, and Third World liberation. These statements in particular highlight the ideological struggles that the TWWA (and other black feminists) waged with segments of the Black Power and women's liberation movements.[46]

For example, the first page of the pamphlet asks, "What is the 'Third World'?" and explains its use as a political designation for people of color in the United States. "Within the confines of the Unites States, the third world consists of the descendants of Africa, Asia, and Latin America. This community is made up of Afro-Americans, Puertoriquenos, Chicanos, Latinos, Asian-Americans, Native-Americans (Indians) and Eskimos." Like many others during the Black Power era, the TWWA drew direct links between the historical experiences of Third World nations and people of color in the United States, seeing American racism and European colonialism as two sides of the same coin. "We have suffered from the same kind of exploitation and colonial oppression as our brothers and sisters in our homelands.... All Third World people have suffered under the yoke of white racism and economic pillage by the white imperialist powers."[47]

With respect to the Black Power Movement, and especially the most strident strains of nationalism within it, the pamphlet addressed the question, "Is a Third World Women's Group Divisive to the National Liberation Struggle?" This can be read as the TWWA's response to the idea put forward by some men (and women) that focusing on "women's issues" would serve as a distraction from the primary goal of black liberation. The TWWA rejected this notion, countering that the different forms of oppression in the lives of black women (and other women of color) could not be separated. "We feel that there is no contradiction in being nationalists, in being feminists, and in being socialists.... The Third World woman must always be fighting against and exposing her triple exploitation in this society." Furthermore, they argued, their struggle would enhance rather than detract from broader political battles. Finally, an "independent Third World women's organization" was especially suited to engage the interlocking bases of oppression: "It is the position of the Third World Women's Alliance that the struggle against racism and imperialism must be waged simultaneously with the struggle for women's liberation, and only a strong independent women's group can ensure that this will come about."[48]

The statement on the women's liberation movement—"Why a Separate Third World Women's Group?"—defended the TWWA's decision to organize autonomously from the women's movement. It made a clear distinction between the political objectives of women of color and those of the women's movement and demarcated the racial limits of sisterhood:

> to white women liberation groups we say ... until you can deal with your own racism and until you can deal with your OWN poor white sisters, you will never be a liberation movement and you cannot expect to unite with Third World peoples in a common struggle.... It is difficult for Third World women to address themselves to the petty problems of who is going to take out the garbage, when there isn't enough food in the house for anything to be thrown away. Fighting for the day-to-day

existence of a family and as human beings is the struggle of the Third World woman. We are speaking of revolution, we don't need reforms.[49]

We can also discern the shape of the TWWA's politics—and especially the group's efforts to negotiate the relationship between racial and gender struggles—from the organization's early activities during the fall of 1970. One of the TWWA's first public acts was to participate in a Women's Liberation Day parade and rally in New York City on August 26, 1970, organized by feminists and the liberal National Organization of Women (NOW). Marking the fiftieth anniversary of the ratification of the Nineteenth Amendment, the event was billed as the "Women's Strike for Equality," a national women's strike demanding abortions on demand, twenty-four hour day-care centers, and equal employment and educational opportunities. The TWWA was initially skeptical about participating because they saw the issues raised by white feminists as distinct from their own. Nonetheless, members decided to join the march as a way of letting more women know of the TWWA's existence.[50]

In November, the TWWA received national exposure when the *New York Times* ran a story about the tensions between black women activists and the women's liberation movement. Beal was interviewed for the story, which described the TWWA as a thriving organization with approximately 200 members. Although this number was almost certainly inflated,[51] the TWWA did experience significant growth that fall. In October, Beal reported that the group was "growing every day," with new recruits participating in a variety of community activities, while continuing to hold weekly political education classes and consciousness-raising meetings. At this time, the group was also in the midst of planning a mass march and rally in Harlem to support global liberation movements and to protest the Vietnam War. In these efforts the TWWA reached out to unions, students, and churches, and worked with Asian American and Latino/a communities.[52] TWWA's activities and literature increasingly brought the group into contact with individuals and other organizations who were interested in their program. However, as the TWWA received requests for information about their positions and about forming other chapters, Beal and others began to identify weaknesses in the organization. Specifically, they found that their administrative structure was inadequate to respond to this growing interest, and despite their earlier efforts, there was "uneven political development" among TWWA members.[53]

To address these problems, the group turned inward and intensified its political education program. As it explained to supporters in December 1970, the TWWA "decided to call a halt to all outside activities and attempt to hammer out a solid ideological platform based on a scientific revolutionary analysis, as well as to formulate a workable structure which would facilitate our growth into a national third world women's organization."[54] For several weeks, a "leadership cadre" of fifteen women met four times a week in political education sessions covering such topics as "revolutionary ideology," "dynamics of imperialism," and "the political thought of Frantz Fanon."[55]

By the spring of 1971, the TWWA had completed an intensive political education program and once again sought to expand its membership and political activity. The group adopted democratic centralism as its organizational structure, placing an emphasis on collective leadership to allow for the development of each member's potential. In the fall, prospective members went through an orientation to introduce them "to the goals and objectives of the organization" and "the ideology of the organization i.e. socialism."[56] The seven orientation sessions were led by various members of the group and focused primarily on studying Marxism and socialist theory. Required reading included Beal's "Double Jeopardy," Linda La Rue's 1970 essay "The Black Movement and Women's Liberation," and essays by Mao and James Forman. Works of Marxist theory by Lenin, Marx, and Engels were suggested reading, and a document called "Why Do We Study?" was used to explore the relationship between theoretical development and political practice.[57]

The organization's most thoroughgoing exploration of the relationship between theory and practice came in the form of its newspaper, *Triple Jeopardy*. Conceived and launched during the fall of 1971 (while the TWWA was conducting the orientation sessions), the paper was in some ways the TWWA's most enduring and important project.

Triple Jeopardy

Triple Jeopardy extended Beal's concept of double jeopardy, adding economic exploitation as the third oppressive force operating in the lives of women of color. The masthead read "Racism, Imperialism, Sexism," naming the interlocking systems of oppression that the members of the TWWA sough to eradicate. They envisioned the paper serving three primary functions. First, it was to be informational. To "clarify what the realities are," the paper would disseminate facts and interpretations of development in the United States with specific emphasis on those issues that concern Third World women. The second function of *Triple Jeopardy* was to engage in current ideological struggles. This included ideas within the Black Power Movement—such as the call for black capitalism coming from some conservative elements—as well as the women's liberation movement, where "some are proclaiming that men are the major enemy and completely reject any analysis based on the class or race to which women belong."[58] Finally, the publication was used as an organizational tool by spreading TWWA's ideology to women across the country and recruiting members.[59]

Published approximately every other month from September 1971 through the summer of 1975, *Triple Jeopardy* contained a range of articles designed to perform these functions. A section called "On The Job" highlighted women's labor market and employment experiences through interviews of women in various workplace settings. The "Skills" column taught women to perform mechanical and technical tasks, such as changing a fuse or a flat tire, that are generally considered to be the province of men. The TWWA identified the learning of such skills as important not only to obtain a measure of independence, but also as a matter of their rights and responsibilities as revolutionaries: "In order to participate in the struggle for liberation, we must develop all possible skills."[60] Local (New York), national, and international news stories filled the paper, covering events and political issues relevant to people of color generally and women in particular. *Triple Jeopardy* often featured articles on the activities of women of color in various settings, especially stories that aimed to show the important and prominent roles that women were playing in Third World and socialist countries. Other frequent topics included women's health and political prisoners (male and female).

Triple Jeopardy's first issue was published in September 1971. It engaged Black Power politics while simultaneously addressing concerns and political developments pertaining specifically to black women and other women of color. For example, it included articles on the recent Attica Prison uprising—where politicized male inmates overtook the prison, held guards hostage, and were eventually stormed by New York State law enforcement officers—and the murder of celebrated black prison intellectual George Jackson by guards in San Quentin Prison. The end of the Jackson article reprinted the text of a telegram that TWWA sent expressing sympathy and revolutionary solidarity to Jackson's mother.[61]

Triple Jeopardy's inaugural issue also exemplifies the way that feminism in general, and black feminism in particular, politicized areas of life not generally within the purview of radical political action. An article titled "Day Care Centers: a problem for whom?" informed readers about a massive demonstration in New York City to protest recent curtailments of child-care services by city, state, and federal authorities. After describing the inadequate and unsafe day-care centers provided by the city, the article asserts: "We need 24 hour free day care centers. We want decent facilities to fit the needs of our children. We demand adequate supervision and adequate trained personnel." We should recall that these issues were also raised during the BWLC's 1969 meeting. Like that discussion, the *Triple Jeopardy* article framed the issue of day care, which is ostensibly a family and thus personal matter, as a public concern. "When the people have day care centers that we control, then we will be able to develop and work in order to further benefit our communities."[62]

Similarly, a report titled "Anatomy and Physiology" illustrates how the TWWA sought to use the paper as a vehicle to empower women of color; the article also provides a glimpse into the organization's collective process of discovery, discussion, and knowledge production. Accompanied by diagrams of the female pelvic and reproductive organs, the article explained how the reproductive system operates in an effort to counter "the lack of information that women receive about their bodies" and thus "begin to conquer the ignorance that has crippled us in the past." The article came from a booklet called "Women and Our Bodies" that the TWWA was using in a health workshop. A sidebar explained that the TWWA's decision to start the workshop was prompted by personal experiences: six members of the organization had recently become pregnant, and as their pregnancies progressed the women realized how little they knew about the reproductive process. After talking to other women they realized that this lack of knowledge was pervasive. They then began to discuss this need for information within the organization, invited a woman doctor to speak at a meeting, and started the workshop "to do some intensive study in the area of health." Thus, very personal experiences and problems were translated into a shared educational and political experience.[63]

Beal wrote the editorial for the first issue. It returns to a persistent concern of the organization, a concern that inspired the formation of the Black Women's Liberation Committee and animated the Black Women's Alliance: affirming the role of black (and all Third World) women as an autonomous, organized force in a movement for revolutionary change. The editorial confirmed the political agency of women of color ("the involvement of women on all levels of struggle is of vital importance") and the necessity of struggling against women's oppression in conjunction with struggles against racism, economic exploitation, and imperialism. Reflecting the TWWA's ideological and organizational evolution, Beal ended the editorial by boldly projecting these ideals:

> The task before us is to develop a sisterhood of women which stretches across all countries—a sisterhood that finds within itself the resolve and strength to actively participate in all phases of the liberation struggle, while at the same time, making sure that the role of women in the new society will be one that will not continue the same kind of stunting attitudes which are still in mode today, among even the most revolutionary of men.
>
> We are women, determined to reap the fruits of our labor. The history of our people in this country portrays the prominent role that the Third World woman has played in the on-going struggle against racism and exploitation. As mother, wife, and worker, she has witnessed the

frustration and anguish of the men, women, and children living in her community. As a revolutionary, she will take an active part in changing this reality.[64]

The urgent tone of the statement and its sense of purpose and possibility remind us of the heady times in which it was written. For many, the early 1970s seemed to promise revolution. As in the preceding decade, these years were filled with dramatic and history-making events that made icons of some individuals and brought many more together in mass movements. By the fall of 1971, when the TWWA released the first issue of *Triple Jeopardy,* Angela Davis had emerged as one such icon, and the TWWA was part of a rising movement in her support, a movement that may have looked to Beal and others like the makings of the sisterhood that she suggested in her editorial.

"Hands Off Angela Davis"

The TWWA ran a full-page announcement in the first issue of *Triple Jeopardy* for an "Angela Davis Day" rally in New York's Central Park on September 25, 1971.[65] The TWWA worked with the New York Committee to Free Angela Davis and other organizations in the area to organize this event, which coincided with similar efforts across the country.[66] The TWWA had stood in defense of Davis as soon as she went "underground" in August 1970 to avoid capture by the FBI, which had placed her on its list of 10 Most Wanted Fugitives.[67] As a public—and contentious—display of this support, the TWWA carried a banner reading "Hands Off Angela Davis" during the Women's Liberation Day March in New York City on August 26, 1970. This earned the condemnation of spectators along Fifth Avenue who called TWWA members "murderers" and "communists." Beal recounted to a reporter that one of NOW's leaders ran up to TWWA members and said angrily, "Angela Davis has nothing to do with women's liberation." Beal responded by saying, "It has nothing to do with the kind of liberation you're talking about but it has everything to do with the kind of liberation we're talking about."[68]

The Third World Women's Alliance continued to support Davis after her arrest, working with the Angela Davis Legal Defense Fund[69] as well as covering her case in *Triple Jeopardy*. The January 1972 issue carried a letter from Davis written from Marin County Jail while she prepared for trial. The cover of the next issue of *Triple Jeopardy* featured a drawing of Davis and jailed Puerto Rican independence activist Lolita Lebron, and pictures of each woman appeared next to a story about international women's day (March 8). The April–May 1972 issue ran an article on the "U.S. Worldwide Campaign Against Sister Angela," carried out by the U.S. Information Agency (USIA). This issue also contained a poem for Davis by Cuban poet Nicholas Guillen. Written in September 1971, Guillen's poetic tribute to Davis sent a message of solidarity and hope:

> I call your name, Angela, louder
> I put my hands together
> not in prayer, plea, supplication or petition
> that they pardon you—
> but to urge you on
> I clap my hands, hard
> hand to hand, harder
> so you'll know I'm with you![70]

After Davis was acquitted on June 4, 1972, several TWWA members had a conversation with her about her case, as well as a range of issues relating to political prisoners and women's liberation. Portions of the conversation—"a one-hour interview [that] stretched into a four-hour rap session"—were published in a series of articles in *Triple Jeopardy*. Davis explained her view that "the victory of my freedom was a people's victory" and that she now saw her "most important contributions to be in the arena of building a movement to free other political prisoners."[71]

Conclusion

The TWWA's involvement in the support movement for Davis was one of several political spaces within which the organization operated during the early and mid-1970s. The group spent much of its energy working on issues related to prisons, establishing a program where they corresponded with prisoners across the country (male and female), sending issues of *Triple Jeopardy* and other literature to inmates, and publicizing the cases of political prisoners. During this period, the group formed a chapter in the San Francisco Bay area, broadening the TWWA's base geographically and attracting more Chicana and Asian American women. In 1972, the TWWA helped to organize the African Liberation Day demonstrations, one of the most effective and important expressions of Black Power–internationalism.

This chapter has presented a preliminary exploration of the TWWA's origins and early development that tells only part of the organization's history. A fuller story remains to be told; nonetheless, the foregoing reveals important insights. First, it begins to chart a new understanding of black feminism during the Black Power Movement. The historical example of the TWWA calls us to recognize that some strains of black feminism in this period emerged largely as a part of, rather than primarily in opposition to, the Black Power Movement. That is to say, black feminist activity arose as part of the political struggles in this period to achieve black liberation. As an emerging social movement, Black Power represented an important dual commitment: to reevaluate the nature and mechanisms of racial oppression in an emerging postsegregation era; and to create new ideas, organizations, and strategies appropriate to new political circumstances. By introducing and integrating the oppression of women into an analysis of black oppression and creating alternative organizational forms, black feminist politics exemplified these commitments. Furthermore, black feminists were centrally engaged in Black Power politics, both in terms of organizational membership and as individual organizers, activists, and thinkers. Beal and others created the TWWA through their simultaneous engagement with both black feminist and Black Power politics.

Second, this overview of the TWWA's formation calls for an understanding of Black Power-era feminism that identifies and conceptualizes the central objective of black feminism as the construction of a political identity. Given the pull of ideological and political forces at play during this period, many of which worked to marginalize black women (and their ideas) as agents of political change, black feminist activism was fundamentally and collectively aimed at the construction of a black woman's political identity and attendant political practice. Developing their own political praxis, black feminists envisioned themselves fighting in concert with other progressive struggles, all as part of a broader project of political struggle and human liberation. Just as some Black Power activists, thinkers, and organizations assigned new political roles to various segments of the black population, such as disaffected youth, workers, or the urban poor, black feminists sought to define a place for black women as agents of revolutionary change. In doing so, black feminists were not simply challenging expressions of male chauvinism, but were also advancing arguments for deeper revolutionary purpose, theory, and commitment; they were, in effect, applying and extending Black Power thought.

Fig. 1 Stokely Carmichael, chairman of Student Nonviolent Coordinating Committee, addresses a crowd of 6,500 at Will Rogers Park, 1966. Los Angeles Times Photographic Archive (collection 1429, box 584, negative 234453, frame 34A). Reproduced with permission from the Department of Special Collections, Charles E. Young Research Library, UCLA.

Fig. 2 Stokely Carmichael (center, wearing dark glasses), during meeting of the Black United Front, Washington, D.C., 1968. © Washington Post. Reproduced with permission of the DC Public Library.

Fig. 3 Alameda County Courthouse, Oakland, CA, 1968. © Roz Payne. Reproduced with permission from Roz Payne Archives (http://www.newsreel.us).

Fig. 4 Demonstration outside courthouse for Panther 21 trial, New York City, 1969. © Roz Payne. Reproduced with permission by the Roz Payne Archives (http://www.newsreel.us).

Fig. 5 Demonstration for Panther 21 trial outside courthouse, New York City, 1969. © Roz Payne. Reproduced with permission from Roz Payne Archives (http://www.newsreel.us).

Fig. 6 Marcher confronts impassive policeman outside Los Angeles Federal Building, scene of picketing in support of San Francisco attempt to free Black Panther leader Huey Newton pending appeal of his conviction for manslaughter, ca. 1968. Los Angeles Times Photographic Archive (collection 1429, box 631, negative 260020, frame 29A). Reproduced with permission from the Department of Special Collections, Charles E. Young Research Library, UCLA.

Fig. 7 Amiri Baraka, poet, black arts leader, and Black Power icon, April 1973. © Washington Post. Reproduced with permission of the DC Public Library.

Fig. 8 Stokely Carmichael, November 1972. © Washington Post. Reproduced with permission of the DC Public Library.

Fig. 9 Huey P. Newton, Black Panther Party cofounder, speaks to reporters, ca. 1970s. Los Angeles Times Photographic Archive (collection 1429, box 715, negative 274691, frame 34A). Reproduced with permission from the Department of Special Collections, Charles E. Young Research Library, UCLA.

Fig. 10 Angela Davis (center) at a press conference, 1976. © Washington Post. Reproduced with permission of the DC Public Library.

THE ROOTS OF BLACK POWER?

Armed Resistance and the Radicalization of the Civil Rights Movement

SIMON WENDT

The publication of Timothy Tyson's *Radio Free Dixie: Robert F. Williams and the Roots of Black Power* represents a milestone in Black Power scholarship. Tyson recounts in vivid detail how North Carolinian civil rights activist Williams emerged in the late 1950s as one of the most ardent advocates of "armed self-reliance."[1] As Peniel Joseph has pointed out, *Radio Free Dixie* laid important groundwork for "reperiodizing" the black freedom struggle "by examining the ways in which black radicals influenced black politics during the 'heroic period' of the Civil Rights movement."[2]

However, Tyson's thesis that the civil rights struggle and what came to be known as Black Power "emerged from the same soil, confronted the same predicaments, and reflected the same quest for African American freedom" raises important questions about its applicability beyond the borders of North Carolina.[3] We now know that armed resistance, the most conspicuous element of Williams's multilayered radicalism, played a far more significant role in the southern civil rights struggle than previously thought.[4] But were the Deacons for Defense and Justice or similar defense units that emerged in Dixie in the first half of the 1960s actually the precursors, or even the natural allies, of Black Power groups such as the Black Panther Party for Self-Defense? Did southern black militancy, as Tyson's argument suggests, constitute a vital part of the roots of Black Power?

A comparative analysis of the role of armed militancy in the freedom movement of the 1960s reveals conspicuous differences between black defense efforts in southern civil rights campaigns and the concept of armed militancy advocated by the Black Panther Party (BPP), the most prominent example of Black Power militancy. Southern protective groups that emerged in Louisiana, Alabama, and Mississippi successfully complemented nonviolent protest and voter registration drives. Although their armed actions provoked heated debates within movement circles, these black men worked in tandem with nonviolent demonstrations. By contrast, the BPP, at least in their public statements, rejected nonviolence and elevated armed resistance to an alternative protest strategy. More important, armed resistance in the Black Power era played a fundamentally different role when compared with the southern freedom movement. Whereas southern activists used their guns solely to repel white attackers, the BPP's concept of self-defense included revolutionary violence and appeared to serve primarily as a symbolic means to defy racist authorities and to nurture notions of militant black manhood. The example of the Black Panthers suggests that the advent of Black Power, at least in terms of armed self-defense, did mark a turning point in the black freedom struggle insofar as it introduced new protest strategies and actively reinterpreted the meaning of revolutionary violence for black liberation.[5]

The Deacons for Defense and Justice are probably the best-known example of armed black militancy in the southern freedom struggle. The Deacons were founded in 1964 in the small town of Jonesboro, located in the northern corner of Louisiana. When members of the Congress of Racial Equality (CORE) began civil rights organizing in the area that spring, the Ku Klux Klan launched a campaign of intimidation against Jonesboro's black community. When city authorities informed CORE that they would provide no protection for civil rights workers, local African Americans were left to defend themselves against white aggression. Shortly after CORE launched a campaign to desegregate public facilities in early July, several armed black men served as guards and two weeks later, in reaction to a nightly Ku Klux Klan procession through the black neighborhood, black residents decided to form a protective agency. White CORE worker Charles Fenton assisted in establishing a highly organized self-defense group, which came to be known as the Deacons for Defense and Justice.[6]

Equipped with rifles, pistols, and walkie-talkies, the defense squad patrolled the black section of town around the clock. Following every white driver who entered the black neighborhood, the Deacons quickly put an end to anti-black violence. The Deacons, whose members were mostly African American Army veterans, also protected civil rights workers and volunteers, assigning Charles Fenton a personal bodyguard. Harassment by local police continued, but white attacks against black homes and civil rights workers ceased almost completely. For several months, the Jonesboro Deacons operated in obscurity. Indeed, few members of CORE's executive National Action Council were aware of the Deacons' existence. That changed in February 1965 when CORE activists and a *New York Times* article first reported the Deacons' activities.[7]

The emerging freedom movement in Bogalusa in southeastern Louisiana finally catapulted the Deacons for Defense and Justice onto the national stage. As in Jonesboro, segregation and discrimination in this little paper mill town had survived the Civil Rights Act of 1964. Dubbed "Klantown USA" by the journalist Paul Good, Bogalusa was a hotbed of Ku Klux Klan activities. But local black activists were determined to challenge Jim Crow, asking CORE to assist them in the struggle. In early February 1965, when a large white mob gathered downtown and vowed to kill the two CORE field workers William Yates and Dave Miller, their host Robert Hicks quickly mobilized a group of armed men to guard his house. The determination of African Americans to defend themselves, together with numerous telephone calls to local authorities, prevented a violent clash. Two days later, armed blacks again rescued Yates and Miller from angry whites in the black neighborhood. As in Jonesboro, CORE's repeated pleas for federal protection had been ignored.[8]

Faced with constant harassment and violent intimidation, local blacks and CORE workers contacted the Jonesboro Deacons to establish a Bogalusa branch of the defense organization. Local leader

A. Z. Young later reflected, "We felt as though that we must protect ourselves and if any blood flows any direction in this city that it'll be both black and white together."[9] At the beginning of March 1965, the Jonesboro Deacons obtained an official state charter, thus affording the defense organization a semi-official status. The organization's "Articles of Incorporation," however, did not mention armed self-defense. Rather, the document portrayed the Deacons' purpose as educating U.S. citizens, and especially minority groups, in the principles of democracy. Somewhat veiling the underlying principles of the group's aims, the document stated that the Deacons would defend American citizens' civil rights and property rights "by any and all honorable and legal means."[10]

The Bogalusa Deacons raised organized black self-defense to a new level of sophistication and notoriety. The new branch's first president, Charles Sims, a former army weapons and judo instructor, expanded the group's arsenal. A young white civil rights activist later recalled in his memoirs that the trunk of Sims's car usually contained "a semiautomatic carbine that looked like a submachine gun, two shotguns, several boxes of shells, and a handful of grenades."[11] Because local authorities often helped in thwarting civil rights activities, the Bogalusa unit also began to monitor police radio communications.[12]

White supremacists soon learned that Bogalusa's defense squad meant business. When several carloads of Klansmen shot into the Hicks residence at the beginning of April, fifteen armed Deacons repelled the attack with several volleys of disciplined gunfire. Sometimes, white hooligans who entered the black section of town suddenly found themselves surrounded by a dozen armed Deacons, quietly emerging from bushes and dark driveways. Few whites dared to enter the black neighborhood after news of the black defense group's existence had spread.[13] Members of the new organization also guarded CORE volunteers day and night. One Berkeley student reported about his stay: "We never crossed the streets without a Deacon. We never drove our car without a Deacon present. Most of our cars were escorted by two carloads of Deacons, one in front and one in back. The homes where we stayed were guarded day and night by Deacons, and our canvassing was protected by Deacons. Our lives were literally in their hands."[14] In addition, the Deacons guarded most of the nonviolent demonstrations that were staged during the summers of 1965 and 1966.[15]

Local blacks as well as civil rights workers agreed that the presence of the Deacons saved many lives. Local leader Robert Hicks told an interviewer: "If it hadn't been for these people, a setup, the idea of people willing to protect themselves—Negroes—I'd say we wouldn't be here today."[16] One student volunteer was convinced that "ten more would have been beaten or shot in Bogalusa if we had relied on these [federal] protection agencies."[17] Ultimately, the crisis that CORE's nonviolent demonstrations and the presence of the Deacons had created compelled the federal government to intervene. Confronted with almost daily violent clashes between blacks and whites, Louisiana Governor John McKeithen, together with Bogalusa activists, appealed to President Lyndon B. Johnson for help. In reaction to this plea, the White House dispatched a representative of the Justice Department to settle the conflict. In spite of the Justice Department's decisive steps in curtailing harassment by Ku Klux Klan and local police, however, the black defense unit remained an essential part of the Bogalusa movement.[18]

For the local African American community, the Deacons signified more than mere protection. The defense group proved to be an enormous source of pride. Journalist Roy Reed noted: "Watching the Deacons in Louisiana, one is struck repeatedly by the pride they inspire among Negroes.... The Deacons have proved to be a natural instrument for building community feeling and nourishing the Negro identity."[19] The historian George Lipsitz similarly points out that the defense unit's "discipline and dedication inspired the community, their very existence made black people in Bogalusa think more of themselves as people who could not be pushed around."[20]

For black men, moreover, the formation of the self-defense unit symbolized an affirmation of their manhood. Deacon organizer Earnest Thomas declared in a speech: "It's not natural to let someone destroy your wife, your kids and your property and not prevent it. If this means battle, then that's the way it has to be."[21] According to Deacon Royan Burris, the defense group's militant stance also won them respect from white Southerners. "They finally found out that we really are men," he declared in an interview. It was clear "that we would do what we said, and that we meant what we said."[22] Defying the southern myth of the submissive and contented Negro, the Deacons powerfully asserted blacks' dignity and their legitimate claim to the rights of American citizenship.[23]

Although some shocked observers denounced the defense squad as dangerous "protection racketeers" or "Mao-inspired nationalists," their strict focus on self-defense clearly distinguished them from the revolutionary nationalists of the late 1960s.[24] Charles Sims emphasized in a speech that "as a Deacon, you cannot fire on a man unless you've been attacked."[25] Reiterating the group's defensive character in an interview, Sims told a reporter: "I believe nonviolence is the only way. Negotiations are going to be the main point in this fight." But, according to Sims, the Deacons were necessary to protect the nonviolent movement.[26] Bogalusa, then, in many ways, epitomized the significant role of both nonviolent direct action and armed resistance in the southern black freedom struggle. Not only did the Deacons work in close alliance with peaceful protest, they also ensured the local movement's survival and contributed to its ultimate success.

The Deacons for Defense and Justice were not the only protective agency that emerged during the era of nonviolent mass protest. In June 1964, black military veterans formed a similar organization in Tuscaloosa, Alabama. In the spring of that year, the black Tuscaloosa Citizens for Action Committee (TCAC), under the leadership of Baptist minister T. Y. Rogers, began to stage nonviolent demonstrations to protest against continued discrimination and segregation. On June 9, 1964, white police officers bloodied almost one hundred demonstrators, most of them women and children, in a brutal attempt to prevent a march to the city's courthouse.[27]

The violent attack, during which policemen and firemen bombarded Rogers's First African Baptist Church with tear gas, used water hoses to disperse protesters, and arrested injured women and children, outraged black Tuscaloosans. A number of angry black men began to arm themselves. Some of them intended to retaliate with violence against both the police and the white community. The city's atmosphere was explosive. During the night, residents could hear gunshots, and scattered violence left two African Americans wounded.[28] Joseph Mallisham, a Korean War veteran and longtime labor organizer at Tuscaloosa's Zeigler meatpacking plant, was one of several older activists who sought to convince the angry hotheads of the futility of violent disorders. Rather than burn down the city, he argued, blacks ought to organize their own protective agency to prevent violent incidents like the one at the church that day and to protect the movement against the Ku Klux Klan. "If we're going to do this," Mallisham told them, "let's do it right."[29]

At a meeting that took place later that night, black activists discussed the possibility of forming a defense unit. During a second gathering the following night, almost three hundred men, including youth gang leaders, workers, teachers, and businessmen, enthusiastically endorsed the plan. A small group of army veterans formed the nucleus of the new organization. Thirty-six-year-old Mallisham was entrusted with the leadership of the group. His military training and service during the Korean War, together with his impressive record of labor activism, made him an ideal choice.[30]

Tuscaloosa's defense organization clearly reflected its leader's army training. Its structure mirrored that of a military combat unit. Mallisham led a small executive board that determined the group's strategy and a group of lieutenants and the rank and file executed specific operations. The organization established strict criteria for membership, accepting only married war veterans, who had served in active combat. In addition, new recruits had to be discreet and were required to conform to a rigid code of morality. If candidates passed the thorough background check, they solemnly pledged to protect fellow blacks at the cost of their lives. Throughout the summer and fall of 1964, about one hundred men took this oath.[31]

Rituals such as the oath reflected the great secrecy that characterized the defense squad. Mallisham believed that avoiding general publicity would lessen tensions in the city and increase the group's effectiveness. For this reason, the new organization never acquired a name. Sworn to confidentiality, members never talked about their activities, which explains why whites remained unaware of the unit's existence. Even among blacks, few had full knowledge of the sophisticated protective system. Police officers, who sometimes encountered members of the group on their nightly patrols, appeared to tolerate its existence, as there were no official attempts to outlaw or disarm Mallisham's men.[32]

The security of the movement's leader, T. Y. Rogers, and other TCAC officers was the defense unit's major concern. By early June, death threats against the minister had become routine, and few nights went by without suspicious cars slowly passing by the parsonage. Only one day after the official formation of Mallisham's group, about twenty armed black men began to guard Rogers's home. Concealing themselves in bushes around the one-story building, the sentries were ready to repel potential Klan attacks. No hooded terrorists showed up that night, but the guards continued to protect the parsonage in two shifts almost twenty-four hours a day.[33] In the following weeks, Rogers's small one-story house became a fortress. Nathaniel Howard Jr. remembered, "Going by T.Y.'s house [was like] going on a military installation."[34] Armed guards requested identification from those who approached the building and cars that passed the checkpoint had to blink a prearranged signal to avert being greeted by a volley of buckshot.[35]

TCAC officer Willie Herzfeld received protection as well. He later remembered that several of Mallisham's men "spent a lot of sleepless nights, some of them sleeping on the top of my house, ... trying to protect me from what would have been the ravages of the Klan."[36] Since death threats against Herzfeld had become common, the Lutheran minister found the armed sentries an immense relief. Rev. T. W. Linton, a Presbyterian minister who became TCAC's main representative in the tense negotiations with white merchants, similarly recalled that a group of about ten men regularly guarded his home. Throughout 1964, armed bodyguards followed Rogers, Herzfeld, Linton, and others wherever they went.[37]

Finally, the defense unit watched over the handful of TCAC's white allies, frequently escorting them to the black neighborhood and back to their homes. Most prominent among them were Jay and Alberta Murphy. Jay was a law professor at the University of Alabama while Alberta worked as a lawyer, and their support for civil rights had earned them a reputation for being dangerous Communist agitators. Like Rogers and other black activists, the Murphys received numerous threats against their lives. Armed blacks made sure that this menace never translated into actual harm. When Alberta ventured into the rural areas of Tuscaloosa County to teach voter registration, for example, members of the defense unit inconspicuously followed her.[38]

University of Alabama sociology professor Harold Nelson not only benefited from similar security measures, but also gained deep scholarly insight into the defense group. Nelson befriended Mallisham in the aftermath of the June 9 incident and subsequently participated in virtually all activities of TCAC and the protection agency. Documenting the activities of the protective agency over the course of several years, he summarized his findings in a sociological article, which he published in 1967.[39]

Those who protected the local movement with rifles and shotguns saw no conflict between their weapons and nonviolent protest. Their leader had never considered himself a pacifist, but he accepted nonviolence as a successful tactic. In fact, Mallisham viewed nonviolent direct action as the only possible strategy in the black freedom struggle. Tuscaloosa's defense agency, he emphasized years later, would have never started a fight. "Our membership," he reminisced, "was a membership of peace..." Protection was the group's main responsibility. "Any violence would be the last resort, and that was stressed," he said.[40] In his article on the organization, Harold Nelson noted that its members sought to defuse rather than aggravate volatile situations, knowing that publicized black violence would jeopardize the nonviolent movement's moral position.[41]

Probably because of the unit's purely defensive character, the TCAC's leadership fully accepted the armed men into their ranks. T. Y. Rogers, despite his deeply felt commitment to philosophical nonviolence, welcomed the group and frequently consulted with Mallisham and his men about movement tactics. In addition, several members of the defense group became an integral part of TCAC's executive board. As in Bogalusa, Tuscaloosa's defense organization not only operated in tandem with the movement's leadership but also successfully complemented its nonviolent campaigns.[42]

In Mississippi, armed defense efforts became a significant auxiliary to voter registration drives and nonviolent protest as well. During the dangerous 1964 Freedom Summer project, which had been organized under the aegis of the Council of Federated Organizations (COFO), African Americans across the state met white supremacist terror with bullets and buckshot. In Holmes County, for example, blacks were well prepared to repel white attackers. "The Movement may be non-violent," white summer volunteer Eugene Nelson wrote to his parents in early July 1964, "but the people here are by no means so when it comes to protecting their families and property."[43]

In the all-black community of Milestone, virtually all families guarded their houses with guns. Volunteers who failed to honk a pre-arranged signal when approaching the neighborhood risked being welcomed with gunfire. In the town of Tchula, by Eugene Nelson's account, a group of white men who had attempted to bomb a private black home "escaped only by the same grace of God that put their bomb out: the owner of the house had them in his sights, but his wife had hidden the shells."[44] In addition, groups of black men protected the county's local churches and meeting places. After a bomb attack on a church in Milestone in August, African Americans guarded the building with rifles and shotguns. The town's community center, which became the hub of movement activities, was similarly pro-tected.[45] Positioning themselves on both sides of the wooden building during mass meetings, armed men controlled the country road next to the building. "An attacker might get in," Nelson explained, "but he'd have little chance of getting out."[46] The strategy was highly successful. In 1965, a car manned with Klansmen was caught in the crossfire of the armed protectors during an attempt to attack the community cen-ter. "[F]rom that day on," local civil rights leader Walter Bruce recalled, "we never had no more problems."[47]

In Leake County, African Americans started similar defense efforts. Like Holmes County, this area had a long tradition of inde-pendent black landownership. When visiting the area around the all-black community of Harmony, journalist Nicholas von Hoffman found many farmers ready to repel white invaders with rifles and pis-tols. According to von Hoffman, the practice was so common that it was "dangerous to drive off the paved highway into the harmony area after sundown if your car is unfamiliar there."[48] Some of the town's residents organized a defense unit to protect the local community center. Built by African Americans and summer volunteers, the thirty by sixty foot frame building housed an office, a library, and one of COFO's freedom schools. After Klansmen fired into private homes and burned several crosses in the area, one volunteer noted in a letter that the black community did "not intend to have all their hard work go up in flames right away." Several men, armed with rifles and shotguns, guarded the community center around the clock.[49]

Like the Deacons for Defense and Justice or Tuscaloosa's protective squad, the Leake County defense group was highly organized. CORE staffer Jerome Smith remembered being stopped by armed sentries on the city line every time he approached the community. Only after identifying himself would the guards let him pass.[50] Similarly, drivers who approached the community center were required to honk a prearranged signal. "If anyone does attempt to bomb or burn the center," a volunteer assessed the efficacy of the guard system, "they haven't got a chance."[51] For many SNCC and CORE staffers, all-black communities such as Milestone and Harmony became what historian Akinyele Umoja has called "haven communities," which provided shelter and security in a dangerous and hostile environment.[52]

Organized protection was not confined to all-black communities. In Meridian, a city of about 50,000 located at Mississippi's eastern border to Alabama, African Americans, who constituted one-third of the city's residents, formed a "mutual protection society" to guard black churches against racist attacks. The defense group served its purpose well. Unlike thirty-eight other black churches that went up in flames in the state in 1964, the First Union Baptist Church of local civil rights leader Rev. R. S. Porter was still intact when the summer project ended. The Meridian defense group also guarded the homes of NAACP leader Claude Bryant, white attorney and movement-ally William Ready, and other local activists. In late July, Claude Bryant's guards exchanged gunfire with a group of white attackers.[53]

In addition to these collective defense activities, there were numerous attempts by individual blacks to protect themselves and the COFO activists that lived in their modest homes. Those who were known to house white summer volunteers became prime targets for Ku Klux Klan attacks. The mother of a white volunteer who visited two Freedom School teachers on a farm near Canton was relieved to know that the young women's host and his sons were prepared to repel white intruders with gunfire. In August 1964, the concerned woman wrote to Assistant Attorney General Burke Marshall: "Cars have stopped there last night; prowlers have been seen. Luckily, no trouble has ensued, because at least one of the homes has four rifles ready, and its owner, a Negro farmer, was quite determined to use them in defense of his home."[54]

Although men were at the forefront of such protection activities, African American women were also prepared to stop white invaders with armed force. There is no evidence of female participation in the activities of the Deacons, Tuscaloosa's protective agency, or the numerous informal defense groups that emerged in Mississippi, but it was not uncommon for Magnolia State women to protect their homes on an individual basis. One COFO volunteer was perplexed to find her host heavily armed. In late July 1964, the young student wrote in a letter: "I met Mrs. Fairly coming down the hall from the front porch carrying a rifle in one hand [and] a pistol in the other. I do not know what is going on…. [All she said was] 'You go to sleep; let me fight for you.'"[55] Working near Canton, SNCC worker Jo Anne Ooiman Robinson was similarly puzzled to hear that her host slept with an ax hidden under her bed. In the past, Robinson learned, she had slept with a gun under her pillow but removed it after nearly shooting a neighbor's son. Sometimes, women fired their weapons at white attackers. In McComb, for example, the wife of local civil rights leader Charles Bryant shot at a car manned with Klansmen who had hurled a bomb toward the couple's home.[56] Throughout 1965 and 1966, similar defense efforts continued in Mississippi, Alabama, and Louisiana.

By 1968, however, as segregation and disfranchisement were on the wane and state and local authorities in the South finally appeared to take seriously their responsibility to protect civil rights protesters, southern defense groups such as the Deacons had outlived their usefulness. In November 1967, FBI agents reported that the Bogalusa Deacons no longer held official meetings. Four months later, federal agents believed the Deacons to be "of little or no significance."[57] By the time the Deacons put their shotguns back on the rack, protective agencies in Alabama and Mississippi had ceased activity. Given the symbiotic relationship between protest and protection in the southern civil rights struggle, the demise of nonviolent demonstrations also sealed the end of the region's era of armed black resistance.

As the examples from Louisiana, Alabama, and Mississippi show, African American civil rights activists resorted to armed resistance on a widespread basis. But what did black defense groups accomplish? Any assessment of self-defense in the southern freedom struggle has to acknowledge the vital role that such militant actions played in local civil rights campaigns. Most important, homegrown southern militancy helped numerous local freedom movements survive in the face of racist aggression. Guarding black communities and protecting the lives of fellow activists, armed blacks made sure that nonviolent protestors and their leaders remained safe once they left the picket line. Armed protection also played a significant role in sustaining the morale of nonviolent protestors. The Ku Klux Klan aimed to erode the confidence and resolve of African Americans through violent terror. In many ways, the actions of black guards neutralized this strategy. Knowing that armed defenders were nearby probably bolstered the determination of many civil rights activists to continue protests despite the omnipresence of menacing whites. A final benefit of armed resistance was that it occasionally became an additional means of coercion in negotiations with white authorities. In Bogalusa, for example, nonviolent demonstrations paralyzed the city and forced the state's segregationist politicians to take seriously black demands. But the prospect of racial warfare between the Ku Klux Klan and the Deacons for Defense and Justice certainly increased the pressure on Louisiana Governor McKeithen and President Johnson to defuse the local crisis.

Such incidents have led historian Lance Hill to overemphasize the role of armed militancy in the Deep South. Thoroughly researched and well written, his *Deacons for Defense: Armed Resistance and the Civil Rights Movement* makes a major contribution to the historiography of the Civil Rights Movement. Unfortunately, the study largely ignores the complementary character of armed resistance and nonviolent protest in the southern freedom struggle and misconstrues the character of the movement's tactical repertoire. According to Hill, the Louisiana group "developed into a highly visible political organization with a clear and compelling alternative to the pacifist strategies promoted by national civil rights organizations." Hill claims that the Deacons ultimately evolved "into a political movement for self-defense," which converted armed resistance "into a principled challenge to nonviolence."[58] In reality, however, neither the Deacons nor other southern defense units considered their armed actions an alternative to nonviolent direct action, which was far from pure pacifism but constituted a pragmatic strategy that relied on both moral suasion and tactical coercion. Rather, their militancy complemented the nonviolent strategy and frequently enhanced its effectiveness at the local level. Armed resistance in the southern movement indirectly contributed to the radicalization of the Civil Rights Movement insofar as it triggered heated debates among nonviolent activists and partially inspired paramilitary Black Power groups such as the Black Panther Party.[59] But for the most part, southern defenders worked hand in hand with nonviolent activism.

By contrast, during the Black Power era, the BPP came to see self-defense as a full-fledged strategy that was deemed a realistic alternative to nonviolence. Compared with southern defense units, moreover, armed resistance played a fundamentally different role in the Oakland-based organization's militant programs. Self-defense remained largely confined to militant rhetoric and appeared to reflect psychological, rather than physical, imperatives. Although defensive efforts in the Deep South had similarly instilled a sense of pride in African American men, the key rationale behind their militant activities was the simple necessity to protect black communities. Of course, the Panthers regarded their armed actions as an effective way to curb police brutality, and ensuing confrontations with law enforcement authorities resulted in the deaths of party members and numerous incarcerations. But protecting black communities was not the most important motivation behind the BPP's militancy. Instead, in large part, the organization's preoccupation with guns and their public pledges to use them to confront racist violence can be understood as gendered symbols of defiance that served to affirm and nurture black masculinity.[60]

Although the BPP's founders Huey Newton and Bobby Seale viewed themselves as the spiritual heirs of black nationalist Malcolm

X, they were also deeply influenced by psychologist Frantz Fanon's analysis of the Algerian freedom struggle. Incorporating Fanon's ideas in their analysis of the problems that confronted urban black America, Newton and Seale likened the situation of African Americans to that of a colonized people. From this perspective, white police officers constituted a foreign occupying army, which served as the military arm of a thoroughly racist system of oppression. The Panthers argued that armed self-defense against police brutality in black enclaves was a justified means to oppose this occupation. Newton and Seale hoped that the BPP's armed patrols in the California's Bay Area would help recruit new members and might ultimately change policemen's brutal behavior.[61]

Equipped with rifles, pistols, and law books, Newton and Seale followed police cars and informed African Americans of their rights in case of arrest. Several armed stand-offs with police in late 1966 and early 1967 bolstered the BPP's reputation in Oakland's black community. A bill proposed by Republican California State Assemblyman Donald Mulford, who sought to prohibit the carrying of loaded firearms in public, was a direct response to the Panther patrols. The BPP's decision to stage an armed demonstration against the Mulford Bill at the California State Legislature in Sacramento on May 2, 1967, marked the beginning of the organization's rise to national fame and notoriety.[62]

Neither Newton nor Seale had expected their demonstration to prevent the passage of the Mulford Bill. Rather they considered their armed protest part of a long-term strategy to establish the BPP as the "vanguard group" of the black revolution. Following a fusion of independent Marxism and black nationalism, Newton intended his organization to raise the consciousness of the black masses to prepare them for the ensuing revolutionary struggle against the racist system of capitalism. Through highly visible, but legal, activities such as the armed protest at the California Capitol in Sacramento, coupled with educational programs, the BPP planned to acquaint blacks with strategies and methods that would enable them to resist seemingly omnipotent white authorities.[63]

In this respect, the Sacramento demonstration was a resounding success. Practically overnight, the Panthers were thrust into the national spotlight. While black militants admired the BPP, the organization's fixation on guns and violent resistance in the early years of its existence frightened white America. Seale insisted in his memoirs that the Panthers "had never used" their "guns to go into the white community to shoot up white people," but their martial rhetoric suggested the exact opposite to white observers.[64] Citing Chinese revolutionary Mao Zedong, the Panthers repeatedly proclaimed that political power grew "out of the barrel of a gun." Given the colonized situation of the black community, moreover, the killing of white police officers seemed a justifiable part of the black revolution. "We have reached the point in history," the BPP told the *National Guardian* in January 1968, "where we must claim that a black man, confronted by a bloodthirsty cop who is out to take his life out of hatred for the black race, has a right to defend himself—even if this means picking up a gun and blowing that cop away."[65]

According to the BPP, even aggressive violence constituted a legitimate form of self-defense. The teachings of Fanon, Mao, and Che Guevara provided the theoretical base for this militant stance. For Algerian, Chinese, or Cuban revolutionaries, as Newton later explained in his autobiography, "the only way to win freedom was to meet force with force," which, according to the BPP's Minister of Defense, was "a form of self-defense although that defense might at times take on characteristics of aggression." Newton concluded that oppressed people never initiated violence but simply responded to the violence that the oppressor inflicted on them.[66] For the colonized people of African descent who resided in the United States, therefore, seemingly aggressive attacks on white racists became justifiable acts of armed resistance. In this spirit, the BPP's ultimate goal was to lead an interracial coalition of revolutionaries in an anticapitalist and anti-imperialist struggle against common enemies.[67]

Such new interpretations of armed resistance stood in sharp contrast to the concept of self-defense that was espoused by southern defense groups. Neither Charles Sims nor Joseph Mallisham would have contemplated attacks on white police officers or revolutionary warfare against the forces of white supremacy, and the theories of Marx, Fanon, or Mao were of little consequence for their activism in the Deep South. The skepticism of southern defenders toward Black

Power militancy did not mean that the idea of black nationalism was unheard of in the Deep South. In 1964, for example, organizers of the Revolutionary Action Movement (RAM) and members of the nationalist Afro-American Student Movement (ASM) met in Nashville, Tennessee, to discuss how to introduce self-defense and black nationalist ideas into the southern freedom movement. In a report on the conference, white activist Anne Braden asserted that she found considerable "unspoken support" for black nationalism among black Southerners.[68] But older activists such as Sims or Mallisham remained adamant in their opposition to the revolutionary rhetoric that was frequently uttered by black nationalists.[69]

A notion that southern black activists and their black nationalist counterparts did share was the conviction that armed self-defense was the prerequisite for attaining true manhood. Martin Luther King Jr.'s assertion in June 1967 that there was "masculinity and strength in nonviolence" was ludicrous to the BPP.[70] "We do not believe in passive and nonviolent tactics," Huey Newton told the *New York Times* in May 1967. From Newton's perspective, nonviolence had not "worked for us black people."[71] The Panthers, by contrast, would provide a model of masculinity that nonviolent protest could never provide. "The black woman found it difficult to respect the black man because he didn't even define himself as a man!" Newton explained in an interview. By contrast, the Black Panthers, "along with all revolutionary black groups" had "regained" African Americans' mind and manhood.[72] Of course, the organization's militancy cannot be reduced to mere symbolism. Armed confrontations with white police and federal agencies' concerted efforts to stop the Panthers testify to the destructive consequences of their self-defense stance on the daily lives of party members. However, given the fact that the BPP neither repelled Ku Klux Klan attacks nor implemented their plans for revolutionary warfare, the organization's self-defense stance seems to have functioned primarily as a way to assert black manhood. Although activists might not have consciously conceived of it as such at the time, armed militancy was transmuted into a vehicle of psychological liberation.

In many ways, the Black Panther Party's militant stance was a tactical alternative to nonviolent demonstrations, but the organization's armed machismo contained serious problems. The Panthers countered white stereotypes and nurtured black self-respect, but they simultaneously appropriated and reproduced dominant notions of masculinity, which were grounded in patriarchal privilege and the subordination of women. Jeffrey O. G. Ogbar has pointed out that "the Panthers were not ideologically static or monolithic chauvinists." Rather, gender relations within the organization were constantly reshaped, in part because of Huey Newton's changing views on women, and because female Panthers repeatedly challenged sexist tendencies among male party members. Still, at least until the late 1960s, the machismo that permeated the party created a largely male-centered organization that regarded women as readily available sexual objects, not as equal party members.[73]

Their public display of armed readiness also impeded the effectiveness of the BPP. Government repression increased in direct correlation to the rhetorical threats of black militants. In 1967, the FBI launched COINTELPRO, a highly sophisticated domestic counter-intelligence program that sought to disrupt and destroy the Black Panthers and other black nationalist groups. FBI agents infiltrated the organization's chapters, attempted to fan animosities between the Panthers and Ron Karenga's Us Organization, and aided authorities to imprison its leadership on fabricated charges. By the early 1970s, twenty-eight members of the organization had been killed in confrontations with police or deadly turf fights with Us, and most of its original leadership was either in prison or in exile. Although the organization lingered on until 1982, the government's repressive tactics had weakened the Panthers considerably by 1972.[74]

Huey Newton was probably one of the very few activists who frankly admitted that the BPP's public self-defense posture had ultimately become counterproductive. As Newton remembered in his memoirs, the police had not started any concerted efforts to disarm the BPP until the Sacramento demonstration. The news media, moreover, distorted the revolutionary message of the Panthers, focusing solely on the group's paramilitary character rather than on the dismal conditions that Newton and Seale intended to improve. The resulting one-sided press coverage obscured the BPP's significance as local community organizers, whose ten-point platform listed the call for self-defense after the demand for self-determination, full employment, decent housing, and education for the black community. As Newton later explained, the platform was a clear reflection of the party's priorities. Indeed, virtually ignored by the white media, BPP chapters provided important social services such as free breakfast programs for school children as well as legal assistance or medical care for African Americans across the nation.[75] As early as 1968, the BPP had dropped the term self-defense from its name to preclude such misinterpretations. By the end of the decade, the party began to make concerted efforts to tone down its violent rhetoric, erroneously hoping that less provocative language would prompt the government to end its repressive tactics and public perception.[76]

In light of these striking differences between southern defense squads and the Black Panther Party, we need to reassess the radicalism of Robert F. Williams. A thorough understanding of his impact on the Black Power movement requires us to explore how Williams's ideology changed over time. In the 1950s, the militant North Carolinian advocated a type of militancy that was virtually identical to that of black defense units in Louisiana, Alabama, and Mississippi. At that time, Williams believed that African Americans "should use or utilize any method that brought results," which included both nonviolent protest and what he called "armed self-reliance." When the NAACP activist and other black veterans repelled Ku Klux Klan attacks in Monroe, North Carolina, in 1957, for example, their defensive actions operated side by side with nonviolent attempts to integrate the local swimming pool. Two years later, when Williams gained nationwide notoriety for publicly declaring that blacks would have to "meet violence with violence" when attacked by white racists, he continued to believe that armed self-defense could complement nonviolent protest strategies.[77]

But in the 1960s, after being forced to live in Cuban, and later Chinese, exile, Williams's ideology underwent a fundamental change. In Havana and Beijing, he devised plans for an apocalyptic struggle with the white oppressor. In interviews with his first biographer Robert Carl Cohen in 1968, Williams insisted that the black revolutionary juggernaut would obliterate America. Black guerrillas would strike at the heart of the capitalist system, such as oil fields and pipelines. Using arson and sabotage, the black underground army would then destroy the nation's cities, and, eventually, the United States itself. In his newsletter *Crusader,* which continued to reach America until the Post Office banned its distribution in the summer of 1967, Williams provided specific advice about how to conduct clandestine guerrilla warfare.[78]

Such doomsday visions propelled Williams to the ideological forefront of the Black Power movement. Together with Malcolm X, he became the idol and major reference point for many black militants. As early as 1964, the founders of the Revolutionary Action Movement claimed Williams as president of their underground organization. Four years later, he was chosen as the president in absentia of the nationalist Republic of New Africa (RNA). In their first pamphlet, the founding members of the RNA praised the "true revolutionary guidance and insight" that Williams and Malcolm X had provided them. Like Williams, the black nationalist RNA was determined to gain independence "by arms if necessary."[79]

Unlike the Deacons for Defense and Justice and similar groups in Dixie, Williams had turned into a fiery advocate of black separatism and revolutionary guerrilla warfare. Talking to Cohen in July 1968, Williams explained that since actual integration was impossible to attain, he now favored "complete separation...."[80] The militant activist had concluded that it was illusory to expect support from the federal government. "[W]e had the illusion," Williams reflected, "that the federal government would actually be sympathetic towards us because we were only fighting the clan [sic] and the racists. ..." The fact that Washington took little interest in the Monroe movement eventually convinced Williams that African Americans would have to prepare for a protracted underground struggle against the racists.[81]

Given this process of radicalization that Williams underwent between 1957 and 1968, the assessment of Malcolm X that the North Carolinian "was just a couple of years ahead of his time" but "laid a good ground work" for others was a fairly accurate assessment.[82] Williams and southern defense units had emerged out of the same tradition of homegrown southern militancy. But in exile the NAACP maverick became one of the first black activists to transform conventional ideas of self-defense into a justification for aggressive guerrilla warfare. The black intellectual Harold Cruse argued as early as 1967 that had Williams been able to stay in Monroe, "his original tactic of self-defense would probably have led him no further than the current position of the Deacons." As Cruse pointed out, Williams was forced to change his views because traditional notions of self-defense were simply not "revolutionary enough."[83] This process of radicalization and the subsequent impact of his ideas on the Black Panther Party and other African American militants make Williams a unique, and in many ways exceptional, bridge figure between the civil rights struggle and the Black Power movement, at least in terms of armed struggle. More case studies of armed black militancy in the Black Power era will be needed until we are able to fully understand the complexities of the black freedom struggle's radicalization and the movement's radical legacy.

7

"A RED, BLACK AND GREEN LIBERATION JUMPSUIT"

Roy Wilkins, the Black Panthers, and the Conundrum of Black Power

YOHURU WILLIAMS

There will be no pictures of Whitney Young being run out of Harlem on a rail with a brand new process. There will be no slow motion or still life of Roy Wilkins strolling through Watts in a Red, Black and Green liberation jumpsuit that he had been saving for just the proper occasion.

—Gil Scott-Heron, "The Revolution Will Not Be Televised," 1971

The NAACP can win court cases, it is said, but the Negroes, the masses, don't live in a court, they live up in Harlem, or down in Oxford, Mississippi.

—Robert Penn Warren, 1965

At approximately 4:45 a.m. on December 4, 1969, fourteen police officers opened fire on an apartment located at 2337 West Monroe Street in Chicago, Illinois. In less than ten minutes, police discharged between eighty and one hundred rounds into the apartment. When the shooting stopped, two men were dead and several others wounded. That morning, steady news reports told of a bloody gun battle between police and the notorious Black Panther Party (BPP). The official story, given to the press by the State District Attorney, was that the police were trying to execute a search warrant when fired on by the Black Panthers. In the following weeks this official version of events began to unravel, replaced by a more disturbing portrait of law enforcement, most notably a Federal Bureau of Investigation (FBI) that had helped facilitate "a northern lynching."[1]

Within days of the attack a special commission began to investigate the shooting. One of the cochairs was Roy Wilkins. As executive director of the nation's oldest and largest civil rights organization, the National Association for the Advancement of Colored People (NAACP), Wilkins seemed an ideal choice. Over the course of his thirty-year career, Wilkins had become practically synonymous with civil rights. He was, however, also the most outspoken critic of the concept of "Black Power," with which many people associated the Black Panthers.

By 1969, Wilkins was also widely considered a "sell-out" and an "Uncle Tom" for his consistent attacks on Black Power, as well as for his close proximity to white power. Among Black Power groups Wilkins represented what Black Panther cofounder Huey P. Newton called an "endorsed spokesmen." On July 3, 1967, while awaiting trial for the murder of an Oakland police officer, Newton issued, from his prison cell, "In Defense of Self-Defense II." Newton outlined the complex relationship between the "endorsed spokesmen," the state, and "the implacables." According to Newton, the "implacables," were an army of the dispossessed whose festering resentment included "a more profound hatred for the endorsed leaders than for the oppressor himself, because the implacables know that they can deal with the oppressor only after they have driven the endorsed spokesmen off the scene."[2]

On the surface, Newton's analysis of the relationship between the three parties fits the popular way in which many still interpret the 1960s and Black Power. On the occasion of the commemoration of a postage stamp honoring Wilkins in the year 2000, for example, a Minnesota journalist proclaimed, "He also weathered the storm of Black Power during the 1960s, which stood at odds to the NAACP's moralist movement."[3] However, Wilkins's understanding and opposition to Black Power were far more multilayered than standard discussion reflects. Huey P. Newton's analysis of the relationship between subjugated people and what he described as "endorsed leaders" begs a much larger question. Although recent scholarship has expanded our understanding of the nuances of Black Power, the role of the endorsed spokesmen criticized by Newton remains elusive. This story, like the history of the Black Power movement itself, is much more complex than how it is represented in the present literature. Nowhere, perhaps is this more evident than in the case of NAACP Director Roy Wilkins, consistently denounced as a tool of the "white establishment" and an uncompromising critic of Black Power.

Given the popular assessment of this era, one would expect to find overwhelming evidence to support this thesis in Wilkins's relationship with the chief government organization devoted to undermining Black Power, the FBI. Rather than exposing him as a spineless tool of "the oppressor," however, Wilkins's FBI file illustrates his struggle to come to grips with Black Power and the evolution in his thinking on the subject after 1966. While Wilkins remained adamantly opposed to the use of the term, he became increasingly sympathetic to the programs its advocates sought to advance. In reevaluating Roy Wilkins's story, comes a much more nuanced portrait of civil rights advocates in the era of Black Power.[4]

* * *

In the early to mid-1950s the NAACP was widely considered, at least by southern segregationists, as one of the most radical organizations in the United States. Its executive director, Roy Wilkins, was labeled one of the most powerful and dangerous Black men in America for his stewardship over the group's demands for full integration of Blacks into American society. By the mid-1960s, however, Wilkins and the NAACP had become synonymous with the "establishment" and "plantation politics." With a tendency to micromanage local branches and singular emphasis on the primacy of the Southern struggle, the NAACP did not win many adherents among poor and lower-middle-class African Americans. The organization's conservative ideology and devotion to maintaining white support further alienated it from a growing number of blacks seeking alternative solutions.

Wilkins in particular became the symbol of NAACP stodginess, making him a favorite target of Nation of Islam Minister Malcolm X, who lumped him together with the remaining members of the so-called Big Six, a group of the most recognizable leaders and spokesmen for the Civil Rights Movement, as unprincipled sell-outs. The Black Panthers similarly denounced established leaders as "boot licking" tools of the "white power structure." Countless other militants expressed related criticism of Wilkins. Wilkins's image as a "Super Tom" and tool of the establishment would be forever memorialized in Gil Scott-Heron's biting social commentary, "The Revolution Will Not Be Televised." Scott-Heron situated Wilkins as an agent provocateur strolling through the streets of Watts cloaked in the symbols of revolution. Unlike the executive director of the Urban League, Whitney Young, whom Scott-Heron proposed would be run out of Harlem "on a rail," Wilkins—despite donning his "red, black and green liberation jumpsuit"—would come to realize the need for a Black revolution too late. By the time he would be ready to join the masses in the streets, Wilkins and his conception of "Black Power" would be irrelevant.

Born in St. Louis, Missouri, in 1901, Wilkins was raised in the home of his aunt and uncle in a modest-income, integrated neighborhood in St. Paul, Minnesota. His early experiences instilled in him the belief that integration was possible through persistent struggle. Wilkins attended college at the University of Minnesota, paying tuition by working in a slaughterhouse and as a waiter on the North Coast Limited Railroad. Graduating in 1923, he worked for the *Kansas City Call*, a black newspaper, where he became managing editor. Thereafter, Wilkins joined the staff of the NAACP, where from 1934 to 1949 he edited *The Crisis*, the organization's official magazine. By 1955, Wilkins had been named the NAACP's executive director, quickly gaining a reputation as an articulate spokesperson for civil rights.

From this vantage point Wilkins presided over the hey-day of the NAACP, including its victories in *Brown v. Board of Education* and Little Rock and its participation, through its local branches, in hundreds of demonstrations throughout the South. By 1960, however, the NAACP found itself slipping in influence to Martin Luther King Jr.'s Southern Christian Leadership Conference (SCLC), and to more militant youthful organizations such as the Student Nonviolent

Coordinating Committee (SNCC) and the Congress of Racial Equality (CORE). Criticized as a moderate organization, Wilkins saw no essential problem with this label. "I know I have been called a moderate," Wilkins remarked to the author Robert Penn Warren in 1965, "but I always reply that our position has sponsored the most radical idea in the twentieth century—the idea of eliminating racial segregation. So I'm not concerned particularly with these labels that latter-day crusaders bring upon us."[5]

What Wilkins belittled as labels represented new ideas—or at least new strategies that were inconsistent with the aims and goals of the NAACP. Calls by militants for all-Black organizations, for example, challenged the very essence of the NAACP. As an interracial organization committed to integration, the NAACP was no stranger to such criticism. In fact, variations of this complaint had dogged the association from its inception. In 1942, for instance, the African American diplomat and future Nobel Peace Prize–winner Ralph Bunche observed, "There can be no doubt that the Negro leaders in the organization have always kept a weather eye on the reactions of their prominent and influential white sponsors." New York Congressman Adam Clayton Powell similarly pondered how an interracial organization with whites in the leadership could legitimately claim to be the "voice of the black masses."[6] SNCC, which drew many of its members from the youth rolls of the NAACP, had been grappling with this same issue before its decision to expel white members in the winter of 1966. Perhaps no event did more to solidify SNCC's radicalism than the Meredith March Against Fear in the summer of 1966.

Typically set as the backdrop for the public airings of the deep divisions that beset the movement, the march took its name from James Meredith, who was the first African American to integrate the University of Mississippi. Before the Meredith March, the NAACP continued to stand on its reputation as the leader of the Civil Rights Movement. However, in hundreds of communities across the nation, local organizations with a strong orientation toward Black Power were emerging. In this sense, Black Power, as a slogan, posed a serious problem for Wilkins and the NAACP. At the moment when civil rights seemed to enjoy its greatest successes, Black Power threatened to fragment not only the coalition of organizations but crucial white support for additional civil rights legislation. The Meredith March coincided with Martin Luther King Jr.'s sojourn north into Chicago, where Blacks loyal to the political machine of Mayor Richard Daley publicly pleaded with King to go home. In Chicago, King encountered indigenous civil rights and Black Power organizations that were unwilling to have their push for equality molded by outsiders. In this context, King and the SCLC began to look more moderate, whereas Wilkins and the NAACP began to look extremely conservative.

Wilkins's public statements concerning Black Power did little to help the situation. His uncompromising stance against the use of the term helped to ensure the NAACP's declining prestige among militants. Interestingly, it was not necessarily the term *power* but the use of the word *black* before it that made Wilkins uneasy. To be sure, Wilkins understood the implications of Black Power. Following Harry Truman's 1948 presidential victory, secured with robust Black electoral support, Wilkins had commented, "The message was plain: white power in the South could be balanced by black power at the Northern polls. Civil Rights were squarely at the heart of national politics."[7]

But, for Wilkins, moral suasion offered the safest and most comfortable dimension of power. As he put it in 1965, "the Negro in this country is a very practical animal, and he has never lost sight of the elementary facts of survival, and he has never forgotten that he's a ten percent minority. He does not have the power, except the moral power."[8] Following Wilkins's concept of Black Power, which clearly fell along more traditional lines, Blacks could rise as a unit to support deserving friends who would deliver political influence.

Wilkins was especially uncomfortable with the separatist tone of some Black Power advocates. Black Power, as loosely articulated by Stokely Carmichael, seemed to equate power with violence and Wilkins was adamant that movement leaders repudiate Carmichael and his slogan. Long before Carmichael provided a description, the Black Power paradigm was already taking shape in hundreds of communities around the nation. Many Blacks viewed it as an opportunity to shape their own destiny. Local groups seeking solutions outside the civil rights mainstream were crafting a new strategy to tackle problems of housing, education, and police brutality.

For Wilkins, angry rhetoric would only stir white animosity. As a result, he moved aggressively to distance the NAACP from Black Power. At the NAACP's 57th National Convention in Los Angeles, California, Wilkins lashed out. "Black Power" he charged, was nothing more than "the raging of race against race on the irrelevant basis of skin color." "It is the father of hatred," he boomed, "and the mother of violence." "We of the NAACP will have none of this," he defiantly told those in attendance. "We have fought it too long." In a follow-up commentary published in the August 1966 *Crisis,* Wilkins declared, "The only possible dividend of 'black power' is embodied in its offer to millions of frustrated and deprived and persecuted black people of a solace, a tremendous psychological lift, quite apart from its political and economic implications." "Now separatism," Wilkins concluded, "whether on the rarefied debate level of 'black power' or on the wishful level of the secessionist Freedom City in Watts, offers a disadvantaged minority little except a chance to shrivel and die."[9]

Indeed, in interviews and private correspondence concerning Black Power, Wilkins consistently expressed his concern that the slogan would lead to anti-Black violence. Simply stated, Wilkins based his rejection of violence on a fear of white reprisals. As he told Robert Penn Warren in 1965, "This so-called Revolution must be conducted in an uncompromising fashion, but it must be conducted in a fashion that recognizes that when it's all over, we have got to live here together in mutual respect."[10] Of equal concern for Wilkins was what he perceived to be Black Power's inherent call to a worldwide Black revolution and the inability of the militants to deliver on spectacular promises. He dismissed the possibility of Black linkages with the Third World and proclaimed armed self-defense as "suicidal." "For all Stokely's reckless talk of guns and power back then," Wilkins later commented, "I still don't think he could tell the difference between a pistol and a powder puff."[11] As Harold Cruse conceptualized the problem in *The Crisis of the Negro Intellectual,* "What Wilkins is really saying is—'Please don't start throwing around power you don't really have, or power which you might have but which you obviously don't know how to use. All you are doing is scaring people (like me) and provoking other people to mobilize white power for a showdown you are not ready for.'"[12]

Wilkins even denied that Black Power could instill racial pride. "I think that the most concrete legacy of the black power movement was to make the term 'Negro' a dirty word," he later wrote. "The rationale for substituting black for Negro was that Negro was a white man's word. That, of course, was true, but I could never see how the word black was much of an improvement." After all, Wilkins concluded, "There's not a word in the English language that couldn't be considered a white man's word."[13] "No matter how endlessly they try to explain it," Wilkins concluded, "the term 'black power' means anti-white power. In a racially pluralistic society, the formation and the exercise of an ethnically tagged power means opposition to other ethnic powers just as the term 'white supremacy' means subjection of all non white peoples."[14]

As executive director of the NAACP, and a featured columnist for a number of newspapers across the country, Wilkins claimed a ready-made platform to express such views, which earned him the praise and gratitude of thousands of whites, many of whom personally thanked him. Typical was a letter from Mrs. W. J. Reichard of Michigan, who wrote, "Many times, I have read one of your columns, said a silent 'amen,' and made a mental note to write you." Echoing Wilkins's own observations about the fruits of Black Power, she declared, "Fear is really what is behind some of the attitudes of some of the white people." "It is not snobbism that made them flee to the suburbs," she concluded, but "raw fear of violence."[15] American ambassador Hugh M. Smyth likewise wrote Wilkins from Yalta, "I have just seen your excellent piece on The Case Against Separatism: Black Jim Crow.... I am glad to see you have never diverged from the basic principle of integration for all Americans." These letters and others certainly encouraged Wilkins in the power of the moral high ground. As the editor of the *Philadelphia Evening and Sunday Bulletin* observed, "Roy we share a common vulnerability: characterization as moderates (or worse) by the fermenting New Breed. But your place in history is secure and unchallenged. Whatever detractors may say, you've paid your dues by getting involved many long trying years ago, and by producing results."[16]

Not all of this correspondence extolled Wilkins. "I have always had the greatest respect for the endeavors and achievements of the NAACP wrote D. Speir. "[I]t's easy to agree with most of your views," "but not with your reaction to the 'black power' slogan."[17] Still, early on, such letters were the exception rather than the rule, and Wilkins had plenty of reason to believe that his position represented the majority of peace-loving whites as well as blacks.

For Wilkins, one of Black Power's difficulties was reconciling the difference between the slogan and violence. Part of the problem stemmed from the manner in which Black Power activists defended the use of violence as a legitimate means of influencing the system. Commenting on urban unrest in the summer of 1967, scholar Charles V. Hamilton, for instance, observed, "And it must be clear that whites will have to bargain with blacks or to continue to fight them in the streets of the Detroits and Newarks." "Rather than being a call to violence," Hamilton continued, "this is a clear recognition that the ghetto rebellions, in addition to producing the possibility of apartheid-type repression, have been functional in moving some whites to see that viable solutions must be sought."[18] Such defenses of riots were problematic for Wilkins, who cautioned, "in attempting to substitute for derelict enforcement machinery, the policy entails the risk of a broader, more indiscriminate crack-down by law officers under the ready excuse of restoring law and order."[19]

At least as far as the state was concerned, Wilkins proved correct. The government looked to crush Black Power and used the rhetoric of its advocates to justify ruthless tactics. Even before the official start of its secret counterintelligence program, COINTELPRO, the FBI maintained surveillance on hundreds of groups and thousands of local individuals involved in militant black organizations. Justification for these actions ranged from possible communist affiliations to racial agitation. With the emergence of Black Power then, the FBI zeroed in on black militants. Publicly, the Bureau consistently claimed that its primary goal was to prevent violence in the form of urban riots that swept the nation in the mid-1960s. Race riots in fact coincided with Black Power; they did not cause it. However, they did provide Black militants a bargaining chip that many unfortunately misused, playing into the popular mind-set that Black militants all supported violence and armed revolution. The public pronouncements of Black leaders like Wilkins against Black Power helped to justify the FBI's ever expanding interest and attempted disruption of militant organizations and contained a special layer of irony.

FBI officials had been monitoring civil rights activists since the 1950s. Under legendary director J. Edgar Hoover, the Bureau was staunchly anti-civil rights, claiming that the movement was a communist plot to embarrass America. In fact, in his hunt for "reds" within civil rights groups, Hoover had found a willing ally in Roy Wilkins, who worried that the discovery of such operatives in the NAACP would ultimately damage the movement. The two men were hardly kindred spirits, but shared a mutual anticommunism. Wilkins's public opposition to Black Power seemed to endorse the FBI director, who consistently referred to it as a call to armed revolution and antiwhite violence. The situation, at least on the surface, recalled the one that developed when a young J. Edgar Hoover had been instrumental in the Greek tragedy that represented Marcus Garvey's devastating spiral during the 1920s.[20]

Wilkins had been an eyewitness to Garvey's spectacular demise. As editor of the St. Paul *Appeal,* Wilkins covered Garvey's celebrated fraud trial. "From my restricted vantage in St. Paul," Wilkins remembered, "I sided with Randolph and Dubois" a duo he admitted "hit below the belt every now and then." "In opposing Garvey," recalled Wilkins later, "I was not just put off by the style of the man; I did not like his ideas of separatism. There was nothing personal in it." "In *The Crisis,*" Wilkins noted, "I watched W.E.B. Du Bois try to come to terms with Garvey.... In 1920 Du Bois was calling Garvey an 'honest and sincere man with tremendous vision, great dynamic force, stubborn determination, and unselfish desire to serve.' In a few years he was calling him 'the most dangerous enemy of the Negro race in America.'" Wilkins also appreciated Garvey's influence over the masses. "His success," Wilkins wrote,

> alarmed black leaders as well as white persecutors. Even then, I thought his back to Africa ideas marched in the wrong direction, but he commanded an awesome power to raise broken spirits and to reach that nine-tenths of the Black population that the Talented Tenth of Du Bois

left out. When Garvey called out, 'Up You Might Race' the people moved. I underestimated that power back in the twenties.[21]

The actions of Black leaders during Garvey's trial seemed to fit the pattern represented by Huey Newton's "endorsed spokesman."[22] Thus, four decades after Garvey, it appeared that Hoover may have found another seriously divisive issue in Black Power. However, the situation in the 1960s would not turn out the same way, for several reasons. All major Black organizations were riddled with informants in the 1960s, but there would be no secret sacrifice, at least not on the part of Roy Wilkins.

The FBI certainly attempted to exploit ideological as well as personality differences in the movement. In his well-documented study of the FBI and Martin Luther King Jr., David Garrow notes that the Bureau made a concerted effort to ensnare Wilkins and other Black leaders in a public feud with King. However, their efforts proved unsuccessful. Despite a bitter and long-standing personal rivalry between himself and Dr. King, fueled largely by Wilkins's jealousy over King's public recognition, Wilkins never betrayed King. In fact, after Hoover referred to King as "the most notorious liar" in America, it was Wilkins, at a meeting with President Johnson and other Black leaders who defended Dr. King and emphasized that many in the Black community shared King's criticisms of the FBI.[23]

The NAACP had been under the scrutiny of the FBI since the creation of the Bureau. Citing the need to monitor possible communist influences within the organization, FBI surveillance reached its peak between 1941 and 1966. The FBI kept close tabs on the NAACP's involvement in national and local civil rights initiatives. Several influential members of the NAACP were on the government's informant list and regularly reported on its activities. In this period, the Bureau employed nearly three thousand wiretaps and over eight hundred electronic eavesdropping devices on "subversive targets," including the NAACP and Roy Wilkins. By the 1950s, the FBI had an extensive file on Wilkins dating to the Great Depression. Although the Bureau claimed to have terminated its NAACP surveillance in 1966, it continued to monitor Wilkins for close to another decade. Despite Hoover's infamous Black Extremist memorandum in which he actually proposed possible "responsible" Black leaders to replace King and others in the civil rights leadership, Wilkins's name was not on the list, despite actively purging the NAACP of radical influences and communists. Although the Bureau would later claim that Wilkins was never a subject of COINTELPRO operation, Bureau records suggest otherwise. A highly redacted memo hints at the FBI's use of dirty tricks against Wilkins. "In view of the above, the NYO feels that there is a tremendous opportunity to cause Roy Wilkins and the NAACP to attack [deleted] and [deleted] at this point. Authority is requested to anonymously call Roy Wilkins of the NAACP under the pretext of [deleted]."[24] Largely unaware of the Bureau's intensive actions against him, Wilkins continued to support the FBI's crusade against communists. Despite his efforts to pacify Hoover's fears about communists in the NAACP, Wilkins still maintained a healthy mistrust of the FBI.

Roy Wilkins would once again be targeted because of his very public opposition to Black Power. This was the case when the New York City police approached him in the summer of 1967 about a purported plot by Black extremists to assassinate him along with Whitney Young of the Urban League, in hopes of inspiring a race war. Working in secret with the Bureau, the NYPD informed Wilkins that the elaborate scheme was the brainchild of a pro-Chinese communist Black militant group called the Revolutionary Action Movement (RAM). Wilkins initially dismissed the idea as "far-fetched." To his surprise, a few weeks later the police announced that they had arrested sixteen suspected conspirators and hauled in "a regular little arsenal of terror" in predawn raids on RAM's New York and Pennsylvania offices. At the trial, Wilkins learned that RAM members possessed a map of his home and made contingency plans to execute him even if his wife was present.[25] This was enough to satisfy Wilkins that disillusioned militants posed a serious threat to the movement. Unbeknown to Wilkins, however, the FBI had targeted RAM for neutralization under COINTELPRO. By the summer of 1967 the organization was highly infiltrated by informants and agent provocateurs. In August agents boasted that, "They were arrested on every possible charge until they could no longer make bail. As a result

RAM members spent most of the summer in jail and no violence traceable to RAM took place."[26]

The FBI's assault against RAM was only the beginning. The following February, the Domestic Intelligence Division expanded COINTELPRO to include surveillance and counterintelligence operations against all militant Black groups. Instructions sent to field offices directed agents to pursue programs that could stop the rise of a Black "messiah." "Martin Luther King, Stokely Carmichael, and Elijah Muhammad all aspire to this position." Hoover was particularly concerned with King, whom he feared "could be a real contender for this position should he abandon his supposed 'obedience' to 'white, liberal doctrines' (nonviolence) and embrace Black Nationalism."[27] But less than a month later King was killed by an assassin's bullet in Memphis, Tennessee, where he marched on behalf of sanitation workers.

Within months of King's murder, in September 1968, Hoover declared the Black Panther Party to be "the single greatest threat to the nation's internal security." The editors of *Time* concurred:

> In the two years since the first tiny pack of Panthers emerged in Oakland, they have seized pre-eminence in the Black Power movement. They are not only militant but militaristic. They have guns, determination, discipline and the makings of a nationwide organization. In a dozen black ghettos, Panthers prowl in uniform: black jackets, black berets, tight black trousers. They proclaim their right to bear arms, and they have an affinity for violence. Committed to revolution, devoted to some hard-line Chinese Communist double-talk, they are gathering notoriety as an American Mao-Mao.[28]

By the fall of 1968, when the FBI and the media were proclaiming the Panthers to be "the most extreme of the black extremists," the Party had already taken numerous steps, including suspending its armed patrols of the police, in order to connect more with local people.[29] While the Panthers did espouse a Marxist-Leninist line, its rallying cry, "All Power to the People," symbolized an internationalist perspective and call for a worldwide freedom struggle. The Panthers were, in short, the embodiment of FBI fears. In the eyes of the Bureau and journalists, they had a viable program and popular appeal beyond the Black community and held the potential to unite revolutionary movements. To stop this, the FBI initiated a campaign of terror against the BPP and worked diligently to drive a wedge between the Panthers and other Black nationalist organizations.

Meanwhile, the assassination of Martin Luther King Jr. in April 1968 had a profound impact on Roy Wilkins and the NAACP. As the nation exploded in flames over King's murder, Wilkins and the NAACP were forced to confront their growing alienation from the "masses." At first, Wilkins and the NAACP responded with even stronger condemnations of Black Power as a divisive force within the movement. A strongly worded *Crisis* editorial, by Henry Lee Moon in November 1968, for instance, called on all responsible Blacks to make a stand against Black Power. "[T]he time has come," Moon wrote, "for speaking out loud and clear lest the entire race be branded as hate-mongers, segregationists, advocates of violence and worse. The silent majority must let its views be known ... the time for silence or muted voices is past."[30] But, in the wake of the assassination of King, the NAACP's anti-Black Power rhetoric proved out of step with the temper of the times. While Moon's words resonated with those in the media who charged that many Black leaders and "moderates are too intimated by the Panthers to speak out," a letter in response to his editorial, published in the *Crisis* the following month, underscored the basic problem. "It is true, the time has come for speaking out loud and clear," the writer observed, "but not against other black groups who are in the same struggle either directly or indirectly." "Since we are to speak out along this line," the author continued, "let it be toward establishing more unity. It is time for us to start claiming instead of disclaiming, owning in lieu of disowning, association, in lieu of disassociation. We must come to realize that just as a family may be disappointed with the actions of one child, they don't chase him out."[31]

This sentiment extended to the NAACP's relationship with other national organizations. As 1968 drew to a close, Wilkins came under fire from militant leaders and groups for contributing to a climate that sanctioned official repression. One of his most outspoken critics was Roy Innis, the national director of CORE. In a December *Manhattan Tribune* editorial, Innis took Wilkins to task for "taking unfortunately anachronistic and detrimental positions on some key issues facing black people." In a follow-up press release, Innis criticized Wilkins for "a continuing history of unenlightened statements and positions that are directly opposed to the interest of Black People."[32] Innis noted that Wilkins was one of the first Black leaders to attack Black Power in 1966. "The fallacious reasoning behind his attack," Innis wrote, "crystallized the fear and suspicions of white racists." He further charged that the *Crisis* had carried out a vicious attack against Black radicals that "predictably, was praised by various segments of the white community."[33]

In January 1969, the NAACP began reaching out to a variety of groups. One of the keys to this new outreach program was a drive to expand the NAACP's nationwide Leadership Development Program to recruit and train volunteer personnel to handle community social and economic problems. As NAACP brass proclaimed, "We will broaden the reach of training to embrace strategic non-member groups in the black community in our effort to encourage and promote the community's capacity for identity and self fulfillment."[34] The NAACP also softened its hard line against Black militancy, acknowledging that there might be some room for compromise. In a memo to Branch Departments dated April 9, 1969, National Director of Chapters Gloster B. Current advised, "The Black Liberation Front is a revolutionary front. In some situations it has provoked some changes. But we will have to give careful study to what is developing around us."[35]

Toward this end, in July 1969, Wilkins reached out to the organization most associated with Black Power, the Black Panther Party. In a telegram to Bobby Seale, Wilkins requested a "conference with officers of militant groups and particularly with you as the Chairman of the BPP." Noting that he was acting on his own initiative, Wilkins assured Seale that the meeting would be "official … but not binding." Explaining the rationale for the meeting, Wilkins noted, "I simply feel very strongly that the present situation of our race requires trying to reach some common ground and arrival at some sort of strategy that will be effective even if productive only in a few areas."[36]

After the Panthers went to the media with the communication from Wilkins, the executive director denied sending the initial telegram to the Panthers. As he explained in a letter to Professor John M. Mecartney, chairman of the Sociology Department at Bluffton College, "At no time did I issue a formal call for a conference." Instead, Wilkins claimed that in the course of an interview with an AP writer in Jackson, Mississippi, he had suggested, among other things, that "there ought to be a dialogue between the militants and the moderates." "The Panthers saw a report of the interview," Wilkins continued, "and sent a telegram in which they stipulated the date, the place and circumstances in which they would like to meet." To further convince Mecartney, Wilkins sent along photocopies of the memo.[37]

Despite his public disavowal of the proposed behind the scenes meeting, Wilkins kept the lines of communications open. After Panther Chief of Staff David Hilliard sent him a Western Union telegram proposing a meeting between Seale and Wilkins at San Francisco City Prison on September 24, 1969, Wilkins responded, "I will be out of the country in the latter half of the September."[38] Nonetheless, Wilkins suggested that "NAACP members would consider a conference of maximum helpfulness if it could be held to a discussion and setting limited to discovering areas of agreement in the program of the two organizations." Cognizant of the Panthers' legal troubles associated with various criminal charges (many of which were a result of the FBI's all-out assault on the Party which began the year before), and perhaps eager to avoid unwanted publicity, Wilkins further suggested that the parties "set a date and a place after November first when your attention to other pressing matters will not impede free discussion or stimulate unwarranted speculation."[39] Before the two organizations were able to reestablish contact, Fred Hampton and Mark Clark were gunned down in Chicago and Wilkins now found himself beseeched by appeals to do something to protest the killings. One woman wrote to express her indignation at the "reckless" and "insatiable arrests and murders of the young men of the Black Panther Party." "I also feel very disturbed," she continued, "that I have read of no protest and outcry by other, more established Black organizations." "I believe that these young men are fighting against the oppression of Black and Puerto Rican groups in their own way," she lectured the NAACP. "Perhaps we elders don't agree with their methods but we should support their sincerity, idealism and goals. It is horrendous to permit, silently, this wholesale imprisonment and murder of an intelligent fighting force among the youth."[40] Roy Innis, almost a year to the day of criticizing Wilkins for his insensitivity to Black Power, sent a telegram concerning "the national pattern of atrocities by police against the Black Panthers" and inviting the "heads of national organizations meet [and] discuss common positions" at the Hamilton House in Brookline, Massachusetts, on December 8.[41]

On December 9, 1969, Roy Wilkins joined Innis on a panel of four speakers, including King's successor at the SCLC, Ralph Abernathy, and Panther Raymond Masai Hewitt at Boston College. At the forum, titled "Who Speaks for the Black Community," Wilkins made clear that his newfound sensitivity toward the campaign against the Panthers was limited to police attacks. FBI reports of the meeting emphasized Wilkins's staunch opposition to the others on the panel. While maintaining that the SCLC was still committed to the philosophy of nonviolence, for instance, Abernathy noted that his organization would forge new alliances with other Black organizations such as the Panthers. Abernathy even announced plans for a new counseling service for boys drafted into the Armed Services to discourage them from participating in a "godless war." Wilkins balked at the panel's radicalism and FBI agents relished his unbridled patriotism after he upbraided panelists for attacking the United States. "I consider it my country," Wilkins declared, "and I'm not giving up on it."[42]

Wilkins's role on the commission did little to ease the tension between the two organizations but would ultimately come to change his perception of the Black Panthers and also of Black Power. Less than two weeks later he was named cochair, along with former Attorney General Ramsey Clark, of a special commission of inquiry into the Black Panthers and the police convened to consider police and FBI misconduct in the Hampton and Clark murders.

The commission exposed Wilkins to a new side of the Panthers and Black militancy generally and pulled him in two directions. It also made Wilkins and the NAACP unlikely defenders of Black militants. The association began fielding numerous requests from Black Power advocates seeking the NAACP's assistance. Mrs. Mabel Robinson of the Morris County Branch of the NAACP, for example, wrote Wilkins, "Naturally, the recent assassinations in Chicago and the shoot-out in Los Angeles are focal points of such an investigation, but we would also suggest that here in New Jersey there has been a terror campaign against the Black Panthers."[43] As the commission began its investigation into the Hampton and Clark killings, one of the nations' premiere Black Power critics found himself in the position of having to justify the actions of the militants and answer pointed questions from white supporters. "I'm very puzzled as to what is going on," Ganelle Taylor penned on the back of an NAACP fundraising letter, "has the NAACP been taken over by the radicals." "I am reluctant to contribute to a group who tries not to disagree with the Black Panthers," she concluded.[44] Simultaneously, Wilkins earned the grudging respect of some militants, as his appointment to the commission seemed to answer their appeals to the NAACP. "Ruby and I are delighted—but not surprised that you raise your voice in defense of equal justice for the Panthers," commended the actor Ossie Davis. "Police seem to find it possible to handle Yippies, and S.D.S.ers without resorting to fire arms."[45]

Suffering from a stomach ailment in late December 1969, Wilkins left many of the responses to these early letters to Assistant Executive Director John Morsell who attempted to do damage control. Morsell assured Mrs. Taylor, for instance, that "our concern about possible police harassment of the Black Panthers in no way constitutes endorsement of the Panthers themselves or their principal methods. We in the NAACP are still dedicated to our long-time philosophy."[46] Despite Morsell's assurances, the NAACP now found itself being approached more frequently to intercede on behalf of Black Power organizations.

Despite several polls, which found that 60 percent of the people surveyed supported both the tactics and philosophy of the BPP, Wilkins was more concerned with a poll appearing in the *St. Louis Globe Democrat* in May 1970, which found that two out of three whites distrusted the Panthers.[47] Wilkins continued to sound the alarm against the dangers of retaliatory violence, but he also demonstrated a degree of understanding missing in his earlier attacks on Black Power.

This included sharing the platform with Black Power advocates that the NAACP would not have dreamed of several years earlier. Such was the case when Wilkins traveled to Augusta, Georgia, to participate in a rally protesting the killing of six blacks by local police on May 11, 1970. Wilkins was scheduled to speak with a local activist named Wilbert Allen, who claimed to represent the Augusta branch of the Black Panther Party.[48]

The FBI compiled a detailed report on the gathering, estimated to be 500 strong. Of particular interest to the reporting agents was the racial composition of the crowd. Of the 500 persons who attended the rally, the FBI noted only "eight or ten whites were present." Despite this, the special agent in charge noted, "the meeting was quiet and orderly with no violence." The Bureau further noted that Allen and the majority of the 15 to 20 Panthers present withdrew before the start of the program, and Wilkins's speech, which called on Augusta Blacks to unite.[49]

That August, Wilkins sent a detailed complaint to Attorney General John Mitchell charging the Hartford, Connecticut, police department with misconduct for its handling of rioters after a civil disturbance erupted over the acquittal of an officer charged in the shooting of two Puerto Ricans. Wilkins informed Mitchell that, "the NAACP has co-operated with local officials and groups and has used radio appeals for sanity," but noted, "all such have been rendered of no force and effect by reports of fresh assaults upon innocent Black citizens."[50] Mitchell turned Wilkins's communiqué over to Assistant Attorney General Jerris Leonard, who contacted the FBI to make an investigation of the charges.[51] The Bureau opened a limited investigation of the matter but ultimately did little but report what they found in the local newspapers concerning the disturbance.

Despite his role in the commission and his sharing platforms with Black militants, as well as his private assistance in places like Hartford, Wilkins continued his public assault on Black Power. In an article in the *Seattle Post-Intelligencer* on August 8, Wilkins issued his strongest critique of government repression against Black protest, along with a forceful condemnation of Black radicals who invited such repression by their actions. Although acknowledging anti-Black racism and white supremacy, Wilkins called on Blacks to challenge "elements in the black community," who "by their rhetoric and their conduct" assisted in white repression. "Without selling out the race," Wilkins argued, "Negroes are now called upon to search out and eliminate those provocative moves within the race that justify to a thoughtless public the repression of millions solely because of skin color." "Such a course," he concluded, "is just as necessary as that of preventing a man from knocking a hole in the bottom of a loaded life-boat."[52]

To this end, Wilkins continued to challenge militant organizations who overstepped what he considered to be the bounds of acceptable rhetoric. In at least one instance, Wilkins came across sounding more like a Black nationalist than he intended. Take the strange example of his critique of Huey Newton in the summer of 1970. After the riots in Hartford, Newton had made headlines when he announced, shortly after release from prison, his intention to send Black Panthers to assist the National Liberation Front in Vietnam.[53] Angered, Wilkins crafted a caustic response. In his *Oakland Tribune* column, Wilkins questioned how, "a young black as smart and articulate as Huey Newton," can be "so overcome with the anguish of a people 9,000 miles from the United States that he downgrades the suffering of his own people in the slums of Los Angeles and the shacks of rural Alabama?" "Of course, Huey Newton knows about this suffering," Wilkins wrote. "It was the resentment over this treatment that led, at least in part, to the founding of the Black Panther Party." "But Huey," Wilkins continued, "for all his talents is a revolutionary. Revolutionaries get confused. They think that following a 'line' is more important than winning an improvement for their people." Reminiscent of Stokely Carmichael's critique of the Party's involvement with the predominately White Peace and Freedom Party two years earlier, Wilkins concluded, "Newton, an attractive and personable young man, is described in one news dispatch as being the darling of White revolutionaries. It Figures."[54]

In typical fashion, Newton struck back hard at the NAACP executive director. In an open letter to Wilkins in the September 26, 1970, issue of the Black Panther Party newspaper, Newton denounced Wilkins's comments as "insidious white baiting" and accused him of being out of touch with the global nature of oppression. Drawing a sharp distinction between the Panthers and the NAACP, Newton challenged, "We recognize that America is no longer a nation but an empire and that the same troops who occupy and kill at Jackson State, Birmingham, Chicago and New Orleans are also occupying and killing in My Lai, in Penom and in many other places."[55]

Significantly, however, the exchange between the two leaders did not end attempts by Wilkins to find some common ground. Over the next twenty-four months, the Panthers would undergo extensive changes, including the closing of all local chapters and a move en mass to Oakland. Wilkins, in the interim, continued to try to bridge the gap between Black Power and civil rights. In a series of exposés about the FBI's clandestine COINTELPRO operation, published in the *Washington Post* in May 1972, the columnist Jack Anderson exposed the Bureau's illegal operations. Anderson charged that no Black leader was immune from federal surveillance, while "Only the most extreme white radicals have come under FBI scrutiny."[56] Anderson listed more than a dozen Black entertainers, activists and civil rights leaders, including Eartha Kitt, Ossie Davis, Floyd McKissick, Ralph Abernathy, and Roy Wilkins, whom the FBI had conducted surveillance on. Indeed, although acknowledging its files on the other leaders, in a subsequent internal investigation the FBI denied maintaining active interest in Wilkins concluding that, "he has not been investigated by the FBI." Instead, the Bureau claimed that its primary source of information on Wilkins was "Information he has furnished and from 'public sources,' which upon requests were made available to the White House, State, Labor, Civil Service, USIA, and military intelligence."[57] Against this backdrop of government revelations, by September 1972 the relationship between the Black Panther Party and the NAACP actually seemed to be improving. Wilkins was ecstatic after Bobby Seale announced a new direction for the Party. In a taped statement broadcast on San Francisco Radio, Seale informed the public of the "evolution" of the Party from a revolutionary organization to one working within the system.[58] After hearing of the announcement, Wilkins applauded the Panthers. FBI intelligence summarized an *Oakland Tribune* article in which Wilkins noted that the BPP was "not the boogeyman" it was often portrayed as and celebrated the Party's move toward the political center. The BPP's move into the electoral arena comforted Wilkins. Though hardly the "Red, Black and Green Liberation Jumpsuit" that Gil Scott-Heron had imagined for Wilkins, the NAACP and the Panthers united, at least on one issue.

Meanwhile, after being buried for nearly two years in May 1973, the commission's findings on the shootings in Chicago were finally released. The tone of the report suggested more growth on Wilkins's part, especially regarding his analysis of the causes of anti-Panther violence. The callous actions of the police and the FBI exposed Wilkins to the grim reality of state-sponsored terror. Wilkins, along with the other members of the commission, did not mince words in their condemnation of the government for its role in the murder of Fred Hampton and Mark Clark. "Whatever their purpose," they began, "those officials responsible for planning the police action and some who directly participated acted with wanton disregard for human life and the legal rights of American citizens." The commission further charged that "Systems of justice—federal, state, and local failed to do their duty to protect the lives and rights of citizens." "Of all violence," they continued, "official violence is the most destructive. It not only takes life, but it does so in the name of the people and as the agent of society." In a statement reminiscent of Huey Newton's lecture to Wilkins a year earlier, the report continued:

There is a common thread that runs through the violence of B-52 raids in Indochina, police shooting students at Jackson State College in Mississippi, and the slaughter of prisoners and guards at Attica State Penitentiary in New York. We do not value others' lives as we do our own. The Vietnamese, the black students, the convicts and the guards are expendable. Until we understand that George Jackson and Mark Clark and Fred Hampton, as well as the victims of Kent State and the nameless and faceless victims of Jackson State and on all sides in the Indochina war, are human beings equal in every way to our children and ourselves, we will see no wrong in using violence to control or destroy them.[59]

The *New York Times* called the document "the source of much wrangling between commission staff members and some of the prominent citizens who agreed to make the investigation. Staff sources said that some commission members wanted the document toned down." Although Wilkins's personal feelings about the wording of the document remain a mystery, the final document does bear his endorsement.[60]

Despite his rapprochement with the Black Panthers, by the mid-1970s Wilkins found himself on the losing side of a competition with a new charismatic leader, the Reverend Jesse Jackson. Adopting the symbols of Black Power, the clenched fist, Afro and dashiki, Jackson anchored his message in more moderate terms while appealing to a much broader audience. Around the same time, Wilkins found himself marginalized within the NAACP. As he would later recall, "All through the middle and late 1960s, when the rhetoric of militancy was hottest, the NAACP's board of directors had stayed right behind me, and their support helped in those terrible years. But suddenly in the middle 1970s, I found that some board members were eager to see me step down."[61] In 1977, Wilkins did just that continuing to offer analysis of the steadily declining movement from the sidelines.

Wilkins would not, however, retire in peace. Although COINTELPRO "officially" disbanded shortly after the release of the commission's report on the Hampton and Clark murders, its reverberations would continue. In 1978, it was Wilkins's turn. That year movement veterans and the public were shocked after a document, released as part of Director Hoover's "Official and Confidential" file on King, implicated Wilkins in the FBI's plot to discredit the slain civil rights leader. The charges were not new. During the Church Committee hearings in 1975 to determine the damage and extent of the FBI's campaign against Dr. King, FBI official Cartha De Loach testified that Wilkins had been briefed about the Bureau's concerns about King. Wilkins, De Loach maintained, also met privately with Hoover in November 1964 and volunteered to help the Bureau have King quietly retire after De Loach shared information with him concerning King's personal life. In sworn testimony, Wilkins vigorously denied the allegations maintaining that he had never met with the FBI regarding any plot against King.[62] But the story seemed plausible enough, especially to Wilkins's critics who viewed him as a "sellout." The historians David Garrow, Kenneth O'Reilly, Athan Theoharis, and Frank Donner, however, present convincing evidence that Wilkins never agreed to help the FBI remove King but instead had contacted the Bureau to ask them to halt the smear campaign against King.[63]

Wilkins died in 1981 shortly after completing his autobiography. In his final column in the *Oakland Register Tribune,* on the Miami Overtown riot, Wilkins revealed an evolved sensitivity and understanding of ghetto misery and violence and the failure of the government and the movement for civil rights to address them. With a cartoon portrait and title, "He's been a Credit," Wilkins's editorial, "Explaining, but not condoning violence," sought to address the issues associated with the riot. "The nation's seeming surprise at the outbreak of racial violence in Miami, Florida," wrote Wilkins, "once again serves notice that most whites still are ignorant about the Negro side of life in America." "Assuming this to be the case," he continued, "the riots in Miami have done what the black leadership had failed to accomplish: focus the population's attention on a long chain of racial inequality." "The economic retrenchment of the 1970s," he observed, "has virtually wiped out the steady racial progress that started in the 1960s." Wilkins summed up a rather bleak outlook:

> They are discouraged by the setbacks. They are rebelling against incidents of police abuse and discrimination in the criminal justice system. And they are bracing themselves in fearful anticipation of a greater explosion.[64]

In spite of this warning, Wilkins cautioned against the use of violence noting, "it will feed on racial hatred and invite repressive measures because the primary interest of the society will be in restoring order."[65]

Wilkins's understanding of the need for Black Power had thus grown over the period of a decade and a half. While he would never champion the slogan itself, he also did not deliberately, so far as we know, help federal officials in an effort to sabotage those who used it. Despite sincere efforts to keep the NAACP at the forefront of civil rights protest, Wilkins remained largely unconnected to the grassroots who continued to explore Black Power as means of addressing the poverty, political inequality, and police brutality that dominated their communities. However, Wilkins came to better appreciate that a degree of militancy might help facilitate the dream of racial equality and equal justice under the law in a nonsegregated society. In this sense, he remained true to the struggle for civil rights, without directly selling out Black Power. Rather than aiding the state in its attacks on Black Power, Wilkins sought, on his own terms, to bridge the gap between the two in hopes of creating some kind of unity. Although his anti-Black Power rhetoric undoubtedly served to bolster the government and white America's fears about Black Power, Wilkins stopped short of condoning the unlawful elimination of Black militants. In the final analysis, over time, Roy Wilkins and Black Power radicals had both matured to an extent that allowed for, if not a cozy relationship, mutual understanding of the hopes and impediments toward a shared goal of Black liberation.

Rainbow Radicalism

The Rise of the Radical Ethnic Nationalism

JEFFREY O. G. OGBAR

The Black Power movement had a profound affect on the symbolism, rhetoric, and tactics of radical activism outside the African American community during the era of tumultuous political and social change in the late 1960s. Scholars have long credited the civil rights movement with fomenting the emerging liberation movements of women, gays, and others in the late 1960s and early 1970s. While the black struggle for civil rights undoubtedly affected the growing efforts of other marginalized and oppressed groups in the United Sates, it was the Black Power movement that had some of the most visible influences on the radical activists struggles of Latinos, Asians, and Native Americans, giving rise to a visible movement of radical ethnic nationalism and new constructions of ethnic identity. Young activists of all backgrounds had been impressed and inspired by the militancy, political analysis, organization, and symbolism of black nationalists and Black Power advocates. No organization influenced these burgeoning militants more than the Black Panther Party (BPP).

The Nation of Islam (NOI), chief benefactor of the Black Power movement and largest black nationalist organization in the country, had long embraced all people of color as members of the family of black humanity. Still, the Nation's language, symbolism, and general cosmology were geared toward African Americans. There were Latinos, Asians, and other who joined the NOI, but for non-African

Americans, the Black Power movement demonstrated that ethnic nationalism had incredible potential for political mobilization and resistance to the oppression and marginalization they experienced. For many, the BPP, in particular, represented the model for revolutionary struggle, resistance, and radical chic.

The party experienced precipitous growth in 1968, with more than thirty chapters emerging across the country. Whereas thousands of African American militants were willing to embrace the party as a vanguard organization to lead the national struggle against oppression, non-African Americans took notice. Conditions that gave rise to the radicalism that characterized Black Power similarly catapulted other minorities and even poor whites into militant activism in the late 1960s. Other people of color had languished under the domination of white supremacy in the United States for more than a hundred years. The militant call for Black Power reverberated in the barrios and ghettoes, engendering such organization as the Brown Berets, Young Lords, Red Guard, American Indian Movement, and others that joined the chorus for liberation and radical political activism. By 1967, the Brown Berets had become the first major organization to model itself after the Black Panthers, emerging as the self-described "shock troops" for a burgeoning Chicano civil rights movement.

Chicano Power

Throughout the West, communities with high concentrations of Mexican Americans passed laws barring Chicanos from attending schools with white children, obtaining municipal jobs, and even owning land.[1] Hundreds of thousands of acres of land were procured from Mexicans by Anglos between 1848 and 1960. Chicanos in the West became sources of cheap agricultural labor for Anglo landlords, much like blacks in the South. In the mid-1960s a movement to organize Mexican farmworkers, led by Cesar Chavez in California, gave birth to the Chicano civil rights movement.

The Chavez-led strike helped generate activism in barrios across the state. East Los Angeles, home to one of the largest Spanish-speaking communities in the nation, became a center of increasing political activism. Chicanos in the city suffered from police brutality and widespread discrimination in housing, education, and employment, as they had throughout the Southwest. Although Chicanos were California's second-largest ethnic group, they had only one state assemblyman and no state senators. In Los Angeles, there were no Chicano city councilmen or representatives on the county board of directors. By 1970 a full 80 percent of Chicanos were high school dropouts, a rate higher than any ethnic group in the city.[2]

In 1967 high school student David Sanchez organized the Young Citizens for Community Action (YCCA) in East Los Angeles. Attempting to meet the needs of the surrounding community, the YCCA surveyed the dilemmas of Latino students and sought Chicano representation on the L.A. board of education, campaigning for Julian Nava. Initially a liberal, youth-oriented reformist organization, the YCCA quickly became affected by the wave of radicalism that swept the country. With the help of Father John Luce, YCCA opened a coffee shop, La Piranya, in September 1967, which provided a meeting place for Chicano youth and others who read poetry and took part in informal political discussion groups. There, young Chicanos talked about the tumultuous political and social climate that had given rise to Black Power, student radicalism and a generally militant mood among many young people. Police brutality, poverty and pervasive discrimination against Chicanos were issues of frequent debate. La Piranya also served as a meeting place for many of the leaders of the Black Power movement, including H. Rap Brown, Stokely Carmichael from the Student Nonviolent Coordinating Committee (SNCC) (who also served as officials of the Black Panther Party), and Maulana Karenga from the Us organization. Books and tapes by and about Malcolm X were exchanged, and, like black people, many Mexican Americans gravitated to a more salient racial and cultural affirmation that was not dependent on whites.[3]

On November 24, 1967, police officers who had been called to a civil disturbance in East Los Angeles beat one man unconscious. According to eyewitnesses, the man's wife and daughter were also beaten, pulled by the hair to a squad car where they were arrested and taken to jail. Similar stories of police brutality had been long known in black and Chicano communities in Los Angeles. It was the new militant climate, however, that moved Sanchez and other members of

YCCA to seek redress, by placing police brutality central to the agenda of Chicano activism.[4]

On December 3, David Sanchez formed the first unit of the Brown Berets, which demonstrated in front of the East Los Angeles Sheriff Station and the Hollenbeck Division of the Los Angeles Police Department. In addition to creating a formal organization to protest police brutality and the general oppression of Chicanos, Sanchez developed a uniform for its membership. Each of the twelve members wore a brown beret as his new uniform, demonstrating to spectators that the group was unified and militant.[5] Many observers knew that the beret had been derived from the uniform of the Black Panther Party for Self-Defense.

The BPP adopted the black beret as part of its uniform in 1966, along with the black leather jacket, black slacks, powder blue shirt, and black shoes.[6] While black militants before the party had worn leather jackets, the beret was the Panthers' unique symbol, and it soon became the icon of militancy and radicalism across the country. For Sanchez, the beret symbolized "the dignity and pride in the color of my skin and race."[7] It also represented his identification with the Panthers' revolutionary program.

While Sanchez spearheaded a new revolutionary nationalist group, Denver-based Rodolfo "Corky" Gonzales cultivated a Mexican-American brand of cultural nationalism and helped popularize the term *Chicano,* which supplanted *Mexican-American.* Although there are different explanations of the word's origin, according to Gonzalez, Chicano was a name with deep historical meaning, rooted in a rich and proud tradition.[8] Like the term *Negro,* Mexican-American, to Gonzalez and others, reflected a confused, culturally ignorant assimilationist, wedded to the system of oppression and exploitation that trampled on the rights of the brown masses. These "Anglo-prones" eagerly defended white supremacy, even to the extent that they accepted their own inferiority. The acceptance of their inferiority was indicative in their eagerness to jettison any cultural trappings of their Chicano heritage and their willingness to idealize whiteness. Speaking Spanish was discouraged, as were holidays, rituals, and other aspects of Mexican culture. Chicano, by contrast, proudly affirmed self-determination.[9]

Like the newly popularized word *black*, Chicano came from the people not the oppressors. It was a word the people chose to identify and define themselves. It also spoke to the myths that characterize cultural nationalist traditions, an essential party of nationality formation, as political scientist Karl Deutch has explained.[10] Like black nationalism, Chicano nationalism celebrated a past envisioned as an almost Edenic pre-European-contact world. That past served as a source of pride and fundamentally undermined the history lessons taught in schools, in which non-Europeans were perennially marginalized and relegated to secondary roles as backdrops to the stage of European history and civilization.

People of Mexican descent in the United States had, like other people of color, sought to approximate the cultural standards of white Americans, despite whites' overt hostility toward them. From the European standard of beauty to the pride that people took in claiming European ancestry (or denying Indian and African ancestry), Mexican people experienced the psychological effects of racism. In a culture where Spanish ancestry and white skin had benefits, Chicano cultural nationalists insisted that they were a "bronze" people, whose native ancestors built great monuments and civilizations, such as Aztlan. They revered the Aztecs for their cultural and material achievements. Some nationalists even dropped their Spanish names, considered symbols of European imperialism and conquest of the Aztec empire. Like the black nationalist adoration for the empires of ancient Egypt, the Swahili, or West Africa, Chicano nationalists conveniently overlooked the fact that the Aztecs had built their massive empire on the backs of subjugated, exploited, and oppressed victims.

In a political climate that saw black nationalists bicker over the role of cultural and revolutionary nationalism, many Chicano nationalists easily merged the two types. Panthers, self-described enemies of cultural "pork chop" nationalism, were able to influence the Berets significantly in their rhetoric and symbolism without substantively affecting the Berets' position on cultural nationalism. The Berets created titles for their leadership that mirrored the party's: minister of information, minister of defense, minister of education, and prime minister, among others. They also adopted eight points of attention, which listed the BPP's eight points verbatim.[11] In their "13 Point

Program" the Brown Berets made eight of the ten demands in the Panthers' Ten-Point Platform and Program, including "an end to the robbery of our community by the capitalist businessmen," exemptions for all Chicanos from military service, the release of all Chicanos from jails, and the immediate end to police brutality.[12] Though supportive of the Chicano cultural nationalism, the Berets were not tolerant of conservative economic programs couched in the seemingly radical rhetoric of "Chicano Power."

In language reflective of the BPP's leftist politics, the Berets were highly critical of the Chicano pride that sought community development through capitalism. "Many so-called Chicanos leach off the people, just because they are Chicanos. Many times the sign that says 'se habla espanol' [Spanish spoken here] really means, 'come in we'll speak in Spanish and I'll charge you 30% credit charge.'"[13] Still, the Berets and other militant Chicanos celebrated cultural nationalism extensively: "Before we could move the system that oppressed us, we first had to realize our own identity. Because of the cultural and psychological genocide suffered by Chicanos, many of us did not realize our own identity. We called ourselves everything from Spanish to American of Mexican ancestry. Many Chicanos were ashamed of being Mexican or Chicano, because the racist system only showed us as bandits or lazy dumb winos. By bringing the true history of Chicanos to light all of La Raza can be proud of a great culture and history."[14]

Control of the public schools was central to the Berets' effort to realize a more appropriate study of Chicano history and culture. Suffering from high drop-out rates and a school board that appeared indifferent, if not hostile, the Berets worked closely with the "Eastside Blowouts" of March 1968. During these blowouts, nearly ten thousand students in five East Los Angeles high schools walked out of classes, demanding better education and Chicano control of schools. The result was an upsurge in Chicano student and youth militancy across the Southwest. Thousands of high school students walked out in cities in California, Texas, Arizona, and Colorado demanding similar reforms.[15] With the increased activism came new police attention. On June 9, 1968, three months after the initial blowouts, police raided the homes and offices of thirteen Chicano activists, who were arrested on charges of "conspiracy to disrupt the

schools." Los Angeles County district attorney Evelle J. Younger
charged the activists with a felony that could have resulted in prison
sentences of sixty-six years for each person convicted. Seven of the
thirteen who were arrested were Brown Berets, including founder
David Sanchez, who was preparing for his high school prom when
police took him to jail.[16] Although all were acquitted of these charges
after two years of appeals, police harassment continued as the Berets
became more militant in their organization of Chicano youth.
Despite the violent gang epidemic of East Los Angeles, police
devoted more attention, including arrests, surveillance, and man-
hours to disrupt the Berets than any gang in the city.[17]

In May 1969, the Berets opened the East Los Angeles Free Clinic on
Whittier Boulevard to serve poor Chicanos in the area. An expansion
of their activities also included the Chicano Moratorium rally held in
December at Obregon Park, which brought together two thousand
people to protest the Vietnam War and the exorbitant death rate of
Chicano soldiers. The Second Chicano Moratorium rally at Laguna Park
produced five thousand marchers, but it was the Third Chicano Moratorium that would make history as perhaps the largest Chicano rally
ever, when between twenty thousand and thirty thousand people
marched on August 29, 1970.[18]

Despite arrests of their leadership, the bombing of their headquarters,
and factionalism, the Brown Berets continued for two more years until they
disbanded in the fall of 1972. At a press conference that October,
David Sanchez announced that the organization of ninety chapters
and five thousand members would dissolve so as to avoid further disruption of the Chicano Power movement by repressive agents of the
state. Subsequent U.S. congressional hearings on the FBI and
COINTELPRO confirmed that the Brown Berets had been targeted
for neutralization. As the hearings revealed, neutralization included,
at times, extralegal activities such as break-ins, false correspondence,
wiretaps, beatings, and even murder.[19]

For many Chicano activists, the Berets' revolutionary program
invited police attention. Much like activists in the black community,
some nationalists found a more subtle celebration of ethnic nationalism more effective in mobilizing militants. Although they were not
afraid of confrontational language, the cultural nationalist elements of

Chicano Power flowered in the late 1960s and early 1970s, without significant cases of violent police repression.

Corky Gonzales helped spearhead a cultural renaissance through the Chicano Arts movement, which provided a scathing critique of white America and paralleled the Black Arts movement. Gonzales's 1967 epic poem, "I Am Joaquin," became a staple of Chicano reading. Luiz Valdez's Teatro Campesino showcased Chicano talent on stage, while skilled Latino artists painted murals depicting romantic and politicized scenes of Aztlan, the Aztecs, and Mexican and Chicano history. In the realm of music, *corrido*, Chicano soul music, grew popular in barrios throughout the Southwest and California.

Like their black counterparts, Chicano nationalists celebrated a new and dynamic language, replete with political meaning. Writer Jose Montoya produced some of the first Chicano literary pieces that used *calo*, or street slang. This use of calo further rejected the white American cultural standard, as had been the case with black poets who freely bastardized standard English with proud and pervasive usage of black vernacular. Relying heavily on Spanish as a language of Chicano nationalism, militants borrowed from the Black Power movement to create terms such as *Tio Taco* (literally, "Uncle Taco"), "Uncle Tom"; *camales*, "brothers"; and *vendidos*, "sell-outs."

In April 1969 Gonzales spoke at the Youth Liberation Conference in Denver and implored *La Raza* (the race/people) to remove themselves from the clutches of the *gabacho* (honky/whitey) and ground themselves in a world where they are in power. In a strong call for nationalism, the conference adopted a declaration, the "Plan Espiritual de Aztlan (Spiritual Plan of Aztlan)," in which people dedicated their efforts to "reclaiming the land of [our ancestors'] birth and consecrating the determination of our people of the sun." They continued to state that "Aztlan belongs to these who plant the seeds, water the fields and gather the crops and not to the foreign Europeans. We are a bronze people with a bronze culture. We are a nation."[20]

Chicano nationalism adopted its own symbols and ideals that embodied the ethos of self-determination and radicalism. Aztlan, as homeland to Chicanos, affirmed their right to the land where they lived—superceding and rejecting the white nativist exhortation to "go back to where you came from" and dismissing any notion that America was a white man's country. Some activists held placards that read "Aztlan: Love it or Leave it."[21] Chicano cultural nationalism simultaneously undermined the traditional Mexican racial and social hierarchy that made Spanish ancestry a source of pride and privilege. White skin had long symbolized prestige in Mexico, as it had in the United States. Chicano nationalists, however, departed from this paradigm and conspicuously celebrated a "bronze" nation, deriding European foreigners. White Americans had been put into the position of explaining their right to the land in North America. Despite this overt nationalism, as the case with Black Power advocates, Chicano militants did not abandon their rights to public or private institutions controlled by white people. Instead, these nationalists sought to carve out their own space within white-dominated domains. No institutions demonstrated this contest for power more than colleges and universities.

Because of the successes of the civil rights movement, white colleges and universities that had long practiced discriminatory policies to curtail the attendance of students of color experienced a significant increase in minority students by the late 1960s. Black students, inextricably connected to the political climate of their communities, clamored for self-determination through Black Power on campus. The cry for Black Power realized black student unions and black studies programs, as well as more recruitment of black faculty and staff. Beginning in California, Chicano students, who were some of the closest allies of African Americans, also demanded changes in the college curriculum. By 1969, Chicano students had created a popular Chicano Power movement on campuses throughout California and the Southwest.

In 1968 black students at San Francisco State College protested and demonstrated in favor of black studies. Other students of color joined their efforts and formed the Third World Liberation Front (TWLF). The TWLF brought together black, Chicano, and Asian American students for the first time in any major student activism. The demands for black studies evolved to include Chicano/La Raza and Asian American studies as well. The TWLF moved across the bay to the University of California at Berkeley and inspired students there to launch a large, protracted, and militant struggle for curriculum and administration changes.[22]

At Berkeley, long a hotbed of student activism, the massive student strike led by the TWLF began on January 22, 1969, and included five demands:

(1) a Third World College to teach the history and current events of "Third World" people;

(2) the hiring of more people of color by the university at all levels of the administration, from faculty to workers;

(3) the recommendations of a selection committee to be composed of people of color and decisions not based on academic achievement alone;

(4) Third World people's control of all programs affecting Third World people; and

(5) no disciplinary action to be taken against the strikers.

The movement was supported by a clear majority of students of color, where protests often attracted more than fifteen hundred students, half of all students of color at the university. White students eager to assist TWLF efforts formed the White Student Support Committee.[23]

The strike lasted for weeks, until the National Guard, San Jose and San Francisco tactical squads, and more than seven hundred Oakland and Berkeley police were mobilized to put it down. Beatings and mass arrests pushed many students into greater radicalism, while others were discouraged from further action. A state of emergency was declared on campus and on the last day of finals in March 1969, nine weeks of confrontation came to a close. Negotiations and a series of compromises produced the Ethnic Studies Program. This process was more or less duplicated across the country, although the rich mix of ethnic groups was generally a California phenomenon.[24]

Asian American Radicalism

Influenced by the political and cultural climate in their respective communities as well as their involvement in the TWLF, Chicano and Asian American students moved closer to radicalism by 1969. Many

Chicano student organizations were born out of this growing political and cultural consciousness. Between 1968 and 1969, numerous organizations representing Chicano students emerged on college campuses in California and the Southwest: Mexican-American Students (MAS), Mexican-American Students Confederation (MASC), Mexican-American Youth Organization (MAYO), Mexican-American Youth Association (MAYA), and United Mexican-American Students (UMAS). The Movimiento Estudiantil Chicano de Aztlan (MECHA) was formed at a conference in October 1969 with a hundred students, scholars, and activists, who envisioned a unified plan to work for the benefit of Chicano students on college campuses.[25] Throughout the region, MECHA organized—often in alliances with African and Asian Americans—for Chicano and ethnic studies programs.

Chicano students, as well as blacks and Asians, created student newspapers that brought attention to current events in their respective ethnic communities—college and otherwise. Such papers reported favorable coverage of the Chicano student movement while denouncing the "gabacho system" and the racism of their "gringo fellow students." Although the Black Power movement influenced them, Chicano student activists were not without conflict with Black Power advocates. In 1970, Stanford University's MECHA chapter submitted a budget of $20,395 for the 1970–71 academic year, but disgruntled Chicano students complained that, "a coalition between conservatives and blacks has offered MECHA a token $5,800 in an attempt to buy us out." The university's Chicano student paper, *Chicanismo*, denounced the "gringos and their lackeys on this campus."[26] The struggle for resources college administrations earmarked for minority students would cause similar spats on other campuses in the state. Still, the occasional friction was overshadowed by the alliances and unity black and Chicano students celebrated. In the same issue in which it condemned black "lackeys," *Chicanismo* found inspiration in the words of black nationalists. Quoting Stokely Carmichael, the paper declared that, "integration is a euphemism for white supremacy." The paper also quoted Black Panther Eldridge Cleaver and found power in the unifying term "Third World people," which included people whose ancestors were from Africa, Asia, and Latin America.[27]

The creation of the TWLF in the Bay Area mobilized and inspired thousands of Asian American students, as it had other students of color and many whites. Berkeley's Asian Student newspaper provided a history of the Asian Student Movement and acknowledged the influence that black students brought to the college arena. "Our black brothers and sisters were the first to cry out in protest in the civil rights movement and were the first to make militant radical demands for the transformation of society. Out of this grew the Asian Student Movement."[28]

Like other people of color, Asians in the United States had long experienced virulent and legally sanctioned racism. Some groups even petitioned the courts for legal status as "whites" in order to avoid the systemic oppression they experienced. They were unsuccessful.[29]

Influenced by the cultural and political currents of black national-ism and Black Power, Asian American militants found themselves consciously transforming the public image of their panethnic "nation." Rejecting the stereotype of the timid, obsequious, and quiet Oriental, young Asian American militants affirmed them-selves as radical harbingers of progress who were no longer enam-ored of whiteness. In 1968 the Asian American Political Alliance (AAPA) was formed at Berkeley and for the first time brought together disparate ethnic groups of Asian students. Richard Aoki, a Japanese American raised in West Oakland, joined the Black Pan-ther Party while at Merritt College with Huey Newton and Bobby Seale. He later joined the AAPA after transferring to Berkeley. Aoki, a field marshal for the Panthers, explains that he "went underground to look into the Asian Movement to see if we could develop an Asian version of the BPP." Aoki soon became the spokesperson for the AAPA. The AAPA developed close ties with the BPP and the Red Guard, an Asian American organization mod-eled after the Panthers.[30] They often co-sponsored demonstrations and panels calling for justice for the Panthers and an end to "the pig repression of the Vanguard Party." With some members donning berets and sunglasses, the AAPA organized students around issues related to both the university and nonuniversity communities. As Vicci Wong, founding member of AAPA notes, "It wasn't just a local thing or just for our little group in college. We identified with the struggles that were going on then. We fought harder because we didn't see it as just our own fight."[31]

Students demanded more faculty and students of color, as well as an end to the Vietnam War, police brutality, and the exploitation of Asian farmworkers. The Berkeley AAPA worked with a growing number of visible Asian American student leaders in the state, such as Jack Wong, a student activist at the University of California at Santa Barbara. These student activists called for more Asian American representation in college administrations, but they also put the politics of these Asian Americans under heavy scrutiny. Asian ancestry was not enough for AAPA support. Wong called the Japanese American acting president of San Francisco State College a "tool of the white power establishment" for resisting demands of the TWLF. Not satisfied with simply calling President Hayakawa an Uncle Tom, Wong and others also called him an "Uncle Charlie," derived from the Charlie Chan detective series.[32] That a Japanese American was derided by using a term derived from a Chinese character also demonstrates that race transcended ethnicity among these student activists. It was clear that the younger generation of Asian Americans had made a break with their parents' popular image as tolerant, apologetic, and meek "permanent foreigners," unwilling to jeopardize their pursuit of white acceptance by complaining too much. As the AAPA declared: "We Asian Americans believe that heretofore we have been relating to white standards of acceptability, and affirm the right of self-definition and self-determination. We Asian Americans support all non-white liberation movements and believe that all minorities in order to be truly liberated must have complete control over the political, economical and educational institutions within their respective communities."[33]

Dedicated to the mission of strong community ties beyond academia, Berkeley students traveled to Agbayni Village, a poor rural California retirement community for farmworkers, half of whom were Filipino men. These elderly were typically without a family and alone. Students provided development work and petitioned for farmworker rights.[34] In 1973 the Asian Student Union formed a community committee responsible for developing student support for issues in Chinatown, Manilatown, and Japantown. Often considered less audacious with their radical politics than their white, black, or Latino counterparts, Asian student activists were visible in the political discourse of the era, particularly on the West Coast. They provided films and sponsored panels on socialism, the Chinese Revolution, and class struggle, as well as antiwar activities. The relations between campus militancy and community militancy were as inextricable in Asian American communities as they were in Chicano and black communities.[35]

Asian Americans were forming radical organizations outside of academia as well. The most visible organization was the Red Guard, which grew out of the Bay Area's dynamic political and cultural climate. Named after Mao Tse-tung's unit of young revolutionaries who burned the property of capitalists and counterrevolutionaries during the Chinese Cultural Revolution, the Red Guard was founded in 1969 in San Francisco. Like the Berets, the Red Guard saw the Panthers as an example of radical resistance to racial and class oppression. Armed, the Red Guard openly declared itself a communist organization, a bold move in Chinatown. Fully aware of the incredible taboo against radical leftist political activity in the Chinese American community, the group initiated a series of projects to meet the people's basic needs. It was able to prevent the closing of a tuberculosis-testing center in Chinatown, exposing the fact that the TB rate in the city's Chinatown was the one of the highest in the country. It also worked with the Asian Legal Services and had a thousand cases of people who resisted the draft, via the Asian American Draft Help Center. The Breakfast for Children program chiefly fed black children from public housing projects in or around Chinatown. The program was modified to feed poor elderly, which attracted many Asian senior citizens.[36]

While the Red Guard saw itself as a Chinese American version of the Black Panther Party, it was also very well aware that the dynamics of the black and Chinese American communities were different. Alex Hing, a Red Guard cofounder who assumed the title minister of information (one of several titles that mirrored those in the BPP) explains that "we tried to model ourselves after the Panthers. When it didn't work, we gave it our own characteristics." To that end, the Guard hoped to serve the people in the same manner the Panthers had, but it also had a strong political and cultural affinity to Asia and was particularly concerned about China's role in global affairs. Moreover, the Guard understood Chinese American anxiety over the tenuous status of Chinese as American citizens. Only in 1965 did the U.S. government lift its more than seventy-year immigration restriction on Chinese. By campaigning for U.S. recognition of Beijing, the Guard demonstrated its political and cultural identification with mainland China; it also invited repression by the FBI and CIA.

The Red Guard's activities, which included efforts to seat China at the United Nations, were firmly connected to the larger leftist community, which proved to be of serious concern for U.S. foreign policy during the cold war. Leftists, influenced by the rapidly changing geopolitical landscape, increasingly assumed the mantle of radicalism in the contextual framework of anti-imperialism. Anti-imperialism had a profound resonance among radicals who were self-described "Third World People." This term declared their affinity with the struggles of people in Africa, Asia, and Latin America. It also postulated that "internal colonialism" was the mechanism by which people of color were subjugated in the United States. This rhetoric invariably found considerable coverage in the press of both communist and capitalist countries.

International news coverage reported on the plight of black people in the United States to millions worldwide and even influenced radicals overseas. The urban rebellions, shoot-outs with police, assassinations, and student upheaval were reported in countries that the United States considered friendly as well as in those it considered hostile, which caused headaches for the State Department. For communist countries, the social and political unrest in the United States indicated the inherent contradictions of a capitalist and imperialist society. Following the assassination of Martin Luther King Jr. in 1968, Mao Tse-tung led hundreds of thousands of Chinese demonstrators to denounce white supremacy in America. Mao was certainly not alone. Fidel Castro, president of Cuba, and other leaders of socialist countries eagerly exploited the news of civil unrest to denounce the United States and its subjugation of black people. The militant struggle of black people received more international media attention as the collective efforts of Black Power advocates provided a subtext to the American cold war dichotomy of "democracy" versus "communism." This was, of course, a false dichotomy that assumed that the United States

was pro-democracy when it was actually pro-capitalism. As it demonstrated in its friendly foreign relations with Zaire, Haiti, South Africa,
Rhodesia, and dozens of other undemocratic states, capitalism was
more favorable than democracy for U.S. foreign policy makers.

For many international observers, the intensification of violent
clashes between Black Panthers and the police through 1969 made
the party the rightful revolutionary vanguard of the country's
bourgeoning left. Communist countries North Korea and China
issued favorable statements regarding the Panthers by 1969. In 1970,
the International Section of the Black Panther Party, led by Eldridge
Cleaver, established an "embassy" in North Korea. David Hilliard,
Panther chief of staff, requested representation from the Red Guard
for the eleven-member trip to North Korea. Alex Hing joined
Hilliard and others in visits to North Korea, Vietnam, and Algeria.
As the Red Guard enjoyed international press and greater visibility,
police harassment led to a steady decline in members.[37]

Like other radical organizations of the era, the Red Guard attracted
a youthful membership, peaking with about two hundred members
before police repression reduced it to a few dozen. Their uniforms,
which included army field jackets and red berets, were instant targets for
the police. Red Guard members complained about systematic police
harassment and their offices were constantly raided, often without sufficient pretense. In a cold war climate of fierce anticommunism, the FBI
and CIA were eager to undermine the Red Guard and the Panthers
for their domestic and international political activism. With joint
efforts between federal and local law enforcement agencies, the Red
Guard experienced significant challenges from police and the intelligence community, leaving the organization moribund by 1971.[38]

Unlike the Panthers, the Red Guard avoided the Custer-like defenses
of their office during police raids, despite one armed standoff that a
member had with police. A March 1969 issue of the Red Guard paper
states that four "pigs" arrested Tyrone Won who was leaving Red Guard
headquarters with a disassembled rifle. Later, while released on parole,
Won joined a Black Panther who was also fleeing police and escaped
to Mexico where they hijacked a plane for Cuba. In 1971 members
decided to disband the Red Guard. Most joined other Asian American

leftist organizations, particularly I Wor Kuen, a New York-based organization that had become national by the early 1970s.[39]

Founded in 1969, the I Wor Kuen (IWK) was named after a secret society of Chinese rebels who tried to expel Westerners from China and dispose the Qing dynasty beginning in 1895. Called "Boxers" in the West, the I Wor Kuen attacked Westerners and Western influence in China, evoking outrage from the West, which eventually repressed what became known as the Boxer rebellion. In the United States, Yu Han and Yu Man, two graduate students from mainland China, led the IWK. The IWK was an extension of the radical ethnic nationalist discourse of the era. It was a Maoist organization that was ideologically modified to adapt to the highly racialized climate of the United States, while simultaneously adhering to the class-centered language of Maoism and Marxism. As former member Lee Lew-Lee explains, "the IWK was like the Black Panther Party, the Young Lords and the Red Guards" and was "patterned after the Red Guards." Like other militant groups, the IWK hoped to form an essential vanguard in its ethnic community to mobilize its people for a class-based revolution that would destroy racial and class oppression. Synthesizing theories of class struggle from Frantz Fanon, Mao, Lenin, and Marx, as well as the ever-dynamic Panthers, the IWK considered U.S. Chinatowns to be internal colonies. Neocolonialism provided them with a sound explanation of the system of oppression that exploited Chinese Americans and other people of color in the United States.[40]

Although attempting to organize the Asian American community, the IWK, like the Red Guard, was confronted by deep-seated hostility from Chinese Americans who rejected communist China and thought that leftist activities would reflect negatively on the Asian American community at large. Hoping to protect the Asian American community against any police state repression or future attempts to relocate citizens into internment camps, the IWK maintained a largely marginal voice in Asian American political discourse, despite its growth, which allowed it to work closely with the Red Guard and eventually absorb many of its remaining members. In 1975 it merged with the predominately Chicano August 29th Movement to form the League of Revolutionary Struggle.[41]

Whereas the Red Guard, AAPA, and IWK pulled heavily from the college-educated middle class, the Yellow Brotherhood (YB), a Los Angeles-based organization that emerged in 1969, like the Panthers attracted many "brothers off the block." Formed out of a nexus of political militancy, ethnic pride, and general social pathos, the YB was the first radical Asian organization of young militants in the city. It comprised former gang members, ex-convicts, and ex-servicemen. Many were Nisei and Sansei—second and third generation Japanese Americans—who were unnerved by the political reticence that seemed to characterize their communities, particularly in an age when other ethnic groups had galvanized around radical ethnic nationalism. Speaking about their parents, one former YB member states that "they're hypersensitive or hyperapologetic. We [younger generation] picked up some of that." According to another, "That is why the Yellow Brotherhood was so controversial. We weren't hyperapologetic." As many Japanese Americans were instructed to resist racism by seeking white approval through cultural assimilation, the YB joined the chorus of black cultural nationalists that vilified assimilation with whites. "We were told to outwhite the whites and groups like the YB ... said 'Fuck the whites. Fuck that shit.'" The time had come for radical political organization in the Asian American community, but for Guy Kurose, it was initially an uphill battle he was not willing to wage.

Guy Kurose, a Japanese American, joined the Seattle branch of the Black Panther Party at age sixteen. Raised in the black community, he naturally gravitated to Black Power with his friends. "I ... listened to [James Brown singing] 'Say it loud, I'm black and I'm proud.' I wanted to be there too." However, unable to fully extricate himself from socially dysfunctional behavior, Kurose, like many other Panthers, carried his lumpen life into the party. "I was a renegade Panther. We were what Bobby Seale called 'jackanapes,' kids that had good intentions but were relating strongly to hoodlumism." Deeply involved with the Black Power movement, Kurose was unaware of any community of young Asian revolutionaries until a visit from Mo Nishida, Victor Shibata, and Warren Furutani from California. His immediate reaction: "I don't need to talk to no Japanese motherfucker who thinks he's white, man." He stayed in the BPP until he entered college, where he joined the Asian Student

Coalition and carried over the radicalism that he had learned in the Panthers, even fighting police on campus.[42]

Kurose later moved to Los Angeles where he worked closely with other Asian radicals in leftist groups such as the Yellow Brotherhood, Joint Communications, and the Asian American Hardcore. While the Yellow Brotherhood pulled heavily from nonacademics, like the Panthers, it also struggled over jackanape activities. Los Angeles had a serious gang presence that extended into the Asian American community. Gangs such as the Ministers, Shokashus, and Constituents became politicized in the late 1960s, as had gangs in the black community, but as YB member Art Ishii noted, "Gangsters don't give a shit about Red Books." The YB challenged the pervasive notion of Asian meekness, yet simultaneously struggled with self-destructive tendencies. Former members take pride in being the "first ones talking shit and kicking ass" but admit that they were marginalized by the larger Asian American community in ways not experienced by black nationalists in their communities. However, this alienation did not stop other militant, street-based Asian organizations from developing.

The Asian American Hardcore, like the Yellow Brotherhood, attracted former junkies, gang members, and convicts. Mo Nishida, a former member, explains that the Hardcore grew out of the tumultuous political and cultural climate of the Black Power movement in general and the Black Panthers in particular. "I think that the idea was percolating around because of the notoriety of the Panthers.... When the Panthers came forward, the idea of trying to get some of our people back from the other side of capitalism came up, so some of us talked about needing to form a group like that. With the Panthers as a model, we could serve the people."[43] The Hardcore established an office on 23rd and Vermont Avenue and began detoxification programs for drug addicts, as well as a political education class, Christmas programs for the poor, and other programs for the elderly. The group, taking a sartorial cue from the Panthers, as others had, wore fatigues and red berets as part of their uniform. Clearly the Panthers loomed large for the small band of revolutionaries in Los Angeles. Members of the Hardcore met with Panthers, including national leaders like Eldridge Cleaver and Bobby Seale. Yet, as Nishida says, "We were small potatoes compared to those guys ... but we never felt that way." Like many self-described revolutionaries of the period, members of the Hard-core believed that the revolution was imminent and that the Panthers would be its vanguard party. "The Panther Party was the basic acknowledged leadership in the Revolutionary Nationalist Movement. They set the whole stage." When the FBI unleashed its unprecedented repression, in concert with local police, the Panthers were decimated as no organization in twentieth-century U.S. history had been. "After the Panthers got wasted by COINTEL-PRO ... there was disillusionment about the political line of the Pan-thers." Nishida explains that despite the Panthers' revolutionary posture, "when they couldn't respond to the killings by the police, it [screwed] everybody's mind up."[44]

After the revolutionary, gun-toting posturing of the Panthers evoked the deadly wrath of the government, many members of the Asian American Hardcore moved into other arenas of political dis-course, no longer desirous of following the Panther line, in toto. As community-based organizations with strong ties to the street, the Yel-low Brotherhood and Asian American Hardcore turned stereotypes of Asian Americans on their ears. Asian-descended young people rejected the term *Oriental* in the late 1960s and embraced a Pan-Asian term for the first time: Asian American. Many organized around a simple Asian identity, unlike the typically nationality-based organizations before the late 1960s, such as the Japanese American Citizens League or the Chinese American Citizens Alliance. Affected by Black Power, they promoted the slogan "Yellow Power" and raised the clenched fist in union with other "Third World People" on college campuses and in streets across the country. While they avoided the type of deadly conflict with law enforcement agencies the Panthers experienced, they offered material and moral support to the Black Panther Party, as well as a scathing critique of the political, social, and economic systems that converged to undermine the Panthers and others.

Native American Ethnic Nationalism

The smallest minority group in the United States, Native Americans, like other people of color, found great inspiration in the examples of radical ethnic nationalism in the Black Power movement. Like Asian

Americans, many Indian ethnic groups organized around narrow ethnic identities until the 1960s where a pan-Indian consciousness was forged in a new and militant effort, the Red Power movement. The general circumstances that led to radical ethnic nationalism were identical to that of other minority groups. Native Americans long suffered under blatant and brutal forms of white supremacy. Killed by wars and disease, displaced from their lands, forced into reservations, Native Americans had by 1970 become the ethnic group with the lowest standard of living in the United States. Rates of alcoholism, high school dropout, unemployment, and death were higher for them than for any other group in the country. Indian teenagers' suicide rate was one hundred times that of whites.[45]

In the mid-1960s the Black Power movement had impressed Clyde Warrior, a Cherokee college student, who envisioned pan-Indian nationalism modeled after SNCC. Warrior helped form the National Indian Youth Council (NIYC) and pushed "red power" in its newspaper, *ABC: Americans before Columbus.*[46] Informed by the new militancy of young people, the NIYC helped spread the message of new activism on college campuses nationwide, providing suffuse radical analysis of Indian political, social, and cultural concerns. The general mood of militancy continued to grow, and Dennis Banks and George Mitchell in Minneapolis founded the American Indian Movement (AIM) in 1968. As Ward Churchill and Jim Vander Wall explain, the Black Panther Party loomed large for Banks and Mitchell. "[AIM] was self-consciously patterned after the Black Panther Party's community self-defense model pioneered by Huey P. Newton and Bobby Seale two years previously in Oakland."[47] In fact, like the Panthers, AIM's first major project, the Minneapolis AIM Patrol, was designed to end police brutality. Like the Brown Berets and others, AIM formed a platform that was influenced by the Panthers, although AIM's twenty-point platform was less dependent on the Panther's platform and program.[48]

Other Native American activists had begun to rely on media-attracting protests such as the occupation of Alcatraz Island in San Francisco Bay. In November 1969 an ad hoc group, Indians of All Tribes, landed on Alcatraz, claiming it "by right of discovery." Two weeks later more people arrived. Reflecting the ubiquitous aim of ethnic nationalists, the protesters announced that "the Indians of Alcatraz want self-determination for all native Americans." Hoping to be "fair and honorable" in their relations with white inhabitants, the new arrivals announced that they planned to "purchase said Alcatraz for twenty-four (24) dollars in glass beads and red cloth, a precedent set by the white man's purchase of a similar island about 300 years ago."[49] The reference to the purchase of Manhattan by Europeans in the seventeenth century reflects the pan-Indian consciousness and new ethnic nationalism that relied on common historical myth and the promotion of a general historical experience that textured the collective consciousness of national identity. This process of pan-ethnic nationality formation was bolstered by the rhetoric of the late 1960s. The new occupants of Alcatraz also demanded "RED POWER to Red People!" Not to be out of step with the larger ethnic nationalist movement, they also insisted that along with red power, there must be "Black, Brown, Yellow and white [power] also." At bottom, they argued that they wanted "All power to the people."[50]

By 1970 AIM had become a national organization and generated considerable media and police attention. The FBI began a rigorous campaign to circumscribe its development, although AIM continued to find larger audiences and sympathy across racial lines, particularly on college campuses. In 1970 the Native American Student Association was founded at the University of California at Berkeley and worked in alliances with MECHA, the Students for a Democratic Society (SDS), and the Black Student Union. Vernon Bellcourt, executive director of AIM, spoke on campus in March 1973 and helped raise funds for Indian children and denounced police harassment of AIM.[51] That same month, U.S. military units, as well as local authorities, interrupted an AIM occupation of Wounded Knee, South Dakota. After a standoff that lasted seventy-one days, two FBI agents and five Native Americans were killed; several more were wounded.[52]

Several AIM members were arrested as a result of the Wounded Knee conflict. Yet despite the violent conflict with law enforcement agencies, AIM alone remained one of a few radical ethnic nationalist organizations of the late 1960s that survived into the 1980s and beyond. Chapters expanded throughout the country and continued to sponsor community development programs aimed at satisfying the political, social, and cultural needs of Native Americans, engendering a more popular base of support as the militant rhetoric subsided.

Puerto Rican Nationalism

Jose "Cha Cha" Jimenez, a leader of the Puerto Rican Young Lords street gang in Chicago, grew more affected by the civil rights movement and the rhetoric of Black Power by 1968. Jimenez brought new members into the organization and began developing community programs such as a community summer picnic, a drug education program, and a Christmas giveaway of food and toys for impoverished people in the Puerto Rican community. The Lords even began dialogue with the largest street gang in the country, the notorious Black Stone Rangers, and cosponsored a "Month of Soul Dances" with them.[53] While these efforts impressed many liberals, Illinois deputy chairman Fred Hampton and the local Panthers hoped to make the Lords into revolutionaries.

In accordance with the party's theories of class, the Panthers viewed the politicization of the Young Lords as an essential process in the political transformation of the country's internal colonies. The urban rebellions that often included the poorest and most maligned elements in the community were the precursors to revolution. The lumpen had guns and were not afraid to use them. Unfortunately, they were not yet politically sophisticated enough to aim in the direction of the "pig power structure" more frequently. These rebellions, insisted Huey Newton, were "sporadic, short-lived, and costly in violence against the people." The task of the Panthers was clear: "The Vanguard Party must provide leadership for the people. It must teach correct strategic methods of prolonged resistance through literature and activities. If the activities of the Party are respected by the people, the people will follow the example."[54] The efforts of the Lords and the Rangers indicated a political transformation that could make them into agents of liberation and harbingers of freedom, justice, and power for the people.

As Hampton began negotiating with Jeff Fort, leader of the Black Stone Rangers, he also met with Jimenez, who was warmer to the idea of revolution than Fort had been. Impressed with the bold and brash militancy that characterized the Panthers, Jimenez envisioned a

Puerto Rican revolutionary organization to realize liberation for Puerto Ricans on the island and in the mainland. The Young Lords began to realize that they had been acting more like social workers by only addressing the symptoms and not the causes of social illness. Like African American gangs, the Lords became critical of their street violence. They initiated a peace treaty with virtually all of their former enemies and advised them to cease the fighting against each other but address anger "against the capitalist institutions that are oppressing us." The Latin Kings, the city's largest Latino gang, began to organize as well, even opening a breakfast program for children. By 1969, the Young Lords had officially joined in a pact with the Panthers and the Young Patriots, a gang of white Appalachian youths from the city's Uptown section on the North Side.[55]

In this new "Rainbow Coalition," the Lords and Patriots dutifully modeled themselves after the Black Panther Party. In their respective communities, the Lords and Patriots held political education classes, sponsored free breakfast programs for poor children, and monitored police activities in an attempt to curb police brutality. They created an organizational structure that reflected Panther influence, which included ministers of information, defense, education and a central committee with field marshals. The Patriots developed an Eleven-Point Program and Platform that borrowed heavily from the Panthers, as did the Lords' Thirteen-Point Program and Platform.[56] All three organizations sponsored events together, providing joint speakers and joint security. It seemed odd for some black nationalists to see Fred Hampton give a typically awe-inspiring speech on revolutionary struggle, while white men wearing berets, sunglasses, and Confederate rebel flags sewn into their jackets helped provide security for him.

The Patriots, led by a seminary student named Preacherman, were quick to denounce racism, despite their proud display of Confederate flags. "We believe that to fight only for the interests of your close cultural brothers and sisters is not in the interest of all the people, and in fact perpetuates racism. We understand the struggle is a class struggle. All power to the poor and working people!"[57] While the Patriots followed the Panther line, which denounced cultural nationalism, they embraced subtle traces of it in their group symbolism (much like the Panthers themselves). The Patriots' tolerance of cultural nationalism was demonstrated in the celebration of their Appalachian and southern heritage. Poor white southern migrants had come to Chicago, as had thousands of poor blacks and Puerto Ricans, and despite their whiteness, experienced ridicule from other whites for their southern drawl and provincial proclivities. Their poor rural background was a source of shame for many who grew up in poor white areas in the city. Joining with the Panthers and Lords, the Patriots were able to bond with blacks and Latinos in class terms in ways that the Students for a Democratic Society or most other white radicals could not.[58]

Just as Chicanos, and African and Asian Americans rejected the cultural orthodoxy that idealized the white American middle-class standard, the Patriots celebrated their poor white southern roots. The Confederate flag was a reminder and symbol of their incessant class struggle. The Patriots found pride in maintaining an affinity for their southern background and found no incongruence in identifying with antiracism and the flag of the blatantly white supremacist Confederacy. The Patriots created a radicalism that found strength and cultural grounding in an odd mix of symbols and rhetoric. At bottom, the Patriots found their radical ethnic nationalism in the glorification of a poor southern white ethos that jettisoned the racism that typified the white South. This was done in the interest of a radical activist ideology that transcended race but did not ignore the centrality of race to political struggle. There were several other white groups that found the Panthers a model for radical struggle; however, the Patriots were the only ones who created a conspicuous radical ethnic nationalism.[59]

By 1969, the Young Patriots and Young Lords were becoming nationally known through their Rainbow Coalition, which was featured in articles in the *Black Panther* and other alternative newspapers. Also that year, the coalition sent representatives to the annual convention of the SDS, where Joe Martinez, an SDS member from Florida, met with Young Lords founders and was granted permission to start a branch in New York.

In New York, Puerto Rican nationalism was still growing. In the context of the militant student protests, some students at City College formed the Sociedad de Albizu Campos (SAC) in early 1969 to bring together the militancy of college radicals with that of the ghetto. In a struggle to bridge the chasm between unorganized street militancy and that of the college campus, community-based activists, Pablo "Yoruba" Guzman and David Perez joined SAC and became the links to the ghetto that the organization desired. Yoruba, with an Afro and dark skin, had a strong cultural nationalist affinity to both Africa and Puerto Rico. Perez, who was born in Puerto Rico and raised in Chicago, had involved himself in radical politics before moving to New York. SAC members were reading the *Black Panther* newspaper regularly and learned of Fred Hampton's Rainbow Coalition. After merging with other local Puerto Rican activist organizations, SAC met with Martinez and on July 26, 1969, a coalition was formed that became the New York State Chapter of the Young Lords Organization.[60]

The Young Lords from New York spread to several cities along the East Coast, including Philadelphia, Newark, and Bridgeport, Connecticut. Within weeks, the Lords captured headlines. In agreement with the Panther dictum to serve the people by meeting their basic needs, Lords asked local residents what they wanted. People informed the Lords that they wanted cleaner streets. The Lords swept streets in Spanish Harlem and put trash in piles in the middle of the street, demanding that the city pay more attention to the barrio. The images of radicals working for the people impressed many who eagerly joined the fledgling organization.[61] A hundred men and women took over Lincoln Hospital on July 17, 1970, to protest inadequate health care for the poor and neglect from the city government. Though the protesters were expelled by the police, the act brought attention to insufficient medical care in poor communities. The mayor of New York, John Lindsay, promised community activists that the city would build a new hospital on East 149th Street to replace the dilapidated Lincoln. The new hospital opened in 1976.[62]

Adherents of Puerto Rican independence, the Young Lords denounced the cardinal "three evils" of revolutionary nationalists: capitalism, racism, and imperialism. They sponsored free breakfast, drug detoxification, and garbage clean-up programs in several states. Their activities were numerous in every major Puerto Rican community. They brought attention to police brutality, worked closely with students on college and high school campuses, and even found success organizing in prisons. During the Attica Prison uprising in September 1971, insurgents issued a list of more than twenty demands to prison officials, including a request for the Young Lords and the Black Panthers to serve as observers and advisers. In many cities, Lords worked in alliances with Black Power advocates and helped realize more community control of police, political reform, and political mobilization for poor and working-class people. Like the Brown Berets, the Young Lords were able to work with organizations openly hostile to the Black Panthers, despite their official pact with the party. In the early 1970s the Young Lords in Newark, New Jersey, established an alliance with the Committee for a Unified Newark, led by Amiri Baraka, a leading cultural nationalist.[63]

The Young Lords and other revolutionary nationalist organizations saw how various communities of color in the United States provided cheap labor and resources for capitalists. Influenced by a theoretical rubric of racism, the capitalists found cheap, expendable labor that provided for improved quality of life for whites by expanding the white middle-class considerably. Increased numbers of people of color in urban areas allowed working-class whites to assume higher socioeconomic status. Because racism was very real, working-class whites, often beholden to white supremacy, refused out of ignorance and cultural tradition to consider the affinities they shared with working-class people of color. The Young Patriots hoped to demonstrate that working-class and poor whites could be mobilized and follow a revolutionary program led by a black organization, but whereas the Patriots, Rising Up Angry, and White Panthers of Michigan modeled themselves after the Black Panther Party, the party and Black Power had a special resonance for radicals of color.

Class exploitation was a major concern for leftists; however, the highly racialized climate of the United States made interracial political organization difficult, particularly with working-class whites, considered by many people of color to be a more overt and crude group of racists than the capitalist class. Moreover, the U.S. tradition of class exploitation was significantly bolstered by white supremacy, which had profound psychological and cultural ramifications.[64] People of color who were involved in the era's leftist liberation

movements were committed to liberate themselves along class and
cultural lines simultaneously.

There was a particular appeal that made the Panthers a model for
many young people of color longing for an end to the racial oppression they had endured. Without doubt, the Black Panthers'
machismo cool typified a revolutionary chic that prompted many to
imitate the party. Like black people, other people of color had long
languished under a system of racial domination that dehumanized,
marginalized, and exploited nonwhites. For men of color, the dehumanization included emasculation, thereby fomenting a hypermasculinity in the age of radical ethnic nationalism.

For Chicanos, the situation was similar. Francisco Ramos, a Brown
Beret, exclaimed that "there is a new breed of Mexican who is getting
tired and angry and frustrated and will no longer ask for tomorrow;
we want it now. We don't want to ride at the back of the bus; we want
to drive it and own it if possible."[65] There was also a clear masculine
emphasis that ran through Chicano power, similar to the language of
Black Power proponents. Chicano students in California warned that
they would vigorously resist the "emasculation" of Chicanos. Others
wrote poetry to liberating Chicano manhood.

> Until yesterday you called me a good Chicano ... I was meek,
> humble, god-damned ignorant.
> I was young, passive. I was a good american.
> I licked the hand that fed me crumbs.
> However, in transition, a new Chicano has emerged from the
> despair:
> A man—re-born a man, has learned to stand up, bear the burden of
> his people on his back.
> I—no longer dead. I—alive. See my people rising, my peasant blood
> sings with pride.
> See my people refuse to bend, prostitutes for an angle dog.
> See a multitude of clenched fists, casting off shackles of death.
> See brothers join hand in hand, muscular and strong, march before
> the sun.[66]

With strong male-centered language, ethnic nationalists attempted
to forge a new identity as "liberated" men. Despite the rhetoric that

celebrated masculinity, largely rendering women invisible, challenges to this patriarchal discourse did not materialize during the earliest years of the ethnic nationalist movement. Women in the Brown Berets were active in all of the group's functions, which included military drills and protests; however, their role remained largely secondary. Women wrote for the organization's newspaper, *La Causa,* but rarely did their articles focus on sexism within society at large or within the Berets in particular. The liberation of La Raza was considered the primary focus, while women's liberation was often viewed as a white women's movement. In 1969–1970 Grace Reyes, a writer for *La Causa,* wrote on subjects of particular concern to women. The birth control pill was an issue that had special significance for women, who could more effectively choose when to give birth. In general, feminists viewed the pill as favorable for women, but like many black nationalists, Reyes saw the pill as an insidious attempt to curb the birth rate of people of color, not as empowering to women.[67] By 1971 Chicano feminism emerged with demands to move women to the center of Beret activities. In a *La Causa* article, one writer complained that Chicanas had been active in all of the group's functions, but their roles in the organization's leadership were peripheral. Women were simply "working for the Beret guys" and not realizing their complete talents and skills.[68]

Women insisted that a successful revolution "must have full involvement from both Chicanos and Chicanas." Not to be confused with the growing Women's Liberation Movement, they declared that "we're not talking about women's liberation because, like that's not ours. That's a white thing. We're talking about our Raza's liberation." Although Chicanas voiced their frustrations via the Berets' official organ, the recalcitrant male leadership made no substantive changes to the organization's relationship with women.[69] A similar movement to challenge patriarchy occurred within the Young Lords, resulting in very different reactions.

By 1970 the Young Lords Organization became the Young Lords Party and launched its bilingual paper *Palante!* in May 1970. Articles in *Palante!* expressed the revolutionary zeal that characterized the organization. Like the *Black Panther* and *La Causa, Palante!* reflected the hypermasculinity of the Puerto Rican nationalist movement.

Moreover, the organization relegated women to peripheral roles in leadership, despite a general policy that granted all members access to all organizational activities. By 1970 a women's caucus was formed and began to meet weekly. Female members shared stories of confronting the sexism of their comrades on a regular basis. The women's caucus issued demands to the central committee for an end to sexual discrimination and full inclusion of women in the Lords' leadership. The all-male leadership reacted swiftly by promoting Denise Oliver and Gloria Fontanez to the central committee. The Lords also adopted a new slogan, "Abajo con Machismo!" (Down with Machismo!), which appeared in the newspaper and other official releases. They also made changes to the party's thirteen-point program to include denouncing sexism as point number five: "Puerto Rican women will be neither behind nor in front of their brothers but always alongside them in mutual respect and love."[70] For many members of the Young Lords, the effort to denounce sexism was an inevitable step in the movement toward liberation.

Some have argued that the Black Power movement was a particularly sexist phenomenon. It clearly lionized black men as macho leaders, fighters, and defenders of black people. The bravado, militant rhetoric, and general character of Black Power were decidedly male-oriented. While Black Power advocates and Latino ethnic nationalists used hyperbolic language to articulate their politics, it must be acknowledged that it was the Black Panther Party that was the first major black organization to align itself with the women's liberation movement as well as the gay liberation movement. The Panthers also denounced sexism on several occasions and appointed women to key leadership positions. By 1973 the chairperson of the party was a woman. The Young Lords similarly accepted the challenge to transcend the narrow confines of patriarchy and made substantive changes to their organization's rhetoric and style. Clearly, the liberation of a nation could not tolerate the oppression of its half.

There was no particular formula or model for ethnic nationalists to respond to sexism. Latino, white, and black Americans all lived in a patriarchal culture that openly advocated male domination. Mainstream black and Latino organizations reflected patriarchal traditions without considerable challenges and upheaval. It was the passion for total liberation that raised the expectations of struggle for many radical ethnic nationalists. Despite their criticism of the white-oriented women's movement, radical ethnic nationalists were aware that women's liberation was intrinsic to national liberation. Some, like the Brown Berets, were less successful than the Lords or Panthers in denouncing sexism.

Similar to the process of psychological oppression experienced by African Americans who lived in a virulently antiblack world, other people of color had to resist the culturally hegemonic forces of white supremacy as well as the de facto policies that discriminated against them. In this rejection of the cultural orthodox there emerged the opportunity to criticize and transform traditional gender roles. Not all ethnic nationalist organizations were as responsive to the challenges to patriarchy as the Panthers and Lords, who were not fully successful in realizing their goals to destroy sexism within their organizations. But the efforts to confront sexism in a very explicit way reflected the ability of the organizations to adapt, grow, and evolve in ways that many so-called mainstream organizations had not. It was their willingness to consider new challenges and ideas that made these ethnic nationalist organizations attractive to young people. In addition, the new militant ethnic pride drew many young people into the movement.

As they rejected terms such as *Negro, Oriental,* and *Spanish,* blacks, Asians, and Chicanos conspicuously celebrated their ethnicity in innovative ways. Part of the drive to adopt new terms for identification grew out of the common call for self-determination. The Nation of Islam had long derided black people for allowing whites to define them as Negroes. *Black* was the term the people chose, not outsiders. It was an inherently defiant term that rejected the negative associations with blackness that were pervasive in American culture. For Chicanos and Asians, the effort for self-identification was twofold. It also marked a departure from the manner in which people viewed these groups.

As one student newspaper stated, "Asian Americans took a turn and began to cast off the chains of complacency. To many Asian Americans there was a need to define ourselves, our history, culture and our roles in society."[71] The new term that affirmed self-definition symbolized a new age for those who resisted oppression. As with the term *Negro,* old terms represented obsequiousness and ignorance. Thus, to reject the old term meant to reject the old manner of politics and political mobilization. The Yellow Brotherhood and Asian American Hardcore created names that represented this transition into a new people. Self-described tough guys, the Brotherhood embraced the era's tendency to colorize races. "Black" and "white" provided an easy dichotomy in the discussion of race, while "brown," "red," and "yellow" conveniently seemed suitable for people seeking new definitions. Yellow, like black, carried negative connotations: weakness, fear, cowardice, and meekness—many of the stereotypes Asians fought. Just as black people had done with slogans such as "black is beautiful," the Yellow Brotherhood systematically created an image for themselves that was anything but meek and cowardly or dependent on conventional definitions. They were proud to come from the street and proved to be no "model minority" for white America. The Asian American Hardcore similarly adopted a name that dismissed the pervasive notion of weak, timid Orientals. They were, after all, hardcore, and certainly not Oriental.

Latino and Asian militants, following the modus operandi of Black Power advocates, made it obvious that they were no longer at the door of white America requesting acceptance. "Now the Chicano no longer relies on the good will or good intentions of the [white] liberal." Students demanded resources, no longer politely asking for them to stroke the ego of the gabacho or *gwai* (literally "demon/ ghost"). These militants also made it very clear that white was not always right and that whites could no longer assume the cultural standard. Chicano students argued that the goal of Chicano studies was ultimately connected to the liberation of Chicano people. The programs must work "toward exposing to Brown students the evil machinery of the capitalist system and turning them on to revolution-ary principles." Some programs were not progressive enough but simply "Coconut studies" (brown on the outside, white inside). A degree in that type of assimilationist program only enabled one to be a "true cocoanut [*sic*]" who "knows how to behave white, talk white, write white, paint white and draw white, in short, perform white tricks in exchange for fat checks acknowledged gratefully in the name of 'La Rahssa.'"[72]

The Chicano Power movement, the Yellow Power movement, and Puerto Rican nationalism were not solely dependent on Black Power for symbolism, political direction, or motivation. The movements necessarily influenced each other in alliances, networks, conferences, and general dialogue. Furthermore, the international dynamics that influenced Black Power similarly formed Latino and Asian struggle in the United States. Mao Tse-tung was an inspiration to Panthers, as well as to the Red Guard. Brown Berets and Young Lords had a particular affinity with Che Guevara, who was also an adored icon for the Panthers. Still, the Black Power movement helped form a period of social and cultural transformation that would have substantive effects on the cultural and political landscape of the country.

The Black Power movement articulated the anger of a generation created by the pervasive and insidious nature of racial subjugation. In no uncertain terms, it challenged the legitimacy of white supremacy—politically, culturally, and socially. The visibility of Black Power meant that militants could not be ignored. They were featured on television shows, in newspapers, on college campuses, and on the radio. Popular culture paid great attention to the cultural transformation of the United States. The country was in a process of upheaval of its long-lasting traditions of racial hierarchy, and no organization caught the media spotlight as did the Black Panther Party.

Although there had been different social, cultural, and political exigencies in the various communities, the BPP proved to be a matrix for Latino, Asian, white, and Native American radicals. Imbued with a profound sense of duty, obligation, resistance, and idealism, these revolutionaries were inspired, motivated, and influenced by the symbolism, rhetoric, and tactics of the Black Power movement in general and the Black Panthers in particular. Black nationalists and Black Power advocates, by example, demonstrated the humanity of white people in ways that Martin Luther King Jr. and nonviolent integrationists did not. Integrationists on a very basic and fundamental level acquiesced to white supremacy by allowing whites to maintain an aura of power and prestige. Despite the overt challenges to the authority of racist laws, there was a pervasive assumption that moderate and liberal whites in the North could be persuaded to assist the southern-based freedom movement. Civil rights leaders constantly made appeals to white lawmakers, capitalist power brokers, and white liberals for moral and material support.

Civil rights activists were certain to attend marches and sit-ins with "respectable" attire. Men wore shirts and ties; women wore dresses. They protested for desegregation and integration. While many clearly fought for human rights, suffrage, and equal access to resources, the overall thrust to the activities, as articulated by its national leadership, was integration. This integration was contingent on white approval. Blacks were instructed to be conscious of their speech, manners, dress, and general presentation in front of whites. The NAACP argued that it was psychologically damaging to a black child to be segregated in public school. No mention was ever made of how psychologically damaging racial segregation was for white children. The implicit belief was that a white presence made things better. As Richard Newman, a professor at Boston University in the late 1960s, said, "When civil rights leaders called for integration of higher education, they were not hoping to send more whites to Howard University. They wanted more blacks at ['white' colleges]."[73] Integration was a one-way street that assumed that majority white was normative and desired.

Black Power rejected the idea that white people's acceptance was desirable. Other people of color and even some poor whites, informed and significantly affected by Black Power, also formed ethnic nationalist paradigms of resistance. As with their black counterparts, these ethnic nationalists organized in their communities, changing the social, political, and cultural landscape. Furthermore, most of these ethnic nationalists copiously developed a theoretical construct of radical self-determination that was not dependent on xenophobia. The radical ethnic nationalism of the Black Panthers, Young Lords, Brown Berets, or Red Guard reflected a conscious effort to culturally affirm people who languished under a dehumanizing system of racial oppression, while it also refused to pander to the convenient race-only discourse that attracted many. These proponents of radical ethnic nationalism glorified their ethnicity while they eagerly embraced a polysemic nationalist framework that pulled from Fanon, Marx,

Lenin, and Mao. Too, they were significantly influenced by the BPP's political analysis and its thesis of revolutionary struggle.

Black Power's influence on non-African Americans altered the popular discourse and public discussion of identity and equality in the United States in significant ways. Outside and inside the radical leftist ethnic nationalist communities were militants who rebuked whiteness and the implications of whiteness, such as status dependent on the subjugation of nonwhites. In this contextual framework, many militants sought to "humanize" whites by stripping them of any trappings of cultural prestige or supremacy. The cornerstone to this reorientation was a rejection of integration. Radical ethnic nationalists struggled for a world where whiteness was no longer the standard by which all else was judged and for a class-free society. Yet rejecting the traditional class-based rhetoric of the Left, the radical ethnic nationalists merged radical interpretations of race and class into their movements.

Radical ethnic nationalism attempted to overturn the white supremacy that had historically denigrated people of color in every arena of American life. To that end, whites were criticized in ways that they had never been. They were openly ridiculed for their smell, lack of rhythm, lack of hygiene, lack of morality, lack of beauty, and, at bottom, lack of humanity. Although these criticisms may appear inconsistent with the ideals of Panther transracialism, some ethnic nationalists' ridicule of whites was an attempt to reconcile the new self-love with generations of self-hate. Whites were pushed off their pedestal of whiteness and all the implied honor, prestige, and respect that skin-privilege conveyed. Black Power and radical ethnic nationalism revealed the vulnerability of whiteness. Whiteness was not sacrosanct or without flaw. It was corrupt and inextricably bound to the frailties of humanity.

Beyond the cultural and psychological effects that radical ethnic nationalism introduced to the New Left of the late 1960s and early 1970s, the movement was truly a unique phenomenon. There are no major examples of ethnic nationalist struggles that established alliances, as had young radicals of the Black Power era. African American, white, Puerto Rican, Chicano, Asian, and Native American radicals merged ethnic nationalist rhetoric with a struggle that emphasized class conflict and interracial coalitions. When the

Black Panther Party coined the slogan "all power to the people," it was attempting to broaden the call for Black Power by transcending race. According to party chairman Bobby Seale, interracial coalitions are powerful examples of the people gaining strength in numbers in their efforts against the "power structure's oppression."[74] At the center of this struggle was the Black Power movement, which provided the earliest examples of cultural nationalism and political organization around ethnic nationalist causes. The BPP served as a paradigm of radical ethnic nationalism and a vanguard party for the revolutionary nationalist movement. The Panthers provided an appeal that was unprecedented in the annals of radical struggle.

Though considered a black hate group by some whites; an irresponsible, careless, and disorganized band of immature radicals by some leftists; or too conciliatory to white radicals by some black nationalists, the Panthers' impact was indelible. A group that reached a peak membership of five thousand members, the party not only influenced radicals from every ethnic community in the United States, it inspired marginalized and oppressed people worldwide who created Black Panther parties. Australian Aborigines, Sephardic Jews in Israel, blacks in Britain, and the Dalit in India all formed organizations that carried the name Black Panther Party, evoking the radical ethnic discourse of the organization. From the legacy of the Black Power movement are ethnic studies programs on college campuses, Kwanzaa, and a rich celebration of ethnic diversity and social activism in Latino, Asian American, and other communities throughout the United States.

9

"A Holiday of Our Own"

Kwanzaa, Cultural Nationalism, and the Promotion of a Black Power Holiday, 1966–1985

KEITH MAYES

The Nguzo Saba (seven principles of Kwanzaa) is the first, the basic, primary teaching. The rest of the doctrine, covering the completeness of modern experience is a Black ideology in toto, a path itself to Blackness and Nationhood. The doctrine now is in the head and hands mostly of organization people, and a few key organizers and student leaders around the country. But soon it will be ... available to most of us. It is the central ingredient of the new Nationalist organization. It will transform Black people and by doing this, transform yes, America. You better get ready for it.

—Amiri Baraka, *The Black Scholar*, 1969

In 1974, at the height of the Black Power movement and five years after Baraka's announcement of the coming of Kwanzaa's seven principles, a black cultural nationalist publication sent out a clarion call to African Americans around the country: "It's time that we as Black People with Black families put down crazy cracker celebrations for something that is for us. Think about it: Easter, Thanksgiving, Passover, Chanukah, X-Mas, Columbus, George Washington, Independence Day, on and on ... Zillions of white holidays and lily white images—but nothing for us. Think about all of the negative effects of all these so-called holidays."[1]

This call to "put down" white holidays and to think about the psychological cost of participating in mainstream American holiday traditions represented a phase in the black consciousness movement interested primarily in the politics of culture. Culture encompassed the literary—the poetry of Amiri Baraka, Sonia Sanchez, and Larry Neal, the stage—the drama of Ed Bullins and Woody King, the song—the music of James Brown, Gil Scott-Heron, and Curtis Mayfield, and sports—the acts of Tommy Smith and John Carlos. But culture also meant language—Kiswahili, clothing—dashikis and bubas, hair—Afros, and new holidays—Kwanzaa. Though disparate, what these multifaceted phenomena underscored was the politicization of black culture, or what I call the ascendancy of "cultural Black Power." Cultural Black Power emerged as that part of the black freedom movement in which culture, identified both in its broadest and narrowest senses, was understood as a remedy for black liberation. Cultural Black Power privileged song and dance, arts and letters, language, clothing, and holiday rituals as agents of social change.[2]

Although Black Power is generally responsible for producing Kwanzaa, the holiday's lineage in history and memory is specifically connected to its creator, Maulana Karenga, and his ideas about African history and culture. Karenga borrowed and synthesized practices from the African continent, then applied them to the African American context. He believed that black American culture originated in African traditions—traditions that could lead to freedom and liberation from white cultural domination.[3]

If Kwanzaa's 1966 birth was a result of the efforts of one man, then the early growth of the holiday from 1967 to 1985 was a community affair. At the forefront of this effort were black cultural nationalists and pan-Africanists affiliated with local community-based organizations.[4] Though Karenga's Us Organization in Los Angeles breathed life into Kwanzaa, the Committee for a Unified Newark (CFUN) in New Jersey, the EAST Organization in New York, and other activist groups in Chicago, Washington, D.C., and Philadelphia nurtured the infant holiday in urban centers. Also instrumental in establishing Kwanzaa in black neighborhoods were an assortment of groups and institutions such as black independent schools, local Kwanzaa committees, black theater companies, and black student unions. In addition, black media, churches, public schools, and museums played a vital role in introducing the holiday to the larger African American community.

This chapter details the black community's efforts to promote Kwanzaa through urban networks of cultural Black Power. Although Kwanzaa is presently celebrated by many African Americans and familiar to some whites and other people of color, what follows examines Kwanzaa's local roots prior to its acceptance into the American mainstream.[5] The popularity that Kwanzaa has enjoyed since its inception is owed not to corporate America, but to black men, women, and indigenous community institutions who took the warning of reveling in "crazy cracker celebrations" very seriously.

The historical context for the rise of Kwanzaa is both simple and complex. Kwanzaa's origins are simple in that we can easily identify one person as its creator, inventor, and major booster—Maulana Karenga. But Kwanzaa's appearance is simultaneously complex in that there exist multiple historical layers to peel back: the Watts rebellion, black nationalism in Los Angeles, and the Us Organization. The Watts rebellion certainly gave birth to the leadership of Karenga, Us, and the new political culture of black nationalism in southern California. Watts, however, did not produce Kwanzaa. Kwanzaa's origin lies specifically in debates within Us over the Christmas holiday.[6]

Kwanzaa was part of a series of alternative holidays and rituals recognized and promoted by Us from 1966 to the group's temporary demise in the early 1970s. Before Kwanzaa emerged as a major holiday for African Americans, it existed alongside other Us organizational rituals such as wedding, funeral, and naming ceremonies.[7] Outside of Us and within the broader Black Power Movement, Kwanzaa was insignificant in comparison to black cultural nationalist and pan-African ceremonies such as Malcolm X commemorations, African Liberation Day parades, and Los Angeles' annual Watts Summer Festival. Despite Kwanzaa's initial obscurity, it quickly grew and evolved beyond Karenga and Us after the first few years of its existence.[8]

The Us Organization and New Holiday Formations

Black Power as a national social movement was in its early stages of articulation when the first official week of Kwanzaa commenced in December 1966. Six months earlier, Stokely Carmichael and others attempted to define to the nation what Black Power truly meant.[9] Only weeks removed from the Meredith March Against Fear, the media and civil rights leaders would not wait for a clear analysis and definition of Black Power from Carmichael and other activists.[10] Critics seized the moment and offered versions of the term immediately at odds with its major proponents.[11] But if confusion abounded about what Black Power meant, no such national bewilderment dictated how Black Power should manifest itself during the Christmas holiday season. That is because no one anticipated Black Power's complexity and the kind of cultural work it would perform on behalf of African Americans. Certainly, no one envisioned Black Power's challenge to the traditional year-end holiday season and its bold reworking of the American calendar.

On December 31, 1966, approximately fifty people packed a house near Washington Street and Tenth Avenue in Los Angeles to celebrate the first Kwanzaa.[12] Smaller gatherings had occurred throughout the week, but on the sixth day of Kwanzaa, weeklong festivities culminated in one grand feast called the Karamu. Most Us members attended, including top leaders. During the first Kwanzaa Karamu, Us members invited family and friends, and even found themselves among nonmembers who had heard about the celebration by word of mouth. The people who filed inside the home that evening experienced a celebration in two parts. From approximately early evening to 12 a.m., the first half of the Kwanzaa Karamu was administered with traditional Africa in mind. Us members wore colorful African dashikis and bubas. Men and women bowed and embraced, using Swahili terms to greet one another. The candles, on a modified Jewish menorah, were lit accompanied by the definition of the seven principles.[13] For children, emphasis was placed on African storytelling and various skits on how to select a king. Adults sat on the floor and ate food with their hands. As the first half of the festivities came to a close, the second part of the Karamu commenced around 12 a.m.[14]

If six to midnight represented an attempt to reconnect with a lost African past, then 12 a.m. to daybreak meant returning to the American present. Twelve a.m. until dawn encompassed the African American portion of the celebration. The early morning hours of January 1, 1967, were mainly reserved for adults as Us members and non-members drank and danced to the latest black music. James Brown blared from the stereo as Karamu attendees took the floor. After officiating the first half of the Karamu, Karenga let the spirit of the moment engulf him as he danced to the music. Elizabeth Campbell, a nine-year-old girl who was allowed to witness some of the adult phase of the Karamu recalls seeing Karenga that night:

> During the celebration, I saw for myself what made Ron Karenga special. I must have been 9 years old, old enough to take an interest in what was going on around me. I was used to seeing Karenga lecturing from a podium, looking so stern in his black clothes and dark-rimmed glasses. But now he was on the dance floor, enjoying himself with everyone else. I was surprised to see someone so serious—a big shot down with the folks and having a good time.[15]

Young Elizabeth Campbell was the daughter of W. D. Campbell—an Us sympathizer who wanted his child to experience what the Karamu had to offer culturally. A second but older non-Us member recalled arriving by chance at the same inaugural Kwanzaa Karamu. Unlike young Elizabeth Campbell, who took notice of the adult phase of the feast, Iya Afin was enthralled by the first half ceremonies, remembering how the event transformed her life:

> I met some people in my apartment building who invited me to a feast. The feast took place at the US organizational meeting house in Los Angeles in 1967. They were celebrating a feast … known as Kwanzaa. The music, the food, the clothes, my people, I was entranced and captivated. For the first time in my life I felt at home in my own skin. I was listening to my people's music and dancing to my people's drums. At last I had a culture of my own. I felt a connection to my ancestors so strong that everything I had ever experienced in my whole life came back to me and I was changed forever.[16]

While traveling on the East Coast in 1968 preparing for the Black Political Convention in Newark and the National Conference on Black Power in Philadelphia, Karenga promoted these major gatherings along with the little-known Kwanzaa. Attempting to raise awareness about the new holiday, Karenga stressed the importance of embracing cultural alternatives in a speech at Howard University. He asked the black student body to consider exchanging long-standing family traditions based on European culture for something more substantive: "if we ask people not to celebrate Christmas then we must be prepared to give them an alternative ... so we did some research and found a Zulu custom where people came together for about a week around the first of the new year."[17] In introducing this Zulu-inspired custom, Karenga did not mean for blacks to completely erase their Euro-American cultural traditions, but to recognize that there existed a black cultural tradition beyond the strictures of American society.

Holiday, festival, and ritual promotion inside and outside of Us went hand-in-hand with Black Power activism on the West Coast. Karenga was known to conduct meetings with various organizations in the Los Angeles Black Congress only to return to the Hekalu (temple and Us's headquarters) later in the day to officiate an harusi—a wedding ceremony, or an akika—the nationalization and naming ceremony for children. From the Hekalu it was on to a black denominational church to officiate a maziko (funeral) for a fallen comrade. But holiday promotion also meant organizing larger public ceremonies in South Los Angeles similar to the Watts Summer Festival, annual Malcolm X birthday and assassination commemorations, and Uhuru (freedom) Day rallies commemorating those who lost their lives in the Watts rebellion.[18]

Interestingly, Us's first public appearance in southern California was not organized around activities in radical umbrella groups like the Temporary Alliance of Local Organizations (TALO) or the Black Congress.[19] Instead, Us appeared publicly for the first time during the inaugural Malcolm X observance in Los Angeles. Named for the Swahili word meaning sacrifice—Dhabihu—the day of Malcolm X's assassination or "martyrdom" proved the most promising out of all Us's new holidays. The first Dhabihu brought 200 people on February 20, 1966, to the Garden of Prayer Church. With Malcolm's widow, Betty Shabazz, unable to attend, many local black nationalists paid tribute to Malcolm who was assassinated just one year earlier.[20] Speeches were given praising Malcolm's legacy, and strident commentary promised to keep his work alive. Additionally, candles were lit and relit honoring Malcolm's memory. Confident about the success of the first Dhabihu, Karenga informed the audience, "this is going to be one of many holidays we are going to substitute for those celebrated by Euro-Americans."[21] Though filled with much certainty about reprioritizing calendar events on behalf of African Americans, Karenga's remarks about a major Malcolm X holiday in subsequent years proved premature. Instead, Kwanzaa would become the most influential Black Power holiday, eventually outlasting the movement that gave it birth.

Kwanzaa on Highway 101

Los Angeles was the birthplace of Kwanzaa. But because of Black Power's growing political and cultural capital, resonating with more African Americans, the city could not keep the holiday to itself. Kwanzaa began traveling in many directions, first making its way onto the entrance ramp of highway 101, heading south and north. A few members of Us with family connections in San Diego brought and celebrated the first Kwanzaa there in December 1967. The first Kwanzaa in San Diego, however, was an extension of Los Angeles and bore the stamp of the Us Organization.[22] More significant is Kwanzaa's move to northern California and the holiday's promotion by other black activists outside of Us. At the center of this story is one of many Black Power gatherings that placed an unknown student organizer from the Bay Area in contact with Kwanzaa's creator.

The Western Regional Black Youth Conference held in Los Angeles in November 1967 was part of the growing Black Power public sphere where discussions about Kwanzaa could be identified alongside more immediate concerns in the movement. The conference's institutional site, the Second Avenue Baptist Church was transformed from a traditional place of worship to a politicized meetinghouse drenched in Black Power conversation and accoutrement.[23]

The major developments and news stories included an altercation leading to gunshots between Karenga's Us Organization and a black Marxist group, the United Front, and a call by the Olympic Committee for Human Rights to boycott the 1968 Mexico City Olympic Games. The Us Organization's confrontation with the United Front posed no serious danger to attendees or the conference itself. The call to boycott the Olympics captured the attention of the public and made front-page news.[24] Black nationalist sociology professor Harry Edwards invited sports luminaries, such as basketball's Lew Alcindor (later Kareem Abdul Jabbar), and track stars Lee Evans and Tommy Smith, to serve notice to the world that African American athletes were preparing to take a stand against black oppression. The boycott's objective said Edwards, was to "put the question" of white supremacy "before the United Nations" and remove it from the "sphere of civil rights ... into the sphere of human rights."[25] Karenga spoke to conference attendees later in the day, concurring with Edwards's assessment about the need for black athletes to use the upcoming games as a forum for political redress. But unlike his Howard University speech where he talked specifically about his alternative to Christmas, Karenga said nothing to the audience about Kwanzaa, speaking instead of a "new culture, a new value system, and a new lifestyle among black people."[26]

On day two of the Western Regional Black Youth Conference, a little known speaker name Harriet Smith from Merritt College in Oakland stood at the podium to address black students' role in the Black Power movement. A native of Berkeley and student body president at Merritt College, Smith talked about organizing on campus and the need for black students at major white colleges to seize control of school budgets and activity fees. Impressed with Smith's presentation, her strategic location in the Bay Area, her mature age of 39, and her relative obscurity within black sectarian politics, Karenga believed the key to Kwanzaa's expansion lay in this black student leader. After Smith's presentation, Karenga approached her to see if she would be willing to start what he described to her as the "community Kwanzaa" in the Bay Area. Smith's unaffiliation with Us or other black nationalist organizations made her an ideal person to further Karenga's plans. Karenga's ambition was driven both by his desire to see Kwanzaa grow and to inject his personal brand of Black Power in areas that the Black Panthers geographically and ideologically controlled. The Us Organization's altercation with the communist United Front at the Black Youth Conference reminded Karenga of the urgency to spread his beliefs of black cultural nationalism. Thus, the "community Kwanzaa" articulated by Karenga to Smith simply meant Kwanzaa celebrations practiced by African Americans outside the sphere of the Us Organization.

The brief meeting about Kwanzaa and its potential efficacy in the Bay Area ended with Karenga giving Smith materials to make African-style clothing, a new name (Sister Makinya), and instructions on how to perform a Kwanzaa ceremony.[27] Name changing was not unusual for Karenga—he had given African-derived names to all members of his organization.[28] Neither was name-changing unusual to the Black Power movement as a whole as it signified a veritable Negro-to-Black conversion experience.[29] Smith's three-day politicization in Black Power ideology and practice ended when she and the Merritt College attendees returned to northern California. The spatial politics of Black Power, however, forced Smith to discard the African attire before reaching Oakland and Berkeley because of the potential danger the clothing posed in areas controlled by the Black Panthers. If the dashikis and bubas did not make it to the Bay Area, then Kwanzaa certainly did, traveling north with Smith on highway 101 as part of a stack of conference papers and flyers collected over the last three days.[30]

One month after meeting Karenga, Sister Makinya decided to attempt a private Kwanzaa celebration among family and friends on December 26, 1967. The first Bay Area Kwanzaa ceremony was held at her Berkeley home, and like the first Los Angeles Kwanzaa a year earlier, proved very experimental. The mimeographed outline provided by Karenga lacked instructions on where to place the holiday's material items. Makinya improvised, arranging the symbols and African-prepared foods on a table according to her own personal taste. Activities integral to Kwanzaa celebrations, such as pouring libation and the passing of the Unity Cup were absent from this inaugural festivity. With only the rudimentary instructions and materials of a new holiday celebration before them Sister Makinya and company "giggled through the first Kwanzaa."[31]

After Kwanzaa's private debut in Berkeley, it did not take long for the holiday to spread throughout the area. From 1968 to 1971, Sister Makinya became the contact person for Kwanzaa celebrations on both sides of the Bay. She created the Kwanzaa Organizers in 1968—a Bay Area consulting group that trained blacks how to perform Kwanzaa celebrations in Berkeley, Oakland, and San Francisco. After providing interested parties with information, Sister Makinya encouraged them to form their own organizations and hold annual Kwanzaa celebrations in their homes and neighborhoods. In Oakland, Fred T. Smith organized a Kwanzaa celebration in 1968. Thomatra Scott, trained by Sister Makinya and a close associate of the Us Organization, began conducting Kwanzaa celebrations in 1969 under the auspices of his group, Young Adults of San Francisco. Other Makinya trainees included Akilimali in 1969, Debbie O'Neal in 1970, and John Hill in 1971, as well as Hurumu and Itibari Zulu, who later helped establish Kwanzaa in Sacramento.[32]

Kwanzaa soon blossomed, becoming the featured annual event in other Bay Area organizations like Oba T'Shaka's Pan-African Peoples Organization (PAPO), the Street Academy (a group of black postal employees), the Bay Area Kwanzaa Committee, the Pan-Afrikan Secretariat, the Kwanzaa Celebrants, the Nairobi Kwanzaa Committee, and the Wo'se Community Church in Oakland. An early PAPO invitation set the tone for 1972's Bay Area Kwanzaa celebrations and future gatherings: "The Pan-African People's Organization proudly extends a warm welcome to all its beautiful Black brothers and sisters at Kwanza and throughout the years to come."[33]

As the Bay Area Kwanzaa representative with the longest history associated with the holiday, Sister Makinya's facilitation of public Kwanzaa celebrations in the 1970s and 1980s made her the unofficial "mother of Kwanzaa." The "mother of Kwanzaa" was able to bring various groups together during the perennial holiday week. When the celebrations were small and manageable, each Kwanzaa organization would pick a day during the seven-day holiday and stage a celebration in a Bay Area city. One group would hold the first day of Kwanzaa in Berkeley, another group in Oakland on the second day of Kwanzaa, another group on the third day in East Palo Alto, the fourth night in San Francisco, and so forth. By the mid- to late 1970s, Kwanzaa celebrations grew so large, sometimes upward of a few hundred persons at a single location, organizers agreed to have Kwanzaa festivities in multiple locations on the same night. Sister Makinya and other organizers turned down many groups that wanted to participate in coordinated Kwanzaa efforts. In just a few short years, Kwanzaa's popularity would explode. Despite Kwanzaa's growth, eventually moving beyond the oversight of Sister Makinya, she is remembered in the Bay Area as the woman who started it all in northern California.[34]

Baraka, the Congress of African People, and Kwanzaa

In the late 1960s and early 1970s, Amiri Baraka embodied Kawaida cultural nationalism and unleashed a flurry of activities in Newark, New Jersey, and around the country. After modeling his Committee for a Unified Newark on Karenga's Us Organization and playing a major role in Newark electoral politics, Baraka attained instant visibility as a major Black Power activist. Conference organizing on the local and national level became a Baraka staple. Realizing that Black Power activists lacked a national structure to continue the work of the three previous Black Power conferences, Baraka, in 1970, gathered a significant group of national and international black political activists in Atlanta, Georgia. The Atlanta meeting featured civil rights veterans Ralph Abernathy, Whitney Young, and the young Jesse Jackson; religious figures such as Louis Farrakhan; newly elected black mayors Richard Hatcher and Kenneth Gibson; and many leaders from African anticolonial struggles. More important than who attended, the Atlanta Congress held workshops on key areas of concern in the Black Power movement. The Political Liberation workshop highlighted pan-Africanism as a possibility for an independent black nation. The workshops also called for releasing African prisoners of war. The education workshop established definitions for education and assessed the viability of Black Studies programs, Black Student Unions (BSUs), black teachers and administrators, black colleges, and independent black schools. Other workshops featured sessions on creativity, black technology, religion, community organization, law and justice, history, and communications. The 1970 African Congress also held a workshop on social organization, which included a seminar on Kwanzaa.[35]

The Kwanzaa seminar began with a short synopsis of the holiday. The presentation emphasized Kwanzaa's fundamental connection to celebrations of the harvest. Kasisi Washao, the seminar's instructor and CFUN member, explained to the class that during the harvest season, "our people in Africa came together to give thanks. Songs were sung, dances danced, food was eaten, and drinks were drunk, in a word, life was lived in sheer enjoyment." Washao also described in detail the symbols of Kwanzaa: the straw mat (mkeka), the candleholder (kinara), the ear of corn (muhindi), and the gifts (zawadi). After a detailed explanation of the symbols, the instructor explained how they were to be arranged: "after the mkeka has been spread out, place the kinara in the center. Then place the muhindi around or on the sides of it. Place the zawadi on the mkeka in any arrangement that is artistic. Finally, the mishumaa (candles) should be placed at the far right of everything so that they might be available for daily lighting." Washao ended the seminar by describing the evening prior to the last day of Kwanzaa, the Karamu. Washao cautioned that the Karamu should be held "at the largest house" among the celebration's participants because it is "traditionally an all night set" mainly for adults, consisting of "food, drink, music, dance, conversation, laughter, and ceremony." Before concluding, Washao told seminar attendees that Kwanzaa is CFUN's "holiday [based] upon tradition and reason.... To us it is a sign of self-determination and self-respect.... Surely by things like this, we provide ... something of value."[36] Thus, in just a few short years, Kwanzaa had graduated from organizational ritual in a small number of community-based groups to an important plenary session at a major Black Power gathering, touching hundreds of people at one time.

The major offspring of the Atlanta meeting was not Kwanzaa, however, but the Congress of African People (CAP). CAP institutionalized Kwanzaa in the United States. Over a hundred groups from more than twenty-five cities attended the 1970 Atlanta meeting, most leaving as local CAP affiliates. A CAP report explained the importance of local organizations: "the base of the CAP operation has been the Local Organizations. Leadership, kazi (work), and policy have emerged from local activities. These bodies based in African communities around the western hemisphere will be carrying out the daily work of CAP. To local folk, these groups represent the CAP message."[37] Part of this message to local affiliates was to return home and promote Kwanzaa in black neighborhoods. CAP locals with a mandate to spread Kwanzaa included Haki Madhubuti and the Institute of Positive Education (Chicago), Jitu Weusi and the EAST Organization (New York), Kalamu ya Salaam and Ahidiana (New Orleans), Reginald Mtumishi and Maisha Ongoza of the Urban Survival Training Institute (Philadelphia), Thomatra Scott and the Young Adults of San Francisco, Ron Daniels of Freedom, Inc. (Youngstown, Ohio), and Vernon Sukumu of the NIA Organization (San Diego). Recalling the importance of his organization's role in the new Black Power holiday, Baraka declared, "if it were not for CFUN and the later Congress of African People ... the seven principles and the holiday Kwanzaa would never have been as widely known as they are."[38]

But Baraka would only be around shortly to take note of the flowering of the holiday he helped promote. On October 7, 1974, Baraka officially made his "public notice to the world of our socialism." Baraka renounced Karenga's doctrine of Kawaida and all of its accompanied rituals, including Kwanzaa, driving a wedge in the movement. Despite Baraka's public departure from Kawaida cultural nationalism, Kwanzaa continued to flourish. The holiday was already entrenched in the Black Power community, remaining behind in local cultural nationalist groups that refused to follow Baraka into Marxist-Leninism.[39]

Kwanzaa and the Black Neighborhood Public Sphere

New York

Organizations such as the EAST Organization in New York, the Institute of Positive Education in Chicago, and the Urban Survival Training Institute in Philadelphia, continued to celebrate Kwanzaa.[40] Others existed solely to promote Kwanzaa. Most, however, tied

Kwanzaa to the larger process of controlling black neighborhoods. The men and women in community-based nationalist and non-nationalist organizations believed in creating their own schools, community centers, and publishing houses, reflecting their own Black Power politics. For them, Kwanzaa was just one in a series of activities that validated their struggle for institutional independence and cultural autonomy. Promoting Kwanzaa was an extension of building an independent school, a community center, or participating in Third World political struggles.

In Brooklyn, New York, home to one of the largest black populations in the United States, the EAST labored diligently to promote Kwanzaa. "If you know something about Kwanza already, spread the word," wrote Basir Mchawi of the EAST, "our greatest communications vehicle is our mouths." For the EAST, no single place proved more appropriate than another for the introduction of Kwanzaa. Members believed Kwanzaa could be held just about anywhere: "Support and initiate Kwanza programs in your community, at day care centers, schools, community centers, your home, etc." All African Americans should "try to make Kwanza a household word."[41]

Promoting Kwanzaa in urban neighborhoods often meant confronting the popularity of Christmas within the black community. EAST publications during the month of December were filled with articles about blacks and Christmas, often chastising African Americans for rampant holiday season consumption: "Now you fool where do you think you're going? Just come back here ... sit down and let us put some sense in your head.... There are over $400 worth of outstanding bills which you still have from last year, including Christmas."[42] The EAST felt that Christmas shopping for blacks was akin to slavery, extolling African Americans to "break the chains." "Once again, its time for us to PLAY THE FOOL.... MAS-X SEASON is here, better known as XMAS. The time for us to sigh, buy, cry, grin, and PURCHASE, purchase, PURCHASE! All for the hippie-dippey Christ and his OLD new year. TAKE THE CHAINS OFF YOUR BRAIN BLACK PEOPLE!!!"[43] The EAST annually called for a boycott from Christmas shopping and asked African Americans to consider the cultural alternative to the main holiday tradition, admonishing: "As the holiday season approaches us again, when our monies are most likely at an all time low, we Afrikans had better seriously consider the alternative to the Christmas rip off—Kwanza." Understanding the generational politics in black families where most members were wedded to the traditional Christmas season, the EAST cautioned black parents, "if you can't handle Kwanza, give it to your children. The young folks will love you for it and respect you more than Santa." The EAST summed up their feelings about Christmas and the new Kwanzaa holiday: "Kill Santa Claus, relive Kwanza, bring forth the cultural revolution."[44]

Public announcements every December notwithstanding, Kwanzaa promotion in black neighborhoods manifested in large public events such as Kwanzaa parades, pre-Kwanzaa workshops, concerts, and large community feasts. In 1974, the EAST moved their traditional Kwanzaa activities from their headquarters on 10 Claver Place to accommodate a larger crowd. After a children's Kwanzaa festival on December 20, and the follow-up family Kwanzaa activities from December 26 through December 29, the EAST reported that on December 31 "over 1,000 Brothers and Sisters ... participated in ... activities held at the Sumner Avenue Armory." By moving to a larger site, the EAST was able to commission nationally known artists, dramatists, and musicians such as poet Sonia Sanchez, musician Lonnie Liston Smith, and actors from the National Black Theater to help promote Kwanzaa at its 1974 celebration. The EAST reminded those unable to attend: "If you missed Kwanza '74, we'll be back when Kwanza lands again. Be sure you catch it this year. Kwanza '75 will be a sure nuff smoka."[45]

While the EAST made Kwanzaa an annual ceremonial event in Brooklyn, other institutions promoted Kwanzaa in different parts of New York City. One of the earliest groups to sponsor public Kwanzaa celebrations was a social service agency called the Harlem Commonwealth Council located on 125th Street. The Harlem Commonwealth Council typically held annual Kwanzaa festivities at the Studio Museum in Harlem and area public schools. In December 1971, the Harlem Council assembled fifty elementary students at the Studio Museum from Public School 68 to teach them about the new holiday. To enliven and embolden the message of roots, identity, and African cultural connection, as well as to reduce the generational gap between the messenger and the students, the Council commissioned a sixteen-year-old ordained minister and director of the National Youth Movement named Al Sharpton to educate students about Kwanzaa. The young, "heavy-set" Sharpton, as the *New York Times* described him, wore an African dashiki and opened his talk by explaining to the students, "today you're going to learn something about Kwanza." In the trademark raspy voice he would become known for as an adult, Sharpton went on to explain in the simplest of terms the holiday's connections with the African past, telling the students, ranging from seven to nine years old, that Kwanzaa is "a spiritual ceremony" and that "harvesting ... is traditional in Africa." After Sharpton provided a lesson on Kwanzaa's material symbols and the correct way to annunciate the holiday's Swahili terminology, the students were provided gifts, and seven of them were chosen to light candles on the kinara. The following year in 1972, the Council gathered 300 more students at the Studio Museum to hear another Kwanzaa lecture.[46]

Chicago

While independent organizational efforts were common among groups like the EAST, coalition-led Kwanzaas were a major feature of year-end holiday ceremonies in some cities. In 1971, the Confederation of Pan-African Organizations formed to stage citywide Kwanzaa galas in Chicago. Haki Madhubuti and a few others had been performing Kwanzaa ceremonies in their organizations since the late 1960s, but the Confederation recruited a broad cross-section of Chicago black nationalists to further popularize the holiday: Madhubuti and the Institute of Positive Education; Hannibal Afrik and the Shule Ya Watoto; Musa Kenyatta and the Republic of New Africa; Ife Jogunosimi and Mansong Kulubally of the Black Body; the United Africans for One Motherland International (UFOMI); the Chicago chapter of the Provisional Government; and Conrad Worrill—educator, columnist, and later the Chicago chair of the National Black United Front.[47]

One of the most significant developments to come out of the Chicago Confederation was the Karamu Ya Imani—a community feast meaning the feast of faith. Proposed by Hannibal Afrik as a communitywide promotional and educational campaign, the first Karamu Ya Imani was held at the Ridgeland Club on January 1, 1973. Typically, children performed in the early afternoon. During the evening, the ritual phase for adults was held. Evening activities included pouring libations to the ancestors, lighting candles, and making commitments for the New Year. As customary, food was prepared by volunteers, delivered, and placed in the center of the room for eating. The 200-person gathering included much of the Chicago nationalist community but also a steady stream of apolitical blacks from Chicago's south and west side. Black cultural nationalists also represented visually, appearing in colorful African clothing, whereas others wore jeans, slacks, suits, and dresses. Remarks about the significance of embracing "African" culture were made by Afrik and Madhubuti, both of whom reiterated how important it was to instill a new set of values in African Americans, particularly black children. All speakers agreed to the efficacy of the Karamu Ya Imani and promised the Confederation would institutionalize Kwanzaa in the windy city by holding the Feast of Faith annually.[48]

In the years following 1971, an increasing number of participants forced the Confederation of Pan-African Organizations to move the Karamu Ya Imani to different locations in Chicago: the Viking Temple, the YMCA, the South Shore Cultural Center, the DuSable Museum, and the Packing House on 49th and Wabash. The growth of the Feast meant that more blacks in Chicago had come to embrace Kwanzaa but also produced setbacks. By late 1978, the Confederation found it increasingly hard to finance the Karamu Ya Imani, resulting in the dissolution of the Confederation of Pan-African Organizations. In 1980, however, a few of the original organizations in the Confederation along with a number of newer groups reorganized as the African Community of Chicago and continued the tradition of the Karamu Ya Imani in the new decade.[49]

Washington, D.C.

In Washington, D.C., the same spirit of cooperation existed among Kwanzaa organizations united to promote the new Black Power holiday. Again, the black cultural nationalist community took the lead in the city's Kwanzaa publicity campaign. The district's first Kwanzaa gathering took place at the home of local activist Sister Woody (Nia Kuumba) in 1970. Wider public festivities soon spread to the black independent school, Ujamaa Shule, under the direction of Baba El Senzengalkulu Zulu, and to nationalist houses of worship like the Temple of the Black Messiah and the Union Temple Baptist Church pastored by the Reverend Willie Wilson. The Museum of African Art under the educational direction of Amina Dickerson, the Reverend Ishakamusa Barashango, Ayo Handy, the D.C. Kwanzaa Committee, the Watoto Shule, and the United Black Community were also instrumental in introducing Kwanzaa in the 1970s. Many of these groups and institutions sponsored coordinated public Kwanzaa celebrations at their respective locations, making the holiday an annual event in the nation's capital.[50]

The harmony prevailing among community groups in Chicago and Washington, D.C., was not always present in other cities. Occasionally, Kwanzaa organizations squabbled over the staging and promotion of events. In vying for the most elaborate Kwanzaa festival, discord sometimes prevailed, forcing organizations to call on Karenga to mediate differences. In Philadelphia, for example, separate organizations, such as the African Community Learning Center, the Marcus Garvey Shule, the Temple of the Black Messiah, and the Ujima Unit participated in individual Kwanzaa activities during the late 1970s.

While there is no evidence that Maulana Karenga ever attempted to settle this particular dispute in Philadelphia, Karenga was familiar with Kwanzaa parades. He had dealt with a similar proposal by members of his own organization in 1968. Parades, like large community feasts and other public displays of the holiday, had been present from the very beginning. One of the earliest was the Bay Area Kwanzaa Parade held in East Palo Alto in the early 1970s consisting of black cowboys, clowns, dancers, drummers, and marchers from a multitude of African American cultural groups.[51] But Los Angeles started its own Kwanzaa parade tradition. Samuel Carr-Damu—a high ranking official in the Us Organization, along with members Yuseff Majahliwa and Karl Key-Hekima originally proposed a plan for a Kwanzaa parade. After Karenga rejected the idea, Damu, Majahliwa, and Hekima—all three who had left the organization by 1970—joined forces with Akile Washington-Kosi and Sheila Ward (two individuals closely associated with the Us Organization but never formal members) to make the parade a reality. Though the parade idea in Los Angeles was hatched in 1968, it would take ten years for the parade to come to fruition. Damu and Hekima stepped aside, which allowed Majahliwa to proceed with Washington-Kosi and Ward in creating an independent Kwanzaa parade organization called the Kwanzaa People of Color. The Kwanzaa People of Color and its annual parade in South Central Los Angeles would represent a major vehicle for Kwanzaa promotion in Los Angeles and one of the few but growing public expressions of Kwanzaa outside of the Us Organization in southern California.[52]

Local Kwanzaa community organizing served as sustained educational campaigns toward African Americans. One of the most common forms of protracted promotional strategies were pre-Kwanzaa celebrations. These celebrations consisted of workshops, forums, and minicelebrations that started at the beginning of December and lasted up to the first day of Kwanzaa. Pre-Kwanzaa ceremonies in the first three weeks of December were designed to spread the word about Kwanzaa events taking place before the official holiday week in addition to publicizing activities during the last week of the year. Pre-Kwanzaa events also became a vehicle to educate African Americans about holiday essentials. Not only did these events allow blacks to purchase hard-to-find Kwanzaa materials, or provide instructions on how to stage a Kwanzaa ceremony, pre-Kwanzaa gatherings helped demystify the holiday in a variety of ways. Some African Americans in Chicago who had never heard of Kwanzaa and did not interact with the city's black nationalist community harbored thoughts about an anti-Christian holiday ritual in their midst. Hannibal Afrik, founder of the black independent school, Shule Ya Watoto, and cofounder of the African Community of Chicago, remembered encountering these obstacles in the 1970s and early 1980s:

In those early years there was some hostility and resentment about Kwanzaa because it was felt by some that it was in opposition to Christmas and therefore was pagan ... and church people should not get involved with it. Because it was African, most people didn't know that much about African culture and so there was some resentment to the terminology, the method of practicing Kwanzaa … so it was important that we take our message to the community to help inform them and to solicit their support.[53]

Afrik and other promoters made and distributed Kwanzaa materials, published calendars in black newspapers, and read them aloud on black radio programs like the Lu Palmer Show on WVON—all to publicize events taking place in the city and help clear up any misrepresentations about the Black Power holiday.[54]

Conclusion

Although Kwanzaa entered the 1980s with institutional vigor via official Kwanzaa week celebrations and December-long pre-Kwanzaa events that gathered more adherents each year, the Black Power movement stumbled out of the 1970s as a result of government repression, the exile of leaders, internal struggles, deaths, and an overall loss of focus by national organizations. But to invoke the death of the Black Power movement in a linear manner is to understand Black Power only in its national dimension. Kwanzaa and local promotional efforts remain examples of Black Power's continued resilience and relevance in black neighborhoods during the decline of the national movement. It can be argued that the Black Power movement survived because its cultural offspring, Kwanzaa, evolved and matured, becoming an independent entity whose charge was to educate a community about the African roots of black American culture. And the enormity of this educational and promotional campaign in black urban neighborhoods was nothing short of extraordinary in the late 1960s, 1970s, and early 1980s. Whether they realized it or not, many persons, organizations, and institutions respectively partook in this Black Power endeavor: Ahidiana in New Orleans, SHAPE Community Center in Houston, Some Positive People in Jacksonville, Florida, the Boston Kwanzaa Committee, and the Metro Atlanta Kwanzaa Association (formerly the Atlanta Kwanzaa Committee). Additional Kwanzaa promoters included black independent schools—the Shule Ya Watota in Chicago, the Uhuru Sasa in New York, the Aisha Shule in

Detroit, the Kazi Shule in Houston, and the Council of Independent Black Institutions (CIBI), which served as an umbrella organization for all black independent schools. Others that publicized Kwanzaa early on were politically conscious black teachers in public schools such as Betty Anne Jackson in Community School District Twelve in the Bronx, New York, and the Department of Elementary and Secondary Education in the Milwaukee Public Schools. Some houses of worship with black nationalist ministers made Kwanzaa part of their institutional politics: Union Baptist in Washington, D.C., Albert Cleage's Shrine of the Black Madonna, Augustus Stallings's Imani Temple, and Jeremiah A. Wright Jr.'s Trinity United Church of Christ. Black Student Unions fighting for Black Studies programs and departments made Kwanzaa a staple activity on white campuses. And finally, black theater groups did much to raise public awareness about Kwanzaa: Baraka's Spirit House in Newark, the Theater of Afro-Arts in Miami, the Sudan Arts/Southwest of Houston, the Kuumba Workshop in Chicago, the Free Southern Theatre of New Orleans, the Mafundi Institute in Los Angeles, and Concept East of Detroit.[55]

The sheer number of community organizations and institutions promoting Kwanzaa annually underscored the holiday's ties to the Black Power movement and a larger black neighborhood public sphere—a counterpublic comprised of political activists, cultural workers, ministers, educators, and others bent on changing the way the larger African American community understood culture, holidays, and themselves.[56] Creating a black holiday ultimately meant capturing the avenues and spaces of publicity: not only the calendar, but community centers, museums, schools, armories, churches, the airwaves, and even the streets. African Americans were both empowered by Kwanzaa and the public spaces the holiday occupied every December. The story of the public Kwanzaa in the late 1960s, 1970s, and early 1980s is not the story of a single individual but a narrative about a community of people that collectively decided to challenge the hegemony of Christmas and stake out new areas for the Black Power movement. Any history of Kwanzaa must take seriously the holiday's connection to this broad-based social movement that was national in scope but local in character.

10

BLACK STUDIES, STUDENT ACTIVISM, AND THE BLACK POWER MOVEMENT

PENIEL E. JOSEPH

Contemporary Black Studies programs owe a large, and largely forgotten, debt to radical social and political movements that resulted in student protest demonstrations across the country at both majority white institutions such as Columbia University, and historically black institutions such as Howard University.[1] During the decade of the 1960s black students demanded education that was relevant to their specific history of racial oppression.[2] These demands were a central component of larger, and at times radically utopian, political, and philosophical imperatives that undergirded the Black Power Movement.[3] The proponents of the Black Studies movement of the 1960s and 1970s argued that educational institutions in American society (with an emphasis on, but not exclusive to, the university) had to be radically transformed for humanity's sake. Historically, Black Studies advocates supported the utilization of scholarship for the larger pursuit of social justice and a broader, more inclusive democracy.[4] However, the "modern Black Studies Movement" represented perhaps the greatest political and pedagogical opportunity to fundamentally alter power relations in American society. Building on the early-twentieth-century "Negro History Movement" pioneered by historians Carter

G. Woodson and J. A. Rogers, the modern Black Studies movement emerged from the hotbed of black radicalism produced during the 1960s. Black Studies provided a practical and political education for a variety of captive, and captivated, audiences during this era. The movement simultaneously promoted community building, black nationalist consciousness, class struggle, education opportunity and restructuring, employment creation, and anticolonial struggles through think tanks and study groups. Although not completely successful, these efforts should by no means be considered a failure. On the contrary, Black Studies programs remain one of the enduring and outstanding legacies of the Black Power Movement.

Efforts at institutionalizing Black Studies have their roots in the heroic work of W.E.B. Du Bois and Carter G. Woodson as well as lesser known, although no less important figures, such as Arturo Schomburg, Hubert Harrison, and others.[5] While ideologically diverse, all of these individuals substantively explored and disseminated African American history through books, editorials, symposia, study groups, and public speeches. Although these pioneers undoubtedly paved the way for contemporary African American Studies, the modern Black Studies movement has its immediate roots in the depths of a Cold War that witnessed unprecedented and unexpected black political radicalism. This chapter explores the origins of the modern Black Studies movement, focusing on the grassroots intellectuals and student activists who sought to utilize intellectual work and political activism to transform American society. If not advocating for Black Studies in the specific institutionalized context that would erupt during the late 1960s, the organizations discussed here provided the intellectual and practical political context, especially consciousness raising, for the political environment that led the Black Studies movement.

The Cold War as Classroom: World Black Studies

The historian Manning Marable has argued that Black Studies is simultaneously descriptive, corrective, and prescriptive.[6] One also may add that the historical development of Black Studies has been experiential. That is to say its evolution has been directly affected by the larger flow of international events. The threat of international communism and its utilization of American antiblack discrimination provided Pan-Africanism with an at times begrudging support from the United States.[7] The Cold War presented a generation of African Americans with a real-world political experience that would effectively undermine anticommunist hysteria by introducing a catalogue of revolutionary figures into the consciousness of African Americans. Revolution was the goal of this new race consciousness, and anticolonialism was its currency. If the 1954 Supreme Court *Brown v. Board of Education* decision signaled the coming of a domestic revolt, then the Afro-Asian Conference in Bandung, Indonesia, in 1955 represented its international counterpart.[8] Part of an emerging Third World solidarity that challenged white supremacy at the global level, Bandung, as well as international conferences such as the meeting of "Negro Writers and Artists," exported race and class consciousness through back channels unimpeded by the Cold War's ideological restrictions.

Indeed, black writers and artists were equally encouraged by the waves of anticolonial movements sweeping through Africa and debated the implications for the United States, the Caribbean, the Soviet Union, Asia, and Latin America. Richard Wright, exiled and living in Paris, published several works during the late 1950s that were firsthand accounts of the liberation of the West African Gold Coast, the Bandung Conference, and the implications for Africans and the West.[9] Of course, Wright was not alone in contemplating the impact of African liberation struggles on the wider political milieu. On this score Wright, along with Aimé Cesairé, Léopold Senghor, and others, published *Presence Africaine*, an extremely important journal committed to the ideas of radical Pan-Africanism, and sponsored the first world conference of black writers and artists at the Sorbonne in 1956.[10]

Several participants provided practical descriptions of what was required for the future. Richard Wright gave the most controversial response. Although passionately committed to African liberation, Wright's vision of African shied away from conventional notions of a diasporic return home. Rather, for Wright, the process of diaspora had paved the way for "the making of black modernity and radical consciousness."[11] This was clearly displayed in Wright's address to the conference. In a paper titled "Tradition and Industrialization: The Plight of the Tragic Elite in Africa," he argued that modernity's brutality had the unintended consequences of sowing the seeds of the modern African states.[12] Although committed to radical internationalism, Wright's ultimate vision was one of transnational humanism that went beyond narrow nationalism of any kind.

> I would like to explain that the Black Nationalism that we, American Negroes, practiced in America, and which we were forced to practice, was a reluctant nationalism, a proud and defensive one. If these implementations of American law continue, the nationalism of itself should be liquidated. I hope, even though I wrote lines to justify Black Nationalism in America, that they need not remain valid for decades to come.[13]

Although Wright was heavily criticized for this speech, his passage should not be viewed as antinationalism sentiment.[14] Rather, he viewed nationalism (and communism) as one step in the advancement of the oppressed peoples of the world. Declaring that freedom was a human right, Wright argued that African leaders required autonomy from Western influence lest Africa be mired in global marginality in the near future. Wright sought to turn the notion of "western civilization" on its head by excluding notions of white supremacy and colonialism from Africa's utilization of modernity. Declaring the interaction between the West and Africa a "ghastly racial tragedy," Wright attempted to utilize the technological innovations associated with the West for African advancement.[15]

Held in Rome in 1959, the second congress of Negro Writers and Artists included future Black Power icon Frantz Fanon, the Haitian intellectual Jean Price-Mars, and Senegalese historian Cheikh Anta Diop. If the first congress had dealt with the need to restore Pan-African culture that had been marginalized under colonialism, the second congress attempted to redefine black culture in a global sense.[16]

> Among the capital sins of colonialism, one of the most pernicious, because it was for a long time accepted by the West without discussion, was the concept of peoples without culture. It had a corollary, which consisted in passing off the culture of a colonized peoples, and especially

of the Africans, in the occasional instances where recognition was granted to it, as a dead thing. The conqueror, faced with a corpse, could find nothing better to do than simply impose his own culture, which for its part could not fail to be an expression of life. But it was commonplace to say that culture is not a mere assemblage of works and norms which can function automatically in every climate and all periods. These works and these norms must have a subject which fires them with its passions, its aspirations, and its genius. The most universal philosophical doctrine or literary work is only valid by virtue of the men who live by it. It is only the people who give it authority and dynamic force.[17]

In the United States, black activists would echo this declaration for political revolution through cultural rebirth. The international energy precipitated by Pan-Africanism and African independence movements dominated the black radical intelligentsia and emboldened and inspired African American political activists. The formal declaration of the Republic of Ghana in 1957 and Prime Minister Kwame Nkrumah's call for skilled African Americans to aid the newly independent nation-state resulted in a black American expatriate community whose decade in Ghana would provide in-depth lessons regarding the euphoria and pitfalls of postcolonial Africa.[18] Even more influential than Ghana in the imagination of U.S. African Americans during the late 1950s were the events in Cuba. Following the 1959 Cuban Revolution, tours of the island were organized for leading black political activists, intellectuals, and artists.[19] Individuals taking these tours ranged from radical activist Robert F. Williams to poet LeRoi Jones and cultural critic Harold Cruse.[20] Moreover, important artists and intellectuals, including Julian Mayfield, John Henrik Clarke, and Tom Feelings, journeyed to Cuba, many of whom recounted their experiences in journals and magazines upon returning. For many of these political activists, Cuba represented a dramatic, and radicalizing, turning point in their lives.

For LeRoi Jones (later Amiri Baraka), Cuba was the lightning rod that spurred a political metamorphosis that would lead him to black cultural nationalism, Pan-Africanism, and finally Marxism. However, immediately after returning from Cuba, Jones started the Organization of Young Men (OYM), a study group comprised of black intellectuals living in Greenwich Village, New York City.[21] Eventually merging with the black Greenwich Village-based group On Guard, international events figured prominently into the minds of formerly apolitical black bohemians, such as Jones, at the start of the 1960s. The organization's newspaper, *On Guard,* carried the subtitle "The Truth Shall Make You Free," and devoted its pages to examining the connection between civil rights and "Third World" revolutions. *On Guard* columnist Calvin Hicks succinctly presented this perspective.

> Afro-Americans are called upon by the Cuban events to think even more seriously and clearly than ever. Profound changes are taking place in the Western hemisphere. The immorality that dominates the foreign relations of those who rule our country has never before been so thoroughly exposed as in the Cuban affair. Most Afro-Americans, however, have regarded the moral decay as limited to the government's relations to its black nationals. Now we can see that immorality permeates all phases of government.[22]

In the same issue, assassinated Congo leader Patrice Lumumba received a moving tribute a few months after his death. For a generation of African Americans, the murdered nationalist leader provided a face for both anti-imperialism and the consequences associated with such political audacity. Lumumba's death propelled the black nationalism sentiment that had been buiding in the wake of Bandung to a fever pitch that led to demonstrations outside the United Nations building in 1961.[23] However, Lumumba's martyrdom carried more than symbolic notions for many of these demonstrators. This assassination, along with the Cuban Revolution and African decolonization efforts, provided the practical and ideological building blocks for a black radical solidarity that was fueled by a resurgence in black nationalism, street corner speaking, study groups, and community organizing. African Americans learned important lessons from these experiences.

In the Tradition: Black Revolutionary Journals

On Guard was just one of many journals and newspapers that radicalized a generation of African Americans. In New York City alone, in addition to *On Guard*, there were influential periodicals, such as African Nationalist Pioneer Movement's (ANPM) *The Street Speaker* and *The Black Challenge*, Shirley Graham Du Bois's *Freedomways*, and Dan Watts's *Liberator*. All of these periodicals raised the international awareness of young black Americans. Moreover, they provided a critical exploration of African American history that encompassed the global implications for past and contemporary black liberations struggles. In short, black revolutionary journals served as critical texts that reached an influential segment of the African American community. It was no accident that many of these journals were based in Harlem. A mecca of black radicalism during the heady days of "New Negro" politics in the 1920s, Harlem was home to influential activists and long-marchers, including ANPM founder Carlos Cooks and bookstore owner Lewis Micheaux. Raising the political consciousness of a generation of young intellectuals, activists, artists, and cultural workers, these journals challenged the very idea of American democracy. They did so by arguing that democracy in the United States would be incomplete and ineffective if white supremacy was not eliminated both domestically and internationally. From this vantage point they redefined democracy as a political ideology that was both racially inclusive and philosophically humanistic. In the process, they questioned some of the goals, strategies, and tactics of mainstream civil rights organizations. Moreover, the varieties of black nationalism articulated in these periodicals revealed currents of internationalism, class struggle, and Pan-Africanism that are often missing from conventional portraits of black nationalism. *Liberator* provided a forum for a diverse group of black writers and political activists ranging from cultural critic Harold Cruse to Harlem activist Bill Epton and journalist William Worthy. Many of the journal's frequent contributors, most notably Harold Cruse, would play important roles during the Black Power era and in debates over Black Studies in institutions of higher education.

In the late 1950s and early 1960s, Harlem experienced a revival of the radical street-speaking that had its heyday in the 1920s during the New Negro militancy personified by Marcus Garvey and Hubert Harrison.[24] Emboldened by African independence movements, Carlos Cooks asserted that "a new day" had dawned wherein Harlem would be "engulfed by Nationalism."[25] Although the African

Nationalist Pioneer Movement kept the embers of Garveyism burning bright, the Nation of Islam (NOI) was undoubtedly the most powerful nationalist organization in Harlem. Publicly disavowing secular political engagement, the NOI nonetheless profoundly influenced black radicals through the political speeches of Malcolm X and the anticolonialism that filled the pages of *Muhammad Speaks*. A master communicator and teacher, Malcolm X understood the power of the press and founded *Muhammad Speaks* as primarily a revolutionary newspaper that advocated an anti-imperialist philosophy that would characterize Black Power politics during the late 1960s and early 1970s. Originally titled *Mr. Muhammad Speaks,* the newspaper was read "religiously," by a variety of students, activists, and intellectuals who appreciated its broad international perspective. For example, at the 1960 Harlem Freedom Rally, Malcolm X articulated the united front politics that he would more explicitly adopt after his break with the NOI, while highlighting the importance of anticolonialism.

> As a collective mass of people we have been deprived, not only of civil rights, but even our human rights, as the right to human dignity … the right to be human beings! This Freedom Rally is to be a united effort by all of our leaders. We have set aside all petty differences, and in the spirit of Bandung we have come together on this same platform, wherein each one can voice his personal feelings and his personal solution to this grave crisis we face.[26]

For many of its readers, *Muhammad Speaks* provided international coverage and analysis that was missing from mainstream and alternative press outlets. More important, the paper provided an incisive political education regarding international issues. In its critical reportage of world affairs and anticolonial struggles, *Muhammad Speaks* provided secular coverage related to some of the most important events of the era. In doing so *Muhammad Speaks* was one of the important conduits that introduced radical African leaders who, according to St. Clair Drake, "were the heroes of the militant black youth for decades before Black Studies programs burgeoned."[27]

The Afro-American Association and the
Radical Black Student Movement

At the very moment that black political radicalism contained a variety of popular outlets on the East Coast, the Bay Area in California was also experiencing a radical political reawakening. Black Power era-politics in the Bay Area had its roots in the Afro-American Association. Inspired by the sit-in movement and the Student Nonviolent Coordinating Committee (SNCC) in the South, the Association began in September 1960 when students at the University of California (UC) at Berkeley began holding regular meetings. The group's members included Donald Hopkins, Otho Green, Henry Ramsey, and Donald Warden.[28] Meeting consistently over the next two years, the Afro-American Association reached hundreds of young people in the Bay Area through street-speaking, rallies, and study sessions. The Association grew out of the alienation and racism experienced by black students attending UC Berkeley.[29] By 1962 the group's leader was Donald Warden, a young black nationalist from Howard University whose speaking style attracted many militant black students. The group primarily served as a consciousness-raising tool for African Americans in California, with a reading list that ranged from W.E.B. Du Bois to texts on ancient African kingdoms.[30] The charismatic Warden became something of a legend in the Bay Area during this time, preaching and teaching African Americans in a way that was seductive and compelling, according to former member Les Lacy:

> Like a prophet calling for the millennium, he walked through the streets of Oakland, Berkeley, and San Francisco, in and out of schools and colleges, office buildings and coffeehouses, telling black peoples where they were. "The time has come to break with white America."[31]

Association leaders frequently challenged white professors (and all comers) to debates related to issues of African American history, white racism, and political oppression. The Association reached out to students at Merritt College and San Francisco State University, several of whom, such as Huey P. Newton and Ron Everett (Maulana Ron Karenga), would go on to play major roles in the Black Power Movement. Discovering the group while a student at Merritt College, Huey Newton was introduced by the members of the Association to the serious and sustained study of African American history.[32] In the early 1960s Maulana Karenga, who would later introduce the influential Kawaida philosophy through his Us organization, remained influenced by aspects of the Association's black nationalist philosophy.[33] Although Newton and many others eventually left the group, the Association taught African history and culture to hundreds of young blacks during the early 1960s. Furthermore, the Association, through its aggressive advocacy of curricula on African American history and culture, was an early and vocal advocate of the modern Black Studies movement.[34] In short, the Afro-American Association provided black students with an ideological and practical platform for a black nationalist-based critique of American society and international political and economic affairs.

Several individuals who had been involved in the Afro-American Association joined the Revolutionary Action Movement (RAM). Initially started by a group of radical college students influenced by revolutionary journals, decolonization movements, and political activists such as Malcolm X and Robert F. Williams, RAM eventually developed chapters in New York, Oakland, Philadelphia, and Detroit. Williams, a burly tough-talking militant NAACP leader from Monroe, North Carolina, was particularly important. A vocal proponent of self-defense, Williams was a national figure in the late 1950s whose exploits inspired many future Black Power activists. In 1961 he fled North Carolina and later the United States as a fugitive pursued by federal authorities on a trumped-up kidnapping charge.[35] The development of RAM relates directly to the growth of SNCC and New Left organizations, such as the Students for a Democratic Society (SDS), during the early 1960s. When they learned of Robert Williams's flight at the National Student Association (NSA) conference in Madison, Wisconsin, radical black students affiliated with SDS and the Congress of Racial Equality (CORE) decided on a plan of action.[36] Led by two Ohio-based college students, Donald Freeman of Case Western Reserve University and Max Stanford of Central State College, the small group started an off-campus SDS group called "Challenge." The group was made of militant students, some of whom "had been expelled from southern schools for sit-in demonstrations."[37] At Freeman's urging, the group studied Harold Cruse's

1962 *Studies on the Left* essay "Revolutionary Nationalism and the Afro-American." This pivotal essay described the need for an indigenous black revolutionary struggle in the United States. Spurred on by Freeman and its study of Cruse, the group transformed itself into the Reform Action Movement (to allay suspicion from college administrators), committing itself to building a mass-based, black nationalist movement focused on direct action, discipline, and self-defense. Eventually forming in Philadelphia as the Revolutionary Action Movement at the end of 1962, RAM was a key black radical organization of the era.

The group operated stealthily and membership was informally defined. Politically, RAM's philosophy was black internationalism—the conjoining of race and class struggle to defeat imperialism and white supremacy. Future Black Power activist Ernest Allen Jr. (Ernie Mkalimoto) encountered RAM members, including Max Stanford (Muhammad Ahmed) and future Panther 21 member Robert Collier, during a two-month visit to Cuba in 1964.[38] In addition to Stanford and Allen, future League of Black Revolutionary Workers (LBRW) member Charles Johnson, Luke Tripp, Charles Simmons, and General Baker were also in Cuba. They had traveled to Cuba through sponsorship from several progressive socialist organizations. During their stay, this group of radical black students enjoyed the opportunity to network with each other, while engaging in political dialogue and debate with exiled leader Robert F. Williams. This meeting established ties that would strengthen the burgeoning radical black student movement through the creation of revolutionary journals and community- and campus-based political organizations. On returning to the United States, RAM members began to publish in Detroit the influential journal *Black America*. In addition to Williams, the organization was mentored by Ethel Johnson, a Monroe, North Carolina, activist, and Queen Mother Audley Moore, who schooled New York members on black nationalism, Marxism, and issues of nationhood.

Black America advocated the national liberation of U.S. African Americans and, in the spirit of *Muhammad Speaks* and Williams's *Crusader*, connected domestic racial crisis with international events.

RAM philosophy may be described as revolutionary nationalism, black nationalism or just plain blackism. It is that black people of the world (darker races, black, yellow, brown, red oppressed peoples) are all enslaved by the same forces. RAM's philosophy is one of the world black revolution or world revolution of oppressed peoples rising up against their former slave-masters. Our movement is a movement of black people who are coordinating their efforts to create a "new world" free from exploitation and oppression of man to man.[39]

Black America featured articles and commentary from a group of veteran radical activists, including James Boggs and Rev. Albert Cleage Jr. In many ways RAM occupied the central agit prop role in a black radical sphere that included the periodicals *Muhammad Speaks, Liberator, Crusader,* and *Revolution;* cultural groups such as the Afro-American Association; and the radical political community organizing of the Freedom Now Party (FNP) and the Detroit-based Group on Advanced Leadership (GOAL). Not directly a RAM publication, but produced by individuals associated with the organization, was the journal *Soulbook*.[40] This journal featured poetry and short stories, in addition to political commentary. Through *Black America, Soulbook, RAM Speaks,* and the *Razor's Edge,* revolutionary black nationalism was promoted to a generation of youthful black militants.

The Grassroots: Motor City Radicalism

An auto worker, labor activist, radical theorist, and community organizer, James Boggs (along with his wife Grace Lee) mentored a generation of black student radicals who would go on to play pivotal leadership roles in the Black Power Movement. Associated with C.L.R. James's Johnson-Forest tendency within the Worker's Party that produced the periodical *Correspondence,* James and Grace Lee Boggs broke with James in the early 1960s and charted their own political path.[41] Boggs gained a lasting measure of political fame and influence among radicals with his 1963 publication *The American Revolution*. The book was widely disseminated in black and white leftist circles throughout the 1960s and served in many ways as one of the key texts of the Black Power Movement.[42] Boggs was active in Detroit's black radical community that included Rev. Albert Cleage

Jr., who would go on to be one of the founders of Black Power theology, and Richard and Milton Henry, who organized the Republic of New Afrika (RNA). These radicals were active in the Michigan chapter of the Freedom Now Party (FNP) that, anticipating 1972's historic Black Political Convention, advocated independent black politics. These Detroiters also started the Group on Advance Leadership that in the aftermath of 1963's Walk for Freedom in Detroit (that featured Martin Luther King Jr. and a turnout of over 125,000), organized a northern base for black radical community organizers.[43]

During the early 1960s, James Boggs also served as a political mentor for a group of young activists that included Max Stanford, General Baker, Gwendolyn Kemp, and Luke Tripp. Tripp, Kemp, and Baker were part of UHURU (Swahili for *freedom*), a group of radical black students who met at Wayne State University. Started in 1962, the group began holding study sessions and protest activities all around the Detroit area.[44] UHURU organized protests against police brutality and advocated class struggle and identification with Third World liberation struggles. In August 1963, just a few months after the spectacularly successful freedom march, UHURU issued an open letter to Detroit's Mayor Jerome Cavanaugh, which announced that the organization was "initiating a militant, uncompromising attack" on police misconduct.[45] UHURU gained an even greater measure of notoriety in local politics when, along with GOAL members, they boycotted Detroit's bid to host the 1968 Olympics. In the aftermath of this demonstration, five of the group's members were arrested for disturbing the peace.[46] During the early 1960s Detroit became ground zero for young revolutionary nationalist student radicals who would play key roles in Black Power organizations by the end of the decade. Most notably, Baker and Tripp would go on to play leadership roles in the League of Black Revolutionary Workers in the late 1960s. Inspired by the radical political activity of James Boggs and Albert Cleage, and through meetings with Malcolm X in preparation for 1963's Northern Grassroots Leadership Conference, black student radicals organized a political conference in Nashville, Tennessee, in May 1964. Held at Fisk University, this political gathering was a clarion call for the radical Black Student movement.[47] According to Max Stanford, the conference "was the ideological catalyst that eventually shifted the Civil Rights Movement into the Black Power Movement."[48] Included in these discussions would be the call for a black curriculum and Black Studies in educational institutions throughout the country.

Conceptualizing and Debating the Black University

Black student radicalism during the early 1960s contributed to the political development and unrest that paved the way for the founding of contemporary Black Studies. While the political impact of radical organizations, study groups, conferences, and periodicals was pivotal, the modern Black Studies movement began in 1967 at San Francisco State with a list of visiting professors that included Amiri Baraka and Sonia Sanchez.[49] By the fall of 1967, student unrest had led to militant scholar Dr. Nathan Hare (who had been recently dismissed from his post at Howard University) being named the new coordinator of Black Studies.[50] Between 1967 and the early 1970s militant black students demanded Black Studies at both predominantly white institutions, such as Yale and Columbia universities, and historically black schools, including Howard University in Washington, D.C., and Southern University in Baton Rouge and New Orleans, Louisiana.[51] During the spring of 1968, black students at Howard took over the administration building.[52] What was remarkable about the takeover was the fact that African American students demanded that a historically black college be more responsive to the needs of the local black community and the increased radical consciousness and nationalism within the student body. That same year, African American students at Northwestern University issued a proclamation that demanded, among other things, increased black faculty and financial aid for black students.[53] Perhaps the most well-publicized moment of student unrest took place when black students took over an administration building at Cornell University in 1969. Although initially unarmed, the students managed to smuggle in firearms after drunken white fraternity members attempted a hostile takeover of the building they occupied. The ensuing crisis led to the appointment of James Turner as director of Black Studies at Cornell and the resignation of the university's president.[54]

These episodes of student unrest exemplified the exponential growth of black radical consciousness by the late 1960s. Moreover, they reflected the impact of the ideological seeds that had been sown by radicals through political education, organizing, and protest. During this era of dramatic protest, calls for the creation of a new infrastructure for black liberation were issued by both an older and a newer generation of black activists.[55] By the late 1960s American universities became sites for ideological and physical confrontations initiated by radicalized black students.[56] Such outbursts were not limited to universities, as witnessed by the growing number of high school students who protested against racism and the lack of Black History courses.[57] In Philadelphia, Black Power consciousness resulted in numerous organized demonstrations that centered in part on the implementation of Black Studies curricula in the city's public schools.[58] At times, increased student radicalism bore the direct imprint of activists who had been influenced by anticolonial struggles of the 1960s. These connections were exemplified at Detroit's Wayne State University where, by 1969, Luke Tripp, the radical founder of UHURU and leader of the League of Black Revolutionary Workers, had become feature editor of the *South End,* turning the school paper into an instrument for revolutionary struggle, with the banner reading "One Class-Consciousness Worker is Worth 100 Students." For many political activists, the university, as a repository of labor, educational, and ideological production and orientation, was increasingly seen as a site of revolutionary struggle and contestation.[59]

A former Marxist who had traveled to Cuba and supported Fidel Castro, Harold Cruse in the early 1960s attempted to outline an indigenous theory of black internationalism that was anticolonialist, but not white-controlled. Cruse's political writings significantly influenced the development of "international revolutionary black nationalists" in RAM and a host of assorted black nationalist groups and organizations.[60] Yet Cruse became increasingly dissatisfied with what he perceived to be the pernicious effects of white encroachment on black-led social movements. A black nationalist who argued for the preeminent role of culture in shaping the African American freedom movement, Cruse became the foremost social critic of the era with the 1967 publication of *The Crisis of the Negro Intellectual.*

At the time of its publication, *The Crisis of the Negro Intellectual* was both a critical and commercial success. The book rescued the then 50-year-old Cruse from relative obscurity, transforming him into an intellectual celebrity. Having struggled for the better part of his career to find venues to publish, Cruse now found outlets for previously unpublished work.[61] Similarly, after having been excluded from the upper echelons of black literary circles, Cruse parlayed fame into considerable success on the lecture circuit and a permanent faculty position at the University of Michigan.[62] Tracing the development of a black intelligentsia from the Harlem Renaissance to black Marxists of the 1940s and militant contemporaries, Cruse's book issued a searing critique of the inability of the black left to forge a cultural movement to end black disenfranchisement in the United States. Part autobiography, part political analysis, and wholly polemical, the book targeted white Marxists and black literary figures. Finally, Cruse, in a stance that would anger many among the black left, forcefully admonished black radicals for being puppets of white Marxists.[63]

Arguing that a cultural reconceptualization of black identity was vital for the development of black liberation in American society, Cruse's book focused on the role of black intellectuals in achieving this task. Black intellectuals, who according to Cruse had the skills to accomplish this difficult undertaking, had abdicated their roles through a slavish adherence to liberal integrationism. Criticizing the 1964 debate between black intellectuals and white liberals sponsored by the Association of Artists for Freedom, Cruse argued that such debates illustrated the theoretical ineffectualness and the political bankruptcy of integrationist black intellectuals.

> The Association of Artists for Freedom came into existence in 1964 as a result of the Birmingham church bombing and killing of six children; but not through any prior intellectual comprehension that Negro writers, artists, and creative individuals had a political role to fulfill in the Negro movement, in any event. Now having assumed this rather belated militant political stance, and attempting to palm it off as super-radicalism, these intellectuals, straining at the leash, find themselves the tactical and programmatic prisoners of their northern roles. They are integrationists, active or implied, with no tangibly visible worlds to

conquer in the North, beyond furthering their own individual careers as creative artists.[64]

Cruse's assessment of the Artists for Freedom represented an attack on black intellectuals for articulating a disingenuous critique of American liberalism. Although he agreed with the criticism of white paternalism, Cruse argued that black intellectuals and white liberals engaged in an unequal relationship, which prevented the creation of critical discourse on black liberation that went beyond the narrow confines of liberalism.[65] Cruse's indictment of black intellectuals reverberated throughout African American politics. The book was eagerly received by a younger generation of black activists angered by what they perceived as the ineffectiveness of black leadership.

Cruse's constant focus on indigenous black culture inspired black nationalists, especially those favoring a cultural rebirth. In the late 1960s, the lines between definitions of black political and cultural liberation, historically intertwined, became increasingly stark. Part of this was the result of an ideological and political turf war between various Black Power organizations laying claim to being the vanguard of the new generation of black militants. Activists who described themselves as "political" gave short shrift, indeed at times lampooned, other groups they regarded as narrowly focused on culture. Some of these sectarian struggles approximated political warfare between rival groups that sometimes turned violent. Most infamously, in 1969 on UCLA's campus two black Panthers, Alprentice "Bunchy" Carter and John Huggins, were shot and killed in a shoot-out with the nationalists in the Us Organization.[66] In contrast to Panther leader Huey P. Newton's derisive label of cultural nationalists as "pork chop nationalists," Cruse's works paved the way for an ideological analysis of African and African American culture that would provide the building blocks for the transformation of democracy in the United States. On this score, the colorful and increasingly popular West African "dashikis," worn by many Black Power activists during this era, became something more than an African American fashion statement.

Cruse's argument that African Americans had to gain control of "cultural institutions" that were misrepresenting African American history and contemporary black life struck a deep cord. In the late

1960s former SNCC activists Charlie Cobb, Courtland Cox, and Jimmy Garrett set up the Drum and Spear Bookstore in Washington, D.C.[67] The bookstore became the heart of a grassroots attempt by D.C. activists to transform black life through education. A key part of this was done through the founding of the Center for Black Education (CBE). CBE offered classes in Black History and culture as a way of empowering black residents. Drum and Spear Bookstore became a major site for meetings, conferences, and information gathering among African Americans in the Washington, D.C., area. The center served as an important hub where C.L.R. James, the legendary Caribbean Marxist, taught a course and debated and dialogued with a wide variety of political activists.[68] Both CBE and Drum and Spear were two examples of efforts by black activists and students to develop indigenous cultural and political institutions during this era. In successfully doing so, for a time at least, they utilized black cultural independence to transform educational institutions and practices in American society.[69]

The organization that attempted to analyze this student consciousness and its relationship to black cultural production guided by a larger vision for social change was the Institute of the Black World (IBW). IBW originated out of conversations between Professors Vincent Harding and Stephen Henderson in 1967. Envisioned as an institute related to Atlanta University Center (AUC), IBW eventually became the most dynamic black "think tank" of the era.[70] In addition to Harding and Henderson, early members of the institute included Gerald McWorter (Abdul Alkilimat), A. B. Spellman, Council Taylor, Howard Dodson, and William Strickland. By 1969, the IBW had formed a close relationship to the Black Studies movement through its summer seminars on research in Black Studies and for directors of Black Studies programs. Comprised of veteran activist-intellectuals, such as Harding, along with young black student radicals represented by Strickland and McWorter, IBW attached black scholarship to a radical vision of social change. According to IBW Director Vincent Harding:

> The main burden of our historical research is on the earlier struggles of black peoples toward manhood, freedom, and liberation from European

domination. The focus of our analysis of the present situation is on the search for an unromantic, systematic understanding of our colonized condition in America and elsewhere so that we may move to reshape it out of a position of authentic knowledge and strength. Our planning towards the future places much emphasis on the development of the educational and political systems which will prepare our children and building their community for their phase of the long struggle. So we struggle in the Institute to move from the privatism of Western intellectual work towards that collective vision which must inform the creativity of all oppressed people.[71]

The role of education in black political struggles was debated over three successive years in special issues of *Negro Digest* (later *Black World*) on the "Black University."[72] Many of the contributors to this special issue of were associated with the IBW, including Gerald McWorter, Vincent Harding, and Stephen Henderson. According to *Negro Digest*'s editors, the "Black University" concept would encompass the "real and total needs" of the black community. They added that the university should be "concerned with the conscious strengthening of those institutions which make the black community viable," while focusing on raising the political consciousness of black students.[73] Tellingly, Harding argued that the Black University would have to be international in its focus, but from an "unashamedly black-oriented prism."[74] Furthermore, Harding stated that such a university should house radical black think tanks:

Think Tanks filled with the varied but constant experience of blackness might be established for the sole purpose of analyzing special conflict situations from Detroit to Angola (and beyond), and suggesting directions of actions and ideology for those who are struggling to break away from the hegemony of the West. From such a university there would go out teams of specialists in development whose primary concerns would not include the opening of wedges for American influence. Rather their search would be for ways in which modernization might be purged of its synonymous relationship with Westernization and Americanization.[75]

One year later, Harding's open letter to northern black students outlined the pitfalls faced in the sometimes frantic search by predominantly white institutions for black faculty.[76] According to Harding, an unintended consequence of northern black student protests had been the raiding of talented black faculty and administrators from historically black colleges and universities (HBCUs).[77] Harding's criticisms raised several important question related to both the Black Studies movement and the larger struggle for American liberation. Namely, did increased black representation and programs at predominantly white institutions enhance or hinder the pivotal role that Black Studies would play in contemporary and future political struggles for education, jobs, and social and political justice? The responses to these questions were the subject of the third issue of *Negro Digest,* concerning the dilemma of the "Black University." The special issue featured commentary from leading activists and intellectuals involved in the development of Black Studies. Most of the contributors focused on the role of the African American community, from student to staff, at the Black University. On this score Chuck Hopkins's "Malcolm X Liberation University" eloquently described the confluence of interest—housing, antipoverty programs, neighborhood improvement—that were directly related to both Black Studies and black politics.[78] Founded in October 1969 in Greensboro, North Carolina, Malcolm X Liberation University had emerged from the radicalization of community activists in Durham, who in turn inspired African American students at North Carolina Central and Duke University.[79] Student-community relationships were further enhanced through an internship program that allowed students to reside in local communities. According to Hopkins, this had a profound effect on black students:

> During this time, black students at Duke underwent some important ideological changes. They began to work more in the community and with black non-academic employees on campus. The students began to think and talk in terms of the critical question of the relevance of the entire educational process to the needs of the black community.[80]

Thus, Malcolm X Liberation University was the direct result of community activism and black student militancy. Once they established solid ties to the local community, African American students grappled with the increasingly profound questions regarding the university's pedagogical, political, and corporate functions. Supporting nonacademic black workers and advocating the university's responsibility to the larger community was a direct result of these developments. Malcolm X Liberation University was a creative response to the limitations of state-sponsored higher education and the perceived needs of the black community.[81]

Throughout the 1970s, the debate over the development of Black Studies programs continued. However, this debate was always guided by more than purely academic impulses. Black Studies was inspired by communities of color seeking substantive changes in their lives related to housing, employment, neighborhood improvements, police brutality, health care, and human rights. Domestic and international developments accelerated these concerns among young African Americans during the 1960s. Many of these currents came full circle during the first half of the 1970s through organizations such as the African Liberation Support Committee (ALSC). Indeed, Black Studies was at the forefront of raising levels of awareness about African liberation struggles. According to the black scholar St. Clair Drake:

> When the Africans defeated the Portugese in 1974, a wave of jubilation swept through the ranks of young people in the black world. For Afro-Americans who admired the Black Panthers this was vicarious identification with blacks who had done what the Panthers were incapable of doing. The Afro-American youth who empathized with the Angolan and Mozambique Freedom Fighters included in their ranks thousands of college students and recent graduates. The newly organized Black Studies programs contributed toward the raising of consciousness with regard to Africa between 1970 and 1974, and to the emergence of the group that had organized a very effective lobby, the ALSC.[82]

In addition to the ALSC, the Black Studies movement impacted national student groups, such as the Youth Organization for Black Unity (YOBU). Starting out in Greensboro, North Carolina, as the Student Organization for Black Unity (SOBU), YOBU became one of the leading anti-imperialist student organizations of the era.[83] Through the publication of their journal *The African World,* the organization advocated a Pan-Africanist political philosophy that grew increasingly Marxian in orientation. YOBU, Malcolm X Liberation University, and leading Black Power radicals, such as Owusu Sadaukai (Howard Fuller) and several members of the ALSC, became increasing radicalized by their attempts to organize workers and students both on and off university campuses in the South during the early 1970s.[84] At the same time, this proliferation of ideologies, activities, and organizations greatly affected the Black Power Movement, and in some cases resulted in political and personal splits and divisions that drained the energies and obscured the focus of radical political campaigns and, to an extent, the Black Studies movement.[85] For example, many student activists had spearheaded efforts to implement new programs and strengthen existing ones; however, splits in organizations such as YOBU diverted their energies from Black Studies programs to community and labor organizing. Although the modern Black Studies movement evolved in a series of ways scarcely imagined by its architects, its historical foundations ultimately lay in the material conditions of the black community, and the unresolved issue was whether the primary site of resistance should be the campus or the society at large.

Conclusion: Contemporary Black Power Studies and the Vocation of the Black Scholar

In many ways, Harding's analysis of the "Black University" described the ad hoc functions of radical black student political organizations during the early 1960s. In enduring ways, the Afro-American Association, RAM, and UHURU utilized unfolding political events as a classroom. Through street-speaking, revolutionary journals, study groups, and overseas travel, radical black students anticipated and contributed to the institutionalization of the Black Studies movement in the U.S. academy. More important, they popularized a level of revolutionary consciousness that threatened to fundamentally transform American and global civil society. Of course, they were by no means alone in this endeavor. Emboldened by the examples of Robert F. Williams, Malcolm X, James Boggs, and Queen Mother Moore, black student radicals connected domestic antiblack racism to a larger colonial reality that was beginning to crumble. International movements that sought the transformation of world culture, such as the Bandung and Negro Writers' Conferences, contributed to this emerging reality as well. Introduced to black nationalism through study groups in cities from Harlem, New York, to Oakland, California, black students became further radicalized as a result of several converging phenomena. These included Third World liberation struggles, the political exploits of Malcolm X and Robert F. Williams, trips to Cuba, close political relationships with veteran radical activists, and the influence of revolutionary journals. Although relatively small in number, the influence of these organizations on black student consciousness throughout the United States was exponential. While black nationalism was the starting point for most of these groups, they studied and were influenced by the politics of class struggle and their relationships with leftist organizations. More important, black nationalist-derived study groups and organizations provided rich beginnings in political education and activism for a generation of black youth. Revolutionary black nationalism conjoined more than aspects of race and class struggle during the first half of the 1960s. It offered a global perspective that allowed black radicals to redefine culture, class, and colonialism on their own terms. As a result, many of these activists and organizations went further to the left, yet continued their fervent commitment to "Black Liberation."

Black student radicalism of the early 1960s anticipated many future political developments, and in many ways was ahead of its time. During this era college campuses, such as Wayne State University in Detroit, Temple University in Philadelphia, and Merritt College in Oakland, became training grounds for radical black internationalism more popularly identified with Black Power organizations, such as the ALSC and Black Panthers. The Black Power Movement emerged as a result of the activities of black political activists calling for a radical restructuring of institutions in American society. An integral part of this vision involved the overhauling of the education provided African Americans. By the late 1960s, the radical political consciousness that was seemingly a blip on the domestic radar screen just a few years earlier became a major thrust within black politics. During the late 1960s and 1970s, the Black Studies movement was one of the most visible manifestations of the success of Black Power radicals' attempt to transform existing American institutions. The immediate results served to increase the number of African American students, staff, and faculty in predominantly white universities; raised the level of political consciousness among blacks, and, to a lesser extent, white students; and continued the process of utilizing the university as an active site of political and ideological struggle.

The modern Black Studies movement complemented, and was an outgrowth of, the radical politics of liberation that was advocated by black activists during the 1960s. The implications of their political activity reverberated throughout the United States and beyond, often with unintended consequences. Yet the very fact that the organizers of the initial Black Studies programs and departments consciously attempted to forge local and international alliances toward a larger vision of radical social change attests to the power of the radical Black Student movement.

The systematic study of the origins of the modern Black Studies movement is an important part of the larger study of the Black Power Movement. During the past three decades, Black Studies has experienced institutionalization and a tenuous measure of legitimacy in the academy. Too often, however, the promise of Black Studies has waxed and waned in correlation with the level of mass protests and disruption.[86] Describing these setbacks, Black Studies scholar William E. Nelson Jr. asserts that even efforts at institutional reform have continued to lag.

In the more than thirty-five years since this reform program was first articulated, the American academy has demonstrated a phenomenal capacity to circumvent black demands for structural and intellectual change. On many campuses, Black Studies programs have been viewed not as vehicles for change but as instruments to placate student arousal and short circuit student demands. The reach of Black Studies across the university has been curtailed by the failure to integrate Black Studies courses into the universitywide basic education curriculum, or to make enrollment in Black Studies courses mandatory for graduation. Promises of support and collaboration from other academic units have not been honored. In the face of mounting economic difficulties, many universities have decided to severely cut the budgets of Black Studies programs and drastically limit their authority to recruit student majors and expand their faculty ranks.[87]

The emerging academic interest in the Black Power Movement provides an important opportunity to critically assess, catalogue, and examine postwar African American history. "Black Power Studies" as a field of academic inquiry must maintain the highest standards of scholarly inquiry, while not being divorced from the historical context that precipitated the historical moment in question. That is to say, the systematic and historical analysis of Black Power is more than just a purely intellectual pursuit. A critical analysis of the modern Black Studies movement requires discussion and debate over the role of black intellectuals, the American university, and the concept of the "revolutionary" in radical social and political change. Most notably, Vincent Harding in his seminal essay, "The Vocation of the Black Scholar and the Struggles of the Black Community," raised the most important issues.[88] In assessing the impact of Civil Rights–Black Power-era politics on American society and culture, Harding problematized the relationship between black intellectuals, the American academy, and grassroots efforts for radical democracy. Written against the backdrop of the Watergate crisis and the waning of Black Power radicalism, Harding argued that black scholars avoided discussing the responsibilities of their vocation at their own peril.[89] According to Harding, the putative success of the Black Liberation movement had endowed black scholars with a mandate to speak truth to power, no matter the cost.

> As part of any truth-speaking about the present condition, our situation and our people demand that there be a sympathetic but hard black analysis concerning the nature and effectiveness of the sometimes strange and valiant approaches to struggle which have arisen out of our own generation. We have yet to see clearly for ourselves the meaning, the connections, and the lessons which emerge out of the furious passage of time and events between the justice-seeking boycott and marches of Montgomery, Alabama, in 1955–56 and the criminal subversion of the political system symbolized by Watergate. For instance, we are called upon to seek at least some tentative understandings of the relationship between the marching songs and prayers in the South and the uprisings of black prisoners across the land. We need to see if there is any chartable way from the lunch counters of North Carolina to the bullets of the

snipers in the cities, any recognizable path from the bombings of Birmingham to the mass graves at My Lai. We must measure the ever-
shortening span between Malcolm X and Martin Luther King.[90]

We are now beginning to see the lessons that only time can impart
with regard to modern black liberation struggles. Harding's essay
imaginatively redefined the Civil Rights–Black Power era by casting
it as a radically humanistic effort at social and political transformation. From such a perspective, seemingly incongruous movements
against legal segregation and unjustified political incarceration com-
prise central elements of American democracy. Similarly, Harding's
assessment of the role of black scholars situated them as beneficiaries
of grassroots struggles who were responsible for critical and lucid
analyses of rapidly unfolding domestic and global developments, and
for providing intellectual and political leadership to address these
shifting circumstances.

Harding asked a central question that perhaps resonates more
powerfully today than ever: What is the role of the black scholar?
According to Harding, black scholars, and by extension Black Studies
programs, are crucial to the creation of a new society. Criticizing
black intellectuals, who, ensconced in the "ebony tower," remained
oblivious to black misery, Harding argued that black scholars must
identify the enemy without and within.

> Educational systems which invariably spawn wretched schools and pow-
> erless officials in black communities are the enemy. Political systems
> which use code words like "busing," "welfare," "no quota systems," and
> "crime in the streets" to signal their fear of black people and their willing-
> ness to hold us powerless as long as they can—these are the enemy. Eco-
> nomic systems which reject so many of the basic human needs of the poor
> and the weak in favor of the wealthy and their subalterns are the enemy.
> Health care systems which provide neither health nor care for the power-
> less and poor are the enemy. Legal and penal systems which persistently
> place us, in large, often overwhelming numbers, behind bars, and which
> places whites in almost all the seats of authority, from the judge's bench
> to the turnkey's—those are the enemy. Energy conservation systems
> which give our needs the lowest priority and literally leave us out in the cold
> are the enemy. A military system which serves as the only "respectable"

alternative available to black youth who have been mangled and rejected by America's other systems, a military force which then is ironically guaranteed to be used in the future only against other non-white people—that is the enemy. Cultural systems which in an age such as this still manage to pretend that humanity began and will end with the peoples of Europe are the enemy. Nor is there any difficulty in recognizing the total interpenetration of these systems. They do not exist in any ultimate tension with each other where the future of black people is concerned; and it is part of the vocation of black scholarship to identify that enemy.[91]

Harding's description of the problems plaguing the African American community still resonate today. The internal enemy was described as selfishly undermining the hope and integrity of the black community.

To identify the enemy is to identify the mesmerizing fear, the debilitating venality, the lack of moral and intellectual self-discipline, the opportunism, the pathological lying, and the self-defeating desire for public recognition and praise which dwell among us. To identify the enemy is to speak truth to our tendency to place all responsibility for black crime upon white people. To identify the enemy is to clarify our unspoken desire for white models, white recognition, white legitimation. To identify the enemy is to point to our failure to believe in ourselves and our tremendous potentials.[92]

Black Power Studies continues to take up Harding's provocative challenge and analysis regarding the role of black scholars in American society. As a living legacy bequeathed by years of struggle, contemporary Black Studies provides the vehicle for examining the individuals and organizations that created this enduring legacy of Black Power-era radicalism. Often ignored, and too often neglected, this connection remains crucial to understanding both the Black Power Movement and Black Studies.

NOTES

Preface

1. Walter Mosley, "What We Forgot about Watts," *Los Angeles Times,* August 9, 2005.

Introduction

1. For the Meredith March, see Henry Hampton and Steve Fayer, eds., *Voices of Freedom: An Oral History of the Civil Rights Movement from the 1950s through the 1980s* (New York: Bantam Books, 1991), 283–295; Clayborne Carson, *In Struggle: SNCC and the Black Awakening of the 1960s* (Cambridge, MA: Harvard University Press, 1981), 206–211; Stephen B. Oates, *Let the Trumpet Sound: A Life of Martin Luther King, Jr.* (New York: HarperPerennial, 1994), 395–405; David J. Garrow, *Bearing the Cross: Martin Luther King, Jr., and the Southern Christian Leadership Conference* (New York: Quill, 1999), 475–489; *Eyes on the Prize Part II:* "The Time Has Come, 1964–1966," Episode 1, 1986, Blackside Productions, Boston, MA; John Dittmer, *Local People: The Struggle for Civil Rights in Mississippi* (Urbana: University of Illinois Press, 1995), 389–407; Adam Fairclough, *To Redeem the Soul of America: The Southern Christian Leadership Conference and Martin Luther King, Jr.* (Athens: University of Georgia Press, 2001), 309–320; Stokely Carmichael with Ekwueme Michael Thelwell, *Ready For Revolution: The Life and Struggles of Stokely Carmichael (Kwame Ture)* (New York: Scribner, 2003), 501–514; and Peniel E. Joseph, *Waiting 'Til the Midnight Hour: A Narrative History of Black Power in America* (New York: Henry Holt, 2006).
2. For a history of the Black Power era that rethinks and challenges much of these assumptions, see Joseph, *Waiting 'Til the Midnight Hour.*
3. The main thrust of Black Power politics was radical in orientation. This is to say that Black Power activists argued that American society needed to be fundamentally altered, rather than reformed. This radicalism was reflected in the politics of a broad range of historical actors and organizations that were black nationalists, Marxists, pan-Africanists, trade unionists, feminists, liberals, or a combination of all or some of these tendencies. Additionally, small strains of black conservatives also were attracted to Black Power's call for self-determination and promotion of black business, self-help, and entrepreneurship.
4. The Black Panthers are the group most identified with this era and the images of violence that are attached to it. See Charles E. Jones, ed., *The Black Panther Party [Reconsidered]* (Baltimore: Black Classic Press, 1998).

5. Bayard Rustin famously described this era as the movement's "classical" phase. Bayard Rustin, "From Protest to Politics: The Future of the Civil Rights Movement," *Commentary* 39 (February 1965), 25–31.

6. For critiques of this narrative see Peniel E. Joseph, "Black Liberation Without Apology: Reconceptualizing the Black Power Movement," *The Black Scholar* 31 (Fall-Winter 2001), 3–19; Van Gosse, "A Movement of Movements: The Definition and Periodization of the New Left," in *A Companion to Post-1945 America,* Jean-Christophe Agnew and Roy Rosenweig, eds. (Malden, MA: Blackwell, 2002), 277–302; Jacqueline Dowd Hall, "The Long Civil Rights Movement and the Political Uses of the Past," *Journal of American History* 91 (March 2005), 1233–1263; and Van Gosse and Richard Moser, eds., *The World the 60s Made: Politics and Culture in Recent America* (Philadelphia: Temple University Press, 2003).

7. There is a substantial secondary literature comprised of memoirs, poetry, anthologies, autobiography, and cultural and political analyses of the Black Power era. However, there is still no comprehensive historical overview of the era. One strain of this literature is comprised of texts that were produced by the movement and serve as primary source material. See, for example, Stokely Carmichael and Charles Hamilton, *Black Power: The Politics of Liberation in America* (New York: Vintage Books, 1992); Toni Cade Bambara, ed., *The Black Woman: An Anthology* (New York: The New American Library, 1970); Eldridge Cleaver, *Soul on Ice* (New York: Ramparts, 1968). Black Power produced major interest in the history and philosophy of black nationalism and recent black social activism. See for example John H. Bracey Jr., August Meier, and Elliot Rudwick, eds., *Black Nationalism in America* (Indianapolis: Bobbs-Merrill, 1970). Some literature analyzed the developing Black Power revolt. See, for example, Robert Allen, *Black Awakening in Capitalist America: An Analytic History* (Trenton, NJ: Africa World Press, 1990); James Boggs, *Racism and the Class Struggle: Further Pages from a Workers Notebook* (New York: Monthly Review Press, 1970); Harold Cruse, *The Crisis of the Negro Intellectual* (New York: Quill, 1984). Historical case studies of specific cities and organizations include Dan Georgakas and Marvin Surkin, *Detroit: I Do Mind Dying: A Study in Urban Revolution* (Boston: South End Press, 1998); James Geshwender, *Class, Race, and Worker Insurgency: The League of Revolutionary Black Workers* (Cambridge: Cambridge University Press 1977). Autobiographies and memoirs of the era abounded, with some being written and published during the era and others released decades later. See, for example, James Forman, *The Making of Black Revolutionaries* (Seattle: Open Hand, 1985); Angela Davis, *Angela Davis: An Autobiography* (New York: International Publishers, 1988); Amiri Baraka, *The Autobiography of LeRoi Jones/Amiri Baraka* (Chicago: Lawrence Hill Books, 1997); and Assata Shakur, *Assata: An Autobiography* (Chicago: Lawrence Hill Books, 2001). The Black Arts Movement produced a number of works of poetry and anthologies that defined the emerging black aesthetic. See, for example, Sonia Sanchez, *We a BadddDDD People* (Detroit: Broadside Press, 1970). For contemporary overviews see William Van Deburg, *New Day in Babylon: Black*

Power and American Culture, 1965-1975 (Chicago: University of Chicago Press, 1992); James Edward Smethurst, *The Black Arts Movement: Literary Nationalism in the 1960s and 1970s* (Chapel Hill: University of North Carolina Press, 2005) and Joseph, *Waiting 'Til the Midnight Hour*.

8. Komozi Woodard, *A Nation Within a Nation: Amiri Baraka (LeRoi Jones) & Black Power Politics* (Chapel Hill: University of North Carolina Press, 1999), 50–155.

9. For an exception, see, for example, Robert C. Smith, *We Have No Leaders: African-Americans in the Post-Civil Rights Era* (New York: SUNY Press, 1996). See also Joseph, *Waiting 'Til the Midnight Hour*.

10. Woodard, *A Nation Within a Nation*, 159–218.

11. See, for example, the way in which the Panthers are referenced in the PBS Documentary *Two Nations of Black America*, (1998); Joy James, *ShadowBoxing: Representations of Black Feminism* (New York: St. Martin's Press, 1999); Kathleen Cleaver and George Katsiaficas, eds., *Liberation, Imagination, and the Black Panther Party* (New York: Routledge, 2001); Hugh Pearson, *The Shadow of the Panther: Huey Newton and the Price of Black Power in America* (Reading, MA: Addison-Wesley, 1994); and Yohuru Williams, "In Defense of Self-Defense, the Black Panther Party in History and Memory." Paper delivered at the Organization of American Historians Annual Meeting, April 2002, Los Angeles.

12. Historical scholarship on the relationship between black Americans, civil rights, and Cold War internationalism has produced major studies over the past two decades. See, for example, Gerald Horne, *Black and Red: W.E.B. Du Bois and the African American Response to the Cold War, 1944–1963* (Albany: State University of New York Press, 1986); *Communist Front?: The Civil Rights Congress* (Rutherford, NJ: Fairleigh Dickinson University Press, 1986); *Black Liberation and Red Scare: Ben Davis and the Communist Party* (Newark, DE: University of Delaware Press, 1994); Martin Duberman, *Paul Robeson* (New York: The New Press, 2001); Van Gosse, *Where the Boys Are: Cuba, Cold War America and the Making of a New Left* (London: Verso, 1993); Mary Dudziak, *Cold War Civil Rights* (Princeton: Princeton University Press, 2000); Renee Romano, "No Diplomatic Immunity: African Diplomats, the State Department, and Civil Rights, 1961–1964," *Journal of American History* 87 (September 2000), 546–579; Thomas Borstelmann, *The Cold War and the Color Line: American Race Relations in the Global Arena* (Cambridge, MA: Harvard University Press, 2001); Azza Salama Layton, *International Politics and Civil Rights Policies in the United States* (Cambridge: Cambridge University Press, 2000); James H. Meriwether, *Proudly We Can Be Africans: Black Americans and Africa, 1935–1961* (Chapel Hill: University of North Carolina Press, 2002); Piero Gleijeses, *Conflicting Missions: Havana, Washington, and Africa, 1959–1976* (Chapel Hill: University of North Carolina Press, 2002); Penny Von Eschen, *Race Against Empire: Black Americans and Anticolonialism, 1937–1957* (Ithaca, NY: Cornell University Press, 1997) and *Satchmo Blows Up the World: Jazz Ambassadors Play the Cold War* (Cambridge, MA: Harvard University Press, 2004); Bill V. Mullen and James Smethurst, eds., *Left of the Color*

Line: Race, Radicalism, and Twentieth-Century Literature of the United States (Chapel Hill: University of North Carolina Press, 2003); Brenda Gayle Plummer, ed., *Window on Freedom: Race, Civil Rights, and Foreign Affairs 1945–1988* (Chapel Hill: University of North Carolina Press, 2003) and *Rising Wind: Black Americans and U.S. Foreign Affairs, 1935–1960* (Chapel Hill: University of North Carolina Press, 1996).

13. Timothy B. Tyson, "Robert F. Williams, 'Black Power,' and the Roots of the African American Freedom Struggle," *Journal of American History* 85 (September 1998), 541.

14. See Joseph, *Waiting 'Til the Midnight Hour* and Ferruccio Gambino, "The Transgression of a Laborer: Malcolm X in the Wilderness of America," *Radical History Review* 55 (Winter 1993), 7–31.

15. See Horne, *Black and Red*; Robert Rodgers Korstad, *Civil Rights Unionism: Tobacco Workers and the Struggle for Democracy in the Mid-Twentieth-Century South* (Chapel Hill: University of North Carolina Press, 2003) and Robin D. G. Kelley, *Hammer and Hoe: Alabama Communists During the Great Depression* (Chapel Hill: University of North Carolina Press, 1990). See also Gerald Horne, *Race Woman: The Lives of Shirley Graham Du Bois* (New York: New York University Press, 2000); Carol Anderson, *Eyes Off the Prize: The United Nations and the African American Struggle for Human Rights, 1944–1955* (Cambridge: Cambridge University Press, 2003); Dudziak, *Cold War Civil Rights;* William Chafe, *Civilities and Civil Rights: Greensboro, North Carolina, and the Black Struggle for Freedom* (New York: Oxford University Press, 1980); Glen Eskew, *But for Birmingham: The Local and National Movements in the Civil Rights Struggle* (Chapel Hill: University of North Carolina Press, 1997); Mark Naison, *Communists in Harlem During the Depression* (Urbana: University of Illinois Press, 1983); Dittmer, *Local People;* Charles Payne, *I've Got the Light of Freedom: The Organizing Tradition and the Mississippi Freedom Struggle* (Berkeley: University of California Press, 1995). Nikhil Singh provides a rich intellectual history of black radicalism during the "long civil rights movement" from the Depression through to the 1970s and Martha Biondi's powerful case study of New York during the postwar freedom movement examines the Black Popular Front and its domestic (and international) impact on black activism. See Nikhil Pal Singh, *Black Is a Country: Race and the Unfinished Struggle for Democracy* (Cambridge, MA: Harvard University Press, 2004) and Martha Biondi, *To Stand and Fight: The Struggle for Civil Rights in Postwar New York City* (Cambridge, MA: Harvard University Press, 2003).

16. For an illuminating discussion of this historiography, see Hall, "The Long Civil Rights Movement and the Political Uses of the Past" and Kevin Gaines, "The Historiography of the Struggle for Black Equality Since 1945," in *A Companion to Post-1945 America*, 211–234.

17. For a discussion of the Black Public Sphere, see The Black Public Sphere Collective, ed., *The Black Public Sphere: A Public Culture Book* (Chicago: University of Chicago Press, 1995).

18. See the essays in the "Black Power Studies: A New Scholarship" special issue of *The Black Scholar* 31 and 32. See also "Radicalism in Black

America" special issue of *Souls* 1 (Fall 1999) and the "Dossier on Black Radicalism" special issue of *Social Text* 67 (Summer 2001).

19. Perhaps the best-known narrative of the Civil Rights Movement is Taylor Branch's two published volumes, the first of which won a Pulitzer Prize, of a projected trilogy. See Taylor Branch, *Parting the Waters: America in the King Years, 1954–1963* (New York: Touchstone Books, 1988) and *Pillar of Fire: America in the King Years, 1963–1965* (New York: Simon and Schuster, 1998). See also Garrow, *Bearing the Cross* and Fairclough, *To Redeem the Soul of America.*

20. See Timothy B. Tyson, *Radio Free Dixie: Robert F. Williams and the Roots of Black Power* (Chapel Hill: University of North Carolina Press, 1999); and Peniel E. Joseph, "Waiting Till the Midnight Hour: Reconceptualizing the Heroic Period of the Civil Rights Movement, 1954–1965," *Souls* 2 (Spring 2000), 6–17. Gambino, "The Transgression of a Laborer." Other examples will be cited throughout this chapter.

21. Tyson, *Radio Free Dixie.*

22. A number of important studies have highlighted the contributions of "local people" to the CRM. However, most of these studies have focused on the South and stop short of examining local participation during the Black Power era. William Chafe's work on Greensboro, North Carolina is an important exception in this regard, tracing the impact of Black Power on local southern civil rights activists. See Chafe, *Civilities and Civil Rights;* Eskew, *But for Birmingham;* Dittmer, *Local People;* Payne, *I've Got the Light of Freedom;* Diane McWhorter, *Carry Me Home: Birmingham, Alabama The Climactic Battle of the Civil Rights Revolution* (New York: Touchstone Books, 2002); and Korstad, *Civil Rights Unionism.* For studies of northern civil rights struggles see James R. Ralph Jr., *Northern Protest: Martin Luther King, Jr., Chicago, and the Civil Rights Movement* (Cambridge, MA: Harvard University Press, 1993); Clarence Taylor, *Knocking at Our Own Door: Milton A. Galamison and the Struggle to Integrate New York City Schools* (New York: Columbia University Press, 1997); and Biondi, *To Stand and Fight.* Although all of the case studies point to tantalizing connections between civil rights and Black Power in the north, new case studies that chart civil rights and Black Power in specific cities will shed new light on the interplay between these two eras. On this score, see Matthew Countryman, *Up South: Civil Rights and Black Power in Philadelphia* (Philadelphia: University of Pennsylvania Press, 2005). Historian Hasan Jeffries has recently offered an illuminating historiography of the evolution of scholarship on the postwar freedom struggle. See Hasan Jeffries, "Searching for a New Freedom," in *A Companion to African American History,* Alton Hornsby Jr., ed., (Malden, MA: Blackwell Publishing, 2005), 499–511.

23. See Joseph, "Black Liberation Without Apology: Reconceptualizing the Black Power Movement," 2–19; Scot Brown, "The US Organization, Black Power Vanguard Politics and the United Front Ideal: Los Angeles and Beyond," 20–30; Rhonda Y. Williams, "'We're tired of being treated like dogs': Poor Women and Power Politics in Black Baltimore," 31–41; Stephen Ward, "Scholarship in the Context of Struggle: Activist

Intellectuals, the Institute of the Black World (IBW), and the Contours of Black Power Radicalism," 42–53; and Yohuru Williams, "No Haven: From Civil Rights to Black Power in New Haven, Connecticut," 54–66 in *The Black Scholar* 31. See also Eddie S. Glaude Jr., ed., *Is it Nation Time?: Contemporary Essays on Black Power and Black Nationalism* (Chicago: University of Chicago Press, 2002).

24. See Tyson, *Radio Free Dixie;* and Smethurst, *The Black Arts Movement;* See also, Kevin K. Gaines, "African American Expatriates in Ghana and the Black Radical Tradition," *Souls* 1 (Fall 1999), 64–71; Peniel E. Joseph, "Where Blackness is Bright?: Cuba, Africa, and Black Liberation During the Age of Civil Rights, *New Formations* 45 (Winter 2001–2002), 111–124; and Robin D. G. Kelley and Betsey Esch, "Black Like Mao: Red China and Black Liberation," *Souls* 1 (Fall 1999), 6–41.

25. See, for example, Smethurst, *The Black Arts Movement;* Williams, "'We're tired of being treated like dogs'; Ward, "Scholarship in the Context of Struggle." Scot Brown, *Fighting For US: Maulana Karenga, The US Organization, and Black Cultural Nationalism* (New York: New York University, 2003). See also Joseph, *Waiting 'Til the Midnight Hour*. Although the Black Panthers have received far more attention than virtually every other Black Power-era group or individual, the BPP still has yet to be the subject of a full organizational history.

26. Sundiata Cha-Jua and Clarence Lang, "Strategies for Black Liberation in the Era of Globalization: Retronouveau Civil Rights, Militant Black Conservatism, and Radicalism," *The Black Scholar* 29 (Fall 1999), 25–47.

27. For a powerful history of the underclass debate, see Michael B. Katz, ed., *The "Underclass" Debate: Views From History* (Princeton: Princeton University Press, 1993). I want to thank Jeanne Theoharis for a conversation that illuminated this connection.

28. See Todd Gitlin, *The Sixties: Years of Hope, Days of Rage* (New York: Bantam Books, 1989); Pearson, *The Shadow of the Panther;* Maurice Isserman and Michael Kazin, *America Divided: The Civil War of the 1960s* (New York: Oxford University Press, 2000).

29. For an example of these new voices, see Jones, *The Black Panther Party [Reconsidered];* Cleaver and Katsiaficas, *Liberation, Imagination, and the Black Panther Party;* Jeanne Theoharis and Komozi Woodard, eds., *Freedom North: Black Freedom Struggles Outside the South, 1940–1980* (New York: Palgrave Macmillan, 2002) and *Groundwork: Local Black Freedom Movements in America* (New York: New York University Press, 2005); Rod Bush, *We Are Not What We Seem: Black Nationalism and Class Struggle in the American Century* (New York: New York University Press, 1999); Clarence Lang, "Between Civil Rights and Black Power in the Gateway City: The Action Committee to Improve Opportunities for Negroes (ACTION), 1964–1975," *Journal of Social History* 37 (Spring 2004), 725–754; Smethurst, *The Black Arts Movement*. Black Arts icons such as Sonia Sanchez and Amiri Baraka enjoyed a renaissance during the 1990s that continues into the present. Baraka, Sanchez, and other Black Arts figures have appeared on HBO's popular spoken word performance show, *Def Poetry Jam,* hosted by some of the leading progressive

voices in Hip Hop. Sanchez's poetry figured in a pivotal scene in the urban romance movie "Love Jones" and Baraka performed during the closing credits of the Warren Beatty directed political satire, *Bulworth*.

30. See Smethurst, *The Black Arts Movement*.

31. Ibid., 110.

32. For discussion of *Presence Africaine*, see Bennetta Jules-Rosette, *Black Paris: The African Writers' Landscape* (Urbana: University of Illinois Press, 1998).

33. Esther Cooper Jackson, ed., *Freedomways Reader: Prophets in Their Own Country* (Boulder, CO: Westview Press, 2000).

34. Ruth Reitan, *The Rise and the Decline of an Alliance: Black Leaders and the Cuban Revolution* (East Lansing: Michigan State University Press, 1999). Tyson, *Radio Free Dixie*; Gosse, *Where the Boys Are*.

35. Joseph, "Where Blackness is Bright?," 114. Robert F. Williams discussed Cuba and his personal tour there in the pages of the *Crusader*. See Tyson, *Radio Free Dixie*. Julian Mayfield, "The Cuban Challenge," *Freedomways* 1 (Summer 1961); John Henrik Clarke, "Journey to Sierra Maestra," *Freedomways* 1 (Spring 1961); LeRoi Jones, "Cuba Libre," *Evergreen Review* 4 (November-December 1960); Harold Cruse, "A Negro Looks at Cuba," in *The Essential Harold Cruse: A Reader*, William Jelani Cobb, ed. (New York: Palgrave, 2002), 7–20.

36. Cynthia Young, "Havana Up in Harlem: LeRoi Jones, Harold Cruse, and the Making of a Cultural Revolution," *Science & Society* 65 (Spring 2001), 31–36. See also Jerry Watts, ed., *Harold Cruse's Crisis of the Negro Intellectual Reconsidered* (New York: Routledge, 2004) and Cobb, *The Essential Harold Cruse*.

37. Carson, *In Struggle*.

38. See Plummer, *Rising Wind*.

39. For the death of Lumumba, see Ludo De Witte, *The Assassination of Lumumba* (London: Verso, 2001). For an autobiographical account of the African American response, see Maya Angelou, *Heart of a Woman* (New York: Bantam Books, 1997). See also Komozi Woodard, "Amiri Baraka, the Congress of African People and Black Power Politics from the 1961 United Nations Protest to the 1972 Gary Convention," in this volume.

40. St. Claire Drake, "Black Studies and Global Perspectives: An Essay," *Journal of Negro Education* 53 (Summer 1984), 226–242. See also Joseph, *Waiting 'Til the Midnight Hour*.

41. Lance Hill, *The Deacons for Defense: Armed Resistance and the Civil Rights Movement* (Chapel Hill: University of North Carolina Press, 2004), 264.

42. See Hill, *Deacons for Defense*; Tyson, *Radio Free Dixie*; Christopher Strain, *Pure Fire: Self-Defense as Activism in the Civil Rights Era* (Athens: University of Georgia Press, 2005); Jeffrey O. G. Ogbar, *Black Power: Radical Politics and African American Identity* (Baltimore: Johns Hopkins University Press, 2004). See also Simon Wendt, "The Roots of Black Power?: Armed Resistance and the Radicalization of the Civil Rights Movement," in this volume.

43. Gaines, "African American Expatriates in Ghana," 66.

44. See Maya Angelou, *All God's Children Have Traveling Shoes* (New York: Random House, 1986).

45. Gaines, "African American Expatriates in Ghana," 66.

46. For the African Liberation Support Committee, see Modibo Kadalie, *Internationalism, Pan-Africanism, and the Struggle of Social Classes* (Savannah, GA: One Quest Press, 2000); Ron W. Walters, *Pan-Africanism in the African Diaspora: An Analysis of Modern Afrocentric Political Movements* (Detroit: Wayne State University Press, 1993); and Cedric Johnson, "From Popular Anti-Imperialism to Sectarianism: The African Liberation Support Committee and Black Power Radicals," *New Political Science* 25 (December 2003), 477–507.

47. For an important discussion of the global nature of black history, see Robin D. G. Kelley, "'But a Local Phase in a World Problem': Black History's Global Vision, 1883–1950," *Journal of American History* 86 (December 1999), 1045–1077.

48. Sharon Harley, "'Chronicle of a Death Foretold': Gloria Richardson, the Cambridge Movement and the Radical Black Activist Tradition," in *Sisters in the Struggle: African-American Women in the Civil Rights-Black Power Movement*, Bettye Collier-Thomas and V. P. Franklin, eds. (New York: New York University Press, 2001), 174–196.

49. Grace Lee Boggs, *Living for Change: An Autobiography* (Minneapolis: University of Minnesota Press, 1998).

50. Diane C. Fujino, *Heartbeat of Struggle: The Revolutionary Life of Yuri Kochiyama* (Minneapolis: University of Minnesota Press, 2005).

51. Ogbar, *Black Power*, 159.

52. Brown, *Fighting For US*.

53. Jeanne F. Theoharis, "'We Saved the City:' Black Struggle for Educational Equality in Boston, 1960–1976," *Radical History Review* 81 (Fall 2001), 61–93. See also Jack Dougherty, *More Than One Struggle: The Evolution of Black School Reform in Milwaukee* (Chapel Hill: University of North Carolina Press, 2004).

54. Robert O. Self, *American Babylon: Race and the Struggle for Postwar Oakland* (Princeton: Princeton University Press, 2003) and "'To Plan Our Liberation': Black Politics and the Politics of Place in Oakland, California, 1965–1977," *Journal of Urban History* 26 (September 2000), 759–792.

55. Yohuru Williams, *Black Politics/White Power: Civil Rights, Black Power, and the Black Panthers in New Haven* (New York: Brandywine Press, 2000).

56. For more on government surveillance of Black Power organizations, see Kenneth O'Reilly, *Racial Matters: The FBI's Secret File on Black America* (New York: The Free Press, 1991) and "The FBI and the Politics of the Riots, 1964–1968," *Journal of American History* 75 (June 1988), 91–114. See also Ward Churchill and Jim Vander Wall, *Agents of Repression: The FBI's Secret Wars Against the Black Panther Party and the American Indian Movement* (Boston: South End Press, 1988).

57. See, for example, Bobby Seale, *Seize the Time: The Story of Huey P. Newton and the Black Panther Party* (New York: Vintage, 1970) and *A Lonely*

Rage: The Autobiography of Bobby Seale (New York: Times Books, 1978); Huey P. Newton, *Revolutionary Suicide* (New York: Harcourt Brace Jovanovich, 1973) and *War Against the Panthers: A Study of Repression in America* (New York: Harlem River Press, 1996); Kuwasi Balagoon et al., eds., *Look for Me in the Whirlwind: The Collective Autobiography of the New York 21* (New York: Vintage Books, 1971); Philip Foner, ed., *The Black Panthers Speak* (New York: Da Capo Press, 1995); Michael Newton, *Bitter Grain: The Story of the Black Panther Party* (Los Angeles: Holloway House, 1991); Pearson, *The Shadow of the Panther;* Elaine Brown, *A Taste of Power: A Black Woman's Story* (New York: Pantheon Books, 1993); David Hilliard and Lewis Cole, *This Side of Glory: The Autobiography of David Hilliard and the Story of the Black Panther Party* (Boston: Little, Brown, and Company, 1993).

58. Jones, *The Black Panther Party [Reconsidered];* and Cleaver and Katsiaficas, *Liberation, Imagination and the Black Panther Party.*

59. Charles E. Jones, "Reconsidering Panther History: The Untold Story," in *The Black Panther Party [Reconsidered]*, 12.

60. Nikhil Singh, "The Black Panthers and the 'Underdeveloped Country' of the Left," in *The Black Panther Party [Reconsidered]*, 85.

61. For the BPP's local legacy, see Williams, *Black Politics/White Power;* Charles E. Jones, "The Political Repression of the Black Panther Party: The Case of the Oakland Bay Area, 1966–1971," *The Journal of Black Studies* 18 (June 1988), 415–434; Judson L. Jeffries, "Black Radicalism and Political Repression in Baltimore: The Case of the Black Panther Party," *Ethnic and Racial Studies* 25 (January 2002), 64–98; Jon Rice, "The World of the Illinois Panthers," in *Freedom North*, 41–64; Reynaldo Anderson, "Practical Internationalists: The Story of the Des Moines, Iowa, Black Panther Party," in *Groundwork*, 282–299 and Robyn Ceanne Spencer, "Inside the Panther Revolution: The Black Freedom Movement and the Black Panther Party in Oakland, California," in *Groundwork*, 300–317. See also, Paul Alkebulan, "The Role of Ideology in the Growth, Establishment, and Decline of the Black Panther Party: 1966 to 1982," (Ph.D. diss., University of California, Berkeley, 2003).

62. See Tracye Mathews, "'No One Evers Asks What a Man's Place in the Revolution Is': Gender and the Politics of the Black Panther Party, 1966–1971," in *The Black Panther Party [Reconsidered]*, 268–304 and Angela LeBlanc-Ernest, "The Most Qualified Person to Handle the Job: Black Panther Party Women, 1966–1982," in *The Black Panther Party [Reconsidered]*, 305–334; Kristen Anderson-Bricker, "'Triple Jeopardy': Black Women and the Growth of Feminist Consciousness in SNCC, 1964–1975," in *Still Lifting, Still Climbing: African American Women's Contemporary Activism*, Kimberly Springer, ed. (New York: New York University Press, 1999), 49–69 and Benita Roth, "The Making of the Vanguard Center: Black Feminist Emergence in the 1960s and 1970s," in *Still Lifting, Still Climbing*, 70–90; Paula Giddings, *When and Where I Enter: The Impact of Black Women on Race and Sex in America* (New York: Bantam Books, 1984); Cynthia Griggs Fleming, "Black Women and

Black Power: The Case of Ruby Doris Smith Robinson and the Student Nonviolent Coordinating Committee," in *Sisters in the Struggle*, 197–213.

63. This article grows out of her larger study of the same title on Black Panther women. See Matthews, "'No One Ever Asks What a Man's Place in the Revolution Is': Gender and the Black Panther Party, 1966–1971" (Ph.D. diss., University of Michigan, 1998). Subsequent references are from her essay.

64. Matthews, "'No One Ever Asks What a Man's Place in the Revolution Is.'"

65. See Kimberly Springer, *Living for the Revolution: Black Feminist Organizations, 1968–1980* (Durham, NC: Duke University Press, 2005). See also Anderson-Bricker, "'Triple Jeopardy,'" 49–69.

66. Roth, "The Making of the Vanguard Center." Farah Jasmine Griffin reconsiders *The Black Woman* and its relationship to black feminism, black women's thought and the Black Power era. See Farah Jasmine Griffin, "Conflict and Chorus: Reconsidering Toni Cade's *The Black Woman: An Anthology*," in *Is it Nation Time?*, 113–129.

67. Duchess Harris, "From the Kennedy Commission to the Combahee Collective: Black Feminist Organizing, 1960–1980," in *Sisters in the Struggle*, 280–305.

68. See especially Williams, "'We're tired of being treated like dogs.'" Of course, an understudied aspect of Black Power's gender politics concerns the era's relationship with definitions and conceptions of "manhood." Some recent works, ones that cover postwar black freedom struggles and the way in which protest movements appropriated (and at times subverted) dominant, patriarchal, conceptions of masculinity, shed new light on an era that has (with some justification) been criticized for basking in macho posturing. However, unlike more polemical works, such as Michele Wallace's *Black Macho and the Myth of the Superwoman* (New York: Dial Press, 1978), this new scholarship examines the complicated historical, social, and political matrices that produced the period's at times aggressively masculine politics and highlight the debates, discussions, controversies, and contestation that enveloped the era's "manhood" politics then and now. See, for example, Tyson, *Radio Free Dixie;* Woodard, *A Nation Within a Nation;* Hill, *Deacons for Defense;* Strain, *Pure Fire;* Ogbar, *Black Power;* Wendt, "The Roots of Black Power?"; and Steve Estes, *I Am a Man!: Race, Manhood, and the Civil Rights Movement* (Chapel Hill: University of North Carolina Press, 2005).

69. Woodard, *A Nation Within a Nation*, 159–218; Smith, *We Have No Leaders;* and Leonard Moore, *Carl B. Stokes and the Rise of Black Political Power* (Urbana: University of Illinois Press, 2003).

70. For scholarship that plumbs the depths of what might be called an "archeology of failure" with regard to Black Power era radicalism, see Adolph Reed, ed., *Race, Politics, and Culture: Critical Essays on the Radicalism of the 1960s* (New York: Greenwood Press, 1986) and *Stirrings in the Jug: Black Politics in the Post-Segregation Era* (Minneapolis: University of Minnesota Press, 1999). See also Jerry Gafio Watts, *Amiri Baraka: The Politics and Art of a Black Intellectual* (New York: New York University Press, 2001); Dean E. Robinson, *Black Nationalism in American*

Politics and Thought (Cambridge: Cambridge University Press, 2001); and Cedric Johnson, "From Popular Anti-imperialism to Sectarianism: The African Liberation Support Committee and Black Power Radicals," *New Political Science* 25, no. 4 (December 2003), 477–507. Although all of these works offer insightful analyses of the era, they are hampered by their quest to find out why the movement failed, rather than a search for the way in which Black Power unfolded historically. The latter objective will be crucial to more comprehensive histories that, rather than seeing the era as an ultimately ill-fated rendezvous with defeat, chronicles more than wins and losses, but the human beings behind the era's protests, marches, organizations, and conferences. Moreover, more historical research is needed to know how—and when—Black Power politics succeeded or faltered in local arenas and whether these victories and setbacks correspond with national conceptions of the movement's high tide and low ebb. See Countryman, *Up South*; Woodard, *A Nation Within a Nation*.

71. See Joseph, *Waiting 'Til the Midnight Hour;* Kadalie, *Internationalism, Pan-Africanism, and the Struggle of the Social Classes;* Haki Madhubiti, *Enemies: The Class of the Races* (Chicago: Third World Press, 1978); Woodard, *A Nation Within a Nation;* Self, *American Babylon;* Williams, *Black Politics/White Power;* Jones, *The Black Panther Party [Reconsidered];* Cleaver and Katsiaficas, *Liberation, Imagination, and the Black Panther Party.*

72. Kadalie, *Internationalism, Pan-Africanism, and the Struggle of Social Classes,* 329–358.

73. See Gosse, "A Movement of Movements" and Hall, "The Long Civil Rights Movement and the Political Uses of the Past."

74. See Joseph, *Waiting 'Til the Midnight Hour.*

75. Lang, "Between Civil Rights and Black Power in the Gateway City."

76. For northern black militancy see Smethurst, *The Black Arts Movement;* Biondi, *To Stand and Fight* and Taylor, *Knocking at Our Own Door.* See also Jeanne Theoharis, "'They Told Us Our Kids Were Stupid': Ruth Batson and the Educational Movement in Boston," in *Groundwork,* 17–44 and Brian Purnell, "'Drive Awhile for Freedom': Brooklyn CORE's 1964 Stall-In and Public Discourses on Protest Violence," *Groundwork,* 45–75. For southern Black Power activists being influenced by SNCC, the southern organizing tradition, and early instances of black protest, see Smethhurst, *The Black Arts Movement,* 319–366 and Fanon Che Wilkins, "'In the Belly of the Beast': Black Power, Anti-Imperialism, and the African Liberation Solidarity Movement, 1968–1975," (Ph.D. diss., New York University, 2001). See also Countryman, *Up South.*

77. Christopher Strain's analysis of civil rights and self-defense implicitly follows the declension timeline by examining the years 1955–1968. See Strain, *Pure Fire.* Jeffrey Ogbar's study of Black Power and racial identity sees the movement as largely over by 1970, slowed down by the chipping away of radical black nationalism and a decline in racial upheavals. See Ogbar, *Black Power.* William Van Deburg's overview of the Black Power

era's cultural politics posits the movement as largely disappearing by the early 1970s. See Van Deburg, *New Day in Babylon.*

78. See Payne, *I've Got the Light of Freedom* and Michel-Rolph Trouillot, *Silencing the Past: Power and the Production of History* (New York: Beacon Press, 1995).

Chapter 1

1. This work was made possible by a Rockefeller Humanities Fellowship through California State University, Los Angeles. My Rockefeller graduate assistants Alfio Saitta and Sam Vong played an invaluable role in the shape, contours, and texture of this research. As activist-scholars themselves, they embraced this project as their own, saw the urgency of getting this story of black activism out, brainstormed continually on where and how to document it, and spent countless hours investigating, reading, and recording this broad-based grassroots movement in L.A. I am indebted to Steve Lang—a Fremont graduate himself who has coached track and taught social studies at Fremont High School for the past three decades—for numerous conversations about the school and the history of South L.A. that have undeniably shaped this study. I also would like to thank Scott Dexter, Peniel Joseph, Alejandra Marchevsky, Pete Sigal, Mark Wild, Komozi Woodard, John Rogers, and the members of the Rockefeller seminar for their thoughtful comments on this work.
2. Chester Himes, *The Quality of Hurt: The Early Years* (New York: Paragon House, 1990), 74.
3. Kirse Granat May, *Golden State, Golden Youth: The California Image in Popular Culture, 1955–1966* (Chapel Hill: University of North Carolina Press, 2002), 160.
4. Charlotta Bass, *Forty Years: Memoirs from the Pages of a Newspaper,* self-published manuscript on file at the Southern California Research Library (Los Angeles, 1960), 118–119. By the early 1930s, most black students in Los Angeles attended Jordan and Jefferson High Schools but these schools did not become all black until after World War II.
5. Charlotta Bass "Stage Mock Lynching of 6 at Local School" *California Eagle,* February 20, 1941, 1.
6. "Mothers Protest Mock Lynching," *California Eagle,* February 27, 1941, 1.
7. "Boy Accuses Principal of Fremont," *California Eagle,* March 27, 1941, 1, 9A.
8. Condemning the events at Fremont, an alliance of UCLA, USC, Occidental, and City College students echoed the Mothers' demands when they spoke before the Board of Education. Pressure was also put on the Board to take action against the principal and faculty who were responsible for the riot along with the students. "Fury at Fremont," *California Eagle,* March 6, 1941, 8A.

9. A very small group of Mexican Americans and Japanese Americans and almost no African Americans attended Fremont in this period; this contrasted with neighboring Jefferson and Jordan High Schools, which were fairly multiracial. Fremont's 1946 yearbook showed no black students except one unidentified black woman. Only a handful of students with Spanish surnames could be counted along with four Asian American students.

10. In her autobiography, Bass conflates the two events, dating the riot in 1941 but bringing in many of the details from the one in 1947. Bass, *Forty Years,* 118–119.

11. Describing a pattern of threats and violence, one girl commented, "They [the school administration] waited so long to do anything about the situation in Fremont that the condition became extreme." "Fremont Girls Tell Story on Sentinel Hour," *Los Angeles Sentinel,* March 27, 1947, 1. "Same Rights, Same Privileges," *Los Angeles Sentinel,* March 31, 1947.

12. C. A. Bass, "White Adults Instigate Riot at Fremont," *California Eagle,* March 20, 1947, 1. Bass characterized the strike as "a culmination of many years of race tension unabated which reached the point of explosion." C. A. Bass "Negro Hanged in Effigy: Editor of Eagle Menaced," *California Eagle,* March 20, 1947, 1.

13. Ibid.

14. G. Simmons, "School Board President Ducks Issue in Fremont High Race Baiting Outbreak," *Los Angeles Sentinel,* March 20, 1947, 1.

15. Indeed, the "Communists" were highlighting the disturbing racial nature of the incidents at Fremont. The local Communist Party (C.P.) had been quite active around issues of racial injustice in the city, willing to organize around community concerns. One local section of the L.A. Communist Party hosted a mass meeting on the events surrounding the racial violence at Fremont. There, a candidate for city council charged that "the recent attacks on Negro children at the Fremont High School" were not an isolated incident but part of a broader effort by "restrictive covenant agitators," white parents and homeowners to keep African Americans in their place. Despite historians' characterization of the C.P. as the driving force of racial organizing in 1940s L.A., however, the C.P. did not initiate this organizing around Fremont but provided a forum for parents and other community members who had already been active around this issue to come together. "Links Fremont School Riot to Racist Covenants," *California Eagle,* March 27, 1947, 8.

16. This local history of black struggle in L.A. has recently come into view through a important body of new research that has begun to revise popular notions about race in the West, about the landscape of race and power in Southern California, and about the meanings of the Watts riot. See Josh Sides, *L.A. City Limits: African American Los Angeles from the Great Depression to the Present* (Berkeley: University of California Press, 2003); Becky Nicolaides, *My Blue Heaven: Life and Politics in the Working-Class Suburbs of Los Angeles, 1920–1965* (Chicago: University of Chicago Press, 2001); Quintard Taylor, *In Search of the Racial Frontier* (New York: W. W. Norton, 1998); *Seeking El Dorado: African Americans in California,*

Lawrence de Graafe et al., eds. (Los Angeles: Autry Museum of Western Heritage, 2001); Douglas Flamming, *Bound for Freedom: Black Los Angeles in Jim Crow America* (Berkeley: University of California Press, 2005); Regina Freer, "L.A. Race Woman: Charlotta Bass and the Complexities of Black Political Development in Los Angeles," *American Quarterly* 56.3 (September 2004); and Josh Sides, "Straight into Compton: American Dreams, Urban Nightmares, and the Metamorphosis of a Black Suburb," *American Quarterly* 56.3 (September 2004).

17. A sample of this metaphorical use among well-regarded histories include the following: William Chafe writes, "Almost immediately, the slogan [Black Power] became a rallying cry for angry blacks as well as a justification for a white backlash against the civil rights movement. In the summer of 1965, race riots had laid waste the Watts area of Los Angeles." William Chafe, *The Unfinished Journey: America Since World War II* (New York: Oxford University Press, 1999), 318. Eric Foner writes, "Even as the struggle achieved its greatest successes, however, violent outbreaks in black ghettoes outside of the South—Harlem in 1964, Watts in 1965 (just a few days after Johnson signed the Voting Rights Act), other cities in ensuing years—drew attention to the fact that racial justice was a national, not southern problem, and to the inequalities in employment, education, and housing that the dismantling of legal segregation left intact." Eric Foner, *The Story of American Freedom* (New York: W. W. Norton, 1998).
Christopher Strain writes, "While making substantial strides toward political equality, the civil rights movement in the South had raised hopes and expectations without providing any real gains for black folks living in cities such as Los Angeles, outside the South. Feelings of resentment and futility ran high…. In fact, the Watts uprising was as much a reaction against the black elite, symbolized by middle-class civil rights leaders, as it was a spontaneous rebellion against white authority." Christopher Strain, *Pure Fire: Self-Defense as Activism in the Civil Rights Era* (Athens: University of Georgia Press, 2005), 134, 143.

18. At some level, this dichotomy is more than a 150 years old, dating back to political discourses around the Civil War. Slavery (and by extension racism) was defined as a Southern problem that the North had corrected for itself and needed to correct in the Confederacy. Although the national imagination reserved a special place for the West—and for the opportunity the West allowed—the narrative of the Watts riot never breaks out of this North–South dichotomy. The riot is not explained as a Western phenomenon but linked to uprisings in Harlem, Detroit, Newark—the urban North.

19. Robert Weisbrot writes, "King and his companions ruefully confessed that the carnage pointed not only to the failures of the wider society but also to the limits of their own movement … Residents of Watts, Harlem, or Chicago's West Side slums could read about Southern Negro triumphs in their local papers and watch Lyndon Johnson declaim about new laws against discrimination. Yet their own lives remained as bleak as before the Greensboro sit-in." Robert Weisbrot, *Freedom Bound: A History of*

American's Civil Rights Movement (New York: Plume, 1990), 159–161. The gendered implications of such framings bear further scrutiny as such paradigms often construct middle-class leaders as effete and ghetto dwellers as hypermasculine.

20. Hasan Jeffries has critiqued how Black Power is too often framed as an outside export to local communities rather than an indigenous process. In charting the rise of a separate black political party in Lowndes County, Alabama, Jeffries concludes "Local people's political awareness was not a result of apocalyptic events or movement messiahs but was the product of a process of critical reflection that began with filtering movement experiences through a framework of premovement memories" in *Groundwork: Local Black Freedom Struggles in America,* Jeanne Theoharis and Komozi Woodard, eds. (New York: New York University Press, 1995), 156.

21. See Theoharis and Woodard, *Freedom North* for an elaboration of this argument.

22. Weisbrot continues, "Had this been a middle-class area like Striver's Row in Harlem, where lawyers, doctors, and businessmen upheld a 'model neighborhood,' rage might have melted away amid concern for property values. But this was Watts, a district fifty miles square that lay beneath the approaches to the city's international airport, a dense, squalid ghetto where more than 250,000 Negroes were crammed into faded stucco buildings. Trash collection was a rare event, so a stroll along any street in Watts meant an encounter with broken glass, rusty cans, rotting food. Two thirds of the residents were on welfare, unemployment among adult males was 34 percent ... These conditions afforded little incentive for 'keeping cool' after the arrest of Marquette Frye. Instead residents went about the cathartic business of destroying their neighborhood" (159). The acclaimed documentary series *Eyes on the Prize I* and *II,* despite its depth and breadth, also treated the riots (L.A. and Detroit) outside of a context of activism within these cities.

23. Taylor, *In Search of the Racial Frontier,* 302.

24. Gerald Horne, "Black Fire: 'Riot' and 'Revolt' in Los Angeles, 1965 and 1992" in *Seeking El Dorado.*

25. No work was more pivotal in legitimating this notion of an underclass than the sociologist William Julius Wilson's *The Truly Disadvantaged* (Chicago: University of Chicago Press, 1987). Wilson took older conservative ideas about poverty, married them to a structural analysis, and recast them as liberal formulations on the underclass. He explicitly connected this new underclass to changes in the U.S. economy (notably deindustrialization and public and corporate divestment from U.S. cities) that improved the incomes of many blacks while leaving the rest of the black community unemployed and increasingly isolated. These structural changes in the economy, according to Wilson, precipitated behavioral and community change in black inner-city neighborhoods. As basic institutions declined the social organization of inner-city neighborhoods—sense of community, positive neighborhood identification, and explicit norms and sanctions against aberrant behavior—likewise declined. Wilson contended that social dislocation and isolation were the

defining traits of the underclass, the problems of poor blacks stemming from class rather than race. The dissolution of the black community and of black families, as men lost their jobs, led to the creation of a permanent underclass whose "behavior contrasts sharply with that of mainstream America." While Wilson took pains to distinguish his analysis from conservatives like Charles Murray by emphasizing the structural roots of black community decline, his focus on "the tangle of pathology in the inner city" legitimated the belief that a profoundly destructive culture had emerged in the nation's inner cities. By the early 1990s, Wilson's theoretical formulations had overtaken American social science.

26. The existence of sustained urban protest movements disrupts current assumptions of a disintegrated black community after the Great Migration of African Americans to the North. For a more extended critique of underclass theory, see Alice O'Connor, *Poverty Knowledge: Social Science, Social Policy, and the Poor in Twentieth-Century U.S. History* (Princeton: Princeton University Press, 2001); Robin D. G. Kelley, *Yo' mama's disfunktional: fighting the culture wars in urban america* (Boston: Beacon, 1997); Alejandra Marchevsky and Jeanne Theoharis, "Welfare Reform, Globalization, and the Racialization of Entitlement," *American Studies*, 41:2/3 (Summer/Fall 2000), 235–265; Adolph Reed, "The Underclass as Myth and Symbol: The Poverty Discourse about Poverty" in *Radical America* 24.1 (1990); and Michael B. Katz, ed., *The "Underclass" Debate: Views from History* (Princeton: Princeton University Press, 1993).

27. Gerald Horne, *Fire This Time: The Watts Uprising and the 1960s* (New York: Da Capo Press, 1997), 132.

28. See Sides, Flamming, Nicolaides, Freer, Taylor, and de Graafe.

29. Regina Freer makes a similar point about Charlotta Bass's early dual membership in the NAACP and the UNIA. See Freer, "L.A. Race Woman."

30. This chapter focuses on postwar efforts of African Americans around schools. Latinos were also organizing in this period. In March 1945, Gonzalo Mendez, William Guzman, Frank Palomino, Thomas Estrada, and Lorenzo Ramirez with the help of the League of United Latin American Citizens (LULAC) sued four local school districts, including Westminster and Santa Ana, for segregating their children. Judge Paul McCormick ruled in *Mendez v. Westminster School District of Orange Count*—later upheld by the U.S. Ninth Circuit Court and an important precedent for *Brown*—that this violated the California constitution and the Equal Protection clause of the 14th Amendment.

31. Partly this stems from the ways that the urban black poor are *not* seen as thinkers—certainly as rebellious, angry, and emotional—but rarely spiritual or intellectual. Endowed with less virtue, their activism has then been cast as "extreme" or "misguided" by numerous scholars and journalists.

32. Regina Freer similarly argues against "truncat[ing] L.A.'s black history by locating its birth in Watts in 1965 and circumscrib[ing] black history making to expressions of hopelessness. Political struggle like that practiced by Bass and other black Angelenos signals hope as much as it

does frustration. Thus resurrecting her legacy is more than an exercise in highlighting a history of disappointment for black Angelenos." Freer, "L.A. Race Woman," 629.

33. Rather, if we are to chart any causality, it is that the riots developed in response to decades of white resistance to civil rights activism. Tom Sugrue demonstrates a similar pattern in his work on Detroit. See Thomas Sugrue, *The Origins of the Urban Crisis: Race and Inequality in Postwar Detroit* (Princeton: Princeton University Press, 1996).

34. A number of scholars have begun to contradict this through their studies of Northern cities, notably Tom Sugrue, Arnold Hirsch, Craig Wilder, and Wendell Pritchett. See Sugrue, *The Origins of the Urban Crisis*; Arnold Hirsch, *Making the Second Ghetto: Race and Housing in Chicago 1940–1960* (Chicago: University of Chicago Press, 1998); Craig Wilder, *A Covenant with Color* (New York: Columbia University Press, 2001); Wendell Pritchett, *Brownsville, Brooklyn* (Chicago: University of Chicago Press, 2002).

35. Nicolaides, *My Blue Heaven*, 165. See Chapter 6 of Douglas Flamming's *Bound for Freedom* for a more detailed history of the Klan in Los Angeles.

36. Interview of Chester Murray and Andrew Murray by Josh Sides. Black Migration and Community in 1940s, L.A. Oral History Transcripts on file at the Southern California Library for Research and Social Science.

37. She had attended Kansas City Bible College, married Joseph Edgar Tackett in 1926 and had two children, and worked in real estate.

38. Marnesba Tackett interview by Michael Balter, Oral History Program, University of California Los Angeles 1988, Department of Special Collections, UCLA, 75.

39. According to the historian Daniel Widener, "On the whole the postwar fortunes of African Americans and Japanese Americans in Southern California differed sharply from the antecedent period.... In 1948, California voters struck down a fair housing ordinance aimed largely at blacks and Mexicans even as the U.S. Supreme Court ruled racial restrictions on Japanese commercial fishermen unconstitutional." Daniel Widener, "'Perhaps the Japanese Are to Be Thanked?' Asia, Asian Americans, and the Construction of Black California" in *Positions* 11: 1 (Spring 2003), 167–168. Also, on Mexicans, see Sides, *City Limits*, 111.

40. Interview with Augustus Hawkins by Carlos Vasquez for the California State Archives, State Government Oral History Program on file at UCLA Special Collections, 1988, 108.

41. The L.A. NAACP's membership had been decimated through anticommunism and through lack of attention to organizing and thus hovered around 5000 members in the early 1950s. By 1956, however, in part through Tackett's efforts spearheading the membership drive, it had climbed back up to 15,000 members. Still, factional disputes in the L.A. chapter (particularly around the perceived threat of communism) continued to fracture the organization, and some middle-class black homeowners left the organization in the 1950s, believing that the NAACP's interests were too tied to renters rather than advocating for the rights of property owners.

42. It was not until 1966 that the State Board of Education required L.A. to conduct a racial census.

43. The NAACP education committee reported, "Though there is the general impression through the city of Los Angeles and throughout the length and breadth of America that there is a great shortage of teachers, it should be emphasized that in the county of Los Angeles, the great majority of school districts and Boards of Education will not hire black teachers." In L.A. County, only 10 out of more than 100 districts had even employed African Americans as teachers. Branch Files of the NAACP microfilm Part 27 Series D, 1956–1965 The West. Reel 3.

44. Malcolm X, "Ballot or the Bullet," *Malcolm X Speaks*, George Breitman, ed. (New York: Grove Press, 1965), 42.

45. A survey of schools across the nation in 1972 showed that Los Angeles schools in particular, and California schools more generally were more segregated than those in Alabama, North Carolina, South Carolina, Virginia, and Louisiana. Sides, *City Limits*, 159.

46. John and LaRee Caughey, *School Segregation on Our Doorstep: The Los Angeles Story* (1966) on file at the Southern California Library for Research and Social Science, 10. See also John Caughey's papers on file at the Department of Special Collections at UCLA. By 1951, Charlotta Bass had sold the *California Eagle* to black lawyer Loren Miller.

47. May, *Golden State, Golden Youth*, 14.

48. Horne, *Fire This Time*, 228.

49. "School Head, Pupil Fight Over Haircut," *Los Angeles Sentinel*, March 8, 1962, A1. Horne, *Fire This Time*, 228.

50. According to the *California Eagle*, "This complaint about text books used in Los Angeles schools is a recurrent one. The claim is frequently made that the evils of slavery are played down, and the slaves are generally depicted as 'happy,' 'content with their lot' and uncomplaining. Virtually nothing is said, the complaints continue, about the continued rebellion of Negroes against the cruel conditions under which they were forced to live; nothing is said about the surpassing courage of those men and women, like Frederick Douglass or Harriet Tubman, who became leaders of their people in their fight for freedom." "'Happy Slave' View In Textbooks Scored," *California Eagle*, November 15, 1962, 1, 4.

51. NAACP Branch Files, Reel 3.

52. Tackett later acknowledged that it was the ACLU rather than the NAACP that was willing to be much more persistent in pursuing school desegregation.

53. Sides, *City Limits*, 157. At two L.A. rallies in June 1962, King called on black Angelenos to "register and vote."

54. John Caughey, *To Kill a Child's Spirit* (Itasaca, IL: Peacock Publishers, 1973), 15–16.

55. Tackett interview, 128–129.

56. "Challenge Board's Boundary," *Los Angeles Sentinel*, September 13, 1962, 1, 3.

57. August Meier and Elliott Rudwick, *CORE: A Study in the Civil Rights Movement 1942–1968* (Chicago: University of Illinois Press, 1973), 74.

"Two CORE Pickets Kicked: D.A. Refuses to Issue a Complaint," May 2, 1963, 1. "1000 Tell Torrance Integration's Coming," *California Eagle,* July 4, 1963, 14. CORE also picketed businesses such as Safeway and KFWB Radio for their hiring policies.

58. Branch Files, Reel 4.
59. "Yorty Calls Racial Situation Tense, Asks Federal Help," *Los Angeles Times,* 1.
60. "Letter to Claude Hudson from Roy Wilkins," September 12, 1962. Branch Files, Reel 4.
61. NAACP Head Blasts Report on Brutality," *California Eagle,* January 9, 1964, 1.
62. Tackett interview; "Greatest Freedom Rally Here Nets Heroes Over $75,000," *Los Angeles. Sentinel,* May 30, 1963, 1.
63. Originally the UCRC was called the NAACP-UCRC. But, according to Tackett, "some of the people of the NAACP felt that we were moving a little farther than they wanted to move. So they withdrew the name." Tackett interview, 106–114. Sides, *City Limits,* 163.
64. Mary Tinglof Smith, "How Crawford Began," *Integrated Education,* XX (1983), 8.
65. Caughey, *School Segregation on Our Doorstep,* 16.
66. Tackett interview, 107, 143.
67. Nicolaides, *My Blue Heaven,* 291.
68. The Board consisted of seven members elected at large for staggered four-year terms: J. C. Chambers, Arthur Gardner, Georgianna Hardy, Ralph Richardson, Charles Smoot, Mary Tinglof, and Hugh Willett. At-large voting made it difficult for the black community to change the make-up of the Board.
69. "L.A. Meeting Proposed to Avert Racial Strife," *L.A. Times,* June 4, 1963, 24.
70. "Los Angeles Choice: End Segregation or Face Mass Action," *California Eagle,* June 13, 1963, 1.
71. Tackett interview, 128–129.
72. "Rights Groups Breaks Off All Negotiations," *California Eagle,* July 25, 1963, 1.
73. Ibid.
74. "3 of 'Big Four' will Lead School March," *California Eagle,* August 8, 1963, 1.
75. Malcolm X, *Malcolm X Speaks,* 30.
76. In August 1963, in response to continued intransigence around equity issues and news that the city was about to commit a million dollars to upgrade the segregated Jordan High School, activists went to the courts in *Crawford v. Los Angeles Board of Education.* Activists resisted the Board's proposal both because they did not want better segregated schools—even this large commitment of money to Jordan was not going to erase the inequities between these two schools—and because they feared this was a token effort to appease protesters and not a systematic effort to improve the conditions of all-black schools. Rejecting the idea of being grateful for such handouts, many community activists did not see

this million-dollar promise as the self-determination and excellence they were seeking. In the *Crawford* case, the plaintiffs argued that LAUSD operated a highly and increasingly segregated system, exacerbated by both the action and inaction of the Board of Education. The Board defended, "the high concentration of minorities in portions of the district widely separated from white students, the complete desegregation of the districts schools would be financially unfeasible and educationally counterproductive." Yet, the district was increasingly segregated: by 1967, 218 of the 544 regular schools in LAUSD were more than 50 percent minority. The *Crawford* case was not heard until 1968 when Judge Gitelson found the district to be "substantially segregated." Gitelson drew on evidence of the Board's citing of new schools, transportation and open transfer policies, feeder patterns, and mandatory school attendance boundaries to establish the intentional nature of LAUSD's segregation.

77. "Negro Students Dodge Eggs During Last Week At South Gate High," *L.A. Sentinel*, July 4, 1963, 1.
78. "Dymally Hits Inequal School Boundary Lines," *Los Angeles Sentinel*, September 6, 1962.
79. "Pickets, Pickets, Pickets," *California Eagle*, September 26, 1963, 1.
80. Report of the Ad Hoc Committee on Equal Education Opportunity, September 12, 1963, found in the John Caughey Papers (Box 164), Department of Special Collections, UCLA.
81. Caughey, *School Segregation on Our Doorstep*, iii.
82. Nicolaides, *My Blue Heaven*, 303.
83. Smith, "How Crawford Began," 9.
84. "USC Dean Won't Let Farmer Speak; He'll Talk at UCLA," *California Eagle*, November 7, 1963, 1.
85. "CORE Launches 'Operation Jericho,'" *Los Angeles Sentinel*, November 21, 1963.
86. Nicolaides, *My Blue Heaven*, 304.
87. "School Board Plan 'Gives Us Nothing,'" *California Eagle*, December 5, 1963, 3.
88. "School Board Okays Feeble Bus Plan to Avoid Double Shifts," *California Eagle*, December 26, 1963, 1.
89. "Marnesba Tackett 'Woman of the Year,'" *California Eagle*, March 19, 1964, 1. "Eagle's Choice of Year" *California Eagle*, April 2, 1964, 3.
90. Celes King interview, by Bruce Tyler and Robin Kelley, Oral History Program, University of California Los Angeles 1988, Department of Special Collections, UCLA.
91. The proposition was worded confusingly: "Neither the State nor any subdivision or agency thereof shall ... limit or abridge ... the right of any person ... to decline to sell, lease or rent property to such ... persons as he, in his absolute discretion, chooses" Nicolaides, *My Blue Heaven*, 308. "NAACP Drafts All-Out Drive For State Fair Housing Bill," *Los Angeles Sentinel*, April 11, 1963.
92. Caughey, *To Kill a Child's Spirit*, 24.
93. Numerous groups joined the fight to defeat it including the Japanese American Citizens League and the Mexican American Political Association.

Hundreds of people demonstrated for fair housing in Pomona, Monterey Park, Van Nuys, Westwood, Pasadena, and at local California Real Estate Associate offices. "Pickets March To Save Fair Housing," *Los Angeles Sentinel,* January 9, 1964. "UCRC Backs Boycott," *Los Angeles Sentinel,* November 21, 1963.

94. C. Marie Hughes, "Housing Foes Picket King, CRB Banquet," *California Eagle,* February 20, 1964, 1.

95. "Hate Pickets Thank God for Chief Parker," *California Eagle,* May 7, 1964, 1. "Rev. King Urges Defeat of Segregating Initiative," *California Eagle,* June 4, 1964, 5.

96. Kurt Schuparra, *Triumph of the Right: The Rise of the California Conservative Movement, 1945–66* (Armonk, NY: M.E. Sharpe, 1998), 105.

97. Pouissant argued that Proposition 14 "had an enormous psychological effect on Negroes in ghetto areas. It made them feel trapped." Nicolaides, *My Blue Heaven,* 324–325.

98. Lisa McGirr has given us an important study of the dominance of race in the rise of the new right in Orange County in *Suburban Warriors: The Origins of the New American Right* (Princeton: Princeton University Press, 2001), 133.

99. Grace Simons, "Baldwin Tells L.A. Bitter Facts on Bias," *California Eagle,* May 16, 1963, 1.

100. Taylor, *In Search of the Racial Frontier,* 300. Frye is often portrayed as an unemployed drunk driver, the archetypal underclass young man.

101. Interview with Cynthia Hamilton. Watts Oral History Project of the Southern California Research Library, 1990.

102. Nicolaides says 50,000; Sides 10,000; May 35,000; Strain 31,000 with upward of 72,000 involved as spectators. The uprising initially garnered little public attention, not even making the front page of the *L.A. Times* the next day. Interestingly, in sharp contrast to how they described the aggressive and demeaning treatment of the police during the riot, many people interviewed by the McCone Commission praised the L.A. County Sheriff's Department, the California Highway Patrol, and especially the National Guard for their role in establishing order. Strain, *Pure Fire,* 137.

103. Caughey, *To Kill a Spirit,* 25.

104. May, *Golden State,* 160.

105. Despite the extensive attention around the Stokes case and the pattern of police brutality against African Americans in the city, Police Chief William Parker had still maintained in the winter of 1964–1965 that there would be no violent upheaval in L.A. and that there was little racial tension. Mayor Sam Yorty had also recently testified to the U.S. Civil Rights Commission that "we have the best race relations in our city of any large city in the United States." Sides, *City Limits,* 169.

106. Horne, *Fire This Time,* 99. The Watts Tower, a 104-feet high artistic mosaic structure by white Italian immigrant Sabatino Rodia, was also left untouched, preserved by the community as something beautiful in Watts.

107. Strain, *Pure Fire,* 124.

108. Celes King interview, 453. King had been the bondsman that movement activists, from CORE to the Nation of Islam, went to when they had been arrested.

109. Celes King interview, 458.

110. Alfred Ligon, interviewed by Ranford Hopkins, Oral History Program, University of California Los Angeles 1988, Department of Special Collections, UCLA. Nearly incessantly at first and for years following the uprising, journalists repeatedly asked King about Watts; highlighting his own shock—in other words, working with the frame that most journalists brought to the subject—gave King more room to expound on the problems endemic to American capitalism and democracy. I am indebted to Karthik Reddy for a series of conversations that helped clarify my thinking on this matter.

111. Maya Angelou, *A Song Flung Up to Heaven* (New York: Virago, 2002), 82–83.

112. Strain, *Pure Fire*, 134.

113. Caughey, *To Kill a Spirit*, 29.

Chapter 2

1. Piero Gleijeses, *Conflicting Missions: Havana, Washington, and Moscow 1959–1976* (Chapel Hill, 2002), 131–132.

2. Ibid.

3. Komozi Woodard, *The Making of the New Ark, Imamu Amiri Baraka (LeRoi Jones), the Newark Congress of African People, and the Modern Black Convention Movement. A History of the Black Revolt and the New Nationalism, 1966–1976* (Ph.D. dissertation, University of Pennsylvania, 1991), 28–29.

4. John Henrik Clarke, "The New Afro-American Nationalism," *Freedomways* 1 (Fall 1961), 286; Woodard, *The Making of the New Ark*, 30.

5. Frantz Fanon, "Lumumba's Death: Could We Do Otherwise?" *Toward the African Revolution* (New York: Grove, 1967), 193; Woodard, *The Making of the New Ark*, 31.

6. Woodard, *The Making of the New Ark*, 32; *New York Times*, February 14, 1961: 1.

7. *New York Times*, February 16, 1961: 11.

8. *New York Times*, February 16, 1961: 1; Woodard, *The Making of the New Ark*, 33.

9. Amiri Baraka interview with author in Newark, New Jersey (January 4, 1986); Amiri Baraka, *The Autobiography of LeRoi Jones* (New York: Freundlich 1984), 181.

10. James Smethurst, *The Black Arts Movement: Literary Nationalism in the 1960 and 1970s* (Chapel Hill: University of North Carolina Press, 2005).

11. Interviews with Vicki Garvin, who lived in China alongside the Williams family during those years (Newark, New Jersey, 1983).

12. Harold Cruse, *The Crisis of the Negro Intellectual* (New York: William Morrow, 1967), 357.

13. Komozi Woodard, ed., *The Black Power Movement, Part 1: Amiri Baraka From Black Arts to Black Radicalism and Beyond* (Bethesda, MD: University Publication Association, 2000).

14. Michael Gomez, *Black Crescent: The Experience and Legacy of African Muslims in the Americas* (Cambridge: Cambridge University Press, 2005).

15. Wilson J. Moses, *The Golden Age of Black Nationalism* (New York: Oxford University Press, 1988).

16. When I asked Larry Neal what to study as the background to the Black Arts movement in 1968, he told me to study Janheinz Jahn's *Muntu*. In his personal papers, students may see his early thinking about the cultural nationalism of the Central European rebels in the 1840s and beyond; those are in his correspondence with James Walker.

17. Interview with A. M. Babu, November 1990; Interview with Amiri Baraka; A. M. Babu in *The Future that Works: Selected Writings of A. M. Babu,* eds. Salma Babu and Amrit Wilson (Trenton, NJ: Africa World Press, 2002).

18. Amiri Baraka, "The Need for a Cultural Base for Civil Rites & Bpower Mooments," in *Raise, Race, Rays, Raze: Essays Since 1965* (New York: Random House, 1971), 39–48.

19. Ibid., 45–46.

20. Baraka, *The Autobiography of LeRoi Jones,* 262.

21. Ron Porambo, *No Cause for Indictment: An Autopsy of Newark* (New York: Holt, 1971), 34–35.

22. Ibid., 35.

23. Baraka, *Raise, Race, Rays, Raze,* 41.

24. Ibid., 40.

25. As with the Shrine of the Black Madonna, the Spirit House, as part of the Black Arts Movement, emerged in 1966; the Black Arts Movement was spurred on by the same dynamics that produced RAM as well as the 1964 Harlem uprising that profoundly affected the thinking of Malcolm X in his last year.

26. See Komozi Woodard, *A Nation Within a Nation: Amiri Baraka (LeRoi Jones) and Black Power Politics* (Chapel Hill: University of North Carolina Press, 1999). The classical black convention movement, also called the Negro Convention Movement, took shape in the nineteenth century. See Howard H. Bell, *A Survey of the Negro Convention Movement, 1830–1861* (New York: Arno, 1969); Jane H. Pease and William H. Pease, *They Who Would Be Free* (New York: Atheneum, 1974); Bill McAdoo, *Pre-Civil War Black Nationalism* (New York: David Walker Press, 1983); Vincent Harding, *There is a River* (New York: Harcourt, Brace, Jovanovich, 1981).

27. 1959 Press Release, Box 3, Folder 8 of Ernest Thompson Papers, Rutgers University Special Collections at Alexander Library: "History was made at Orange City Hall Monday night."

28. See Baraka Papers at Howard University for extensive and detailed meeting minutes as well as deliberation of an admissions committee for the exchange program and the applications.

29. *National Black Political Agenda* (Washington, D.C.: National Black Political Convention, Inc., 1972), 14; also in Komozi Woodard, ed., *The Black Power Movement*, Part 1 (Bethesda, MD: University Publication Association, 2000).
30. *National Black Political Agenda.*
31. For background on A. M. Babu, see *The Future That Works* and Don Petterson, *Revolution in Zanzibar: An American's Cold War Tale* (Boulder, CO: Westview Press, 2002).

Chapter 3

I would like to thank the following people for reading drafts of this chapter in its numerous iterations and providing constructive feedback for revision: Peniel E. Joseph, Kevin Gaines, Tracye Matthews, Karen Sotiropoulos, and Robyn Spencer. Any shortcomings are mine alone.

1. Mary Roger Thibodeaux, S.B.S, *A Black Nun Looks at Black Power* (New York: Sheed & Ward, 1972), 42.
2. "What SNCC's Stokely Carmichael Said At Morgan," *Baltimore Afro-American*, January 21, 1967.
3. This essay expands upon my article, "'We're Tired of Being Treated Like Dogs': Poor Women and Power Politics in Black Baltimore," *The Black Scholar* 31 (Fall/Winter 2001), 31–41, and information in Chapters 5 and 6 in Rhonda Y. Williams, *The Politics of Public Housing: Black Women's Struggles Against Urban Inequality* (New York: Oxford University Press, 2004). For other scholarly studies that explore low-income black women's struggles, see Christina Greene, *Our Separate Ways: Women and the Black Freedom Movement in Durham, North Carolina* (Chapel Hill: University of North Carolina Press, 2005); Felicia Kornbluh, "'To Fulfill Their Rightly Needs': Consumerism and the National Welfare Rights Movement," *Radical History Review 69* (Fall 1997), 76–113; Lisa Marie Levenstein, "The Gendered Roots of Modern Urban Poverty: Poor Women and Public Institutions in Post-World War II Philadelphia" (Ph.D. diss., University of Wisconsin-Madison, 2002); Premilla Nadasen, "Expanding the Boundaries of the Women's Movement: Black Feminism and the Struggle for Welfare Rights," *Feminist Studies 28* (Summer 2002), 271–301 and *Welfare Warriors: The Welfare Rights Movement in the United States* (New York: Routledge, 2004); Nancy A. Naples, *Grassroots Warriors: Activist Mothering, Community Work, and the War on Poverty* (New York: Routledge, 1998); Annelise Orleck, *Storming Caesar's Palace: How Black Mothers Fought Their Own War on Poverty* (Boston: Beacon Press, 2005).
4. Goldie Baker, interview by author, January 29, 1997.
5. Ibid.
6. In recent years, numerous scholars have engaged in the important work of charting black women's participation in and shaping influence of black nationalist groups in general and 1960s' Black Power organizations

specifically. Kathleen Cleaver, "Women, Power, and Revolution," in *Liberation, Imagination, and the Black Panther Party*, Kathleen Cleaver and George Katsiaficas, eds. (New York: Routledge, 2001), 123–127; Angela D. LeBlanc-Ernest, "'The Most Qualified Person to Handle the Job': Black Panther Party Women, 1966–1982," and Tracye Matthews, "'No One Ever Asks, What a Man's Role in the Revolution Is': Gender and the Politics of the Black Panther Party, 1966–1971," both in *The Black Panther Party [Reconsidered]*, Charles E. Jones, ed. (Baltimore: Black Classic Press, 1998); *Sisters in the Struggle: African American Women in the Civil Rights—Black Power Movement*, edited by Bettye Collier-Thomas and V. P. Franklin (New York: New York University Press, 2001); Ula Yvette Taylor, "'Negro Women are Great Thinkers as well as Doers': Amy Jacques-Garvey and Community Feminism in the United States, 1924–1927," *Journal of Women's History* 12 (Summer 2000), 104–126 and *The Veiled Garvey: The Life and Times of Amy Jacques Garvey* (Chapel Hill: University of North Carolina Press, 2002); Williams, "'We're Tired of Being Treated Like Dogs.'" Also, see Ruth Feldstein, "'I Don't Trust You Anymore': Nina, Simone, Culture, and Black Activism in the 1960s," *Journal of American History* 91 (March 2005), 1349–1379; Farah Jasmine Griffin, "Conflict and Chorus: Reconsidering Toni Cade's *The Black Woman: An Anthology*," *Is It Nation Time?: Contemporary Essays on Black Power and Black Nationalism*, Eddie S. Glaude Jr., ed. (Chicago: University of Chicago Press, 2002), 113–129; Darlene Clark Hine and Kathleen Thompson, *A Shining Thread of Hope: The History of Black Women in America* (New York: Broadway Books, 1998), 296–299.

7. Sharon Harley, "'Chronicle of a Death Foretold': Gloria Richardson, the Cambridge Movement, and the Radical Black Activist Tradition," in *Sisters in the Struggle*, 174. Also see Cynthia Griggs Fleming, "Black Women and Black Power: The Case of Ruby Doris Smith Robinson and the Student Nonviolent Coordinating Committee," in *Sisters in the Struggle*, 197–213.

8. Harley, "'Chronicle of a Death Foretold,'" 182–183.

9. Michael Flug, "Organized Labor and the Civil Rights Movement in the 1960s: The Case of the Maryland Freedom Union," *Labor History* 31 (Summer 1990), 345.

10. Harley, "'Chronicle of a Death Foretold,'" 189–190. The Northern Negro Grass Roots Leadership Conference is often remembered for Malcolm X's famous speech, "Message to the Grass Roots." See Angela D. Dillard, "Religion and Radicalism: The Reverend Albert B. Cleage, Jr., and the Rise of Black Christian Nationalism in Detroit," *Freedom North: Black Freedom Struggles Outside the South, 1940–1980*, Jeanne F. Theoharis and Komozi Woodard, eds. (New York: Palgrave, 2003), 169.

11. "Gloria Richardson: Lady General of Civil Rights," *Ebony* 19 (July 1964), 23–31, Folder: Richardson, Gloria, Afro-American Vertical Files (AAVF), Enoch Pratt Free Library (EPFL), Baltimore, Maryland.

12. John T. McCartney, *Black Power Ideologies: An Essay in African-American Political Thought* (Philadelphia: Temple University Press, 1992), 1. James H. Cone argued that Black Power went through "stages of development"

and "various manifestations of reality." Cone, *Black Theology and Black Power* (New York: Seabury Press, 1969), 5, 6. Also see, for instance, Timothy B. Tyson, "Robert F. Williams, 'Black Power,' and the Roots of the African American Freedom Struggle," *Journal of American History* 85 (September 1998), 540–570.

13. For specific historical discussions of Black Power as part of the long struggle for black freedom, see, for instance, Dillard, "Religion and Radicalism," 153–175; Peniel E. Joseph, "Black Liberation Without Apology: Reconceptualizing the Black Power Movement," *The Black Scholar* 31 (Fall/Winter 2001), 2–19; Robert O. Self, "'To Plan Our Liberation': Black Power and the Politics of Place in Oakland, California, 1965–1977," *Journal of Urban History* 26 (September 2000), 759–792.

14. "Civil Rights," *Time*, July 15, 1966, Folder: CORE, Baltimore Chapter, AAVF, EPFL.

15. "Dr. King Coming Here to Address CORE Meeting," *Baltimore Afro-American*, June 28, 1966.

16. Manning Marable, *Race, Reform, and Rebellion: The Second Reconstruction in Black America, 1965–1990* (Jackson: University Press of Mississippi, 1991), 96.

17. Ibid., 94.

18. CORE-Target City, *The Soul Book*, in Folder: CORE, Baltimore Chapter, AAVF, EPFL.

19. Quotes appear, respectively, in Flug, "Organized Labor and the Civil Rights Movement in the 1960s," 333–334, and August Meier and Elliott Rudwick, *CORE: A Study in the Civil Rights Movement, 1942–1968* (New York: Oxford University Press, 1973), 409.

20. On the founding of the Target City project, see George H. Callcott, *Maryland & America, 1940 to 1980* (Baltimore: Johns Hopkins University Press, 1985), 163; Marable, *Race, Reform, and Rebellion*, 94, 96–97. Also see Self, "To Plan Our Liberation," 759–792.

21. "McKeldin Says Rights Bill 'Monument,' Makes it Law," *Baltimore Afro-American*, February 29, 1964; quote appears in Ralph Matthews Jr., "Captives Hurt by Rats, Trash, Horses," *Baltimore Afro-American*, August 15, 1964.

22. Meier and Rudwick, *CORE*, 57, 304–305.

23. Self, "'To Plan Our Liberation,'" 759; Williams, *The Politics of Public Housing*, Chapter 5 and "'We're Tired of Being Treated Like Dogs'"; Yohuru Williams, "No Haven: From Civil Rights to Black Power in New Haven, Connecticut," *The Black Scholar* 31 (Fall/Winter 2001), 54–66.

24. Richard V. Oliver, "'Power for Poor People' Should Be Our Slogan," *Baltimore Afro-American*, June 20, 1967.

25. "Mayor Says Target City Could be Summer's Safest," *Baltimore Afro-American*, July 5, 1966.

26. Between May and June 1967, for instance, CORE's Target City director was fired by national headquarters, reinstated, and then resigned. The local project would have two more directors between July and September. See Stephen J. Lynton, "C.O.R.E. Returns Brooks To Post," *Baltimore Sun*, May 24, 1967; Stephen J. Lynton, "Brooks Resigns Target City

Post," *Baltimore Sun,* June 28, 1967; Stephen J. Lynton, "Perot Appointed C.O.R.E. Director," *Baltimore Sun,* July 16, 1967; Stephen J. Lynton, "C.O.R.E. Working to Revitalize Target City Project," *Baltimore Sun,* September 29. 1967, all in Folder: Congress of Racial Equality, Maryland Vertical Files (MDVF), EPFL.

27. R.B. Jones, "Civil Rights Leaders of the 60's Today," *Baltimore Afro-American,* December 27, 1983. Also see Meier and Rudwick, *CORE,* 377.

28. For a definition of cultural nationalism, see William L. Van Deburg, *Modern Black Nationalism: From Marcus Garvey to Louis Farrakhan* (New York: New York University Press, 1997), 215.

29. Rev. Henry J. Offer, "Black Power: A Great Saving Grace," January 21, 1968, Folder: Civil Rights—Part II, Box 14, Governors Records, Maryland State Archives (MDSA), Annapolis, Maryland. A few months after Offer's statement and about thirty days shy of the uprisings following Martin Luther King Jr.'s assassination, black activists "covering all shades of beliefs," including Lively of U-JOIN, and Olugbala of the Soul School, participated in a conference that resulted in the formation of the Black United Front (BUF). Goldie Baker became a member of BUF, which she described as "a fighting group" in the forefront of the black struggle. Baker maintained that the Black United Front and black grassroots organizers like Lively and Carter, who were mentors alongside her mother and grandmother, unabashedly challenged "Uncle Toms," stood up for black equality, and poor people's economic power. See Goldie Baker, interview by author, January 29, 1997.

30. Gladys Spell, interview by author, November 4, 1993.

31. "Attempt to Organize Black Student Unions," *Baltimore Afro-American,* January 25, 1969; "What is BSU?" *Baltimore Afro-American,* August 2, 1969.

32. "Nun Who Stayed for Black Power," *Baltimore Afro-American,* February 8, 1969. For more detail, see the section, "Black Nuns and Community Power," on pp. 91–94 of this book. The Oblate Sisters of Providence had its counterparts in the Holy Family Sisters in New Orleans and the Handmaids of Mary in New York. Also see Offer, "Black Power," 11.

33. Gladys Spell, interview by author, November 4, 1993. For a slightly longer narrative version of this event, see Williams, "'We're Tired of Being Treated Like Dogs,'" 35–37, and *The Politics of Public Housing,* Chapter 5.

34. The term "blue-eyed devils" was made popular by Malcolm X before he separated from the Nation of Islam. In 1969, black theologian and intellectual James Cone wrote: "The demonic forces of racism are *real* for the black man. Theologically, Malcolm X was not far wrong when he called the white man 'the devil.' The white structure of this American society, personified in every racist, must be at least part of what the New Testament meant by demonic forces." Cone, *Black Theology and Black Power,* 40.

35. Armed self-defense tactics and strategies did not simply emerge with the Black Power Movement, but also had its strategic place in the Civil Rights Movement, and the long black freedom struggle more broadly. See, for instance, Emilye Crosby, "'This Nonviolent Stuff Ain't

No Good. It'll Get You Killed': Teaching About Self-Defense in the African-American Freedom Struggle," *Teaching the American Civil Rights Movement: Freedom's Bittersweet Song,* Julie Buckner Armstrong, Susan Hult Edwards, Houston Bryan Roberson, and Rhonda Y. Williams, eds. (New York: Routledge, 2002), 159–169; Lance Hill, *The Deacons for Defense: Armed Resistance and the Civil Rights Movement* (Chapel Hill: University of North Carolina Press, 2004); George Lipsitz, *A Life in the Struggle: Ivory Perry and the Culture of Opposition* (Philadelphia: Temple University Press, 1988); Timothy B. Tyson, *Radio-Free Dixie: Robert F. Williams and the Roots of Black Power* (Chapel Hill: University of North Carolina Press, 1999); Simon Wendt, "God, Gandhi, and Guns: The African American Freedom Struggle in Tuscaoloosa, Alabama, 1964–1965," *Journal of African American History* 89 (Winter 2004), 36–56.

36. Marian Johnson as told to Michael Davis, "Mother of 4 with Shotgun Vows to Stand Up to KKK," *Baltimore Afro-American,* May 2, 1967.

37. For detailed information on the tenants' struggles that resulted in the formation of the Resident Advisory Board, see Williams, *The Politics of Public Housing,* Chapter 5.

38. Williams, "No Haven," 61.

39. Self, "'To Plan Our Liberation,'" 769; Williams, "No Haven," 61.

40. Steve D. McCutcheon, "Selections from a Panther Diary," *The Black Panther Party [Reconsidered],* 117.

41. Stephen J. Lynton, "Head of Baltimore Panthers Resigns Following Demotion," *Baltimore Sun,* July 13, 1969, Folder: Negroes, MDVF, EPFL. Also see "Black Panthers Step Up Activity," *Baltimore Sun,* January 1, 1969, Folder: Negroes, MDVF, EPFL.

    In 1969 the Black Panther Party experienced heightened police scrutiny, raids, and harassment nationwide, especially in new and unstable chapters. In Detroit, a twenty-year-old Panther was found dead, shot in the head. Bobby Seale was jailed on murder charges in Berkeley, California. In one year, police killed an estimated twenty-eight Panthers. See Williams, "No Haven," 61; "Cops Raid Panthers Pad," *Baltimore Afro-American,* May 31, 1969; "Panther, 20, Found Shot in Head," *Baltimore Afro-American,* June 28, 1969; "Top Panther Jailed on Murder Rap," *Baltimore Afro-American,* August 23, 1969; "Robert Williams Faces Arrest," *Baltimore Afro-American,* August 30, 1969; "Solons Ask Panther Death Probe," *Baltimore Afro-American,* December 13, 1969; "Chicago Panther Probe Set," *Baltimore Afro-American,* December 20, 1969.

42. Harold A. McDougall, *Black Baltimore: A New Theory of Community* (Philadelphia: Temple University Press, 1993), 58. Also see "UMBC Group Launches Drive to Aid Panthers," *Baltimore Afro-American,* December 27, 1966.

43. On New Haven, see Williams, "No Haven," 55. On Baltimore, see McCutcheon, "Selections from a Panther Diary," 126.

44. This discussion of women in the Baltimore BPP just brushes the surface. Significantly more work needs to be done on Baltimore's Black Panther Party, in general, and women's involvement and gender dynamics, specif-

ically. See McCutcheon, "Selections from a Panther Diary"; LeBlanc-Ernest, "'The Most Qualified Person to Handle the Job,'" 307; Matthews, "'No One Ever Asks, What a Man's Role in the Revolution Is,'" 227.

45. Sharon Dickman, "Ochiki Fills Freedom with Work for Pardon," *Baltimore Evening Sun,* May 15, 1975, Folder: Young, Irving H. (Ochiki), AAVF, EPFL.

46. Marable, *Race, Reform, and Rebellion,* 95.

47. Quote from Self, "'To Plan Our Liberation,'" 767–768.

48. Although McKeldin approached the Black Power insurgency with aplomb, the new governor, Spiro T. Agnew, responded brashly. Agnew refused to meet and negotiate with black militants. In the wake of the 1968 rebellions, which exploded days after Martin Luther King Jr.'s assassination, Agnew made public his venom. A racial moderate, who ran as a racial liberal against George P. Mahoney, Agnew became belligerent with politically moderate black civil rights leaders and exposed his dislike of black radicalism and political confrontation. In a meeting he called with moderate black leaders, he made a point to exclude "the circuit-riding, Hanoi-visiting type of leader" and "the caterwauling, riot-inciting, burn-America-down type leader." Agnew further argued that "the looting and rioting which has engulfed our City during the past several days did not occur by chance. It is no mere coincidence that a national disciple of violence, Mr. Stokely Carmichael, was observed meeting with local black power advocates and known criminals in Baltimore on April 2, 1968—three days before the Baltimore riots began." He called Carmichael and Brown "twin priests of violence" and "agents of destruction" and compared them with white supremacists and their organizations. "They will surely destroy us if we do not repudiate them and their philosophies—along with white racists such as Joseph Carroll and Connie Lynch—the American Nazi Party, the John Birchers, and their fellow travelers." See Opening Statement by Governor Spiro T. Agnew, April 11, 1968, Folder: Civil Rights—Part 1, Box 14, Governors Records, MDSA.

49. Cleaver, "Women, Power, and Revolution," 125. Also see Matthews, "'No One Ever Asks, What a Man's Role in the Revolution Is,'" 243–247. On Baltimore programs, see McCutcheon, "Selections from a Panther Diary," 116; Adam Kline, "Panthers Here Chart Resistance," *Baltimore Afro-American,* February 8, 1969.

50. For instance, for Panther women's voices that challenge this view, see "Panther Sisters on Women's Liberation," in *Modern Black Nationalism,* 258–268.

51. McCutcheon, "Selections from a Panther Diary," 116, 119.

52. See similar discussion by Matthews, "'No One Ever Asks, What a Man's Role in the Revolution Is,'" 290–291.

53. "Panther Sisters on Women's Liberation," 258.

54. McCutcheon, "Selections from a Panther Diary." For information on Ochiki, see Folder: Maryland—Governor, 1969–77 (Marvin Mandel), MDVF, EPFL; "Young Granted Parole," *Baltimore Sun,* November 16,

1974; Sharon Dickman, "Ochiki Fills Freedom with Work for Pardon," *Baltimore Evening Sun*, May 15, 1975, Folder: Young, Irving H. (Ochiki), AAVF, EPFL.

55. The free-born black woman, Sister Mary Elizabeth Clarisse Lange, had the help of three other free-born black women compatriots, and the support of a French priest, James Hector Nicholas Joubert de la Muraille. See Diane Batts Morrow, *Persons of Color and Religious at the Same Time: The Oblate Sisters of Providence, 1828–1860* (Chapel Hill: University of North Carolina Press, 2002); Vernon C. Polite, "Making A Way Out of No Way: The Oblate Sisters of Providence and St. Frances Academy in Baltimore, Maryland, 1828 to the Present," *Growing Up African American in Catholic Schools*, edited by Jacqueline Jordan Irvine and Michele Foster (New York: Teachers College Press, 1996), 62–75.

56. "Nun Who Stayed for Black Power," *Baltimore Afro-American*, February 8, 1969. This discussion of Black Power and black nuns is not an attempt to characterize the beliefs of all black nuns or entire nun orders. My point is to expose how several black nuns, who were connected with historically black nun orders, also connected with Black Power struggles, iconography, and philosophies. This is yet another area ripe for research.

57. Quotes appear respectively in "Nun Who Stayed for Black Power," *Baltimore Afro-American*, February 9, 1969; Sherry H. Olson, *Baltimore: The Building of an American City* (Baltimore: Johns Hopkins University Press, 1997), 95; Georgia Samios, "Black Nun Hopes to Build an Oasis in the Ghetto," *Baltimore News American*, January 17, 1971, Folder: St. Frances Academy, AAVF, EPFL.

58. Linell Smith, "Ordered Lives: Oblate Sisters Serve God by Teaching Black Children," Baltimore *Sun*, February 20, 1994, Folder: Oblate Sisters of Providence, AAVF, EPFL. Also see Michelle Singletary, "Answering Call to Serve: Oblates Reach Out to City Blacks," *Baltimore Evening Sun*, April 29, 1985.

59. Cone, *Black Theology and Black Power*, 31.

60. "Nun who Stayed for Black Power," *Baltimore Afro-American*, February 8, 1969. Also see Smith, "Ordered Lives," *Baltimore Sun*, February 20, 1994.

61. Thibodeaux, *A Black Nun Looks at Black Power*, 5, 7. Thibodeaux was born in 1938 in Louisiana. In Philadelphia, she was a sociology graduate student at Temple University and a member of the Philadelphia Archdiocesan Human Relations Committee in Education.

62. The Oblate Sisters order, founded by Haitian women, also had a legacy of celebrating age-old black religious icons. The Oblate Sisters celebrated the 22 Catholic Martyrs of Uganda, hanging their pictures in the Sisters' Chapel at either side of the main altar in 1939. They also acknowledged St. Benedict the Black, a sixteenth-century "Italian Negro" who was born in Sicily and freed at the age of eighteen, and the Blessed Martin de Porres, who hailed from Lima, Peru. Porres's mother was a freed slave and his father was a Spanish nobleman and adventurer. "Paintings Tell Story of Colored Saints," *Baltimore Catholic Review*, November 17, 1939,

in Folder: St. Frances Academy, AAVF, EPFL. On Albert Cleage, see Dillard, "Religion and Radicalism," 153–175.

63. Thibodeaux, *A Black Nun Looks at Black Power*, 25.
64. Ibid., 67.
65. Ibid., 68.
66. "Nun Who Stayed for Black Power," *Baltimore Afro-American*, February 8, 1969.
67. "Nun Who Stayed for Black Power," *Baltimore Afro-American*, February 8, 1969; Samios, "Black Nun Hopes to Build an Oasis in the Ghetto," *Baltimore News American*, January 17, 1971, Folder: Oblate Sisters of Providence, AAVF, EPFL.
68. Samios, "Black Nun Hopes to Build an Oasis in the Ghetto," *Baltimore News American*, January 17, 1971.
69. Polite, "Making a Way Out of No Way," 68; Frank P. L. Somerville, "State's Oldest Black School Reborn," Baltimore *Sun*, July 18, 1979. Allen Quille, a parking lot owner, helped to spearhead the "Restoration Plus" project and to raise most of the money in three phases of $875,000, $775,000, and $750,000. The city's provision of $75,000 in historic preservation money spurred debate about church-state relations in the City Council. See Somerville article in the *Baltimore Sun* cited above. Today, St. Frances Academy continues its work with black children who live in impoverished conditions. See Gary Gately, "In a Grim Corner of Baltimore, a High School Offers a Haven," *New York Times*, May 22, 2005.
70. Margaret "Peggy" McCarty, interview by author, June 21, 2003.
71. Ibid.
72. For an examination of the national movement, see Nadasen, *Welfare Warriors*.
73. Carol Honsa, "Welfare Bill Called 'Betrayal of Poor,'" *Washington Post*, August 29, 1967; Betty James, "Welfare Rally Threatens Riots," *The Evening Star*, August 20, 1967, Folder 7: Founding Meetings, Box 7, George Wiley Papers, Wisconsin Historical Society, Madison, Wisconsin.
74. McCarty, interview by author, June 21, 2003.
75. Clarence "Tiger" Davis, interview by author, October 9, 2002.
76. Roger Nissly, "Poor Demanding Role in 'Demonstration' Project," *Baltimore Afro-American*, March 18, 1967.
77. Johnnie Tillmon, "Welfare is a Woman's Issue," *Ms. Magazine* (Spring 1972), 111–112, 114–116, Folder 9: Women's Movement, 1971–1972, Box 36, George Wiley Papers.
78. Salima Marriott, interview by author, November 4, 2002.
79. Ibid. A black Vietnam veteran who served nineteen months, Paul Coates, on his return to Baltimore, had tried SNCC and the Republic of New Africa. Ultimately, the Philadelphia-born man decided to join the Black Panthers, which focused on inner cities. He began working with the free breakfast program, headed the local BPP from 1970 to 1971, and stayed a member until 1972. McDougall, *Black Baltimore*, 58–59; "Black Success Stories Aside," *Baltimore Sun*, April 4, 1978, Folder: Civil Rights—Baltimore, AAVF, EPFL.

80. Frances Beale, "Double Jeopardy: To Be Black and Female," (1970), 146–155; The Combahee River Collective, "A Black Feminist Statement," (1977), 232–240, both in *Words of Fire: An Anthology of African-American Feminist Thought*, Beverly Guy-Sheftall, ed., (New York: New Press, 1995); Toni Cade Bambara, ed., *The Black Woman: An Anthology* (New York: New American Library, 1970). Also see Nadasen, "Expanding the Boundaries of the Women's Movement," 271–301.

81. Marriott, interview by author, November 4, 2002. Marriott, nee Louise Siler, became a Democratic member of the Maryland House of Delegates for District 40 in Baltimore in 1991. See http://www.mdarchives.state.md.us/msa/mdmanual/06hse/html/msa12265.html (Accessed July 15, 2005).

82. Marriott, interview by author, November 4, 2002. Reflecting back on her experience, Marriott argued that she probably did not stay longer with the BWRO, because of class politics and personalities clashes. She said she felt "beaten upon." Referring to the then BWRO chair, Rudell Martin, who also grew up and at the time still lived in Cherry Hill, Marriott said: "I'm sure she did not identify with me like a sister in the struggle from Cherry Hill, because I wasn't. I'd been out of Cherry Hill. I had chosen a different path. I was not a welfare recipient. I was [a] college graduate working on a masters degree in social work…. So, anyway, I think, that class stuff probably came in. And she wasn't like Goldie and Geneva [Clark]." Marriott served as Clark's case worker and together they started an organization for welfare clients. Moreover, Marriott argued that unlike with Martin, she had an established relationship with Goldie Baker, whom she organized with at the grassroots.

83. Marriott, interview by author, November 4, 2002.

84. Ibid.

85. See note 80; Collier-Thomas and Franklin, *Sisters in the Struggle;* Paula Giddings, *When and Where I Enter: The Impact of Black Women on Race and Sex in America* (New York: Quill, 1984), especially Part III; Guy-Sheftall, *Words of Fire;* Kimberly Springer, ed., *Still Lifting, Still Climbing: African American Women's Contemporary Activism* (New York: New York University Press, 1999); Deborah Gray White, *Too Heavy a Load: Black Women in Defense of Themselves, 1894–1994* (New York: W. W. Norton, 1999), Chapter 7.

86. Quote in "Black Women's Liberation," in *Modern Black Nationalism,* 257. For examples of the "crimes against black humanity" referred to by Assata Shakur, see "To My People," *Modern Black Nationalism,* 269–272.

87. Patricia Hill Collins, *Black Feminist Thought: Knowledge, Consciousness, and the Politics of Empowerment* (New York: Routledge, 1991), 230, 224.

88. Samios, "Black Nun Hopes to Build an Oasis in the Ghetto," *Baltimore News American,* January 17, 1971.

89. Ibid. James H. Cone makes similar arguments regarding the relationship among Jesus Christ, Christianity, and Black Power. He writes that "the message of Black Power is the message of Christ himself." Cone, *Black Theology and Black Power,* 37.

90. Baker, interview by author, January 29, 1997.

91. Ibid.

92. McCarty, interview by author, June 21, 2003.

93. For instance, Goldie Baker argued that the Black Panthers and other Black Power groups had a right "to express themselves" and to not be persecuted. Referring to the systematic government-sponsored counterintelligence attacks on black radical groups such as the Black Panthers, Baker stated: "The white man destroyed them. They acted as persecutors, infiltrators.... They got Black Panthers still locked up in jail just like they had Mandela. In jail for years and years and years, because they said they were teaching hatred." Baker questioned why antiblack groups like the Ku Klux Klan could spread racist propaganda and act on their hatred with seeming impunity, while some groups like the Black Panthers faced attacks for conveying publicly the inescapable realities of historical white oppression. They "weren't lying." White people did serve as "slave masters. They were oppressors.... And you got some white people hate poor white people, poor white trash.... And they hate white people that is in friendship with black people. They call them nigger lovers." Baker, interview by author, January 29, 1997.

94. For instance, Cone also wrote: "Black Power is hope in the humanity of black people," Cone, *Black Theology and Black Power*, 29.

Chapter 4

1. Deborah King, "Multiple Jeopardy, Multiple Consciousness: The Context of Black Feminist Ideology," *Words of Fire: An Anthology of African-American Feminist Thought*, Beverly Guy-Sheftall, ed. (New York: New Press, 1995), 295–296.

2. Janie Nelson, "Attitude-behavior Consistency among Black Feminist and Traditional Women" (Ph.D. diss., Kent State University, 1981). In addition to surveys conducted by Nelson, the often-cited Harris/Virginia Slims American Women Poll measured women's attitudes during peak years for the contemporary feminist movement: 1970, 1972, 1974, and 1980.

3. Komozi Woodard, *A Nation Within a Nation: Amiri Baraka (LeRoi Jones) and Black Power Politics* (Chapel Hill: The University of North Carolina Press, 1999).

4. See Marika Sherwood, *Claudia Jones: A Biography* (London: Lawrence & Wishart, 1999) and Ula Yvette Taylor, *The Veiled Garvey: The Life and Times of Amy Jacques Garvey* (Chapel Hill: University of North Carolina Press, 2002).

5. See Deborah Gray White, *Too Heavy a Load: Black Women in Defense of Themselves, 1894–1994* (New York: W. W. Norton & Company, 1999); White explains that although Black women may have appeared to favor race over gender, or gender over race, these prioritizations were strategic

and dependent on the urgency of the issue. Nevertheless, both race and gender were addressed.

6. For fuller explications of Black Power periodization, ideology, culture, and organizations, see Scot Brown, *Fighting for US: Maulana Karenga, the US Organization, and Black Cultural Nationalism* (New York: New York University Press, 2003); Peniel Joseph, "Black Liberation Without Apology: Reconceptualizing the Black Power Movement," *The Black Scholar* 31 (Fall/Winter 2001), 2–19; William Van Deburg, *New Day in Babylon: The Black Power Movement and American Culture, 1965–1975* (Chicago: University of Chicago Press, 1992).

7. Safiya Buhkari-Alston, for instance, maintains that, "The error everyone seems to be making, supporters and detractors of the Black Panther Party alike, is separating the party from its time and roots and looking at it in a vacuum." Saifya Buhkari-Alston, "On the Question of Sexism Within the Black Panther Party," *Panther Sisters on Women's Liberation*, March 9, 1995, http://www.anarco-nyc.net/anarchistpanther/otherwriting6.html. Accessed February 16, 2005.

8. Buhkari-Alston, "On the Question of Sexism Within the Black Panther Party"; Cole and Guy-Sheftall offer a meaningful update to the thoughts and motivations of African American men active in the 1970s and their reflections on sexism and patriarchy during the Black Power era. Johnetta Cole and Beverly Guy-Sheftall, *Gender Talk: The Struggle for Women's Equality in African-American Communities* (New York: One World/Ballantine Books, 2003).

9. For example, Marcus Garvey's question, "Where is the Black Man's government?" is assumed to be gender-neutral, but in the context of Garveyism, this query clearly relates to blacks who are male, not female.

10. I borrow this subtitle from Collins's excellent examination of the tensions between the terms "black feminist" and "womanist." Patricia Hill Collins, "What's in a name? Womanism, Black Feminism, and Beyond." *The Black Scholar* 26 (Spring 1996), 9–17.

11. King, "Multiple Jeopardy, Multiple Consciousness," 299.

12. Guy-Sheftall, *Words of Fire*, 2.

13. For increasingly sophisticated analyses of the TWWA, see Kristin Anderson-Bricker, "'Triple Jeopardy': Black Women and the Growth of Feminist Consciousness in SNCC, 1965–1974," in *Still Lifting, Still Climbing: African American Women's Contemporary Activism*, Kimberly Springer, ed. (New York: New York University Press, 1999) and Robin D.G. Kelley, *Freedom Dreams: The Black Radical Imagination* (Boston: Beacon Press, 2003).

14. For broader explications of black women and reproductive issues, see Angela Y. Davis, *Women, Race and Class* (New York: Random House, 1983) and Dorothy Roberts, *Killing the Black Body: Race, Reproduction and the Meaning of Liberty* (New York: Vintage Books, 1997).

15. Third World Women's Alliance, "History of the Organization and Ideological Platform," *Triple Jeopardy* 1 (September-October 1972), 8.

16. For the purposes of this chapter, I use masculinism to denote the tendency to universalize the black experience as the black *male* experience.

As I explain later, just as white women universalized the category "woman," some within the Black Power movement universalized the category "black," assuming that black meant all black people, when it, in fact, meant black men or the reassertion of black patriarchy.

17. National Alliance of Black Feminists, "Philosophy of NABF." *Alternative School Bulletin.* (Chicago, IL: The Black Feminist Press, n.d.).

18. White, *Too Heavy a Load.*

19. A partial collection of Smith's archives, located at the Lesbian Herstory Archives in Brooklyn, NY, reflects the seeds of this anthology in minutes for a series of black feminist retreats sponsored by the Combahee River Collective; Barbara Smith, ed., *Home Girls: A Black Feminist Anthology* (Albany, New York: Kitchen Table Women of Color Press, 1983).

20. The evolution continues as black feminism faces stagnation and institutionalization within sites of higher learning. The most pressing question, in my opinion, is how to keep black feminism relevant to black communities-at-large. Many activists and scholars are doing this, particularly men such as Kevin Powell and Mark Anthony Neal, continuing the tradition of black male feminist positions in their analysis and writings on masculinity.

21. Woodard, *Nation Within a Nation,* xii–xiii.

22. Toni Cade Bambara, ed., *The Black Woman: An Anthology* (New York: The New American Library, 1970), 11.

23. Beverly and Barbara Smith, "'I am not meant to be alone and without you who understand': Letters from Black Feminists, 1972–1978." *Conditions* 4 (1978), 64.

24. *Black Is, Black Ain't,* California Newsreel (Marlon, Riggs, 1995). For a personal account of the book's reception, see Michele Wallace, *Black Macho and the Myth of the Superwoman* (New York: Verso Books, 1990) and "Anger in Isolation: A Black Feminist's Search for Sisterhood" in *Words of Fire.*

25. Brenda Eichelberger Papers. "National Alliance of Black Feminists," Chicago Historical Society.

26. It is important to note also the unprecedented success of black women writers during this era and the possible impact of that success on gender relations in the black community. Black women were accused of being somehow more acceptable or "safer" than black men, playing into black nationalist rhetoric of black masculinity as dangerous and more of a revolutionary threat.

27. Woodard, *A Nation Within a Nation,* 181–182.

28. Ibid., 183–184; The Third World Women's Alliance, the Combahee River Collective, and the National Black Feminist Organization all engaged in similar campaigns.

29. Margaret Sloan, "Address given by Gloria Steinem and Margaret Sloan on Women," Carleton College Audio-Visual Department, March 5, 1973.

30. Barbara Smith, interview with author, July 15, 1998.

31. Woodard, A *Nation Within a Nation,* 8.

Chapter 5

1. Recent studies that examine key organizations or individuals in the Black
   Power Movement, or that explore the development of the movement,
   include: Jeffrey O. G. Ogbar, *Black Power: Radical Politics and African
   American Identity* (Baltimore: Johns Hopkins University Press, 2004);
   Scot Brown, *Fighting for US: Maulana Karenga, the US Organization, and
   Black Cultural Nationalism* (New York: New York University Press,
   2003); Komozi Woodard, *A Nation Within a Nation: Amiri Baraka (LeRoi
   Jones) and Black Power Politics* (Chapel Hill: University of North Carolina
   Press, 1999); Peniel E. Joseph, *Waiting 'Til the Midnight Hour: A Narra-
   tive History of Black Power in America* (New York: Henry Holt, 2006);
   Matthew Countryman, *Up South: Civil Rights and Black Power in Phila-
   delphia, 1940–1975* (Philadelphia: University of Pennsylvania Press,
   2005); Clarence Lang, "Between Civil Rights and Black Power in the
   Gateway City: the Action Committee to Improve Opportunities for
   Negroes (ACTION), 1964–75," *Journal of Social History* 37 (Spring
   2004), 725–54; Cedric Johnson, "From Popular Anti-Imperialism to
   Sectarianism: The African Liberation Committee and Black Power Rad-
   icals," *New Political Science* 25 (December 2003), 477–507; and Peniel E.
   Joseph, ed., "Black Power Studies: A New Scholarship," a special issue of
   The Black Scholar 31 (Fall/Winter 2001). In the first book-length historical study of the Black Power Movement, Van Deburg examines the cultural, artistic, and psychological dimensions of the movement: William
   L. Van Deburg, *New Day in Babylon: The Black Power Movement and
   American Culture, 1965–1975* (Chicago: University of Chicago Press,
   1992). Two important recent studies that elucidate the culture and politics of the Black Power period by examining the Black Arts Movement
   are: James Edward Smethurst, *The Black Arts Movement: Literary Nationalism in the 1960s and 1970s* (Chapel Hill: University of North Carolina
   Press, 2005), and Melba Joyce Boyd, *Wrestling With the Muse: Dudley
   Randall and the Broadside Press* (New York: Columbia University Press,
   2003). The following works also treat some aspect of the history of Black
   Power: Timothy Tyson, *Radio Free Dixie: Robert F. Williams and the
   Roots of Black Power* (Chapel Hill: University of North Carolina Press,
   1999); Betty Collier-Thomas and V. P. Franklin, eds., *Sisters in the
   Struggle: African American Women in the Civil Rights–Black Power Move-
   ment* (New York: New York University Press, 2001); Jeanne F. Theoharis
   and Komozi Woodard, eds., *Freedom North: Black Freedom Struggles Out-
   side the South, 1940–1980* (New York: Palgrave Macmillan, 2003) and
   Groundwork: Local Black Freedom Movements in America (New York: New
   York University Press, 2005); Lance Hill, *The Deacons for Defense: Armed
   Resistance and the Civil Rights Movement* (Chapel Hill: University of
   North Carolina Press, 2004); Robert O. Self, *American Babylon: Race and
   the Struggle for Postwar Oakland* (Princeton: Princeton University Press,
   2003); Eddie S. Glaude Jr., ed., *Is it Nation Time? Contemporary Essays on
   Black Power and Black Nationalism* (Chicago: University of Chicago
   Press, 2002); Judson L. Jeffries, *Huey P. Newton: The Radical Theorist*

(Jackson: University Press of Mississippi, 2002); Rod Bush, *We Are Not What We Seem: Black Nationalism and Class Struggle in the American Century* (New York: New York University Press, 1999); Robin D. G. Kelley, *Freedom Dreams: The Black Radical Imagination* (Boston: Beacon Press, 2002); Dean E. Robinson, *Black Nationalism in American Politics and Thought* (New York: Cambridge University Press, 2001); Jerry Watts, ed., *Harold Cruse's The Crisis of the Negro Intellectual Reconsidered* (New York: Routledge, 2004); Kathleen Cleaver and George Katsiaficas, eds., *Liberation, Imagination, and the Black Panther Party: A New Look at the Panthers and Their Legacy* (New York: Routledge, 2001); Charles Jones, ed., *The Black Panther Party [Reconsidered]* (Baltimore: Black Classic Press, 1998).

2. Woodard, *A Nation Within a Nation,* p. 260.

3. As the scholarship on Black Power grows, historians will begin to outline the key historical questions, interpretive stances, and methodological issues of the field. I am thinking, for example, of questions relating to periodization of the movement, Black Power's relationship to civil rights, and the use of sources, including nontraditional sources, among others. Peniel E. Joseph begins to chart some of these historiographical questions in his introduction to this volume. See also Joseph, "Black Liberation Without Apology" and the "Introduction" to Stephen Ward, "Ours Too Was a Struggle for a Better World: Activist Intellectuals and the Radical Promise of the Black Power Movement, 1962–1972" (Ph.D. diss., University of Texas, 2002). By way of contrast (and thus illustration), the voluminous literature on the Civil Rights Movement has produced important historical insights along with debates over interpretations of the movement. For recent analyses of these insights and debates, see Jacquelyn Dowd Hall, "The Long Civil Rights Movement and the Political Uses of the Past," *The Journal of American History* 91(March 2005), 1233–63 and Kevin Gaines, "The Historiography of the Struggle for Black Equality Since 1945," in Jean-Christophe Agnew and Roy Rosenzweig, eds., *A Companion to Post-1945 America* (Malden, MA: Blackwell, 2002).

4. For a good overview of the ideas and activism of radical black feminists during this period, see Kelley, *Freedom Dreams,* Chapter 5. For a discussion of radical black feminism as an important force in recent black political history, see Rose M. Brewer, "Black Radical Theory and Practice: Gender, Race, and Class," *Socialism and Democracy* 17 (Winter–Spring 2003), 109–122. An argument for the recognition of black women activists (focusing on Sojourner Truth and Charlotta Bass in particular) within traditions of black radicalism is presented in Ula Taylor, "Read[ing] Men and Nations: Women in the Black Radical Tradition," *Souls* 1 (Fall 1999). For other works that both emphasize the need to recognize ideological distinctions between black feminisms and explore expressions of radical black feminism, see Joy James, *Shadowboxing: Representations of Black Feminist Politics* (New York: St. Martin's Press, 1999); and Helen A. Neville and Jennifer Hamer, "'We Make Freedom': An Exploration of Revolutionary Black Feminism," *Journal of Black Studies* 31 (March 2001), 437–61.

5. Two important recent studies discuss the TWWA as part of their analyses of the development of black feminism during this period: Kimberly Springer, *Living for the Revolution: Black Feminist Organizations, 1968–1980* (Durham, NC: Duke University Press, 2005), and Benita Roth, *Separate Roads to Feminism: Black, Chicana, and White Feminist Movements in America's Second Wave* (New York: Cambridge University Press, 2004). See also Kristin Anderson-Bricker, "'Triple Jeopardy': Black Women and the Growth of Feminist Consciousness in SNCC, 1964–1975," in Kimberly Springer, ed., *Still Lifting, Still Climbing: African American Women's Contemporary Activism* (New York: New York University Press, 1999).

6. The publication of "Double Jeopardy" coincided with other essays exploring the intersections of race and gender in black women's lives and, more specifically, the political agency of African American women. See, for example, Linda La Rue, "The Black Movement and Women's Liberation," *The Black Scholar* 1 (May 1970), 36–42; Mary Ann Weathers, "An Argument for Black Women's Liberation as a Revolutionary Force," in Mary Lou Thompson, ed., *Voices of the New Feminism* (Boston: Beacon Press, 1970); and Pauli Murray, "The Liberation of Black Women," in *Voices of the New Feminism*. All three of these essays as well as Beal's "Double Jeopardy" are reprinted in Beverly Guy-Sheftall, ed., *Words of Fire: An Anthology of African-American Feminist Thought* (New York: The New Press, 1995).

7. For the development of intersectionality in black feminist thought, see Toni Cade Bambara, ed., *The Black Woman: An Anthology* (New York: New American Library, 1970); Kimberle Williams Crenshaw, "Mapping the Margins: Intersectionality, Identity Politics, and Violence Against Women of Color," *Stanford Law Review* 43 (July 1991), 1241–99; Kimberle Williams Crenshaw, "Demarginalizing the Intersection of Race and Sex: A Black Feminist Critique of Anti-Discrimination Doctrine, Feminist Theory, and Antiracist Politics," *The University of Chicago Legal Forum* (1989),139–67. Patricia Hill Collins, *Fighting Words: Black Women and the Search for Justice* (Minneapolis: University of Minnesota Press, 1998) and *Black Feminist Thought: Knowledge, Consciousness, and the Politics of Empowerment* (New York: Routledge, 2000); Deborah K. King, "Multiple Jeopardy, Multiple Consciousness: The Context of a Black Feminist Ideology," *Signs* 14 (Autumn 1988), 42–72; Bonnie Dill Thornton, "Race, Class, and Gender: Prospects for an All-Inclusive Sisterhood," *Feminist Studies* 9 (Spring 1983), 131–50. Writing in 1983, black feminist scholar and activist Barbara Smith asserted that the concept of the simultaneity of oppressions was "still the crux of a black feminist understanding of political reality." A decade later, Rose Brewer wrote that the "conceptual anchor of recent Black feminist theorizing is the understandings of race, class, and gender as simultaneous forces." In her 1999 study of black feminist politics, Joy James reports: "In their efforts to synthesize emancipation theories, various black feminisms improvise integrative analyses of race, gender, sexuality, and class that focus on commonalities in liberation struggles. The utility of black femi-

nisms in progressive movements is largely determined by their capacity to illustrate and analyze the intersections and multidimensionality of oppression and freedom. They forgo one-dimensional liberation theories that focus on patriarchy *or* white supremacy, or transnational capitalism *or* homophobia, as isolated phenomena. Liberation workers contextualize the meanings of progress and resistance by understanding space and time in ways that reflect the intersecting realities of black women's lives." In 2001, Linda Burnham, a former member of the TWWA (and co-founder of the Women of Color Resource Center, which grew out of the West Coast chapter of TWWA) challenged what she saw as a lack of recognition of the Black Power-era origins of contemporary black feminism. She sought to "provide a corrective to the misperception that intersection theory has its genesis in the academy, or, worse still, that it can be attributed to a single discipline, sub-discipline, or individual." Rather, she argued that "the core concepts of black feminism" were born not in the academy but in "the rich political ferment of the late 1960s and early 1970s" when "Black women whose activism in the civil rights and Black Power movements had centered on the issue of racial injustice began to discuss their situation as women." Citing the TWWA and the Combahee River Collective as examples, she asserted that "the struggle for social transformation" was "a powerful generator of theoretical insight." These and other women participated in discussions and political struggles out of which "emerged the concepts of the both/and of Black women's reality, the simultaneity of oppression, and the intersection of race, class, and gender." Quotations from: Barbara Smith, ed., *Home Girls: A Black Feminist Anthology* (New Brunswick, NJ: Rutgers University Press: 2000), xxxiv; Rose M. Brewer, "Theorizing Race, Class, and Gender: The New Scholarship of Black Feminist Intellectuals and Black Women's Labor," in Stanlie M. James and Abena Busia, eds., *Theorizing Black Feminisms: The Visionary Pragmatism of Black Women* (New York: Routledge, 1993), 13; James, *Shadowboxing;* Linda Burnham, "The Wellspring of Black Feminist Theory," *Southern University Law Review* 28 (2001), 265–270.

8. Author's interview with Frances Beal, Oakland, CA, June 14, 2003 (tape recording). Hereafter cited as Beal interview.
9. Beal interview.
10. James Forman, *The Making of Black Revolutionaries* (Seattle: Open Hand, 1985), 504–552; Beal interview. SNCC was one of the first civil rights/Black Power organizations to formally declare its opposition to the war in Vietnam. See "Statement by the Student Nonviolent Coordinating Committee on the War in Vietnam, January 6, 1966," Debbie Louis Civil Rights Movement Collection, Box 10, Department of Special Collections, Charles E. Young Research Library, UCLA. For a discussion, see Clayborne Carson, *In Struggle: SNCC and the Black Awakening of the 1960s* (Cambridge: Harvard University Press, 1981), 183–189. Beal recalls that Vietnam had a big impact on SNCC's internationalism, especially in the New York office of the organization, out of which the international affairs commission developed. As discussed below, a member of the New York

SNCC office, Gwen Patton, who would also become one of Beal's main collaborators in the Black Women's Liberation Committee, organized the National Black Anti-War Anti-Draft Union (NBAWADU).

11. On the differences among black nationalists in this period, see Alphonso Pinkney, *Red, Black, and Green: Black Nationalism in the United States* (New York: Cambridge University Press, 1976); John H. Bracey Jr., August Meier, and Elliot Rudwick, eds., *Black Nationalism in America* (New York: Bobbs-Merrill, 1970); Robinson, *Black Nationalism in American Politics and Thought*; Glaude, *Is it Nation Time?;* William L. Van Deburg, ed., *Modern Black Nationalism: From Marcus Garvey to Louis Farrakhan* (New York: New York University Press, 1997) and *New Day in Babylon.*

12. For works that specifically address gender ideology within black nationalist discourses, the resulting tensions in the Black Power Movement, and responses by black women activists, see E. Frances White, *Dark Continent of Our Bodies: Black Feminism and the Politics of Respectability* (Philadelphia: Temple University Press, 2001), Chapters 1 and 3; Tracye Matthews, "'No One Ever Asks What a Man's Place in the Revolution is': Gender and the Politics of The Black Panther Party, 1966–1971," in *The Black Panther Party [Reconsidered];* M. Rivka Polatnick, "Poor Black Sisters Decided for Themselves: A Case Study of 1960s Women's Liberation Activism," in Kim Marie Vaz, ed., *Black Women in America* (Thousand Oaks, CA: Sage Publications, 1994); M. Rivka Polatnick, "Diversity in Women's Liberation Ideology: How a Black and a White Group of the 1960s Viewed Motherhood," *Signs* 21 (Spring 1996), 679–706; Lauri Umansky, "'The Sister Reply': Black Nationalist Pronatalism, Black Feminism, and the Quest for a Multiracial Women's Movement," *Critical Matrix* 8 (December 1994), 19–50; Paulette Pierce, "Boudoir Politics and the Birthing of the Nation: Sex, Marriage, and Structural Deflection in the National Black Independent Political Party," in Brackette F. Williams, ed., *Women Out of Place: The Gender of Agency and the Race of Nationality* (New York: Routledge, 1996); Roth, *Separate Roads;* Springer, *Living for the Revolution;* Angela Davis, "Black Nationalism: The Sixties and the Nineties," in Joy James, ed., *The Angela Y. Davis Reader* (Malden, MA: Blackwell, 1998); Paula Giddings, *When and Where I Enter: The Impact of Black Women on Race and Sex in America* (New York: William Morrow, 1984), 314–324.

13. Katy Gibson, "Letter to Black Men," *Liberator*, July 1965; "The Role of the Black Women in a White Society" (panel discussion from Fifth Anniversary Writers' Conference: "Black Writers at the Crossroads," June 19, 1965), *Liberator*, August 1965; Evelyn Rodgers, "Is Ebony Killing Black Women," *Liberator*, March 1966; Amerlia Long, "Role of the Afro-American Woman," *Liberator*, May 1966; Louise R. Moore, "When a Black Man Stood Up," and Betty Frank Lomax, "Afro-American Women: Growth Deferred," *Liberator*, July 1966; Louise Moore, "Black Men vs. Black Women," *Liberator*, August 1966. See also the several responses to these articles in the letters to the editor in these and subsequent issues.

14. Cleaver's statement is cited in Philip S. Foner, ed., *The Black Panthers Speak* (Cambridge, MA: Da Capo Press, 2002), 145. Matthews borrows Cleaver's phrase as the title of her excellent essay (cited above) exploring gender ideology and dynamics in the Black Panther Party. Kathleen Cleaver discusses these dynamics in her essay, "Women, Power, and Revolution." Reflecting on the question of women's role, she writes: "Back then I didn't understand why they wanted to think of what men were doing and what women were doing as separate. It's taken me years, literally about twenty-five years, to understand that what I really didn't like was the underlying assumption motivating the question. The assumption held that being a part of a revolutionary movement was in conflict with what the questioner had been socialized to believe was appropriate conduct for a woman." See Cleaver and Katsiaficas, *Liberation, Imagination, and the Black Panther Party*, 124. For another thoughtful autobiographical analysis by a black woman activist from the period, see Toni Cade Bambara, "On the Issue or Roles," in *The Black Woman*.

15. See Simone M. Caron, "Birth Control and the Black Community in the 1960s: Genocide or Power Politics?" *Journal of Social History* 31 (Spring 1998), 545–569; Toni Cade Bambara, "The Pill: Genocide or Liberation?" in Bambara, *The Black Woman;* Robert G. Weisbord, *Genocide? Birth Control and the Black American* (New York: Greenwood Press, 1975); Umansky, "'The Sister Reply'"; Polatnick, "Poor Black Sisters Decided for Themselves"; Polatnick, "Diversity in Women's Liberation Ideology"; Dorothy Roberts, *Killing the Black Body: Race, Reproduction, and the Meaning of Liberty* (New York: Vintage, 1997), 98–103.

16. "Birth Control for Whom—Negro or White?" *Muhammad Speaks,* July 2, 1965; "The Deadly Pill for Negroes and Indians?" *Muhammad Speaks,* July 9, 1965; "The Sins of Birth Control," *Muhammad Speaks,* July 16, 1965; and "The Safety of the Black Man in World Crisis," *Muhammad Speaks,* July 23, 1965. For discussions of the Nation of Islam's gender politics, see Paulette Pierce and Brackette F. Williams, "'And Your Prayers Shall Be Answered Through the Womb of a Woman': Insurgent Masculine Redemption and the Nation of Islam," in *Women Out of Place;* and Ula Y. Taylor, "Elijah Muhammad's Nation of Islam: Separatism, Regendering, and a Secular Approach to Black Power After Malcolm X (1965–1975)," in *Freedom North*.

17. See Lee Rainwater and William L. Yancey, eds., *The Moynihan Report and the Politics of Controversy* (Cambridge. MA: MIT Press, 1967), and John H. Bracey Jr., August Meier, and Elliot Rudwick, eds., *Black Matriarchy: Myth or Reality?* (Belmont, CA: Wadsworth Publishing Co., 1971).

18. Beal interview. Issues of sexism had been raised in SNCC in the mid-1960s, particularly by two position papers (one was "anonymous") written by two white women in the organization, Casey Hayden and Mary King. Beal was not in the organization during this period. See Sara Evans, *Personal Politics: The Roots of Women's Liberation in the Civil Rights Movement and the New Left* (New York: Vintage Books, 1979). For a discussion of the relationship between these two expressions of feminist consciousness in SNCC—the episodes in 1964 and 1965 of women in

SNCC challenging sexist ideas and practices in the organization, and Beal and other black women in raising issues of gender equity in 1967 and 1968, see Anderson-Bricker, "Triple Jeopardy."

19. Linda Burnham makes a strong case for the importance of SNCC in the intellectual and political development of the other women who formed the Black Women's Liberation Committee: "The significance of their start in SNCC is that these were women who had developed a sense of their own power to create change in the course of the civil rights movement. And they were women who had helped develop the ideas about racism central to that movement, most relevantly, that racism is not about individual aberrational behavior, but a matter of deeply structured institutional arrangements that must be fought through collective political action. In the course of their civil rights/Black Power activism they had learned the all-important lessons of how to mobilize people, how to run a meeting, how to engage in collective processes of reflection and decision making, and how to draft 'who we are and what we want' statements. In other words, SNCC served as an organizational container within which Black women not only matured politically vis-à-vis the issue of race, but also a site wherein women came to identify sexism as a major factor in their lives." See Burnham, "The Wellspring of Black Feminist Theory," 266.

20. Beal interview.

21. In "Double Jeopardy," Beal described these practices as "outrageous Nazi-like procedures," and she expressed indignation that "the sterilization experiments carried on in concentration camps some twenty-five years ago have been denounced the world over, but no one seems to get upset by the repetition of these same racist tactics today in the United States of America—land of the free and home of the brave." A decade later a scholarly study confirmed Beal's analogy, pointing out that the sterilization rates of black women under federally funded programs equaled the rate reached by Nazi sterilization programs in the 1930s. See Roberts, *Killing the Black Body*, 93.

22. Roberts, *Killing the Black Body*, 89–98; Angela Y. Davis, *Women, Race, and Class* (New York: Vintage, 1983), 215–218; Weisbord, *Genocide?* 158–174. During the 1970s, Beal was involved with the Committee to End Sterilization Abuse (CESA) and the effort led by Puerto Rican physician Helen Rodriques-Trias to develop guidelines for hospitals performing tubal ligations. Beal interview; Laura Briggs, *Reproducing Empire: Race, Sex, Science, and U.S. Imperialism in Puerto Rico* (Berkeley: University of California Press, 2002), 147–148.

23. Women in SNCC may have been particularly sensitive to the issue of sterilization abuse. In 1964, SNCC fought against a proposed Mississippi statute known as the "sterilization bill"—and which SNCC activists called the "genocide bill"—that was designed to stem the rise of Mississippi's black population and its perceived threat to the state's racial status quo and its economic progress. The bill would have made it a felony for a parent on welfare to have subsequent illegitimate children. The punishment was to be a one- to three-year term in the state penitentiary for the

first offense and three to five years for repeat convictions, but the person could agree to be sterilized in exchange for the prison term. Nationwide pressure forced supporters of the bill to abandon the sterilization provision. However, illegal sterilizations continued. One of the victims was Mississippi native and SNCC activist Fannie Lou Hamer. In 1961, while she was hospitalized to have a small cyst in her stomach removed, a doctor performed a complete hysterectomy without Hamer's knowledge or consent. Though she said little about her own experience publicly or privately, Hamer made public statements about the forced sterilization of rural black women in Mississippi. See Chana Kai Lee, *For Freedom's Sake: The Life of Fannie Lou Hamer* (Urbana: University of Illinois Press, 1999), 21–22, 80–81.

24. Briggs, *Reproducing Empire,* Chapter 5.
25. Alice Echols, "Nothing Distant About it: Women's Liberation and Sixties Radicalism," in *The Sixties: From Memory to History,* David Farber, ed. (Chapel Hill: University of North Carolina Press, 1994), 158. As Ellen Willis explains, the struggle over abortion was the first major public effort of women liberationists because, "more than any other issue, abortion embodied and symbolized our fundamental demand—not merely formal equality for women but genuine self-determination." For black women however, debates and struggles over abortion played out differently. As the feminist historian Alice Echols writes, "for the young, mostly-white middle-class women who were attracted to women's liberation, the issue was forced reproduction. But for women of color, the issue was as often forced sterilization." See Ellen Willis, "Foreword" to Alice Echols, *Daring to Be Bad: Radical Feminism in America, 1967–1975* (Minneapolis: University of Minnesota Press, 1989), vii–viii; and Echols, "Nothing Distant," 171.
26. "General Resolution of Unincorporated Association, First National City Bank, New York," February 21, 1969, in the Records of the National Council of Negro Women, Series 24, Box 3, Folder 24, National Park Service—Mary McLeod Bethune Council House NHS, Washington, D.C. (Hereafter cited by document title or description, date, box, folder, NCNW—Beal Series).
27. Letter from Gwendolyn Patton to unknown recipient, January 16, 1969, Box 3, Folder 24, NCNW—Beal Series.
28. Manning Marable, *Blackwater: Historical Studies in Race, Class Consciousness, and Revolution* (Niwot, Colorado: University of Colorado Press, 1993), p.125; Peniel E. Joseph, "Waiting Till the Midnight Hour: Black Political and Intellectual Radicalism, 1960–1975" (Ph.D. diss., Temple University, 2000), 142–143; Gwendolyn M. Patton, "An Open Letter to Marxists," *The Black Scholar* 6 (April 1975); Beal interview.
29. There is no evidence that the liberation schools and draft counseling centers came to fruition. It is difficult to know how soon or how fully the members of BWLC expected to carry these projects, but a nationwide effort such as this proved to be beyond the resources of the fledgling organization.

30. Letter from Gwendolyn Patton to unknown recipient, January 16, 1969, Box 3, Folder 24, NCNW—Beal Series.

31. The questions were listed under seven headings: Female, Male-Female, Black-White, Family, Philosophy, and Revolution.

32. Letter from Gwendolyn Patton to Sisters, January 6, 1969, Box 3, Folder 24, NCNW—Beal Series.

33. Neither Patton nor Beal recalls this meeting taking place, and I found no evidence suggesting that it occurred. Beal did, however, recall a smaller meeting around this time on the East Coast. Author's conversation with Gwendolyn Patton, March 8, 2003, Bronxville, NY; Beal interview.

34. Bambara, *The Black Woman*. For example, the transcript of the conversation documents Beal describing the social and economic position of black women as "kind of being like the slave of a slave." In "Double Jeopardy," she wrote: "Let me state here and now that the Black woman in America can justly be described as a 'slave of a slave (112).'" Similarly, during the conversation Beal critiqued notions of black manhood that called for black women to "step back" in deference to black men, calling this "a very counter revolutionary position." In "Double Jeopardy" she declared that "[t]hose who are exerting their 'manhood' by telling Black women to step back into a domestic, submissive role are assuming a counter-revolutionary position" (113). "Transcript," April 17, 1969, p. 2, Box 3, Folder 24, NCNW—Beal Series.

35. "Transcript," April 17, 1969, p. 1, Box 3, Folder 24, NCNW—Beal Series.

36. Ibid., 3, 8.

37. Ibid., 4, 7.

38. Evans, *Personal Politics,* especially 133–134, 137. As Ellen Willis explains, the woman's movement developed a critical consciousness and understanding "that sexuality, family life, and the relations between men and women were not simply matters of individual choice, or even of social custom, but involved exercise of personal and institutional power and raised vital questions of public policy." See Echols, *Daring to Be Bad,* ix. For a brief discussion of black women and consciousness-raising, see Angela Davis, *Blues Legacies and Black Feminism: Gertrude "Ma" Rainey, Bessie Smith, and Billie Holiday* (New York: Pantheon, 1998), 28–29, 54–55, 64.

39. "Women in the Struggle," *Triple Jeopardy* 1 (September-October 1971), 8.

40. Letter from Fran Beal to Sister, April 30, 1970, Box 3, Folder 24, NCNW—Beal Series.

41. Bambara explains in the preface to *The Black Woman* that she saw the book as part of a groundswell of activity among black women attempting to collectively define and determine their political perspectives and objectives. These activities marked the development of a collective political consciousness and feminist organizing among black women, and *The Black Woman* sought to give them voice and legitimacy by documenting their activism: "Throughout the country in recent years Black women have been forming work-study groups, discussion clubs, cooperative nurseries, cooperative businesses, consumer education groups, women's workshops on the campuses, women's caucuses within existing organizations, Afro-American women's magazines. From time to time they have

organized seminars on the Role of the Black Woman, conferences on the Crisis Facing the Black Woman, have provided tapes on the Attitude of European Men Toward Black Women, working papers on the Position of the Black Woman in America; they have begun correspondence with sisters in Vietnam, Guatemala, Algeria, Ghana on the Liberation Struggle and the Woman, formed alliances on a Third World plank" (9–10).

42. Letter from Toni Cade to Fran Beal, August 26, 1969, in the Frances Beal Papers, Series 1, Box 1, Folder labeled "Double Jeopardy Permission to Publish Letters, 1969–1973," National Park Service—Mary McLeod Bethune Council House NHS, Washington, D.C. In 1970, Toni Cade added Bambara to her name. The letter cited here was signed Toni Cade, but I have chosen to identify her as Toni Cade Bambara because she adopted the name shortly after the letter was written and this is the name to which she has subsequently been known. See Toni Cade Bambara, *Deep Sightings Rescue Missions: Fiction, Essays, and Conversations,* Toni Morrison ed. (New York: Vintage, 1996), 205–206.

43. In his analysis of black women writers of the 1950s and the roots of black feminism, Kevin Gaines writes: "*The Black Woman* contains pointed critiques of patriarchal articulations of black militancy. But in retrospect it was also part of that vast literature of the Black Power era whose purpose was to define the future objectives, strategies, and agendas of the black freedom movement ... As historians continue to assess the legacy of Black Power, Toni Cade Bambara's *The Black Woman* will be recognized as being among the most valuable and influential contributions of that period." See Gaines, "From Center to Margin: Internationalism and the Origins of Black Feminism," in *Materializing Democracy: Toward a Revitalized Cultural Politics,* Russ Castronovo and Dana D. Nelson, eds. (Durham, NC: Duke University Press, 2002), 307, 310.

44. Beverly Guy-Sheftall cites *The Black Woman* as one of four books published in 1970 which "signaled a literary awakening among black women and the beginning of a clearly defined black women's liberation movement." According to bell hooks, the book single-handedly "placed black women at the center of various feminist debates" and "legitimized looking at black life from a feminist perspective." Furthermore, she says, "the publication of this anthology not only helped compel the publishing industry to recognize that there was a market for books by and about black women, it helped to create an intellectual climate where feminist theory focusing on black experience could emerge." Farah Jasmine Griffin explains that the book reflects "the vibrancy, excitement, politics, and rhetoric of the time," adding that it "is one of the first major texts to lay out the terrain of black women's thought that emerged from the civil rights, Black Power, and women's liberation movements." Quotations from *Words of Fire,* 14; bell hooks, *Remembered Rapture: The Writer at Work* (New York: Henry Holt, 1999), 231–232; Farah Jasmine Griffin, "Conflict and Chorus: Reconsidering Toni Cade's *The Black Woman: An Anthology,*" in *Is it Nation Time?,* 116–117. The other three books that Guy-Sheftall cites are: Shirley Chisholm's autobiography, *Unbought and Unbossed* (New York: Avon Books, 1970); Toni Morrison's first novel

The Bluest Eye (New York: Washington Square Press, 1970), and Audre Lorde's second collection of poetry, *Cables to Rage* (London: Paul Breman, 1970).

45. Beal interview; "Third World Women's Alliance: Our History, Our Ideology, Our Goals," p. 4, Box 4, Folder 29, NCNW—Beal Series.

46. This search for legitimacy within and relative to the larger black political community was not unique to the TWWA, rather it was a general theme of Black Power-era feminist political activity. For a discussion, see Kimberly Springer, "Practicing Politics in the Cracks; The Interstitial Politics of Black Feminist Organizations," *Meridians* 1 (Spring 2001), 155–91. Elsewhere, Springer argues that this dynamic of justification and defense has endured beyond the Black Power era: "Black Feminists in the 1970s expended disproportionate amounts of energy attempting to legitimize themselves in the eyes of Black communities—so much so that often their organizing suffered. It is compelling to note similarities between 1970s Black feminists and those writing in the 1990s. Writings in the 1990s continue to refute the idea that working against gender oppression is somehow counter to antiracist efforts. Both attempt to strike a balance between adequately theorizing race and gender oppression as they intersect in the United States. Black feminists writing then and now struggle with advocating a love for Black men while passionately hating Black sexism." Quotation from Kimberly Springer, "Third Wave Black Feminism?" *Signs* 27 (Summer 2002), 1059.

47. "Third World Women's Alliance: Our History, Our Ideology, Our Goals," 1–2, Box 4, Folder 29, NCNW—Beal Series.

48. Ibid., 3–4.

49. Ibid., 5–6.

50. Charlayne Hunter, "Many Blacks Wary of 'Women's Liberation' Movement in U.S.," *New York Times,* November 17, 1970, 60; "Women Strike But Equal to What?" *National SNCC Monthly* 1 (September–October 1970), 3; Echols, *Daring to Be Bad,* 4.

51. Springer reports that the TWWA actually only had about 12 core members at this time (Springer, *Living for the Revolution,* 81). In the memo cited in the next note, Beal reported that the organization had 150 active members.

52. Letter from Frances Beal to All SNCC Workers, October 9, 1970, Box 3, Folder 20, NCNW—Beal Series; Letter from TWWA to Friends, December 1, 1970, NCNW—Beal Series.

53. Letter from TWWA to Friends, December 1, 1970, Box 4, Folder 21, NCNW—Beal Series.

54. Ibid.

55. Fran Beal to Sandy Scott, December 14, 1970, NCNW—Beal Series, Box 4, Folder 2; Fran Beal to All SNCC Workers, October 9, 1970, NCNW—Beal Series.

56. "Madame Binh Orientation Group," n.d., 2, Box 5, Folder 15, NCNW—Beal Series.

57. Ibid., 2–4. The document listed nine reasons why ideological development was important to the organization. The first reason was "to equip

ourselves with the knowledge of the art and science of making a revolution." Others reasons included: to develop an understanding of Third World women's relationship to the nation and how they fit into the struggle against exploitation and oppression; to train cadres who can organize a revolutionary mass organization; to fight "petty bourgeois tendencies: such as individualism, greed, liberalism, and elitism; and to build "a firm commitment to a life of struggle for world socialism."

58. Untitled document about *Triple Jeopardy* 1, Box 5, Folder 37, NCNW—Beal Series.
59. Ibid., 1–2.
60. *Triple Jeopardy* 1 (September–October 1971), 12.
61. The text of the telegram read: "Your son did not keep quiet nor did he bow down. He is a symbol to all third world people of the strength we must maintain in the face of our oppressors. We will continue our work in the spirit of George Jackson." *Triple Jeopardy* 1, 13.
62. Ibid., 6.
63. Ibid., 7.
64. Ibid., 16.
65. Ibid., 15.
66. Letter from Louise Patterson to Fran Beal, October 29, 1971, Box 4, Folder 21, NCNW—Beal Series.
67. Davis was charged with conspiracy, kidnapping and murder based on the assertion that guns registered to her were used in the August 7, 1970, courthouse raid in Marin County, California, led by Jonathon Jackson, younger brother of "Soledad Brother" George Jackson. Davis was active in the Soledad Brothers Defense Committee and had grown close to the Jackson family. Two months after the raid, Davis was arrested in New York and eventually extradited back to California to stand trial. As Davis was denied bail and charged in connection with a crime for which she was not present, it was clear to her supporters that she was being persecuted for outspoken politics, including her membership in the Communist Party and especially her work with the Soledad Brothers Defense Committee. On Davis and her case, see Bettina Aptheker, *The Morning Breaks: The Trial of Angela Davis* (New York: International Publishers, 1975); Angela Y. Davis, *Angela Davis: An Autobiography* (New York: International Publishers, 1988); Angela Y. Davis (and other political prisoners), *If They Come in the Morning* (New Rochelle, NY: The Third Press, 1971); and James, *The Angela Y. Davis Reader.*
68. "Women Strike But Equal to What?" 3. Charlayne Hunter, "Many Blacks Wary of 'Women's Liberation' Movement in U.S.," 60.
69. Letter from Marvel Cooke to Frances Beal, May 10, 1972, NCNW—Beal Series; "An Evening for Angela Davis," Box 2, Folder 35, NCNW—Beal Series.
70. *Triple Jeopardy* 1 (April–May 1972), 12, 15.
71. *Triple Jeopardy* 2 (January–February 1973), 4.

Chapter 6

1. Timothy B. Tyson, *Radio Free Dixie: Robert F. Williams and the Roots of Black Power* (Chapel Hill: University of North Carolina Press, 1999). This is not to diminish or overlook historian Komozi Woodard's equally important, groundbreaking study of Amiri Baraka and New Jersey published around the same time. Tyson's work, which follows the archaeology of self-defense in the South and its relationship to Black Power's origins, serves as a point of departure for my discussion of self-defense and the Deacons. See Komozi Woodard, *A Nation Within a Nation: Amiri Baraka (LeRoi Jones) & Black Power Politics* (Chapel Hill: University of North Carolina Press, 1999).
2. Peniel E. Joseph "Black Liberation Without Apology: Reconceptualizing the Black Power Movement," *Black Scholar* 31 (Fall/Winter 2001), 9.
3. Tyson, *Radio Free Dixie*, 3.
4. A growing number of historians have begun to explore the role of armed resistance in the southern civil rights struggle. The most important works include Tyson, *Radio Free Dixie*; Lance E. Hill, *The Deacons for Defense: Armed Resistance and the Civil Rights Movement* (Chapel Hill: University of North Carolina Press, 2004); Christopher Strain, *Pure Fire: Armed Self-Defense as Activism in the Civil Rights Era* (Athens: University of Georgia Press, 2005); Akinyele O. Umoja, "The Ballot and the Bullet: A Comparative Analysis of Armed Resistance in the Civil Rights Movement," *Journal of Black Studies* 29, no. 4 (March 1999), 558–78; "'We Will Shoot Back': The Natchez Model and Paramilitary Organization in the Mississippi Freedom Movement," *Journal of Black Studies* 32 (January 2002), 271–94; and "1964: The Beginning of the End of Nonviolence in the Mississippi Freedom Movement," *Radical History Review* 85 (Winter 2003), 201–26; Simon Wendt, "'Urge People *Not* to Carry Guns': Armed Self-Defense in the Louisiana Civil Rights Movement and the Radicalization of the Congress of Racial Equality," *Louisiana History* 45 (Summer 2004), 261–86 and "God, Gandhi, and Guns: The African American Freedom Struggle in Tuscaloosa, Alabama, 1964–1965," *Journal of African American History* 89 (Winter 2004), 36–56.
5. This is not meant to suggest that the Black Panther Party was representative of the entire Black Power Movement, which was a mélange of different ideologies and agendas. However, many elements of the BPP's concept of armed resistance could also be seen in the programs of other Black Power groups such as the Revolutionary Action Movement (RAM), the Us Organization, or the Republic of New Africa (RNA). Similarly, Black Power cannot be reduced to the advocacy of self-defense. Political empowerment, self-determination, antiracism, radical internationalism, to mention just a few themes, were equally important aspects of Black Power programs. Yet these social and political goals were frequently eclipsed by the public advocacy of self-defense. On the various ideological strands of Black Power ideologies, see James Edward Smethurst, *The Black Arts Movement: Literary Nationalism in the*

1960s and 1970s (Chapel Hill: University of North Carolina Press, 2005); William L. Van Deburg, *New Day in Babylon: The Black Power Movement and American Culture, 1965–1975* (Chicago: University of Chicago Press, 1992); Woodard, *A Nation Within a Nation*. On US, see Scot Brown, *Fighting for US: Maulena Karenga, the US Organization, and Black Cultural Nationalism* (New York: New York University Press, 2003). On the RNA and RAM, see Van Deburg, *New Day in Babylon,* 144–49, 165, 168.

6. Daniel Mitchell, "A Special Report on Jonesboro Louisiana with Reference to Voter Registration Activities involving the Congress of Racial Equality," July 1964, CORE-Jackson Parish Files, box 1, folder 10, State Historical Society of Wisconsin (hereafter cited as SHSW); "Reports on Desegregation of Public Facilities 1964–1965 in Jonesboro," CORE-Jackson Parish Files, box 1, folder 5, SHSW; Daniel Mitchell, "Jackson Parish and Jonesboro, Louisiana: A White Paper," CORE-Monroe, Louisiana Chapter Files, box 4, folder 4, SHSW.

7. Hamilton Bims, "Deacons for Defense and Justice," *Ebony,* September 1965, 25–30; *New York Times,* February 21, 1965, 52; "Louisiana-October 1964 through April 1965-Summary Field Reports," CORE Southern Regional Office Files (hereafter cited as CORE-SRO), box 4, folder 2, SHSW; "Summary of Events in Jonesboro, Louisiana, March 8 through March 16," press release, March 16, 1965, CORE Papers, microfilm, reel 17, frame 00258; "National Action Council Minutes, National CORE Office, February 6–7, 1965," CORE Papers, series 4, box 2, folder 1, SHSW.

8. Steve Miller to Shirley Mesher, February 12, 1965, CORE–Louisiana 6th Congressional District Files (hereafter cited as Sixth Congressional District Files), box 1, folder 8, SHSW; *New York Times,* January 9, 1965; Paul Good, "Klantown USA," *The Nation,* February 1, 1965, 110–14; Nancy Gilmore, "Louisiana Field Report, January through June 1965," CORE-SRO, box 7, folder 5; "Bogalusa, Louisiana, Incident Summary: January 25–February 21, 1965," CORE-SRO, box 7, folder 5; *Afro-American* [Baltimore], July 31, 1965; Ronnie Moore to Robert Kennedy, July 25, 1964, Sixth Congressional District Files, box 1, folder 12.

9. A. Z. Young, interview by Miriam Feingold, ca. July 1966, Bogalusa, LA, tape recording, Miriam Feingold Papers (hereafter cited as Feingold Papers), SHSW.

10. "Articles of Incorporation of Deacons of Defense and Justice, Inc.," March 5, 1965, CORE-SRO, box 5, folder 4.

11. Peter Jan Honigsberg, *Crossing Border Street: A Civil Rights Memoir* (Berkeley: University of California Press, 2000), 33, 52.

12. Fred L. Zimmerman, "Race and Violence: More Dixie Negroes Buy Arms to Retaliate Against White Attacks," *Wall Street Journal,* July 12, 1965, 18.

13. *New York Times,* April 8, 1965; Robert Hicks, interview by Miriam Feingold, ca. July 1966, Bogalusa, LA, tape recording; Gayle Jenkins, interview by Miriam Feingold, ca. July 1966, Bogalusa, LA, tape recording, both in Feingold Papers; "The Deacons," *Newsweek,* August 2, 1965, 28.

14. "The Problem in Focus," *Campus CORE-Lator* [Berkeley] 3 (1965): 26, CORE Papers, Addendum, microfilm, reel 17, frame 0293.

15. Royan Burris, interview by Miriam Feingold, ca. 1966, Bogalusa, LA, tape recording, Feingold Papers; *New York Times,* July 9, 1965; *Louisiana Weekly,* July 17, 1965; Hattie Mae Hill, interview by Miriam Feingold, ca. 1966, Bogalusa, LA, tape recording, Feingold Papers.

16. Robert Hicks interview by Feingold.

17. Carl Hufbauer, "Bogalusa: Negro Community vs. Crown Colony," *Campus CORE-Lator* [Berkeley] 3 (1965): 21.

18. See Adam Fairclough, *Race and Democracy: The Civil Rights Struggle in Louisiana, 1915–1972* (Athens: University of Georgia Press, 1995), 370–78.

19. Roy Reed, "The Deacons, Too, Ride by Night," *New York Times Magazine,* August 15, 1965, 22.

20. George Lipsitz, *A Life in the Struggle: Ivory Perry and the Culture of Opposition* (Philadelphia: Temple University Press, 1988), 96.

21. Quoted in "Deacons Take Aim at Klan in North; Locate in Chicago," *Baltimore Afro-American,* October 23, 1965, 1.

22. Roy Reed, "The Deacons, Too, Ride by Night," 11.

23. A. Z. Young, interview by Feingold.

24. Shana Alexander, "Visit Bogalusa and You Will Look for Me," *Life,* July 2, 1965, 28.

25. "Speech by Charles Sims, Pres. of Bogalusa Chapter at Meeting of New York Militant Labor Forum on Dec. 17," *The Militant,* December 27, 1965, 5.

26. "The Deacons—and their Impact," *National Guardian,* September 4, 1965, 5.

27. *New York Times,* June 10, 1964; *Tuscaloosa News,* June 9, 1964; Odessa Warrick, interview by Alan DeSantis, tape recording, Tuscaloosa, AL, July 6, 1987; Ruth Bolden, interview by Alan DeSantis, tape recording, Tuscaloosa, AL, June 16, 1987; Willie Herzfeld, interview by Alan DeSantis, telephone, Tuscaloosa, AL, August 12, 1987, all in Alan DeSantis Collection (hereafter cited as DeSantis Collection), W.S. Hoole Special Collections Library (hereafter cited as HSCL), University of Alabama, Tuscaloosa, AL.

28. *New York Times,* June 10, 1964; *Tuscaloosa News,* June 9, 10, 1964; Warrick interview; Herzfeld interview by DeSantis; Nathaniel Howard Jr. interview by Alan DeSantis, tape recording, Tuscaloosa, AL, June 29, 1987, DeSantis Collection; T. Y. Rogers, interview by Harvey Burg, Tuscaloosa, AL, summer 1964, transcript, 44; Anonymous black teenagers, interview by Harvey Burg, Tuscaloosa, AL, transcript, 8, 22, 26–27, 37–39, 61–63, 76–79, both in Civil Rights Movement in Tuscaloosa, Alabama Collection (hereafter cited as Tuscaloosa Collection), Oral History Research Office, Columbia University, New York; Harold A. Nelson, "The Defenders: A Case Study of an Informal Police Organization," *Social Problems* 15 (Fall 1967), 130; Joseph Mallisham, interview by author, tape recording, Tuscaloosa, AL, March 22, 2002; *Tuscaloosa News,* June 10, 1964.

29. Mallisham interview by author, March 22, 2002; Mallisham quoted in Nelson, "The Defenders," 131.

30. Nelson, "The Defenders," 130–131; Joseph Mallisham, interview by Alan DeSantis, tape recording, Tuscaloosa, AL, July 22, 1987, DeSantis Collection; Mike Williams, "Smiles and Guns: The Fragile Sensitivity of Race Relations in the South," Honors Thesis, Amherst College, 1978, 121–22, 127; *Tuscaloosa News,* May 17, 1985; Mallisham interview by author, March 22, 2002.

31. Nelson, "The Defenders," 131–33.

32. Mallisham interview by author, March 22, 2002; Mallisham interview by author, March 19, 2002; Nelson, "The Defenders," 146.

33. LaPelzia Rogers, interview by Alan DeSantis, by telephone, tape recording, August 19, 1987; L.V. Hall, interview by Alan DeSantis, tape recording, Tuscaloosa, AL, June 23, 1987, both in DeSantis Collection; *New York Times,* June 13, 1964; Mallisham interview by author, March 22, 2002.

34. Howard interview.

35. Olivia Maniece, interview by Alan DeSantis, tape recording, Tuscaloosa, AL, June 24, 1987, DeSantis Collection; Bolden interview; Mallisham interview by DeSantis; "7-9–76 Interview Martha O'Rourke, Head Librarian, Stillman College," Anthony J. Blasi Collection (hereafter cited as Blasi Collection), HSCL.

36. Mallisham interview by DeSantis; Herzfeld interview by DeSantis.

37. Mallisham interview by DeSantis; Herzfeld interview by DeSantis; Rev. T. W. Linton, interview by Alan DeSantis, tape recording, Tuscaloosa, AL, July 22, 1987, DeSantis Collection; LaPelzia Rogers interview.

38. Joyce Mahan, "Alberta Brown Murphy," in *A Collection of Biographies of Women Who Made a Difference in Alabama,* edited by Miriam Abigail Toffel (Birmingham, AL.: League of Women Voters of Alabama, 1995), 104–9; Alberta Murphy, interview by Alan DeSantis, tape recording, Tuscaloosa, AL, August 4, 1987, DeSantis Collection.

39. "6–25–76 Interview with Joe Mallisham," Blasi Collection; Mallisham interview by author, March 22, 2002; Nelson, "The Defenders," 128–29. Published only three years after the defense group was founded, Nelson's article used pseudonyms for both Tuscaloosa and Joseph Mallisham to protect black activists against possible repercussions from the white community.

40. Williams, "Smiles and Guns," 128; Nelson, "The Defenders," 144; Mallisham interview by author, March 22, 2002.

41. Nelson, "The Defenders," 138.

42. Nelson, "The Defenders," 140; Mallisham interview by author, March 22, 2002.

43. Eugene Nelson to Dear Parents, July 3, 1964, Eugene Nelson Papers, SHSW.

44. McLaurin interview; Bingham, "Mississippi Letter," 14; Eugene Nelson to Dear Parents, August 2, 1964, Nelson Papers.

45. Youth of the Rural Organizing and Cultural Center, *Minds Stayed on Freedom: The Civil Rights Struggle in the Rural South, an Oral History*

(Boulder, CO: Westview Press, 1991), 87, 135; Steven Bingham, "Mississippi Letter," 19, Steven Bingham Papers, SHSW; Mary Brumder, "Holmes County, Nov. 21, 1964," box 1, folder 5, Ewen Papers, SHSW.

46. Griffin McLaurin, interview by Harriet Tanzman, tape recording, Milestone, Miss., March 6, 2000, Civil Rights Documentation Project (hereafter cited as CRDP), L. Zenobia Coleman Library (hereafter cited as Coleman Library), Tougaloo College, Tougaloo, MS; Eugene Nelson to Dear Parents, July 3, 1964.

47. Walter Bruce, interview by Harriet Tanzman, tape recording, Durant, Miss., October 8, 1999, CRDP.

48. Nicholas von Hoffman, *Mississippi Notebook* (New York: David White Company, 1964), 95.

49. Hoffman, *Mississippi Notebook*, 94; Ms. Winson Hudson, interview by John Rachal, by telephone, August 31, 1995, transcript, 103, Mississippi Oral History Program (hereafter cited as MOHP), McCain Library and Archives, University of Southern Mississippi; Rims Barber, interview by Kim Lacy Rogers and Owen Brooks, tape recording, n.p., August 30, 1995, Delta Oral History Project, Coleman Library; "Harmony Builds Center," *Student Voice*, August 12, 1964, 3; Elizabeth Sutherland, ed., *Letters from Mississippi* (New York: McGraw-Hill, 1965), 115.

50. Jerome Smith, interview by Tom Dent, tape recording, New Orleans, LA, September 25, 1983, Tom Dent Collection, Coleman Library.

51. Sutherland, *Letters from Mississippi*, 115. Both John Dittmer and Akinyele Umoja have called attention to the significance of armed black resistance in Leake County. See John Dittmer, *Local People: The Struggle for Civil Rights in Mississippi* (Urbana: University of Illinois Press, 1994), 257; Umoja, "1964," 211–12.

52. Umoja, "1964," 210.

53. Jack Nelson, *Terror in the Night: The Klan's Campaign against the Jews* (New York: Simon & Schuster, 1993), 108–9; George Wiley to Melvin S. Cohen, January 27, 1965, box 1, folder 7, Currier Papers; Obie Clark, interview by Don Williams, tape recording, n.p., March 13, 1999; Repr. Charles L. Young, Sr., interview by Don Williams, tape recording, Jackson, MS, November 14, 1998, both in CRDP.

54. Alice Lake to Mr. Burke Marshall, August 21, 1964, Ellen Lake Papers, SHSW.

55. Quoted in Doug McAdam, *Freedom Summer* (New York: Oxford University Press, 1988), 90.

56. "Diary," entry 7/14/64, box 2, folder 1; "Mississippi Negroes Near Violence, Says Knox Grad," newspaper clipping [n.d.], box 1, folder 9, both in Jo Anne Ooiman Robinson Papers, SHSW; Sutherland, *Letters from Mississippi*, 45; "WATS Line Digest," July 26, 1964, 2, unprocessed accessions, Mary E. King Papers, SHSW.

57. Letterhead Memorandum, "Deacons of Defense and Justice, Inc.," November 27, 1967; Memorandum, W.C. Sullivan to R.W. Smith, March 26, 1968, Deacons of Defense and Justice Federal Bureau of Investigation File 157–2466–266. In early 1970, the FBI terminated

its investigation of the group. SAC, New Orleans to Director, FBI, February 17, 1970, Deacons FBI File 157–2466–279.

58. Hill, *The Deacons for Defense*, 2, 54, 58.

59. For a more detailed discussion of the symbiotic relationship between armed resistance and nonviolent protest in the southern civil rights movement, see Simon Wendt, *The Spirit and the Shotgun: Armed Resistance and the Struggle for Civil Rights* (Gainesville, FL: University Press of Florida, forthcoming). On debates on armed resistance in CORE, see Wendt, "'Urge People *Not* to Carry Guns,'" 277–81. On debates in SNCC, see "Staff Meeting Minutes June 9–11, 1964," 12–13, box 2, folder 7, Howard Zinn Papers, SHSW; Mary King, *Freedom Song: A Personal Story of the 1960s Civil Rights Movement* (New York: Morrow, 1987), 318–24. On the inspiring effect of Robert Williams and the Deacons on the Black Panthers, see Tyson, *Radio Free Dixie*, 298; Bobby Seale, *A Lonely Rage: The Autobiography of Bobby Seale* (New York: New York Times Books, 1978), 130; Huey Newton, *Revolutionary Suicide* (New York: Harcourt Brace Jovanovich, 1973), 111–12.

60. Several historians have called attention to the "performative" elements of the BPP's self-defense stance, but except for Steve Estes, these scholars tend to neglect the significance of manhood in black militants' symbolic actions. See Joel P. Rhodes, *The Voice of Violence: Performative Violence as Protest in the Vietnam Era* (Westport, CT: Praeger, 2001); Nikhil Pal Singh, "The Black Panthers and the 'Underdeveloped Country' of the Left," in *The Black Panther Party Reconsidered*, edited by Charles E. Jones (Baltimore: Black Classic Press, 1998), 83. For Estes's excellent analysis of the BPP's "masculinist" organizing strategies, see Steve Estes, *I Am a Man!: Race, Manhood, and the Civil Rights Movement* (Chapel Hill: University of North Carolina Press, 2005), 155–62.

61. Newton, *Revolutionary Suicide*, 111–12, 120; Seale, *A Lonely Rage*, 130; Bobby Seale, *Seize the Time: The Story of the Black Panther Party and Huey P. Newton* (New York: Vintage, 1970), 25; Robert L. Allen, "Panthers Assert Right to Armed Self-Defense," *National Guardian*, January 6, 1968, 6; Bobby Seale, interview by Robert Wright, Berkeley, Cal., November 14, 1968, transcript, 9, Ralph J. Bunche Oral History Collection, Moorland-Spingarn Research Center, Howard University, Washington, D.C.

62. Sol Stern, "The Call of the Black Panthers," *New York Times Magazine*, August 6, 1967, 10–11; *New York Times*, May 3, 1967; Seale, *Seize the Time*, 153–56.

63. Newton, *Revolutionary Suicide*, 120–27, 146; Seale, *Seize the Time*, 85–101; *New York Times*, July 19, 1967. Huey P. Newton, "The Correct Handling of a Revolution: July 20, 1967," in Huey P. Newton, *To Die for the People: The Writings of Huey P. Newton* (New York: Random House, 1972), 15–16.

64. Seale, *Seize the Time*, 71.

65. Quoted in Allen, "Panthers Assert Right to Armed Self-Defense," 6.

66. Newton, *Revolutionary Suicide*, 111.

67. It is important to emphasize that the BPP's ideology evolved over several stages, beginning with a black nationalist analysis that was based on racial solidarity, but incorporated elements of Marxist class analysis. From 1968 to 1970, the organization advocated a fusion of Marxist socialism and revolutionary nationalism that called for class alliances. After 1970, the BPP sought to establish global socialism through revolutionary intercommunalism, which would overthrow U.S. imperialism and capitalism through alliances among revolutionaries around the world. See Floyd W. Hayes, III and Francis A. Kiene, III, "'All Power to the People': The Political Thought of Huey P. Newton and the Black Panther Party," in *The Black Panther Party Reconsidered*, 157–76.

68. William W. Sales Jr., *From Civil Rights to Black Liberation: Malcolm X and the Organization of Afro-American Unity* (Boston: South End Press, 1994), 129–30; Anne Braden, "Nationalist," [n.d.], box 1, folder 9, Carl and Anne Braden Papers, SHSW.

69. "Naw," Charles Sims recalled his reaction to the ambiguous slogan, "that wasn't down my alley at all, 'cause the cats that was hollerin' Black Power, I was protectin' and guardin' they damn ass. I don't see nothin' they was doin' to even talkin' 'bout no Black Power." Transcript of an interview with Charles Sims, in *My Soul Is Rested: Movement Days in the Deep South Remembered*, edited by Howell Raines (New York: G. P. Putnam's Sons, 1977), 423. Joseph Mallisham, too, was highly critical of the posture of Black Power militants and condemned what he termed a "destructive" program. Mallisham interview by author, March 19, 2002.

70. King quoted in David J. Garrow, *Bearing the Cross: Martin Luther King, Jr. and the Southern Christian Leadership Conference* (New York: Random House, 1986), 566.

71. Newton quoted in Wallace Turner, "A Gun is Power, Black Panther Says," *New York Times*, May 21, 1967, 66.

72. "Interview with Huey Newton," in *Black Protest Thought in the Twentieth Century*, edited by August Meier, Elliot Rudwick, and Francis L. Brodwick (Indianapolis: Bobbs-Merrill Company, 1971), 508.

73. Jeffrey O.G. Ogbar, *Black Power: Radical Politics and African American Identity* (Baltimore: Johns Hopkins University Press, 2004), 102, 103–6; Erika Doss, "Imaging the Panthers: Representing Black Power and Masculinity, 1960s-1990s," *Prospects* 23 (1998), 493; Tracye Matthews, "'No One Ever Asks What a Man's Place in the Revolution Is': The Politics of Gender in the Black Panther Party, 1966–1971," in *The Black Panther Party Reconsidered*, 269, 278; Norbert Finzsch, "'Picking Up the Gun': Die Black Panther Party Zwischen Gewaltsamer Revolution Und Sozialer Reform, 1966–1984," *Amerikastudien* 44, no. 2 (1999), 239.

74. Ward Churchill, "'To Disrupt, Discredit and Destroy': The FBI's Secret War Against the Black Panther Party," in *Liberation, Imagination, and the Black Panther Party: A New Look at the Panthers and their Legacy*, edited by Kathleen Cleaver and George Katsiaficas (New York: Routledge, 2001), 78–117; Kenneth O'Reilly, *"Racial Matters": The FBI's Secret File on Black America, 1960–1972* (New York: Free Press, 1989), 293–324.

75. Newton, *Revolutionary Suicide*, 149–50; Van Deburg, *New Day in Babylon*, 160.

76. Seale interview, 1; John A. Courtwright, "Rhetoric of the Gun: An Analysis of the Rhetorical Modifications of the Black Panther Party," *Journal of Black Studies* 4, no. 3 (March 1974), 249–67. It is important to note that the Panthers later emulated the revolutionary Pan-African institution building that other Black Power militants such as Amiri Baraka initiated in the late 1960s and early 1970s. See Woodard, *A Nation Within a Nation* and Robert O. Self, *American Babylon: Race, Power, and the Struggle for the Postwar City in California* (Princeton, NJ: Princeton University Press, 2003).

77. Tyson, *Radio Free Dixie*, 84–89, 137–65.

78. Robert Carl Cohen, "The Negro Che Guevara: Will He Turn the U.S.A. Into Another Viet Nam?," 19–21, 27, box 5, folder 3, Robert Carl Cohen Papers (hereafter cited as Cohen Papers), SHSW; *New York Times,* August 24, 30, 1967.

79. Tyson, *Radio Free Dixie*, 297–98; *New York Times,* April 1, 1968; "Now We Have a Nation: The Republic of New Africa," 12, Third National Black Power Conference Papers, SHSW. For a more detailed account of RAM's activities, see Maxwell C. Stanford, "The Revolutionary Action Movement (RAM): A Case Study of an Urban Revolutionary Movement in Western Capitalist Society," M.A. thesis, Atlanta University, 1986; Robin D. G. Kelley and Betsy Esch, "Black like Mao: Red China and Black Revolution," *Souls* 1(Fall 1999), 6–41.

80. Robert F. Williams, interview by Robert Carl Cohen, July 20, 1968, Dar Es Salaam, transcript, 22, box 1, folder 4, Cohen Papers.

81. Robert F. Williams, interview by Robert Carl Cohen, ca. 1968, transcript, 12, box 1, folder 12, Cohen Papers.

82. "His Best Credentials: On the Air with Joe Rainey," in *Malcolm X as They Knew Him,* edited by David Gallen (New York: Caroll & Graf, 1992), 164–65.

83. Harold Cruse, *The Crisis of the Negro Intellectual* (New York: William Morrow, 1967), 382, 390.

Chapter 7

1. Comments of unidentified black woman in *Eyes on the Prize II: America at the Racial Crossroads, 1965–1985.* Episode 5, "A Nation of Law? (1968–71)"; Producers: Blackside, Inc. Distributor: Alexandria, VA, PBS Video.

2. "In Defense of Self-Defense II," in Huey P. Newton, *To Die for the People* (New York: Writers and Readers, 1995), 88–90.

3. "New stamp to honor Roy Wilkins for his civil rights activism," Seth Woehrle, *Minnesota Daily Online,* 2000 http://www.daily.umn.edu/daily/2000/11/10/news/new6/

4. Over the past three decades, the story of the FBI's campaign against Black Nationalist organizations has been well documented in a number

of studies including Frank J. Donner, *The Age of Surveillance* (New York: Vintage Books, 1981); Frank J. Donner, *Protectors of Privilege: Red Squads and Police Repression in Urban America* (Berkeley: University of California Press, 1990); Athan Theoharis, *Spying on Americans: Political Surveillance from Hoover to the Huston Plan* (Philadelphia: Temple University Press, 1978); Nelson Blackstock, *Cointelpro* (New York: Vintage, 1976); Kenneth O'Reilly, *Hoover and the Unamericans: The FBI, HUAC and the Red Menace* (Philadelphia: Temple University Press, 1983); Ward Churchill and Jim Vander Wall, *Agents of Repression: The FBI's Secret Wars Against the Black Panther Party and the American Indian Movement* (Boston: South End Press, 1988) and *COINTELPRO Papers: Documents from the FBI's Secret Wars Against Dissent in the United States* (Boston: South End Press, 1989); Robert J. Goldstein, *Political Repression in Modern America, 1870 to Present*, 2nd edition (Rochester, VT: Schenkman Books, Inc., 1978).

5. Robert Penn Warren, *Who Speaks for the Negro* (New York: Random House, 1965), 155.

6. Ibid., 145.

7. Roy Wilkins, *Standing Fast: The Autobiography of Roy Wilkins* (New York: Penguin, 1984), 202.

8. Wilkins's interview with Penn Warren, *Who Speaks for the Negro*, 152.

9. Roy Wilkins, "Wither Black Power," *The Crisis*, August–September 1966, 354.

10. Wilkins's comments here are instructive for several reasons. First, they demonstrate, for civil rights advocates at least, the inadequacy of the term revolution as applied to their campaign for inclusion into American society. What they were really engaged in is what long-time Howard University historian Arnold H. Taylor has called a Second Civil War. That is, they were fighting to reclaim the rights lost to them after the first Civil War. Penn Warren, *Who Speaks for the Negro*,157.

11. Wilkins, *Standing Fast*, 317.

12. Harold Cruse, *The Crisis of the Negro Intellectual* (New York: Quill, 1984), 546.

13. Wilkins, *Standing Fast*, 320.

14. Roy Wilkins, "Wither Black Power," 353–354; see also August Meier, et al., eds., *Black Protest Thought in the Twentieth Century* (New York: Macmillan, 1987), 597.

15. To Roy Wilkins from Mrs. W. J. Reichard, October 28, 1973 NAACP Papers Part VI Box A: 45 Folder Roy Wilkins columns correspondence 1965–1980.

16. NAACP Papers VI Box A: 45 To Roy Wilkins from Orin, March 10, 1970, NAACP Papers Part VI Box A: 45 Folder Correspondence Jan–Apr 1970.

17. To Roy Wilkins from D. Speir, February 23, 1967, NAACP Papers Box A: 43 Folder Roy Wilkins Correspondence 1961–1969.

18. Charles V. Hamilton, "An Advocate of Black Power Defines It," *New York Times Magazine*, April 14, 1968, reprinted in Meier, et al., *Black Protest Thought in the Twentieth Century*, 554.

19. Wilkins, "Wither Black Power," 354.

20. On government repression of the Garvey movement see Churchill and Vander Wall, *The Cointelpro Papers*, 11–13; Kenneth O'Reilly, *Racial Matters: The FBI's Secret File on Black America, 1960–1972* (New York: The Free Press, 1989), 13–14.
21. Wilkins, *Standing Fast*, 52.
22. Ibid., 89.
23. David Garrow, *The FBI and Martin Luther King* (New York: W. W. Norton & Co. 1981), 124.
24. To Director of FBI from SAC, New York Subject CP, USA, February 7, 1964.
25. Wilkins, *Standing Fast*, 325. To SAC, Albany from Director FBI, March 4, 1968, see page 2 of this memo the section marked background for the information on RAM; For more information on RAM and the FBI see Churchill and Vander Wall, *The Cointelpro Papers*, 109; Ward Churchill and Jim Vander Wall, *Agents of Repression*, 45–47; Manning Marable, *Race, Reform and Rebellion: Black America's Second Reconstruction, 1945–1990* (Jackson: University Press of Mississippi, 1991), 124–125; O'Reilly, *Racial Matters*, 280–281. In many cases this led the Bureau and local police to collect intelligence on local groups that espoused a more militant ideology than their national counterparts or that challenged more mainstream civil rights groups in influence. In New Haven, Connecticut, this took the form of the Hill Parents Association; in Wilmington, Delaware, a politicized street gang called the Blackey Blacks were the target. In New York, the Bureau set its sites on an offshoot of the Black Muslims called the Five Percent Nation or Five Percenters. The FBI first became aware of the organization after an altercation in 1965. Taking its cues from local police, the Bureau first categorized the organization as a gang but nonetheless opened an investigation of its leader, a Korean War veteran named Charles 13X Smith. Capitalizing on a highly sophisticated system of information sharing, including state and local law enforcement as well as military intelligence, within a few weeks the Bureau was able to furnish the New York City police with a dossier on Smith. Although often overlooked, military intelligence was one of the key sources of information for the Bureau. The widespread military service of many Black militants provided the government with an abundant source of information that could be used for counterintelligence initiatives. Despite the fact that Smith's records indicated that he had been a highly decorated infantryman with excellent service rating, the NYPD, which had initially been unable to uncover any negative information on him, began an aggressive campaign of harassment against the Islamic youth organizer. After the media began to question the police interest in the organization, the NYPD pressed the FBI not to divulge that it had supplied the police with intelligence under the auspices that such a disclosure might compromise their investigation of the organization. Smith was ultimately tapped by New York Mayor John Lindsay to head the Tension Reduction Fund, a statewide initiative to keep New York calm. In 1969 Smith was gunned down in the basement of a New York tenement. Many Five Percenters maintain that the FBI and the police were

involved in Smith's murder. Although there is little available evidence to corroborate this, the FBI certainly did not regret his death. For information on the FBI's campaign on the Five Percent Nation access the electronic reading room of the FBI Freedom of Information Act Web site http://foia.fbi.gov/foiaindex/5percent.htm

26. The FBI used the alleged bomb plot to discredit RAM. In 1972, for instance, the FBI attempted to link Muhammad Ahmed, chairman of the African People's Party and a founder of Revolutionary Action Movement to the alleged 1967 plot to blow up the Statue of Liberty and to assassinate Roy Wilkins and Whitney Young.

27. Memorandum from Director, FBI to Special Agents in Charge March 4, 1968.

28. "The Black Panthers," *Time,* September 20, 1968, 29.

29. Ibid.

30. "Time to Speak Up," *The Crisis,* November 1968, 310; on the NAACP's position on the suspensions of Smith and Carlos see same issue, "The Olympic Suspensions," 312.

31. Letter to the editor, *The Crisis,* March 1969, 150.

32. CORE Press Release, January 21, 1969 NAACP Papers Part VI: Box A: 35 Folder: Congress of Racial Equality 1968–1969.

33. Ibid.

34. The NAACP's program was funded by a Rockefeller Foundation grant to expand the association's activities in the development of grassroots leadership in the black community. "New Leadership Development Program," *The Crisis,* January 1969, 30.

35. Memorandum to Branch Department Staff from Gloster B. Current Re: Black Panthers and Liberation Movement, April 9, 1969 NAACP Papers Part VI: Box A 35 Folder: Black Panthers.

36. Director, FBI and New York via Washington from San Francisco, Black Panther Party (BPP), Racial Matters, July 1, 1969.

37. To Professor John M. Mecartney from Roy Wilkins, August 1, 1969, NAACP Papers Part VI: Box A 35 Folder: Black Panthers.

38. Western Union Telegram to David Hilliard from Roy Wilkins, September 4, 1969, NAACP Papers Part VI: Box A 35 Folder: Black Panthers.

39. Western Union Telegram to Roy Wilkins from David Hilliard, August 31, 1969 NAACP Papers Box A 35 Folder: Black Panthers; To David Hilliard from Roy Wilkins, September 4, 1969, NAACP Papers Part VI: Box A 35 Folder: Black Panthers.

40. To NAACP from Ruth W. Katz, December 7, 1969, NAACP Papers Part VI: Box A 35 Folder: Black Panthers.

41. Western Union to Roy Wilkins from Roy Innis, December 6, 1968, NAACP Papers Part VI: Box A 35 Folder: Black Panthers.

42. "Black Leaders See New Racial Strife," *The Boston Herald Traveler,* December 9, 1969; Roy Wilkins FBI file, Part 9 of 11, FBI Memorandum, To Director, FBI from SAC, Boston Subject: Racial Black Panther Party (BPP) Racial Matters, December 9, 1969.

43. To Roy Wilkins from Mrs. Mabel Robinson, December 16, 1969, NAACP Papers Part VI: Box A 35 Folder: Black Panthers.

44. To Mr. Wilkins from Ganell Taylor, December 20, 1969, NAACP Papers Part VI: Box A 35 Folder: Black Panthers.

45. Ossie Davis's comments suggest another possible motive for the killing of Fred Hampton. Even though Hampton distanced himself from the indiscriminate violence practiced by the Weathermen of SDS as counter-revolutionary, the police and FBI saw Hampton and the Panthers as partly responsible for the rampage of the Days of Rage because of the Weathermen's identification with black militant groups. This certainly warrants further scholarly investigation.

46. To Ganelle Taylor from John A. Morsell, January 20, 1970 NAACP Papers Part VI: Box A 35 Folder: Black Panthers.

47. Between 1968 and 1971 several polls were published which indicated growing support for the Panthers, especially after the Party announced its serve the people initiatives. For a detailed discussion of these polls, see Charles W. Hopkins, "The Deradicalization of the Black Panther Party, 1967–1973," (Master's Thesis, University of North Carolina at Chapel Hill, 1978), 1–10. For a general discussion of the Party's transformation after 1968 see Yohuru Williams, *Black Politics/White Power: Civil Rights, Black Power, and the Black Panthers in New Haven* (Brandywine, St. James, New York, 2000), 117–119.

48. Roy Wilkins FBI File Part 9 of 11, FBI Memorandum Disturbance, Augusta, Georgia, July 20, 1970.

49. Ibid.

50. Telegram to Hon. John N. Mitchell from Roy Wilkins, August 4, 1970, Roy Wilkins FBI File Part 4 of 11; Wilkins, *Standing Fast*, 313.

51. Ibid.

52. Roy Wilkins, "Blacks Fear Repression," *Seattle Post-Intelligencer*, August 8, 1970, Contained in NAACP Papers Part VI: Box A 45 Folder: Black Panthers. Folder column texts 1967–80.

53. In rejecting the need for Black Power while defending some of its advocates, the NAACP at times appeared schizophrenic. The Association, for instance, vigorously challenged the Olympic suspensions of Tommie Smith and John Carlos for their Black Power protest in Mexico City while denying the need for such displays at all. On the NAACP's position on the suspensions of Smith and Carlos see "The Olympic Suspensions," *The Crisis*, November 1968, 312.

54. Roy Wilkins column in the *Oakland Tribune*, August 1970, reprinted in Newton, *To Die For The People*, 186–187.

55. "Open Letter to Roy Wilkins," *The Black Panther*, September 26, 1970, 11.

56. "Black Activists Are FBI Targets," Jack Anderson, *The Washington Post*, May 16, 1972.

57. FBI Memorandum to Mr. E. S. Miller from T. J. Smith Subject: Jack Anderson's Columns 22 May 1972.

58. FBI Memorandum, San Francisco, California, *The Black Panther*, "International Relations-Canada," November 7, 1972 see also *Black Panther*, September 30, 1972.

59. *Search and Destroy Commission of Inquiry into the Black Panthers and the Police: A Report,* Roy Wilkins and Ramsey Clark, chairmen (New York: Applied Research Center, INC, 1973).

60. "Report Assails Inquiry on Slaying of Black Panthers," Thomas A. Johnson, *New York Times,* March 17, 1972.

61. Wilkins, *Standing Fast,* 340.

62. George Lardner, "Black Reportedly Worked with FBI to Discredit King," *Washington Post,* May 29, 1978, 1; George Lardner, "Wilkins Denies Any Link to FBI Plot to Discredit King," *Washington Post,* May 31, 1978, A6; Garrow, *The FBI and Martin Luther King,* 271.

63. Garrow, *The FBI and Martin Luther King,* 13; Churchill and Vander Wall, *Cointelpro Papers,* 95.

64. Ibid.

65. Ibid.

Chapter 8

1. Rodolfo Acuna, *Occupied American: A History of Chicanos,* 3d ed. (New York, 1988), 180, 254–55.

2. "Border Crossings," *L.A. Weekly,* June 24–30, 1988, 22; "The Los Angeles Chicano Area—Cultural Enclave," *San Francisco Chronicle,* October 10, 1970, 12.

3. "Hail 'La Raza' and Scorn the Establishment," from http://www.brown-beret.org/ bbraza.html (accessed July 16, 1999).

4. "Border Crossings," 22; "Cultural Enclave," 12; Marguerte Viramontes Marin, "Protest in an Urban Barrio: A Study of the Chicano Movement" (Ph.D. diss., University of California, Santa Barbara, 1980), 123–24.

5. Ibid., 124–25.

6. Bobby Seale, *Seize the Time: The Story of the Black Panther Party and Huey P. Newton* (Baltimore, 1991), 115.

7. "Hail 'La Raza.'"

8. Some have argued that the word Chicano evolved from sixteenth-century Castilian pronunciation of Mexico, where the "x" had a "sh" sound: Meh-shee-ko. For the people, Meh-shee-kanos, "Chicanos" emerged among isolated rural peasants whose pronunciation was unmodified into the nineteenth century. Conservative and moderate Mexican Americans, hostile to the new word for identity, however, insisted that the word is a Castilian word, meaning "one who practices fraud." Still, others said that it was a blend of two words, reflecting the demographic makeup of the new militants: Mexicano and Chico, literally meaning "Young Mexican." Yet others argued that it had historically been a pejorative term for poor Mexicans. See Tony Castro, *Chicano Power: The Emergence of Mexican America* (New York, 1974), 131; "Cultural Enclave," 12; Acuna, *Occupied American,* 338.

9. Elio Carranza, *Pensamientos on Los Chicanos: A Cultural Revolution* (Berkeley, 1969), 4–5; Castro, *Chicano Power,* 13.

10. Boyd C. Schafer, *Nationalism and Internationalism: Belonging in Human Experience* (Malabar, FL, 1982), 41–47.

11. Marin, "Protest in an Urban Barrio," 128.

12. *La Causa*, December 1970.

13. Marin, "Protest in an Urban Barrio," 131.

14. Ibid., 135.

15. Ibid., 55.

16. Ibid., 143; Castro, *Chicano Power*, 12–14.

17. Acuna, *Occupied American*, 337–38.

18. Castro, *Chicano Power*, 13–17; "In Memory of 1970 Protest," *Los Angeles Times*, August 31, 1980.

19. "Police Spying on L.A. Activist Groups," *Los Angeles Times*, July 19, 1978, B2. There is a growing body of literature on the illegal activities of the FBI and its program, COINTELPRO. See especially Ward Churchill and Jim Vander Wall, *Agents of Repression: The FBI's Secret Wars against the Black Panther Party and the American Indian Movement* (Boston, 1988), and Brian Click, *War at Home: Covert Action against U.S. Activists and What We Can Do about It* (Boston, 1989).

20. Castro, *Chicano Power*, 133.

21. Acuna, *Occupied American*, 348.

22. *The Asian Student* (Berkeley) 3, no. 1 (November 1974): 3; 2, no. 1 (March 1974): 3, 9–10.

23. *The Asian Student* 2, no. 1 (March 1974): 9–10.

24. Ibid.

25. *La Causa* 1, no. 1 (November 1, 1993): [4]. Note that this is a different newspaper created under the same name as the original Brown Beret organ of 1969–73.

26. *Chicanismo* 1, no. 6 (1970): [1].

27. Ibid., 2.

28. *The Asian Student* 1, no. 1 (November 1973): 13.

29. Ronald Takaki, *Strangers from a Different Shore: A History of Asian Americans* (New York, 1989), 13–15.

30. Some have argued that Richard Aoki is a cofounder of the Black Panther Party with Newton and Seale. Such a position conflicts, however, with official party history. Bobby Seale states that Aoki was a "consultant" and comrade to him and Newton but not a founder. Bobby Seale, conversation with author, April 18, 2002; "Yellow Power," *Giant Robot no.* 10 (spring 1998): 71; Seale, *Seize the Time*, 72–73, 79.

31. "Yellow Power," 71.

32. *Hokubei Manichi*, December 9, 1968, [2].

33. Asian American Political Alliance, flier, ca. 1969, Social Protest Collection, CU-309, the Bancroft Library, University of California, Berkeley (UCB-SPC), 18: 25.

34. Asian Student Union, flier, n.d., UCBSPC 18: 27.

35. Ibid.

36. "Yellow Power," 79–80.

37. Ibid.

38. Ibid.

39. Ibid.

40. Ibid., 76.

41. Ibid., 79–80; Robin Kelley and Betsy Esch, "Black Like Mao: Red China and Black Revolution," *Souls* 1, no. 4 (fall 1999): 26.

42. "Yellow Power," 76.

43. Ibid., 74.

44. Ibid., 75.

45. Alvin M. Josephy Jr., *Red Power: The American Indians' Fight for Freedom* (New York, 1971), 3.

46. Churchill and Vander Wall, *Agents of Repression*, 118.

47. Ibid., 119.

48. Russell Means with Marvin J. Wolf, *Where White Men Fear to Tread: The Autobiography of Russell Means* (New York, 1995), 228–30.

49. Churchill and Vander Wall, *Agents of Repression*, 119.

50. Native American Solidarity Committee, flier, UCBSPC 18: 37c.

51. Native American Solidarity Committee, flier, UCBSPC 18: 37b.

52. *Minneapolis Star*, June 28, 1975, 5; Native American Solidarity Committee, flier, UCBSPC 18: 37c.

53. Young Lord Organization, flier, n.d., UCBSPC 18: 33.

54. Huey P. Newton, *Essays from the Minister of Defense*, pamphlet, 1967, Black Panther Party, political pamphlets, P201234, Northwestern University Special Collections, Evanston, 111, 11.

55. "From Rumble to Revolution: The Young Lords," *Ramparts*, October 1970; Young Lord Organization, flier, n.d., UCBSPC 18: 33; see also David Hilliard and Lewis Cole, *This Side of Glory: The Autobiography of David Hilliard and the Story of the Black Panther Party* (Little, Brown: 1993), 229.

56. Ibid.

57. Ibid.

58. There was a strained relationship between the Chicago Panthers and the primarily white Weather Underground, an offshoot of the Students for a Democratic Society. In 1968 Minister of Information Eldridge Cleaver directed Fred Hampton to apologize to the SDS and other local white radicals for comments considered offensive to Panther allies. Hampton refused. The friction developed after Hampton rejected a request that the local Panthers support tactics to protest the 1968 Democratic National Convention in Chicago. One of the tactics rejected was to throw urine-filled balloons on police. The Panthers were also unwilling to dissuade youths from breaking into an SDS office in a poor black Southside neighborhood. The SDS, Chicago Panthers argued, should have an office in a white community. In the white community they could work to eradicate racism from among their white brothers and sisters. Some Weather Underground members, including Bernardine Dohrn, were physically intimidated and berated as "bourgeois mother country radicals," whereas the largely working-class Young Patriots were "respected" by Panthers. Interview with Akua Injeri, July 1996. See also Elaine Brown, *A Taste of Power: A Black Woman's Story* (New York: Pantheon Books, 1993), 198.

59. Some of the white radical organizations that modeled themselves after the Panthers are the White Panther Party of Michigan, the John Brown Party

of California, and Rising Up Angry in Chicago. Steve Tappis, a founder of Rising Up Angry, explains that "It seemed like the only ones around that did what we wanted to do, and did it well, were the Panthers." Rising Up Angry used the Panther paper as a model for its own, as did the John Brown Party, which also adopted a ten-point program modeled after the Panthers' program. Dozens of white organizations created alliances with the Panthers. Many adopted the rhetoric of the Panthers, as had the young radical left in general. Slogans and terms such as "All power to the people" and "pigs" came into common use in radical circles. Hilliard and Cole, *This Side of Glory*, 230–33; misc. fliers, UCBSPC 18: 1.

60. "Palante Siempre Palante! A Look Back at the Young Lords," at http://netdial.caribe.net/~dfreedma/beginnin.htm (accessed July 30, 1999).
61. Felipe Luciano, speech, St. Lawrence University, April 1997.
62. "Palante Siempre Palante!"
63. Komozi Woodard, *A Nation Within a Nation: Amiri Baraka (LeRoi Jones) and Black Power Politics* (Chapel Hill, 1999), 138–40.
64. See David R. Roediger, *The Wages of Whiteness: Race and the Making of the American Working Class* (New York, 1991).
65. *La Causa* 1, no. 1 (May 23, 1969): 2.
66. Adelante Tigeres Angelines, flier, March 1968, UCBSPC 18: 30.
67. *La Causa* 1, no. 2 (July 10, 1969): 3.
68. Marin, "Protest in an Urban Barrio," 144.
69. Ibid., 144–45.
70. *Palante Siempre Palante: The Young Lords*, documentary written, produced, and directed by Iris Morales, Latino Education Network (New York, 1996); *Young Lords Party, Palante, Young Lords Party* (New York, 1971), 117.
71. *The Asian Student* 1, no. 1 (November 1973): 13.
72. Los Siete, flyer, ca. 1970, UCBSPC 18: 32.
73. Richard Newman, interview with author, August 4, 1999.
74. Seale, *Seize the Time*, 210–11.

Chapter 9

1. Basir Mchawi, "Kwanzaa, By Any Means Necessary," *Black News*, December 1974, reprinted in *Black News*, December 1976, 6–8.
2. For an assessment of the Black Power movement's impact culturally see William Van Deburg, *New Day in Babylon: Black Power in American Culture, 1965–1975* (Chicago: University of Chicago Press, 1992) and James Edward Smethhurst, *The Black Arts Movement: Literary Nationalism in the 1960s and 1970s* (Chapel Hill: University of North Carolina Press, 2005).
3. The best expressions of Karenga's ideas on the redemptive power of African culture are contained in Clyde Halisi and James Mtume, eds., *The Quotable Karenga* (Los Angeles: Us Organization, 1967); Maulana Karenga, *Kwanzaa: Origin, Concepts, Practice* (Inglewood, CA: Kawaida Publications, 1977); Maulana Karenga, *Kwanzaa: A Celebration of Family, Community, and Culture* (Los Angeles: University of Sankore Press,

1998); Maulana Karenga, *Odu Ifa: The Ethical Teachings* (Los Angeles: University of Sankore Press, 1999). Also see Karenga's own theoretical explanation of African tradition he named Kawaida. Maulana Karenga, *Kawaida Theory: An Introductory Outline* (Inglewood, CA: Kawaida Publications, 1980); For Kawaida see also Imamu Clyde Halisi, ed., *Kitabu: Beginning Concepts in Kawaida* (Los Angeles: Temple of Kawaida, 1971); Imamu Amiri Baraka, *Kawaida Studies: The New Nationalism* (Chicago: Third World Press, 1972); and Scot Brown, *Fighting for US: Maulana Karenga, the US Organization, and Black Cultural Nationalism* (New York: NYU Press, 2003).

4. In the first historical treatment of Kwanzaa, Elizabeth Pleck writes about Kwanzaa as part of the black nationalist tradition but fails to place the holiday within this Black Power and black nationalist historical milieu. Her Kwanzaa is more a product of the black middle class in the 1980s. Pleck writes, "To historicize Kwanzaa is to place the holiday within the dual contexts of black nationalism of the 1960s and the development of the black middle class in the 1980s." To examine Kwanzaa "in this dual context," she argues, shows why "Kwanzaa could address the needs and anxieties of the burgeoning black middle class in the post-civil rights era." But Pleck failed to address the "needs and desires" of the black cultural nationalist community and to situate and examine Kwanzaa as a product of the Black Power movement and black neighborhood organizations and institutions. Without this broad-based community effort during the Black Power period Kwanzaa may not have survived the 1970s. Elizabeth Pleck, "Kwanzaa: The Making of a Black Nationalist Tradition, 1966–1990," *Journal of American Ethnic History* 20 (Summer 2001), 6.

5. The data on the number of Kwanzaa celebrants varies. One reason is the difficulty in defining Kwanzaa "celebrant." What distinguishes a committed celebrant as oppose to a casual observer—seven days, three days, one day? What about people that perform Kwanzaa celebrations in their home vis-à-vis those who attend public Kwanzaa ceremonies? These unaddressed questions have produced a plethora of numbers, some publicized by the holiday's creator. In 1979, Karenga reported that over 10 million people celebrated Kwanzaa. In 1998, he reported that over 20 million blacks worldwide celebrated the holiday, both times without attribution. *U.S. News & World Report* and *Newsweek* provided a more conservative number: 5 million in 1992. Maritz Marketing Research in *American Demographics* reported in 1997 that 2 percent of American adults celebrate Kwanzaa. See Dr. M. R. Karenga, "Creator of Kwanzaa: Interview," *Black News* (December 1979), 5; Karenga, *Kwanzaa: A Celebration of Family, Community, and Culture*, xv; Tibbett L. Spear, "Stretching the Holiday Season," *American Demographics*, November 19, 1997, 42–49.

6. On December 25, 1965, three months after the founding of the Us Organization, Samuel Carr-Damu, one of the original members visited Karenga's home to present his daughter with a black doll for Christmas. Karenga rejected the gift, stating that Us members should not celebrate Christmas. Since the entire rank-and-file recognized some form of

Christianity and were life-long celebrants of Christmas, the potential elimination of the holiday posed a serious problem for the organization, especially those with young children. The future of Christmas in the organization would have to include an additional year-end celebration at the very least. It is not entirely clear in what manner the Us Organization celebrated Christmas in 1965, but Karenga spent much of the following year researching African cultural practices, trying to find a suitable alternative for Christmas of 1966. Karenga scoured books on African history and culture, noticing in particular the ubiquity of festivity and gaiety on the African continent around agricultural and harvest celebrations. The search for the cultural alternative to Christmas meant returning to the source, or as Karenga became fond of saying, "going back to black." Going back to black was Karenga's idea of returning to what he understood as African tradition, an idea similarly postulated by Guinea President Sekou Toure called "re-Africanization." While reading books on the Zulu culture in South Africa, Karenga came across one particular harvest festival known as Umkhosi. Umkhosi was one of many first fruit ceremonies practiced in the Natal and Zululand regions of South Africa. The culmination of the harvest in Natal and Zulu regions usually occurred during the end of the year and at the beginning of the next, prompting the people in these areas to stop their daily activities and partake in an agricultural celebration. There were many ritual elements in the Umkhosi ceremony but Karenga excluded components of the Zulu custom unfeasible in an American setting and instead appropriated several others including ancestor veneration, feasting, in-gathering of villagers, and the festival's appearance at year's end. "Kwanzaa then became for Us and Black people," Karenga said, "a time and week of the gathering-in of ourselves rather than the agricultural harvests of our ancestors." Now armed with the building blocks of an authentically African tradition, Karenga instituted a new holiday for the Us Organization and black America. Karl Key-Hekima, telephone interview with author, April 24, 2001, 4; Clyde Daniels-Halisi, interview by author, Altadena, CA, April 30, 2001, 5; Eileen Jensen Krige, *The Social System of the Zulus* (Pietermaritzburg: Shuter & Shooter, 1965), 249–260; Henri A. Junod, *The Life of a South African Tribe*, vol. 2 (New Hyde Park, NY: University Books, 1966), 28; Although Karenga drew heavily from Zulu harvest ceremonies, other first fruit festivals in other parts of Africa also inspired him. See D. G. Coursey, "The New Yam Festival Among the Ewe," *Ghana Notes and Queries* (December 1968), 18–23; M. Ron Karenga, *Kwanzaa: Origin, Concepts, Practice* (Inglewood, CA: Kawaida Publications, 1977), 25; Dr. M. Ron Karenga, "Kwanzaa: Concepts and Functions," *Black Collegian* (December/January 1979): 127–128. For an assessment of returning to traditional African sources and ways of doing implied in the concept "going back to black," see Sekou Toure, *Toward Full Re-Africanization* (Paris: Presence Africaine, 1959).
7. Brown, *Fighting for US*, 69.
8. Pleck makes Kwanzaa's historical trajectory synonymous with Karenga's direct involvement with the holiday when she argued, "Kwanzaa rose,

fell, and floundered in relation to Karenga's alliances and schisms." But Karenga's "alliances and schisms" as well as his legal entanglements had virtually no impact on Kwanzaa's development. By the early 1970s, Kwanzaa had already moved beyond the scope and reach of Karenga. It is for this reason why I argue for a de-centering of Karenga when accounting for a social history of Kwanzaa. Pleck, "Kwanzaa: The Making of a Black Nationalist Tradition," 6.

9. Stokely Carmichael said in the summer of 1966, "Political and economic power is what black people have to have." *Time,* July 1, 1966.

10. James Meredith, one of the first African Americans to bring national attention to the issue of desegregation in higher education, integrated the University of Mississippi in 1962, becoming the first black to attend. As a result of Meredith's further politicization and his ongoing participation in southern civil rights protests, he decided to conduct a "March Against Fear" in June 1966. On his 200-mile journey from Memphis, Tennessee, to Jackson, Mississippi, he was shot and wounded. Civil rights leaders, such as Martin Luther King Jr. and Stokely Carmichael decided to continue the march for Meredith. In Greenwood, Mississippi, Student Nonviolent Coordinating Committee (SNCC) field secretary Willie Ricks and Carmichael engaged in a call-and-response routine with marchers that involved discontinuing the famous civil rights slogan, "Freedom Now" for the new "Black Power" chant. During a rally in Greenwood, Carmichael announced: "The only way we gonna stop them white men from whuppin' us is to take over. We been saying freedom for six years and we ain't got nothin.' What do you want?" The marchers yelled, "Black Power! Black Power! Black Power!" The new Black Power chant would quickly move from slogan to a sophisticated analytical assessment about the direction of the black freedom movement. For Carmichael's longer and more thoughtful reflection on Black Power, see Stokely Carmichael and Charles Hamilton, *Black Power* (New York: Vintage, 1967).

11. "Negro Cry: 'Black Power!'—What Does it Mean?," *U.S. News & World Report,* July 11, 1966.

12. The memory of some original Us members is faint as to the name of the gentleman who opened his home to the very first Karamu in 1966. Scot Brown's book on the Us Organization mentions a man name Noble Hanif, but no clear consensus on the name of the man was reached by original Us members when interviewed by the author. The only consensus was that the man was an Us supporter who attended Sunday afternoon Soul Sessions, but not an official member of the organization.

13. Two original Us members recall Karenga searching for a candleholder with seven holes during the early part of 1966 before the inaugural Kwanzaa in December. Unable to find a seven-hole candleholder in the Los Angeles area, Karenga and Us members used a nine-hole Jewish menorah and broke off two of the openings for the Karamu. The first Kwanzaa candleholder, the kinara, was made for the following year's Kwanzaa in 1967 by Us member Buddy Rose-Aminifu. Both undertakings—using a modified menorah and creating a special candelabra for Kwanzaa cohered with the holiday's sixth principle—kuumba (creativity).

Buddy Rose-Aminifu, telephone interview with author, May 23, 2001, 1; Clyde Daniels-Halisi, interview by author, Altadena, CA, April 30, 2001, 4–5.

14. Karl Key-Hekima, telephone interview with author, April 24, 2001, 6; Clyde Daniels-Halisi, interview by author, Altadena, CA, April 30, 2001, 3.

15. Elizabeth Softky, "A Kwanzaa Memory: Growing Up with Dr. Karenga," *Washington Post,* December 20, 1995, E4.

16. Iya Afin and Ayobunmi Sangode, *Rites of Passage: Psychology of Female Power* (Brooklyn, NY: Athelia Henrietta Press, 1999), 9–10.

17. "In Perspective: Karenga's Mission is for Posterity," *The Hilltop,* January 5, 1968, 3.

18. Quincy Troupe, "Festival Welcomes Uhuru Militants," *Los Angeles Free Press,* August 18, 1967, 3; Bruce Tyler, "The Rise and Decline of the Watts Summer Festival, 1965–1986," *American Studies* 31 (1990), 61–81.

19. TALO and the Black Congress were organizations that attempted to unify local civil rights, black nationalist, and black leftist organizations under a single consortium after the Watts rebellion. See Brown, *Fighting for US,* 82–84.

20. Most of the major organizations attended this event including the Black Panthers and the Los Angeles branches of SNCC and CORE.

21. "Observance Set for Malcolm X," *Los Angeles Sentinel,* February 3, 1966, A1, A4; "First Annual Memorial Staged for Malcolm X," *Los Angeles Sentinel,* March 3, 1966, 11; Former Us member Hakim Jamal staged Malcolm X commemorations on the black Muslim leader's birthday with his former colleagues in Us, but particularly after his departure from the organization in 1967. Hakim Jamal, "Celebration Planned for Malcolm X," *Los Angeles Sentinel,* May 16, 1968, B9. For the Us Organization's first public appearance, see Clay Carson, "A Talk with Ron Karenga, Watts Black Nationalist," *Los Angeles Free Press,* September 2, 1966, 12.

22. Vernon Sukumu, future chair of the US chapter in San Diego remembered the first Kwanzaa in 1967: "We had it in [Joe] Chochezi's house, some brothers from Los Angeles came down and officiated the ceremony." Vernon Sukumu, interview by author, Carson, CA, May 12, 2001, 3. For an assessment of San Diego's Us chapter see Brown, *Fighting For US,* 44.

23. Angela Davis was a graduate student at UCLA. She remembered attending the conference and captured the mood in her autobiography: "The Second Avenue Baptist Church in Watts glowed with colorful African patterns and fabrics—the woman wore traditional long dresses of red, purple, orange, and yellow; the men wore bubas that rivaled in every way the fiery beauty of the women's clothes. The walls of the registration room were alive with poster art that hailed Blackness as an ancient and peerless beauty.... I walked around calling everyone sister and brother, smiling and elated, high on love." Angela Davis, *Angela Davis: An Autobiography* (New York: International Publishers, 1988), 158.

24. Douglass Hartmann, *Race, Culture, and the Revolt of the Black Athlete: The 1968 Olympic Protests and Their Aftermath* (Chicago: University of Chicago Press, 2003), 56–59; Amy Bass, *Not the Struggle But the Triumph:*

The 1968 Olympics and the Making of the Black Athlete (Minneapolis: University of Minnesota Press, 2002), 90–92, 203.

25. Quote taken from Hartmann, *Race, Culture, and the Revolt of the Black Athlete*, 57.

26. Davis, *Angela Davis*, 159.

27. Makinya Sibeko-Kouate, telephone interview with author, December 29, 2000, 20.

28. See Brown, *Fighting for US*, 58–60.

29. William E. Cross Jr., "The Negro-To-Black Conversion Experience: Toward A Psychology of Black Liberation," *Black World* (July 1971).

30. "When we got back here," said Sister Makinya, "we realized we were in Panther territory ... so we lost it ... I never in my life saw the material again." Makinya Sibeko-Kouate, telephone interview with author, June 26, 2000, 2.

31. Makinya Sibeko-Kouate, telephone interview with author, June 26, 2000, 3.

32. Sister Makinya, [Harriet Smith—Slave Name], "Asante Sana for the Organizing of the Kwanza Ceremonies in the San Francisco Bay Area," (1972?), personal papers of Makinya Sibeko-Kouate; Itibari Zulu, interview by author, Los Angeles, CA, February 10, 1999.

33. "An Invitation From the Pan-African People's Organization," (1972?), personal papers of Makinya Sibeko-Kouate.

34. Delvin Walker, "Kwanzaa, An Original Afro-American Holiday Just For You," *Pamoja*, December 1980, 23; "Bay Area Communities Celebrate Kwanzaa," *California Voice*, December 19, 1986, 1–2; Marilyn Bailey, "Kwanzaa, An Afro-American Holiday Evolves," *Oakland Tribune*, December 26, 1992, E1, E5; Makinya Sibeko-Kouate, telephone interview with author, June 26, 2000, 18; Hurumu Zulu, telephone interview with author, April 12, 2000, 2; Itibari Zulu, interview by author, Los Angeles, CA, February 10, 1999, 3. The Zulu Brothers, natives of Oakland, California, were introduced to Kwanzaa in 1970 as young children when Sister Makinya was invited to explain the new holiday to the youth at Bethlehem Community Church—a black Lutheran church in Oakland. I thank Itibari and Hurumu for helping me locate Sister Makinya.

Throughout the 1980s, Sister Makinya continued to train individuals and promote Kwanzaa while working as an educator in the Berkeley Unified School District after graduating with a B.A. from California State University, Hayward in 1972. Downstate, in southern California, Kwanzaa continued despite Karenga's incarceration in 1971 but not with the intensity and the same coordinated fashion as it had in the Bay Area. But Kwanzaa began mushrooming in other cities as it had in Oakland, Berkeley, and San Francisco. The early growth of Kwanzaa in the Bay Area, however, was something of an anomaly. First, it began under the direction of a non-Us member even though Karenga wished it would move in that direction. Second, Sister Makinya, though politically conscious, was not a Kawaida cultural nationalist—a follower and practitioner of Us Organization doctrine. And finally, she was an older woman in a public arena dominated by younger black men. Kwanzaa provided Sister Makinya with a tremendous amount of agency, particularly in terms of organizing and educating. But most high-profile spokespersons that promoted Kwanzaa in the late 1960s and early 1970s were men. Though she promoted Kwanzaa with zest and zeal, achieving notoriety in the Bay Area nationalist community, Sister Makinya in many ways remained an outsider to the history of Kwanzaa. This pivotal woman has been marginalized in the history and memory of Kwanzaa's early development. When asked by the author about the role Sister Makinya played in popularizing Kwanzaa in the Bay Area, Karenga said he did not remember her. He recalled being more familiar with the efforts of Thomatra Scott (known as Scotty) of the Young Adults of San Franscisco in relation to the spread of Kwanzaa. Maulana Karenga, interview by author, Los Angeles, CA, February 9, 1999, 8. The organizations and spokespersons remembered as having sustained Kwanzaa in the early Black Power period were Kawaida cultural nationalists—groups affiliated with the Congress of African People in major cities across the United States.

35. Imamu Amiri Baraka, ed., *African Congress: A Documentary of the First Modern Pan-African Congress* (New York: William Morrow & Co., 1972); Congress of African People, "Structure Report, 1972"; Alex Poinsett, "It's Nation Time!: Congress of African People Proposes Models for Worldwide Black Institutions," *Ebony,* December 1970; for a complete assessment of the Atlanta Congress and Baraka's political endeavors, see Komozi Woodard, *A Nation Within a Nation: Amiri Baraka (LeRoi Jones) and Black Power Politics* (Chapel Hill: University of North Carolina Press, 1999). I thank Komozi Woodard for bringing my attention to Kwanzaa's appearance at the African Congress.

36. Baraka, ed., *African Congress,* 183–186. In the late 1960s and early 1970s, CFUN and later the Congress of African People spelled Kwanzaa with one 'a' as did other groups. There were some organizations that spelled Kwanzaa with two a's during this early period. The spelling of Kwanzaa appeared to remain an organizational choice in the 1970s.

37. Congress of African People, "Structure Report, 1972"; For a list of cities and organizational attendees at the Atlanta meeting see Baraka, ed., *African Congress,* 469–475.

38. Amiri Baraka, *The Autobiography of LeRoi Jones* (Chicago: Lawrence Hill Books, 1984), 387.

39. Baraka, *The Autobiography of LeRoi Jones,* 433–436; 445; Amiri Baraka, "Why I Changed My Ideology: Black Nationalism and the Social Revolution," *Black World* 24 (July 1975), 30–42; Kalamu ya Salaam, "Tell No Lies, Claim No Easy Victories" and Haki Madhubuti, "Enemy: From the White Left, White Right, and In-Between," *Black World* 23 (October 1974), 18–34 and 36–47.

40. Jitu Weusi wrote, "In 1970, The EAST had a brief alliance with Amiri Baraka's Committee for a Unified Newark (CFUN), a group based in Newark, New Jersey. We adopted Kwanzaa from that relationship and thus became the first institution east of the Hudson River to practice and observe Kwanzaa." Jitu Weusi, "The EAST Legacy," *International*

African Arts Festival-25 Anniversary, Brooklyn, NY 1996 (brochure), personal papers of Segun Shabaka.

41. Basir Mchawi, "Which Way Kwanza," *Black News,* December 1975, 8.

42. "Christmas Nigger," *Black News,* November 15, 1969, 1.

43. "Black People and the X-MAS Ripoff," *Black News,* December 1973, reprinted in *Black News,* December 1976, 4–5.

44. Segun Shabaka, "Kwanza," *Black News,* December 1975, 16.

45. "Kwanza in Brooklyn," *Black News,* January 31, 1975, 2; Segun Shabaka, "Symbols of Kwanza," *Black News,* December 1975, 16.

46. Charlayne Hunter, "Spirit of Kwanza—Time of Giving: Harlem Pupils Told of Ritual Celebrating Harvest," *New York Times,* December 24, 1971, 28; Barbara Campbell, "Harlem Pupils Get Early Start on Kwanza," *New York Times,* December 20, 1972, 47; Judith Cummings, "City Blacks Begin Fete of Kwanzaa," *New York Times,* December 27, 1973, 41; Carrie Mason-Draffen, "In Kwanzaa, Two Festive Traditions," *New York Times,* December 24, 1986; Cedric McClester, "Editor's Comments," and "Kwanzaa: A Cultural Reaffirmation," *Kwanzaa Magazine* (1984–1985 edition), 6, 13. By the time the Harlem Commonwealth Council and the EAST Organization began to lose institutional muscle in the late 1970s and early 1980s, Jose Ferrer, Malik Ahmed, and the New York Urban Coalition emerged as one of New York City's major organizers of public Kwanzaa celebrations, particularly Ferrer with his annual Kwanzaa Fest—a perennial economic bazaar and exposition.

47. Baba Hannibal Afrik and Conrad Worrill, "The History, Origin, and Development of Kwanzaa in the City of Chicago," November 26, 1999 (unpublished manuscript), 1–2, personal papers of Conrad Worrill; Mansong Kulubally, telephone interview with author, October 10, 2000, 2–3; Conrad Worrill, interview by author, Chicago, IL, December 13, 2000; Haki Madhubuti published one of the earliest Kwanzaa pamphlets, Haki Madhubuti, *Kwanzaa* (Chicago: Third World Press, 1972).

48. Afrik and Worrill, "The History, Origin, and Development of Kwanzaa in the City of Chicago," 3–5.

49. Ibid., 3–5.

50. Joann Stevens, "A Lifestyle Called Kwanzaa, Black Maryland Families Celebrate a Week of Ceremonies That Reflect Age-Old African Traditions," *Washington Post,* December 27, 1979, Md3; Edward D. Sargent, "Alternative Festival, 'Kwanzaa' Celebrates Spirit of Community and Heritage," *Washington Post,* December 25, 1980, DC4; Eugene L. Meyer, "Kwanzaa Reaffirms Roots, Holiday Lets Americans Honor African Heritage," *Washington Post,* December 26, 1986, C1; Pam Carroll, "Celebrating an African Companion to Christmas," *Washington Post,* December 24, 1987, DC1; Rev. Ishakamusa Barashango, *Afrikan People and European Holidays: A Mental Genocide,* Book I (Silver Spring, MD: Fourth Dynasty Publishing, 1979), 81.

51. Delvin Walker, "Kwanzaa: An Original Afro-American Holiday Just For You," *Pamoja,* December 1980, 20–24.

52. Melva Joyce Parhams, "Kwanzaa and Its People," *LA Community Coupon Clipper,* December 1989; "Life Story of One Who Has Departed—In

Love and Memory of Ngao Damu," Obituary, January 27, 1995, personal papers of Ngoma Ali. The first Kwanzaa Gwaride Parade was held in December of 1978, beginning on Adams Street and Crenshaw Boulevard, terminating at Leimert Park with an all-day festival. Another example of Kwanzaa's growing appeal beyond the Us fold in Los Angeles was the birth of a charity organization called the Kwanzaa Foundation in 1973 started by actresses Marla Gibbs and Esther Rolle.

53. Afrik and Worrill, "The History, Origin, and Development of Kwanzaa in the City of Chicago," 4.

54. Afrik and Worrill, "The History, Origin, and Development of Kwanzaa in the City of Chicago," 8, 12; "Kwanzaa Happenings in the City," *Chicago Defender*, December 27, 1997, 15.

55. Mtumishi St. Julien and Kalamu ya Salaam, "Ahidiana Operating Principles," (1973) contained in Mtumishi St. Julien, *Upon The Shoulders of Elephants We Reach the Sky* (New Orleans: Runagate Press, 1995); "The Occasion of the 30th Anniversary of the S.H.A.P.E. Community Center," House of Representatives, 106th Congress, 2 Session, *Congressional Record Extensions*, May 11, 2000; Mansong Kulubally, ed., *We Must Come Together*, vol. 4 (1992); Some Positive People, "Kwanzaa Flyer," December 1982, personal papers of Mansong Kulubally; "Seventh Kwanzaa Celebration to be Held at Edward Waters College Dec. 26," *Jacksonville Free Press*, December 23, 1998, 1; "A Kwanzaa Vision for Atlanta," Resource Guide & Souvenir Book, Metro-Atlanta Kwanzaa Association, 1993; Ronald Roach, "Area Blacks Celebrating Kwanzaa Days," *Atlanta Journal-Constitution*, December 31, 1988, C03; David G. Yosifon, "Kwanzaa Taking Root in Boston Community," *Bay State Banner*, December 24, 1998, 1; the BSU at the University of Wisconsin—Madison used Kwanzaa's seven principles as a rallying cry for organizing black student strikers, *Black Journal Strike Bulletin*, February 1969.

56. Jurgen Habermas, *The Structural Transformation of the Public Sphere: An Inquiry Into a Category of Bourgeois Society* (Cambridge: MIT Press, 1993). For a black-adapted theorization of Habermas's concept, see The Black Public Sphere Collective, ed., *The Black Public Sphere: A Public Culture Book* (Chicago: University of Chicago Press, 1995). In the "Afterword," Thomas Holt writes, "Theoretically, speech communities are democratic forums in which public opinion takes shape, opinion aimed at directing or influencing public policy, norms of behavior, or political consensus. Although these are idealistic and perhaps unrealistic goals for counter-publics, which are by definition divorced from substantial control over how public power is deployed, they define the point of analytic exercise nonetheless: not only speech but also action. In the case of an oppositional public, the goal quite simply is oppositional action. This, then, is the standard, the gauge of the relevance, value, and importance of various forms of contemporary publicity," 328.

Chapter 10

1. I use the term "Black Studies" in its broadest sense throughout this essay. The field that began as Black Studies in the late 1960s has come to be known as Afro-American Studies, African American Studies, or Africana Studies at various colleges and universities. For a recent discussion of Black Studies programs, see Delores P. Aldridge and Carlene Young, eds., *Out of the Revolution: The Development of Africana Studies* (Lanham, MD, 2000).

2. I use the term the "1960s" not in the conventional chronological sense of a decade that spanned ten years. Rather I utilize this term as a metaphor for the period of radical global political activity. Historically specific movements and politics often associated with the "1960s" predate this decade and continue to proliferate after. Therefore it is imperative to resist foreshortened time frames that view this era as simply the "protest decade."

3. Peniel E. Joseph, "Black Liberation Without Apology: Rethinking the Black Power Movement," *The Black Scholar* 31 (Fall/Winter 2001): 2–19.

4. Manning, Marable, "Black Studies and the Racial Mountain," *Souls* 2 (Summer 2000): 17–36. See also Manning, Marable, *Dispatches from the Ebony Tower: Intellectuals Confront the African-American Experience* (New York, 2000).

5. For a discuss of Harrison's importance, see Jeffrey B. Perry, ed., *A Hubert Harrison Reader* (Middleton, CT, 2001), 1–130.

6. Marable, "Black Studies and the Racial Mountain," 17–18.

7. St. Clair Drake, "Black Studies and Global Perspectives: An Essay," *Journal of Negro Education* 53 (Summer 1984): 226–28.

8. Peniel E. Joseph, "Waiting Till the Midnight Hour: Reconceptualizing the Heroic Period of the Civil rights Movement, 1954–1965," *Souls* 1 (Spring 2000): 6–17.

9. See Richard Wright, *Black Power: A Record of Reactions in the Land of Pathos* (New York, 1954); *The Color of Curtain: A Report on the Bandung Conference* (New York, 1956); and *White Man Listen!* (New York, 1957).

10. Margaret Walker, *Richard Wright: Daemonic Genius* (New York, 1988), 274.

11. Kevin K. Gaines, "Revisiting Richard Wright in Ghana: Black Radicalism and the Dialectics of Diaspora," *Social Text* 67 (Summer 2001): 75–101.

12. Richard Wright, "Tradition and Industrialization: The Plight of the Tragic Elite in Africa," *Presence Africaine* 8–9–10 (June–November 1956): 355–69.

13. Ibid., 355.

14. See V. P. Franklin, *Living Our Stories, Telling Our Truths: Autobiography and the Making of the African-American Intellectual Tradition* (New York, 1995), 279.

15. Wright, "Tradition and Industrialization," 634.

16. See the special triple issue of the proceedings from the First International Conference of Negro Writers and Artists, *Presence Africaine* 8–9–10 June–November 1956.

17. "The Policy of Our Culture," *Presence Africaine* 24–5 (February–May 1959): 3–5.

18. Kevin Gaines, "Africa-American Expatriates in Ghana and the Black Radical Tradition," *Souls* 1 (Fall 1999): 64–71 and "Revisiting Richard Wright in Ghana," 75–101.

19. Joseph, "Waiting Till the Midnight Hour," 10–11; Robin D.G. Kelley, "Black Like Mao: Red China and Black Revolution," *Souls* 1 (Fall 1999): 6–41.

20. For a discussion of LeRoi Jones and Harold Cruse's experiences in Cuba see Cynthia Young, "Havana Up in Harlem: LeRoi Jones, Harold Cruse and the Making of a Cultural Revolution," *Science & Society* 65 (Spring 2001): 12–38. See also Peniel E. Joseph, *Waiting 'Til the Midnight Hour: A Narrative History of Black Power in America* (New York: Henry Holt, 2006).

21. Jerry Gafio Watts, *Amiri Baraka: The Politics and Art of a Black Intellectual* (New York, 2001), 85.

22. *On Guard* 1 (May 1961): 1.

23. Komozi Woodard, *A Nation Within a Nation: Amiri Baraka (LeRoi Jones) & Black Power Politics* (Chapel Hill, NC, 1999), 54–58.

24. E. U. Essien-Udom, "The Nationalist Movements of Harlem," *Freedomways* 3 (Summer 1963): 335–342.

25. *The Black Challenge* (Fall 1960): 9, 17.

26. *Mr. Muhammad Speaks,* September 1960, 2.

27. Drake, "Black Studies and Global Perspectives," 230.

28. Donald R. Hopkins, "Development of Black Political Organizations in Berkeley since 1960," *Experiment and Change in Berkeley: Essays on City Politics, 1950–1975,* eds. H. Nathan and S. Scott (Berkeley, CA, 1978), 107–109.

29. Leslie Alexander Lacy, *The Rise and Fall of a Proper Negro* (New York, 1971), 98–99.

30. Khalid Abdullah Tariq Al Mansour (Donald Warden), *Black Americans at the Crossroads: Where do We Go from Here?* (New York, 1990), 70–75 and 122–33.

31. Lacy, *The Rise and Fall of a Proper Negro,* 98–99.

32. Kelley and Esch, "Black Like Mao," 16.

33. Scot Brown, "The US Organization, Black Power Vanguard Politics, and the United Front Ideal: Los Angeles and Beyond," *The Black Scholar* 31 (Fall 2001): 21–30.

34. Lacy, *The Rise and Fall of a Proper Negro,* 105.

35. Timothy Tyson, *Radio Free Dixie: Robert F. Williams and the Roots of Black Power* (Chapel Hill, NC, 1999), 262–286.

36. The following discussion of RAM is based on oral histories and Maxwell C. Stanford, "Revolutionary Action Movement (RAM): A Case Study of Urban Revolutionary Movement in Western Capitalist Society," M.A. Thesis, Atlanta University, 1986.

37. Ibid., 75.

38. Ernest Allen, telephone conversation with the author, August 21, 2001.

39. Max Stanford, "Towards a Revolutionary Action Movement Manifesto," *Correspondence,* March 1964, 3.

40. *Soulbook* 1 (Winter 1964).

41. Grace Lee Boggs, *Living for Change: An Autobiography* (Minneapolis, MN, 1998), 107–109.

42. James Boggs, *The American Revolution: Pages from a Negro Worker's Notebook* (New York, 1963).

43. Suzanne E. Smith, *Dancing in the Street: Motown and the Cultural Politics of Detroit* (Cambridge, MA, 1999), 41–42.

44. "Militant Stand Taken By New All-Black Young Group," *Young Socialist*, September 1963, 1.

45. *Riots, Civil and Criminal Disorders,* Hearings before the Permanent Subcommittee on Investigations of the Committee on Government Operations, Part 6, March 1967, 1461.

46. "Detroit Cops Raid University and Arrest Uhuru Leaders," *Young Socialist*, November 1963, 2.

47. Radical black students contributed to the burgeoning Black Studies movement through organizing conferences, students, groups, and protesting for Black Studies curriculum on campuses during the early 1960s.

48. Stanford, "Revolutionary Action Movement," 91.

49. Woodard, *A Nation Within a Nation*, 70.

50. William E. Nelson Jr. "Black Studies, Student Activism, and the Academy," in Aldridge and Young, *Out of the Revolution*, 79–91.

51. In 1968, Yale University sponsored a symposium on Black Studies, the proceedings of which were published as a book. See Armstead Robinson, Craig C. Foster, and Donald H. Ogilvie, eds., *Black Studies in the University* (New Haven, CT, 1969).

52. Henry Hampton and Steven Fayer, eds., *Voices of Freedom: An Oral History of the Civil Rights Movement from the 1950s through the 1980s* (New York, 1991), 425–448.

53. Northwestern University Black Students, "If Our Demands Are Impossible, then Peace Between Us Is Impossible Too," in *Black Nationalism in American*, eds., John Bracey Jr. et al. (Indianapolis, IN, 1970), 476–485.

54. James Turner, "Black Students and their Changing Perspective," *Ebony*, August 1969, 135–40.

55. The most famous and controversial was Harold Cruse's *The Crisis of the Negro Intellectual: A Historical Analysis of the Failure of Black Leadership* (1967; reprinted New York, 1984); for an example of young black writers advocating the creation of radical black institutions, including Black Studies centers, see Askia Muhammad Toure, "We Must Create a National Black Intelligentsia in Order to Survive," in Bracey et al., *Black Nationalism in America*, 452–62.

56. For a discussion of this phenomenon, see Harry Edwards, *Black Students* (New York, 1970), 61–96.

57. "Black High School Students Revolt Against School Administration," *Rebellion News*, October 1967, 1.

58. The impact of Black Power and Black Studies on high school-age youth has received important scholarly attention. See Special Issue of *The Journal of African American History* 88, no. 2 (Spring 2003). See also V. P. Franklin, "Black High School Student Activism: An Urban Phenomenon?"

Journal of Research in Education 10 (Fall 2000): 3–8; Matthew J. Country-man, *Up South: Civil Rights and Black Power in Philadelphia* (Philadel-phia: University of Pennsylvania Press, 2005).

59. *The South End,* January 23, 1969, 1.

60. Max Stanford, "Revolutionary Nationalism and the Afro-American Stu-dent," *Liberator,* January 1965, 15.

61. Harold Cruse, *Rebellion or Revolution?* (New York: Morrow, 1968).

62. *New York Times,* December 29, 1968.

63. Cruse, *Crisis of the Negro Intellectual,* 137.

64. Ibid., 203.

65. Ibid., 200.

66. Brown, "The US Organization, Black Power Vanguard Politics, and the United Front Ideal," 28.

67. Colin A. Beckles, "Black Bookstores, Black Power, and the F.B.I.: The Case of Drum and Spear," *The Western Journal of Black Studies* 20 (1996): 63–70.

68. Fanon Che Wilkins, "'In the Belly of the Beast': Black Power, Anti-imperialism, and the African Liberation Solidarity Movement, 1968-1975," Ph.D. diss., New York University, 2001, 120.

69. For an in-depth discussion on this, see Joseph, *Waiting 'Til the Midnight Hour.*

70. Stephen Ward, "'Scholarship in the Context of Struggle': Activists Intel-lectuals, the Institute of the Black World (IBW) and the Contours of Black Radicalism, 1967–1975," *The Black Scholar* 31 (Fall 2001): 42–53.

71. Institute of the Black World, ed., "The History of the Institute of the Black World," in *Education and Black Struggle: Notes from the Colonized World* (Cambridge, MA, 1974), 145–48.

72. *Negro Digest* 17 (March 1968): 4–97; 18 (March 1969): 4–97; and 19 (March 1970): 4–97.

73. *Negro Digest* 17 (March 1968): 97.

74. Ibid., 34.

75. Ibid., 36.

76. Vincent Harding, "An Open Letter to Black Students in the North: New Creation or Familiar Death?" *Negro Digest* 18 (March 1969): 5–14.

77. Ibid., 5–9.

78. Chuck Hopkins, "Malcolm X Liberation University," *Negro Digest* 19 (March 1970): 39–43.

79. Ibid., 40.

80. Ibid.

81. Malcolm X Liberation University ceased to operate in the mid-1970s. Underfunded and operating on a precarious budget, MXLU nonetheless provided a model for short-lived alternative education centers that briefly flourished during the late 1960s and early 1970s. See Wilkins, "In the Belly of the Beast.'"

82. Drake, "Black Studies and Global Perspectives," 231.

83. Historian Fanon Che Wilkins has provided the most in-depth historical examination of the evolution of SOBU/YOBU and the group's relationship

to Malcolm X Liberation University. See Wilkins, "'In the Belly of the Beast,'" 123–134.

84. *The African World*, November 30, 1974, 3–4.
85. Rod Bush, *We Are Not What We Seem: Black Nationalism and Class Struggle in the American Century* (New York, 1999), 211–213.
86. Philip W. Semas, "Shortages of Money, Faculty, Time Plague Black Studies Programs," *The Chronicle of Higher Education*, May 4, 1970, 1–2; Edward Simpkins, "Black Studies—Here to Stay?" *Black World* 24 (December 1974): 26–59.
87. Nelson, "Black Studies, Student Activism, and the Academy," 87.
88. Vincent Harding, "The Vocation of the Black Scholar and the Struggles of the Black Community," *Education and the Black Struggle*, 3–29.
89. Ibid., 5.
90. Ibid., 12.
91. Ibid., 15.
92. Ibid., 16.

CONTRIBUTORS

Peniel E. Joseph teaches in the Department of Africana Studies at SUNY-Stony Brook. His work has appeared in *Souls, New Formation, The Journal of African American History*, and *The Black Scholar*. He is the author of *Waiting 'Til the Midnight Hour: A Narrative History of Black Power in America*.

Keith Mayes is Assistant Professor of African American Studies at the University of Minnesota, Twin Cities. He is working on a book-length study of the history of Kwanzaa.

Jeffrey O. G. Ogbar is Associate Professor of History and Director of the Institute for African American Studies at the University of Connecticut. He is the author of *Black Power: Radical Politics and African American Identity*.

Kimberly Springer teaches American Studies at King's College London. She is the author of *Living for the Revolution: Black Feminist Organizations, 1968–1980* and editor of *Still Lifting, Still Climbing: An Anthology of Contemporary Women's Activism*.

Jeanne Theoharis teaches Political Science at Brooklyn College. She is coauthor of *These Yet to Be Free United States: Civil Rights and Civil Liberties in America since 1945* and coeditor, with Komozi Woodard, of *Freedom North: Black Freedom Struggles outside the South, 1940–1980* and *Groundwork: Local Black Freedom Movements in America*.

Stephen Ward is Assistant Professor of Afro-American Studies at the University of Michigan. He is working on a book manuscript about Black Power radicalism in Detroit.

Simon Wendt teaches history at the University of Heidelberg. He is the author of *The Spirit and the Shotgun: Armed Resistance and the Struggle for Civil Rights*.

Rhonda Y. Williams is Associate Professor of History at Case Western University. She is the author of *The Politics of Public Housing: Black Women's Struggles Against Urban Inequality* and coeditor, with Julie Buckner Armstrong, Susan Hult Edwards, and Houston Bryan Roberson, of *Teaching the American Civil Rights Movement: Freedom's Bittersweet Song* (Routledge, 2002).

Yohuru Williams is Associate Professor of History and Director of Black Studies at Fairfield University. He is the author of *Black Politics/White Power: Civil Rights, Black Power, and the Black Panthers in New Haven.*

Komozi Woodard is Professor of American History and Public Policy at Sarah Lawrence College. He is the author of *A Nation Within a Nation: Amiri Baraka (LeRoi Jones) and Black Power Politics* and coeditor, with Jeanne Theoharis, of *Freedom North: Black Freedom Struggles outside of the South, 1940–1980* and *Groundwork: Local Black Freedom Movements in America.*

INDEX

Notes are referred to by page number, the letter n for note, and the note number.

Marches, *see* Demonstrations, marches, rallies

Marchevsky, A., 290n1

Marcus Garvey Schule, 244

Marriage, interracial, 34

Marriott, Salima, 97–99

Marshall, Burke, 156

Marshall, Paule, 132

Martin, Rudell, 309n82

Martinez, Joe, 217

Marx, Karl, 105, 137, 209, 226

Marxism, *see* Socialism/Marxism

Masculinism (term), 312–313n16; *see also* Gender dynamics/relations

Masculinity/manhood issues, *see* Manhood/masculinity/machismo

Matriarchy, Black, 125, 132

Matthews, Tracye, 18, 19

Mayfield, Julian, 13, 15, 61, 255

Mayoral elections, 5, 20, 72

McCarty, Margaret, 94–95, 96, 97, 101

McCone Commission, 52–53

McCutcheon, Steve, 90, 91

Mchawi, Basir, 242

McKeithen, John, 149, 157

McKeldin, Theodore R., 86, 307n48

McKissick, Floyd, 84, 90, 187

McMillan, Benjamin, 86

McWorter, Gerald (Abdul Alkilimat), 268

Mecartney, John M., 182

MECHA (Movimiento Estudiantil Chicano de Aztlan), 203, 214

Media reports

  black activism, 81

  Black Panther Party, 162–163, 179

    Hampton and Clark killings, 167–168

    NAACP and Roy Wilkins outreach to BPP, 181–182

  Black Power activism, 207–208

  Deacons for Defense and Justice, 147

  independence movements in Africa, 57

  Kwanzaa, 248

  Mississippi demonstration, June 1966, 2

  NAACP and Roy Wilkins, 168, 174, 181–182

  Olympic boycott, 236

  tensions between white and black women's organizations, 136

  Tuscaloosa defense organization, avoidance of publicity, 151

  United Front–Us confrontation, 236

  Watts uprising, 52

Medical care programs, Black Panthers and, 163

Meetings, *see* Conventions, congresses, conferences; *specific congresses*

Mendez, Gonzalo, 294n30

Mendez v. Westminster School District of Orange County, 294n30

Meredith, James, 1, 2, 344n10

Meredith March, 169–170, 171–172, 344n10

Meridian, Mississippi, 155

Merritt College, 204, 237, 259, 273

Mexican Americans, 294n30, 338n8

  busing of school children, 45–46

  at Fremont High School, 291n9

  liberation movements, 117

  rainbow radicalism, 23–24, 194–202, 221

  student organizations, 203

  Third World Women's Alliance (TWWA), 134, 143

Miami Overtown riot, 190

Micheaux, Lewis, 257

Middle class blacks, 293n19, 293n22

  Kwanzaa and, 342n4

  Watts uprising and, 292n17

Middle East policy, 74

Migration, Northern, 31, 106, 294n26

Milestone, Mississippi, 154, 155

Militancy, *see also* Defense, armed resistance, and radicalization of Civil Rights movement

  Fremont High School incident and, 29–30

  historiographic representations, 30

  Marnesba Tackett and, 41

  radicalism of R. F. Williams, 6, 163–165

  Soul School, 87

  Watts uprising and, 47

Military service, 276–277

Miller, Dave, 147

Miller, Loren, 39

Ministers, *see also* Churches; *specific ministers*

  and Kwanzaa, 249

  Los Angeles police brutality, 39

Ministers gang (Los Angeles), 211

Misogyny, 9, 18–19

Mississippi

  case studies, 24

  defensive units and activities, 146, 153–154

  first occurrence of term "Black Power," 1

Mississippi 1964 Freedom Summer project, defensive units and activities, 153–154

Mississippi Freedom Democratic Party, 20

Mitchell, John, 185

Mkalimoto, Ernie (Ernest Allen Jr.), 261

black nuns and community power,
    91–94
Black Panthers, police infiltration,
    arrests, murder charges, 89–91
Cambridge, Maryland, Gloria
    Richardson, 82–83
CORE, 83–86
engendering black power, 87
expansive power agendas, 99–101
male authority, 97–99
Mother Rescuers from Poverty, 94–95
public housing activism, 87–89
U-JOIN, 86–87
Women's Liberation Day rally, 136, 141
Women's Liberation Movement, 105
Won, Tyrone, 208
Wong, Jack, 205
Wong, Vicci, 204–205
Wood, Herbert, 29
Woodard, Komozi, 4, 5, 7, 22, 106, 117, 119,
    290n1
Woodson, Carter G., 251–252
Woody, Sister (Nia Kuumba), 246
Worker's Party, 262
Workplace issues, *see* Employment/
    employment issues
Worldliness, 7
Worrill, Conrad, 244
Worthy, William, 13, 257
Wo'se Community Church, 238
Wretched of the Earth, The (Fanon), 123
Wright, Jeremiah A., 249
Wright, Richard, 122, 253–254

Y

Yale University, 264
Yates, Miriam, 147
Yellow Brotherhood, 210, 211, 212, 224
Yellow Power, 212, 225
Yorty, Sam, 39, 299n105
Young, A. Z., 148
Young, Irving, 90
Young, Sister Mary Paraclete, 92, 94, 100
Young, Whitney, 62, 239, 336n26
Young Citizens for Community Action
    (YCCA), 195
Young Lords, 194, 215, 216, 217, 218–219,
    221–222, 225, 226
Young Lords Party, 221
Young Patriots, 216–217, 340n58
Youngstown, Ohio, Kwanzaa in, 241
Youth Organization for Black Unity
    (YOBU), 271, 272, 353–354n83
Yu Han, 209
Yu Man, 209

Z

Zanzibar Revolution of 1964, 65, 76
Zhou En Lai, 59
Zimbabwe, 72, 73, 76
Zulu, Baba El Senzengalkulu, 246
Zulu, Hurumu and Itibari, 238, 346n34
Zulu customs, 234